Judy Andre

Feminist Approaches to Bioethics

Feminist Approaches to Bioethics

Theoretical Reflections and Practical Applications

ROSEMARIE TONG
Davidson College

WestviewPress
A Division of HarperCollins*Publishers*

Chapter 2 draws from material previously published in Rosemarie Tong, *Feminine and Feminist Ethics* (Belmont, CA: Wadsworth, 1982).

Chapters 5–8 draw from material previously published in Lawrence J. Kaplan and Rosemarie Tong, *Controlling Our Reproductive Destiny: A Technological and Philosophical Perspective* (Cambridge: MIT Press, 1994).

Published in 1997 in the United States of America by Westview Press, 5500 Central Avenue, Boulder, Colorado 80301-2877, and in the United Kingdom by Westview Press, 12 Hid's Copse Road, Cumnor Hill, Oxford OX2 9JJ

Library of Congress Cataloging-in-Publication Data
Tong, Rosemarie.
Feminist approaches to bioethics : theoretical reflections and practical applications / Rosemarie Tong.
p. cm.
Includes index.
ISBN 0-8133-1954-4.—ISBN 0-8133-1955-2 (pbk.)
1. Human reproductive technology—Moral and ethical aspects.
2. Feminist ethics. 3. Medical ethics. I. Title.
RG133.5.T65 1997
176—dc20 96-43491
CIP

The paper used in this publication meets the requirements of the American National Standard for Permanence of Paper for Printed Library Materials Z39.48-1984.

10 9 8 7 6 5 4 3 2 1

Contents

Acknowledgments

Many people have helped me think through the issues in this book but two deserve particular mention: Susan Peppers, a philosophy graduate student at the University of Pennsylvania, and Anna M. Kirkland, a graduate student in the Department of Government and Foreign Affairs at the University of Virginia. Susan's critical comments and good stylistic suggestions are especially apparent in Chapter 4, and Anna's skills as a research assistant, manuscript editor, and philosophical thinker enhanced some of the content and form of the manuscript as a whole. I also want to thank all my typists—Jean Newman, Pat Richart, and Frances Alexander—and my copy editor, Christine Arden. Each of them suffered though many a revision with me. Finally, I want to thank Spencer Carr, Cindy Rinehart, and Melanie Stafford of Westview Press. Each of them is an extraordinary editor and an exceptionally supportive human being. Without their persistent encouragement and long-suffering patience, I would not have brought this manuscript to term.

Rosemarie Tong

Prologue

For a long time now, I have struggled to articulate what a feminist approach to bioethics is and how such an approach to bioethics differs from a nonfeminist one. In Part 1 of this book I aim to locate feminist approaches to bioethics within a larger ethical context. I first explain and critique some so-called dominant and alternative nonfeminist approaches to ethics. Among the dominant traditions I discuss in Chapter 1 are classical virtue-centered ethics (Aristotle), utility-oriented ethics (Jeremy Bentham and John Stuart Mill), duty-focused ethics (Immanuel Kant and W. D. Ross), sentiment-motivated ethics (David Hume), law-based ethics (discussed under the rubric of Natural Law), and contract-grounded ethics (John Rawls). Among the alternative traditions I discuss are contemporary virtue theory (Alasdair MacIntyre), contemporary sentiment theory (Larry Blum), existentialism (Jean-Paul Sartre), communitarianism (Michael Sandel, Charles Taylor, Roberto Unger, and Michael Walzer), pragmatism (John Dewey and William James), conceptualism (Robert L. Holmes), and communicative ethics (Jürgen Habermas and Richard Rorty).

Although feminists are eager to distinguish their approaches to ethics from those of nonfeminists, they do not wish to reject all the moral principles, concepts, and virtues that have guided the Western tradition for centuries. Even if it were possible for feminists to interpret ethics entirely *de novo*, it would be very foolish for them to do so. For all their flaws, the Principle of Utility and the Categorical Imperative, for example, have much to recommend them. After all, who does not think it is important to minimize pain and to maximize pleasure, to promote individual and societal well-being, to treat each person as worthy of equal respect and consideration, and to do one's duty because it is one's duty? Nevertheless, feminists insist that many of the Western tradition's principles, concepts, and virtues need to be reinterpreted, reassessed, and transformed in order to reflect women's as well as men's perspectives. For this reason, feminists are particularly attracted to those alternative nonfeminist approaches to ethics that describe moral decisionmaking as the consensual result of an ongoing conversation among a *diverse* group of people. Although these emerging nonfeminist approaches to ethics do not emphasize gender issues, they are sympathetic to the claim that gender as well as race, ethnicity, and class affect one's mode of moral reasoning.

Among the specifically feminist approaches to ethics that feminists have developed are the two basic kinds I describe in Chapter 2: so-called ethics of care (often labeled "feminine" ethics) and so-called ethics of power. Whereas a care-focused feminist approach to ethics emphasizes values that have been culturally associated with women (e.g., nurturance, care, compassion), a power-focused feminist approach to ethics emphasizes the need to eliminate those social, economic, political, and cultural systems and structures that maintain patriarchal domination and work against the establishment of a gender-equitous world. Although there are real differences between care-focused and power-focused feminist approaches to ethics, they uniformly demand that nonfeminist approaches to ethics (1) attend to women's moral interests and issues as much as to men's; (2) treat both women and men as full moral agents; (3) affirm the cultural values that have been associated with women (interdependence, community, connection, sharing, emotion, body, trust, absence of hierarchy, nature, immanence, process, joy, peace, and life) as strongly as the cultural values that have been associated with men (independence, autonomy, intellect, will, wariness, hierarchy, domination, culture, transcendence, product, asceticism, war, and death); and (4) value women's moral experiences and modes of moral reasoning as much as men's.[1] There is, after all, room in ethics for a way of thinking (call it "female," if you will) that focuses on relationships, particularity, partiality, and emotion as well as a way of thinking (call it "male," if you will) that focuses on rules, universality, impartiality, and reason. Finally, there is in both care-focused and power-focused feminist approaches to ethics not only women's different moral voice but women's commitment to creating the kind of society in which culturally associated "female" values as well as culturally associated "male" values can thrive.

Understanding the relationship between nonfeminist and feminist approaches to *ethics* brings us a step closer to understanding the relationship between nonfeminist and feminist approaches to *bioethics*. In Chapter 3 I discuss both dominant and alternative nonfeminist approaches to bioethics. Among the former are deductivism, inductivism (particularly casuistry), principlism, and specified principlism. Among the latter are virtue ethics, care ethics, and postmodern ethics.

Interestingly, with the exception of casuistry, most dominant approaches to bioethics emphasize the role played by the principles of autonomy, beneficence, nonmaleficence, and justice in the process of biomedical decisionmaking. For centuries, most deductivists viewed beneficence as the chief among these four principles, the old assumption being that physicians not only want but also know what is best for patients. In more recent times, however, many deductivists have switched their loyalty from physicians' beneficence to patients' autonomy, the new assumption being that patients have the right to control their own destiny—that they are the preferred judges of their own best interests. Unlike deductivists, principlists and specified principlists have refused to give automatic pride of place to any one of Western medical ethics' four major principles. As they increasingly see it, depending on the context in which a moral conflict takes place, one principle will emerge to assume moral priority over the others.

In contrast to dominant nonfeminist approaches to bioethics, alternative nonfeminist approaches to bioethics do not focus so much on the standards of human reason as on the standards of human judgment. *Virtue ethicists* suggest that, since good persons typically make wise judgments, it is imperative that physicians and other health-care professionals cultivate character traits such as honesty, courage, and justice. *Care ethicists* build on some of the insights of virtue ethics, affirming that good persons are not only honest, courageous, and just but also caring. In particular, what makes physicians and other health-care practitioners caring is their desire to treat patients as unique individuals rather than as "diseases," "conditions," or "problems." Finally, *postmodern ethicists* take attention to detail and difference to their full length. In suggesting, for example, that health and disease have plural meanings and that there is no way to objectively assess whether life is better than death, postmodern ethicists threaten the traditional notion that medicine is an art and science that must always be used to restore health or to preserve life.

Although feminist bioethicists have generally affirmed various aspects of most alternative nonfeminist approaches to bioethics, especially those aspects that are sensitive to human diversity, they have almost always faulted the dominant nonfeminist approaches to bioethics for emphasizing rules over relationships, norms over virtues, and justice over caring. As principlism has become more "specified," however, many feminist bioethicists have reached an accommodation with it. Provided that the principles of autonomy, beneficence, and justice address gender-related issues in historical context, feminist bioethicists find these principles useful. For example, in our society, it is important to make certain that women's reproductive "choices" are truly autonomous. The fact that a woman decides to have an abortion does not mean she has freely chosen to do so—not if social and personal support systems for single mothers are lacking; the fact that a woman enters an in-vitro fertilization (IVF) program does not mean she has freely chosen to do so—not if she has been made to feel that a woman who cannot have a child is not really a woman; the fact that a woman agrees to be a commercial surrogate mother does not mean she has freely chosen to do so—not if she is relatively poor and needs extra money to support herself or her own children. The point here is that bioethicists need to attend to persons' gender (as well as race, ethnicity, class, and so forth) in order to distinguish between true autonomy and coercion masquerading as choice.

Like *nonfeminist* approaches to bioethics, *feminist* approaches to bioethics are not all cut from the same cloth. In fact, in Chapter 4 I note that, to date, the only factor that has united all feminist approaches to bioethics is not a common politics, ontology, epistemology, or ethics but instead a shared methodology. All feminist approaches to bioethics have sought to ask the so-called woman or gender question, to raise women's (and men's) consciousness about women's subordinate status, and to eliminate gaps between feminist theory and practice. Having made this assertion, I then add the disclaimer that at present many feminist bioethicists seem to be in the process of shaping a new philosophical framework in which they can use their tried-and-true methodology more effectively on behalf of women. As I see it, this emerging perspective, which consists of four recent developments in philosophical thought—eclecticism in politics, autokoenomy in ontology, positionality in epistemology, and relationality in ethics—is enabling feminist bioethicists to offer multiple rather than unitary solutions to the ethical and political problems that gender creates for women in particular.

In Part 2 of this book, I move from theory into practice. Chapters 5 through 9 focus on a cluster of issues related to procreation: the reproduction-controlling technologies (contraception, sterilization, and abortion); the reproduction-aiding technologies (artificial insemination, in-vitro fertilization, and surrogate motherhood); and genetic screening, diagnosis, counseling, and therapy. Originally, I had intended to show how feminist and nonfeminist bioethicists differently approach not just issues related to procreation but also issues related to aging, dying, medical research, health-care reform, and so on. I soon realized, however, that I could not do justice to all of these issues, even though I passionately cared about them all. I comforted myself with the thought that, after all, no other cluster of medical issues affects the genders *quite as* differently as do those related to procreation and that I might as well begin with the familiar rather than the unfamiliar in attempting to explain to a diverse audience the unique function of feminist approaches to bioethics.

Throughout Part 2 of this book, then, I make a deliberate effort to show in detail how feminist analyses of the new reproductive and genetic technologies differ from nonfeminist ones. I also draw repeated attention to the fact that feminist bioethicists frequently disagree not only with nonfeminists' views on procreative matters but also with one another's perspectives. Some feminist bioethicists stress the importance of women making autonomous choices—being free to choose to serve as surrogate mothers or egg donors, for instance. Other feminist bioethicists emphasize the ways in which society seeks to control women's reproductive capacities—by limiting access to certain reproduction-assisting technologies (e.g., intrauterine insemination and in-vitro fertilization) as well as to certain reproduction-controlling technologies (e.g., abortion). These feminist bioethicists are especially attuned to the ways in which some policymakers use the rhetoric of choice to oppress rather than liberate women—when, for example, they offer women the "choice" to continue their pregnancy, all the time reminding them how little they will be able to offer their child in terms of food, clothing, and shelter. Still other feminist bioethicists underscore the value of women's traditional capacities for creating and sustaining human relationships, claiming that experiences such as pregnancy are paramount examples of just how powerful women's connecting capabilities are.

Although I affirm moral diversity among feminist bioethicists and delight in the ways that they variously emphasize considerations of *choice*, *control*, and *connection*, I also realize that moral diversity can, and sometimes does, generate undesirable political fragmentation among feminist bioethicists. It is fortunate that not all feminist bioethicists have the same thing to say—that would be boring indeed—but it is unfortunate that feminists sometimes raise so many different considerations about each and every woman's separate "best interests" that they leave the policy table having failed to address the most important interests of the widest range of women possible. Because I believe that feminist bioethicists cannot always afford to indulge their differences, my ultimate aim in this book is to argue that even when feminist bioethicists have strong ideas about the best way to resolve a moral issue, they should be willing to forge a public policy that is good enough (i.e., "moral" enough, "feminist" enough) for nearly all women to accept. It is crucial, after all, that feminist bioethicists have something to say about key bioethical issues—or a perspective less appealing to women may fill in the gap. Convinced of this, I offer the present volume as one feminist's approach to bioethics. I hope it serves as a catalyst not only for present action but also for future thought.

Part One

Theoretical Overview

1

Nonfeminist Approaches to Ethics

In order to appreciate what distinguishes feminist from nonfeminist approaches to *bioethics,* we must first understand what distinguishes feminist from nonfeminist approaches to *ethics.* Although this is not a simple task, it is a necessary one. Tracing the similarities and differences between feminist and nonfeminist approaches to ethics will ultimately enable us to identify what feminist approaches to bioethics do and don't have in common with nonfeminist approaches to bioethics. It will also help us to formulate moral critiques of actions, practices, and institutions in the realm of biomedicine that reinforce women's subordination; to develop morally justifiable methods of countering such actions, practices, and institutions; and to imagine morally ideal ways to restructure the realm of biomedicine in a women-liberating and women-affirming fashion.

Nonfeminist Approaches to Ethics: Some Dominant Perspectives

Western philosophers generally define ethics as a rational effort to systematize the rules, principles, and ideals to which we appeal in justifying our actions as right and our moral characters as good.[1] For the most part, these norms arrange themselves in several familiar dyads: justice / benevolence, rights / responsibilities, individual freedom / group well-being, and so forth. Minimally, most of us wish to pursue our own goals without being harmed by other individuals; maximally, most of us also desire to live and work with other individuals who regard our goals as good ones for all human beings. Supposedly, ethics provides us with a number of analytic tools and action-guides with which to pursue our individual and collective goals "rightly"—whether these goals be minimalistic ones such as personal survival or maximalistic ones such as universal love. At the low end of the moral spectrum, ethics tells us what we must *not* do to other individuals: Do not kill, cheat, lie, steal, inflict unnecessary pain or suffering, and so on. And at the high end of the moral spectrum, ethics advises us as to how we can benefit other persons by contributing to their happiness or to the process of their perfection.

As I noted in the Prologue, the most widely recognized and therefore dominant systems of Western ethics include classical virtue-centered ethics (Aristotle), utility-oriented ethics (Jeremy Bentham and John Stuart Mill), duty-focused ethics (Immanuel Kant and W. D. Ross), sentiment-motivated ethics (David Hume), law-based ethics (for our purposes discussed as the Doctrine of Natural Law), and contract-grounded ethics (John Rawls). By briefly examining each of these systems of moral philosophy, we can identify some of the weaknesses as well as the strengths of nonfeminist approaches to ethics. The better we understand traditional Western ethics, the more we will be able to appreciate feminists' quarrels with it.

Classical Virtue-Centered Ethics

The Greek philosopher Aristotle (384–322 B.C.) was one of the earliest proponents of virtue ethics. He claimed that the ultimate goal of human action is personal happiness (*eudaemonia*), explained as "an active life in accord with excellence, or if there are more forms of excellence than one, in accord with the best and completest of them"[2]—that is, reason. Depending on our physical and psychological constitutions, we might obtain satisfaction from any number of human activities—for example, from parenting, teaching, or healing. What distinguishes these undertakings from, say, eating an ice-cream sundae, is that each is not only a satisfying activity but also one that makes use of our rational powers. In order to be truly happy persons, we have to use what Aristotle called the virtue of "practical wisdom" to prioritize and coordinate our human activities, organizing them in ways that serve the good of society as well as our own personal good.

In the course of describing the virtue of practical wisdom, Aristotle claimed that it has two indispensable functions. First, it enables us to identify which *ends* (i.e., aims, goals, or purposes) are really worthy of human desire and to pursue them only. Second, it helps us attain not only the *specific goods* internal to any worthy practice (e.g., medicine, law, business) but also the *general good* toward which all worthy practices tend—namely, the good of flourishing as an individual in a community. Unless

we are practically wise, we will exhibit not virtue but either its excess or its defect. So, for example, the practically-unwise woman will act not courageously but either recklessly or in a cowardly way. Likewise, the practically-unwise man will act not generously but in either a stingy or ostentatious manner.

Practically-wise individuals are moral geniuses because they consistently strike at the mean between the excesses and defects that frame each virtue. This, too, is no easy task. It requires a person to coordinate reason with emotion in much the same way that a jockey becomes comfortable with a racehorse. As soon as the rider feels at one with the horse, she or he can compel it forward or rein it in without incurring any rebellion. For Aristotle, then, reason is like a jockey who uses the emotions to help individuals become experts in ethics, consistently running well in the race of life by making morally appropriate decisions. Commented Aristotle: "It is the expert, not just anybody, who finds the center of the circle. In the same way, having a fit of temper is easy for anyone; so is giving money and spending it. But this is not so when it comes to questions of 'for whom?' 'how much?' 'when?' 'why?' and 'how?' This is why goodness is rare."[3] But critics of Aristotle's approach to ethics have objected that it errs by relying too heavily on practical wisdom, a virtue that requires consensus about what is truly valuable. Since individuals in a heterogeneous society such as ours do not typically agree on the moral worth of various ends (aims, goals, or purposes), it is highly unlikely that they will all strive to do the same "right thing." On the contrary, insist the critics: The more heterogeneous a society is, the more necessary it is to create an ethics of rules that provides clear guidance about how far any one individual can go in the pursuit of her or his own unique good. Unless everyone's rights, general responsibilities, and specific duties are precisely delineated, too much will be left to individual judgment, and no society set on surviving can afford to trust its members with their own moral governance.

Conceding that the critics' objection is a serious one, Aristotle's defenders nonetheless insist that it is not a devastating one. They point out that although ancient Greece was a relatively homogeneous society, there was considerable disagreement as to what constituted the good life. Some thought it was material prosperity; others, power or prestige; yet others, the life of the mind. Still, Aristotle's "great-souled man," whom we might instead term a "right-minded person," managed to settle moral disputes wisely, serving as an example for the majority of his contemporaries.

If Aristotle's defenders are correct, ideals as well as rules play a crucial role in our moral development. The power of an ideal, however, is quite different from the force of a rule. Whereas rules tell us what is forbidden, permitted, or required and threaten us with punishments for noncompliance, ideals encourage us to put our best foot forward even when we are not *required* to do so. This is not to suggest that ideals, compared to punishment-backed laws, are a weak means of behavior control. On the contrary, by requiring ourselves to live up to a set of self-imposed moral ideals, we might become the human analogues not of tiny bonsai trees but of giant redwoods. For the Aristotelian, ethics is fundamentally the struggle to become one's best self.

Given the fact that ideals have guided the practice of healing through the ages, Aristotelian ethics should appeal to health-care practitioners. According to such classical texts as the Hippocratic Oath and the Prayer of Maimonides, as well as to such contemporary documents as the Principles of Medical Ethics statement of the American Medical Association (AMA), medicine's moral foundation depends on the cultivation, by physicians in particular, of a certain set of virtues. Among these essential virtues are respect for human dignity, compassion, and respect for human life.[4] Displaying what seems to be these virtues may result in great professional success, esteem, and even patient satisfaction; but in the Aristotelian system, pretending to be good is a far cry from actually being good. The *appearance* of moral conduct is not an acceptable substitute for the *reality* of moral conduct. Physicians must really care about their patients; faking concern is an unacceptable substitute.

Utility-Oriented Ethics

Like Aristotelians, utilitarians believe that happiness is a fundamental human goal; however, they link happiness not with the achievement of *personal* perfection but with the attainment of the most good for the most people. Because utilitarians are committed to performing whichever action is most likely to net the most good (happiness minus unhappiness, benefit minus cost, pleasure minus pain) for the most people, they consider both the utility-producing and the disutility-producing consequences of each of several alternative actions before deciding on one. For example, a woman choosing between aborting or not aborting her fetus must decide whether she will produce more *overall* utility by terminating or not terminating her pregnancy. Let us assume that this woman's parents and friends are opposed to abortion and that her husband wants a child more than anything else in life. Let us also assume that this woman's chances of achieving her career goals will be severely limited if she has a child at this time. If more unhappiness will accrue to her parents, friends, and husband if she has the abortion than will accrue to her if she does not have the abortion, utilitarian tenets require her to continue the pregnancy. What ultimately matters is not an individual's happiness or rights but what is best for *everyone* on the whole.

Some critics of utilitarianism object that individuals are not necessarily morally required to prefer the group's interest over their own interests. They find utilitarianism's emphasis on "self-sacrifice" unsettling. They reason that if ethics grants rights to individuals, then it is flagrantly wrong to disregard these rights simply because the majority's pleasure or happiness is served by doing so. Other critics of utilitarianism object that it is impossible to construct a moral scale so finely calibrated that it can objectively weigh, for example, a woman's career goals against her husband's "paternal instincts." In particular, they ridicule Jeremy Bentham's (1748–1832) "hedonic calculus," which he designed to enable people to measure the utility of their actions in terms of duration, intensity, certainty, propinquity, fecundity, purity, and extent.[5] Few—if any—people were able to use Bentham's calculus successfully, having apparently proved unable to "quantify" their various and sundry happinesses and unhappinesses.

Bentham's failure provoked his successor, John Stuart Mill (1806–1873) to distinguish between *quantity* and *quality* of goods.[6] Mill's followers would advise the woman in our previous example to determine not only the *amount of happiness* that the fulfillment of her career goals would bring her but also the *relative human worth* of such an achievement. Since no reasonable person ever deliberately chooses an inferior good over a superior good, she or he would also advise the woman to use as her criterion for action the judgments of reasonable women who have had to make similar judgments under comparable circumstances in the past. If reasonable women who have experienced both childbearing (to make their husbands happy) and career-pursuing (to make themselves happy) rate the latter happiness as much better than the former, then the woman in our example should have the abortion she wants.

Mill's critics, however, are not confident that anyone, including the woman in our example, should use Mill's experienced judges as moral guides. In their view, there are no criteria for membership in this select group other than to be "reasonable." Thus, they caution that Mill's experienced judges are not *reasonable* judges but, instead, *partisan* judges, intent on affirming their particular values as universally right and good.

To avoid the problem of relying on partisan judges, twentieth-century preference utilitarians suggest that the most democratic way to make intersubjective comparisons of utility is to construct a scale on which all people can rank their pleasure preferences from highest to lowest. Yet as appealing as this suggestion seems, it is doubtful either that such a scale can be devised or that most people would truthfully rank their actual preferences on it. When people are polled about their preferences, they tend to distinguish between their ideal and actual preferences, often reporting the former rather than the latter to pollsters. For example, knowing that for ideological reasons feminists ought to prefer *Ms.* magazine to Harlequin romances, a feminist might reveal her *ideal* preference (*Ms.*) rather than her *actual* preference (Harlequin) to pollsters. After all, it would probably be too embarrassing for her to admit publicly that she enjoys reading novels that portray women as "sex kittens" more than reading journals that highlight women's professional accomplishments.

Yet, even if preference utilitarians were able to construct a perfect preference scale on which persons would rank only their actual preferences, they, like all utilitarians, would still need to prove that individuals should sacrifice their own good to that of the group if doing so would produce more total good. It is this assumption, more than any other, that threatens the moral credibility of utilitarianism in its critics' estimation. Consider, for example, the hypothetical case of Sally, a dying patient, whose bodily organs could be used to save the lives of five other patients. Let us assume that Sally is unemployed and that she is without family and friends, whereas the other five patients are powerful persons with large families and many friends. Let us also assume that only Sally can provide the needed organs, since alternative organ sources are unavailable. Finally, let us assume that Sally has only a few more weeks to live, but that the other five patients will die within hours unless Sally's organs are immediately transplanted in them, in which case they will live for several years. Under such circumstances, so-called *act* utilitarians (who directly apply the principle of utility to each and every case as it arises) would defy the ordinary moral judgment according to which Sally should not be killed even if it means that five "worthier" people will die. They would seek to justify killing Sally by viewing her and the five other patients who need her organs as some sort of collective superperson whose aggregate utility demands to be maximized. *Individual* rights, even Sally's right not to be killed, must give way to the *group's* interest in life.

In contrast to act utilitarians, so-called *rule* utilitarians would probably not view killing Sally as a morally appropriate action. Rule utilitarians directly apply the principle of utility to general rules of action rather than to specific actions. For this reason, they would most likely argue that even if the specific *act* of violating Sally's right to life produces overall utility in the immediate circumstances, a general *rule* permitting—let alone requiring—such a violation would not produce more overall good in the long run. On the contrary, it would lead to radical social instability, to a fear that the abuses initially inflicted on the Sallys of this world might one day be inflicted on one's own family, friends, or self.

In its emphasis on rules, rule utilitarianism represents an improvement over act utilitarianism. Still, it is doubtful whether rule utilitarians always obey the rules they have identified as utility-maximizing. Consider the utility-maximizing rule "Always respect *each* person's interest in life." Although rule utilitarians embrace this rule as a very important one, they concede that some circumstances not only permit but actually require us to break it. As an example, let us assume that the lives of thousands of newborns could be saved by depriving one octogenarian of a marginally life-extending but extremely costly organ transplant. Faced with this scenario, rule utilitarians would argue that in making an exception to the rule "Always respect *each* person's interest in life," they are adhering to an even more important rule, "Always respect each person's interest in life unless that interest is incompatible with a multitude of other persons' interests in life." But in making such an argument, rule utilitarians give at least the appearance of engaging in moral sleight of hand.

Whatever contortions in moral reasoning may be invited by utilitarianism, it has nonetheless been adopted by physicians during certain emergency situations such as wartime. In situations where hundreds or perhaps thousands of soldiers require immediate medical attention, the relatively few physicians available group the wounded by the rules of triage to determine who gets treatment first. Those who would die immediately unless treated are cared for as a first priority, followed by those whose treatment may be delayed without great risk, those with slight injuries, and finally those who seem doomed to die no matter what. Using this sorting system, physicians supposedly maximize the number of successfully treated patients, thus maximizing utility for the entire group of soldiers.

To be sure, the desperate conditions of war are mercifully rare. As medicine is typically practiced in the United States, most physicians have the luxury of practicing "nonutilitarian" medicine. They are able to focus on maximizing the good for each of their individual patients without worrying how this focus affects the patient population as a whole. The interests of the *individual* patient are paramount in current medical practice and will probably remain so, unless physicians adopt (or are forced to adopt) another ethos that requires them to be more attentive to the interests of the collective patient population than to the interests of any one of their own patients.

Duty-Focused Ethics

The question of balancing individual rights against group well-being brings us to a discussion of deontology (from 'deon', the Greek word for duty), an ethical system that relies heavily on the work of Immanuel Kant (1724–1804). As noted in the triage example above, utilitarian theory sometimes allows the sacrifice of individuals so that the group can, in some important way, benefit. The end, it seems, would justify the means.

In Kant's version of deontology, by contrast, respect for individuals and their rights is key: One must never treat another person merely as a means to some other person's happiness.

A second contrast between utilitarianism and Kant's deontology is that the former is a consequentialist ethical theory (which holds that the intended or actual consequences of an ethical choice determine its goodness), whereas the latter is a nonconsequentialist ethical theory (which holds that not consequences but adherence to principles determines the goodness of an ethical choice). In other words, unlike utilitarians, who insist that what makes an action wrong or right is its utility-maximizing consequences, deontologists maintain that an action's moral worth depends on one's reasons for doing it. Actions performed *against* duty are immoral; actions performed merely *in accord* with duty are morally nonsignificant or neutral; and actions performed *from* duty are moral. For example, if a physician deliberately kills a dying child she could cure, that physician acts in a *morally unworthy* or wrong manner. If the same physician cures a dying child simply because she loves children or wants to increase her renown in the medical community, that physician acts in a *morally nonsignificant* or neutral manner. Although the physician's action has good (utility-maximizing) consequences, her imperfect motives for committing the action cancel out its moral worth. Finally, if the same physician cures a dying child simply because that is what a good physician is supposed to do under the circumstances, the physician acts in a *morally worthy* or right manner.

Because obedience to moral rules plays such a large role in deontological thought, it is tempting to conclude that deontologists are not different from rule utilitarians in any significant way. But in fact they do differ. For Kant a genuine moral rule is not a rule that necessarily has good (utility-maximizing) consequences; rather, it is one that meets all three conditions of the so-called Categorical Imperative:

1. Act only on that maxim through which you can at the same time will that it should become a universal law;
2. Act in such a way that you always treat humanity, whether in your own person or in the person of another, never simply as a means but always at the same time as an end; and
3. Never . . . perform an action except on a maxim such as can be a universal law, and consequently such that the will can regard itself as at the same time making universal law by its maxim.[7]

The Categorical Imperative encodes the essence of Kant's moral theory. It tells us what general rules to use in deciding what to do. But it does not tell us *why* we should follow them.

In his attempt to explain why we should obey the Categorical Imperative, Kant argued that if happiness were our highest good, as the Aristotelians and utilitarians suggest, God would have done better to create us as "mindless" beings. Blind instinct, programmed to achieve its specific goals no matter what, would have suited us better. Reason is a spoilsport that deflects our appetites from their chosen aims. Instead of being distressed by the way in which we have been structured, however, Kant recommended that we count our rational capacities as a plus rather than a minus. The movement of all nonhuman beings—animate as well as inanimate—is determined simply by the laws of nature. Rocks do not decide to fall; they fall by virtue of the law of gravity. Animals do not decide to mate; they mate by virtue of certain sexual drives over which they have no control. In contrast, human beings are not entirely determined by externally imposed laws. We have the capacity to make laws for ourselves—to decide how we will act. Thus, Kant insisted that our fundamental goal is not to be happy—any sentient creature has this aim—but, rather, to act autonomously, to free ourselves from the blandishments of our inclinations.

Like utilitarianism, deontology is not an unproblematic approach to ethics. If moral rules are as absolute and exceptionless as deontologists deem them to be, how are we supposed to handle conflicts between moral rules? For example, let us assume that a social worker agrees to hide a battered woman from her husband. If this man, brandishing a loaded gun, comes to the social worker and demands to know the location of his wife, she can either lie to him or tell him where his wife is. No matter which choice she makes, however, she will do something "wrong." She will break *either* the rule "Never tell a lie" *or* the rule "Never bring harm to another person." To be sure, deontologists might argue that one or the other of these rules is not really absolute; or that God would never permit two *really* absolute moral rules to conflict; or that the social worker has a third option—she can refuse to say anything to the husband, risking her own life rather than that of the woman she agreed to shelter. None of these responses, though, provides us with a clear procedure by which to prioritize *genuinely absolute* but nonetheless *conflicting* moral rules.

Moreover, some versions of deontology, particularly Kantian ones, claim that our feelings neither add to nor subtract from the moral worth of our actions. It is this point, more than any other, that weakens the credibility of deontology in the estimation of its critics. As they see it, doing the right thing for duty's sake is a morally worthy action, but an even *more* morally worthy action is to do the right thing with the right feelings. For example, feeding our children nutritious food, providing them with quality health care, and sending them to good schools only out of a sense of duty cannot make up for a lack of emotion and love on our part. Our children do not want us to view them simply as moral burdens for which we are responsible. Thus, Kant's critics contend that feelings can and do contribute, positively or negatively, to the moral worth of human actions. As they see it, a sense of duty is not enough to make an action morally worthy; indeed, conscientiousness devoid of kindness may be worse than no sense of duty at all.

In the twentieth century, the English philosopher W. D. Ross (1877–1940) modified Kant's deontology. To avoid irresolvable conflicts between two supposedly absolute moral duties such as "Never tell a lie" and "Never bring harm to another person," as in the case of the battering husband who demands access to his wife, Ross distinguished between actual moral duty and *prima facie* ("at first sight") moral duty. Ethical conflicts are born when two *prima facie* duties (not two actual duties) conflict. For example, physicians have a *prima facie* duty not to lie to their patients about their medical condition. But they also have a *prima facie* duty not to harm their patients. Thus, if the only way for a physician to avoid driving a cervical-cancer patient toward suicide is to hide from her the fact that she has only a few months to live, the physician will have to decide what his actual duty is under the circumstances. This crucial decision will depend on what the physician's moral intuitions tell him about the importance of lying/not lying to the cervical-cancer patient. No matter what he decides, however, the physician will have to defend his choice to his peers by appealing to their moral intuitions—to what they would have judged to be their actual duty in the same situation.

For Ross, moral intuitions play a role not only in helping us decide which of our *prima facie* duties are "actual" but also in revealing our *prima facie* duties to us in the first place. Ross claims that we just know by means of our moral intuitions that fidelity, reparation, gratitude, justice, beneficence, self-improvement, and nonmaleficence are our *prima facie* duties. Although critics concede that Ross's list of *prima facie* duties is a plausible one, they nonetheless doubt that *all* rational persons would necessarily accept it as authoritative for them. In other words, critics view Ross as an ethical elitist who mistook the particular values of his own social circle for universal values. As they see it, such a mistake is of enormous consequence in the biomedical realm where appeals to "our" moral intuitions could easily invite abuses of power in the name of some dominant group's self-proclaimed ethical superiority. For example, given their status and prestige, health-care practitioners might be sorely tempted to place more confidence in their own moral perceptions than in those of "underprivileged" patients whom they tend to regard as "ignorant."

Sentiment-Motivated Ethics

In contrast to rule- or principle-driven systems of ethics, and in partial accordance with the ideas of W. D. Ross, David Hume and his followers claim that a very accurate reason or judgment "is not alone sufficient to produce any moral blame or approbation."[8] Indeed, Humeans maintain that when we judge an act to be morally "right," it is not because we can consistently will it as a law of nature (Kant) but, rather, because we feel a sentiment like approbation or esteem. Not some quality inherent in the action, but some emotion in us, causes us to label the act as "right." For Humeans, then, human feelings are not in opposition to moral duties. Quite the contrary: Moral rectitude arises from properly cultivated moral sentiments that prompt us to treat one another with some measure of respect and consideration.

In contrast to many other philosophers, Hume believed that the foundation of human moral sentiments is not self-love but love of others. He claimed that in reflecting upon our own moral sentiments, we will discover that we approve of beneficent, other-directed actions not only when they affect our lives positively but even when they affect our lives negatively or not at all.[9] Because we know how we feel when we are happy or miserable, we are capable of rejoicing or commiserating with others; and it is this capacity for sympathy that explains why we praise or blame people for certain actions. We praise people if they make others happy, but we blame them if they make others miserable.

Hume provided a list of the character traits that we generally praise. Significantly, all of these are either useful to the human community or immediately agreeable to ourselves or to others. For this reason, Hume claimed that "utility ... is the *sole* source of that high regard paid to fidelity, justice, honor"[10] and a host of other major virtues. Hume ably defended his position by noting that rules of distributive justice, for example, exist only in those worlds where they prove *useful*. That is, rules governing the allocation of resources would prove useless in a world of total abundance, or in a world of normal scarcity populated by supergenerous people. So too would they prove useless in a world of total scarcity, or in a world populated by exceptionally vicious people. The only worlds in which rules of distributive justice apply are worlds like our own, in which normal scarcity exists and in which people are neither totally good nor totally bad. Our rules of distributive justice are designed to help us cooperate so we can all at least survive. The more deeply we internalize these rules so that they become second-nature, the more frequently we will follow them in a nearly spontaneous matter. Thus, Humeans claim that if we cultivate the sentiment of justice in ourselves, we will not have to *reason* long and hard about whether, for example, it is fair to let an indigent mother and her child go hungry as a rich local banker and his wife sit down to a $500 gourmet meal. Rather, our *feelings* of outrage and disgust will swiftly determine that such a scenario is unjust.

Not surprisingly, many health-care professionals consider sentiment-motivated systems of ethics to be consistent with their worldview. Contrary to those who advocate professional detachment as the best frame of mind within which to approach a treatment situation, Humeans praise compassionate health-care professionals: those who bring kindness as well as knowledge, concern as well as expertise, to the bedside. In response to Kantian critics who bemoan the ephemerality of our sentiments, Humeans retort that only our emotions have the power to evoke *active* moral responses within us. Conversely, all that cool reason enables us to do is to think and then think some more.

Law-Based Ethics

As I have noted, Hume's ethics is based on a favorable view of human nature: Human beings are naturally inclined toward being good. Provided with the proper socializing structures, they tend to cultivate a set of human-hearted sentiments. And these cultivated sentiments, in turn, enable the individuals who possess them to create and maintain good human relationships. Significantly, theories about human nature—such as Hume's and certainly Aristotle's—have played a large role in the development of several ethical systems, preeminently the one termed "natural law." According to traditional natural-law thinkers, God establishes rules of human conduct that individuals come to know either through rational reflection on human nature or through divine revelation. Supposedly, when we reflect on our essential nature as human beings, we come to the conclusion that God has created us to live, to procreate, to learn, to love, and so forth. We also conclude that because God has given us the capacities to actualize our human potential, it is our duty to choose life over death, procreating over not procreating, learning over ignorance, loving over hating, and so on. With rare exception, then, we defy the natural law whenever we ignore or refuse to fulfill our human destiny. Thus, according to natural law, it is wrong to use contraceptives, to be sterilized, or to have an abortion. All of these actions frustrate our supposedly God-implanted orientation toward procreation.[11]

Critics of natural law point out that not everyone believes either that God exists or that each part of the human body has a universally recognized natural function. For example, many natural-law theorists claim that the main or only function of our sexual organs is to procreate children. Yet our sexual organs arguably have other functions as well—that of adding to the quantity of human pleasure, for one. Our mouths are certainly designed for chewing food, thus aiding the digestion process; but it would be absurd to insist that everything else we can do with our mouths—such as talking, singing, and kissing—is immoral.

In defense of more secular versions of natural-law ethics that jettison the divine command element, supporters note that, for better or worse, certain principles of natural law have shaped and will continue to shape the practice of medicine. Among these is the principle of totality, according to which it is morally permissible for human beings to sacrifice parts of their bodies, but only for the good of their entire selves. Thus, for example, it is morally permissible for a woman to have a cancerous uterus removed. It is also morally permissible for her to give one of her kidneys to someone who needs it on the grounds that such an act of altruism is compatible with her overall personal good. It would be morally forbidden, however, for her to give her heart to someone who needs a heart transplant. Such an action would be incompatible with her overall personal good.[12]

Another major principle of natural law, and one that is commonly used in the world of medicine, is the principle of double effect. According to this principle, if an action has two effects—namely, an intended good one and an unintended bad one that is nonetheless foreseen as occurring—then the action may be performed for the sake of the good effect, provided that (1) the good effect is at least equal in value to the unintended bad effect and (2) the bad effect is not the means of producing the good effect. Thus, for example, it is morally acceptable for physicians to administer adequate pain relief to suffering patients, even if their doing so might depress the respiration of some patients enough to hasten their death.[13]

Another appeal of natural-law theory is precisely its emphasis on the *natural*. Physician-bioethicist Leon Kass claims that an enlightened understanding of our nature as human beings would lead to much-improved medical attitudes and practices:

> Appreciating the meaning of our embodiment, institutionalized already in our taboos on cannibalism and incest, would lead us to oppose the buying and selling of human organs or the practice of surrogate motherhood. Understanding the virtues of mortality would show us the folly of seeking to prolong life indefinitely and the wisdom of self-sacrifice against the narcissistic prejudices connected with a strictly survivalist principle of life. Recognizing our body's immanent and purposive activities toward wholeness and well-working would instruct and restrain our willful self-manipulation by illuminating which possible alterations of bodies and media might be helpful or harmful to human well-being.[14]

Critics are swift to point out, however, that what Kass regards as a proper understanding of nature is not necessarily shared by all good people. Many good people support organ-selling, surrogate motherhood, elective cosmetic surgery, and/or aggressive medical treatment for people destined to die in a matter of days—even hours. The fact that natural-law theory requires that all good people share the same values helps explain why it functions poorly in heterogeneous societies where one person's "unnatural desire" is another person's "natural inclination."

Contract-Grounded Ethics

Although many contemporary moral philosophers would describe their approach to ethics as virtue-oriented, utility-oriented, duty-focused, sentiment-motivated, or law-based, even more would describe it as contract-grounded. Indeed, the idea of a social compact, agreement, or contract pervades the moral and political imagination of both past and present. It is certainly no accident that a wide range of eighteenth- and nineteenth-century thinkers presented contracts as the procedural means enabling human beings to move out of the so-called Hobbesian state of nature, in which life is "nasty, brutish, and short" for all but the strongest of individuals, and into civil society where life is fairly pleasant, peaceful, and long for most individuals.[15] This concept has been more fully developed by twentieth-century philosopher John Rawls in *A Theory of Justice* (1971).[16] Although Rawls describes as fanciful the idea of an *actual* social contract signed by individuals seeking release from the "state of nature," he nonetheless believes that the idea of a *hypothetical* social contract is a useful heuristic device. Thus, Rawls proposes that we test the merits of existing governments by asking ourselves what kind of social contract a perfectly rational group of individuals would sign if they were brought together to set up a government *de novo*.

To help us comprehend the contours of a truly just society, Rawls asks us to imagine ourselves in an "original position" whereby we would know little about ourselves except that we are rational creatures who wish to be as free and happy as possible:

> Among the essential features of this situation is that no one knows his place in society, his class position or social status, nor does anyone know his fortune in the distribution of natural assets and abilities, his intelligence, strength, and the like. . . . [T]he parties do not know their conceptions of the good or their special psychological propensities. The principles of justice are chosen behind a veil of ignorance.[17]

Rawls suggests that, under such uncertain circumstances, we should first appeal to the "maximin" (short for *maximum minorum*) rule of choice—a rule that directs our attention to the worst possible outcome for ourselves—and then construct our ideal society in light of that worst possibility.[18] According to Rawls, if we focus on the "maximin" rule, we will conclude that the two most fundamental principles of justice are as follows: "First, each person is to have an equal right to the most extensive liberty compatible with a similar liberty for others. Second, social and economic inequalities are to be arranged so that they are both (a) reasonably expected to be to everyone's advantage and (b) attached to positions and offices available to all."[19]

Rawls's contract-based politics thus establishes a *theoretical* structure from which the idea of just human relations can emerge. What remains for us to consider is whether any actual human society can devise the *practical* means to actualize this idea—to move it from the abstract to the concrete realm.

One philosopher who has done much to develop contractarianism as a moral as well as political philosophy is David A.J. Richards. In *The Moral Criticism of the Law,* he envisions a group of perfectly rational persons convened to legislate *de novo* the moral principles that will govern them.[20] Because the contractors exhibit the same degree of liberty and ignorance about their "specific situations, values, or identities,"[21] Richards claims that each contractor will self-interestedly decide to be ruled by the principles of mutual respect, universalization, and minimization of differences. Similar to the Golden Rule, the principle of mutual respect instructs us to treat others as we would like to be treated by them—that is, as persons whose interests deserve as much consideration as anyone else's. The principle of universalization, a version of Kant's Categorical Imperative, maintains that unless our proposed course of action is right for everyone in our situation to perform, it is not right for us to perform it. Finally, the principle of minimization of differences requires, to whatever degree is practicable, that we not take into account people's differences (race, gender, class) when judging them or distributing society's benefits and burdens among them.

To accept these three principles as morally binding upon all rational persons is to accept the idea that the "right" has some priority over the "good." In other words, a just society is one that provides persons with precisely the freedoms (of thought, expression, and religion), safeguards (due process, equal protection, and equal opportunity), and benefits (health care, education, and welfare) they need in order to pursue their own particular versions of the "good life."[22] So, for example, if Mr. and Mrs. Jones are family-oriented whereas Mr. and Mrs. Smith are not, the two couples will have very different procreative priorities, yet both will treasure their right to make their own procreative decisions. To be sure, not every conception of the "good life" (e.g., the neo-Nazi or sadist conception) can be pursued unrestrictedly within the framework of a just society. Rather, only those conceptions of the good life that do not threaten the freedoms, safeguards, and benefits that make their pursuit possible can be unambiguously affirmed.

Although Rawls's ideas continue to dominate most discussions of contemporary moral philosophy, they have been faulted. Some critics doubt that it is possible for people in the "original position" to agree on principles to regulate their lives, since they are *utterly* ignorant of their particular needs and wants. According to these critics, Rawls does not give his

contractors *enough* information to make rational decisions about what might be good for everyone in general as well as for themselves in particular. Other critics wonder whether Rawls's contractarian theory of justice actually differs from the utilitarian theory of justice. They note that Rawls's second principle of justice, the one that tells us how to distribute society's benefits and burdens, is operational only when his first principle of justice, the one that guarantees equal liberty, can be established and maintained. Indeed, when circumstances are such that everyone cannot be guaranteed equal liberty, Rawls apparently permits governments to act in a utilitarian fashion—that is, to restrict individual liberties, provided that the restrictions are for the benefit of all.

Yet however strong these philosophical criticisms of both Rawls and Richards may be, they are not strong enough to defeat the general usefulness of contractarian thought in the medical world. For example, when decisions about how to allocate scarce medical resources must be made, most people sitting behind the "veil of ignorance" favor a health-care system that guarantees all citizens at least *basic* protection. Most men and women, when they lack knowledge about their own circumstances, reason in a self-interested manner (the union of these two human motivations, reason and self-interest, is the beauty of Rawls's system), envisioning themselves to be perhaps poor, alone, and physically handicapped or mentally ill. Thus, they are inclined to accept only those inequalities in a health-care system that benefit individuals in the position of greatest need.

Nonfeminist Approaches to Ethics: Some Alternative Perspectives

Currently, rule-focused approaches to ethics such as utilitarianism, deontology, and contractarianism so dominate the field of ethics that even Aristotle, Hume, and some natural-law thinkers are perceived as challengers to the tradition they helped generate. In particular, virtue-oriented ethics and sentiment-based ethics are viewed as an attack on their rule-focused counterparts. Among the thinkers who espouse contemporary versions of virtue and/or sentiment theory are Alasdair MacIntyre and Larry Blum. As they see it, there is far more to ethics than rules; and, whatever else it might be, ethics is not science.

Contemporary Virtue Theory

In his book *After Virtue*, MacIntyre develops some basic concepts of Aristotelian virtue theory.[23] Unlike Aristotle, however, MacIntyre believes that the good for an individual cannot be determined in advance by appealing to reason—that is, by asking one's self what rational persons desire in general. There is no *one* story to tell about the human species; rather, each human life is a unique "narrative quest" for self-fulfillment and personal integrity—a story about trying to make sense of one's existence. This narrative project is no easy task. We carve our path as we go along, constantly redirecting ourselves in response to the events that befall us as well as to those we make happen. There are as many roadblocks as windows of opportunity. We become confused about who we are and what we want. We have, therefore, great need for what MacIntyre terms "virtues"—namely, those qualities of character without which our search for personal happiness and perfection cannot end successfully.

We do not conduct our search for meaning alone, however. Each of us is a member of one or more communities that either help or hinder us in our struggle to make sense of human existence. Many of the basic components of our search for meaning derive from what MacIntyre identifies as social practices—namely, cooperative human activities that have their own internal standards of excellence. These practices encompass gameplaying (e.g., chess, football, tennis), professional activities (e.g., medicine, law, teaching), and personal activities (e.g., parenting). But if such practices are to flourish, their practitioners must, in MacIntyre's estimation, appreciate the satisfactions or goods internal to them. For example, what ultimately makes medicine truly worthwhile for health-care practitioners is not the money to be earned but the intellectual challenges it provides and the deep human relationships it enables. And, indeed, most of the individuals who choose a medical career do so because they are attracted to a life devoted to healing people—to making patients' bodies, minds, and spirits whole again. This grander project is what gives meaning to health-care practitioners' lives.

To fully appreciate the goods that are internal to a practice, those who embark upon it must agree to accept and obey its standards of excellence. Comments MacIntyre: "To enter into a practice is to accept the authority of those standards and the inadequacy of my own performance as judged by them. It is to subject my own attitudes, choices, preferences, and tastes to the standards which currently and partially define the practice."[24] Thus, when individuals decide to become health-care practitioners, they must willingly submit to the performance criteria established by the reigning authorities in the field. They must also agree to relinquish any idiosyncratic ideas they might have about the practice of medicine. They are not permitted to practice voodoo or psychic healing, for example.

It is one thing to *decide* to become a health-care practitioner, however, and quite another to *persevere* long enough in the practice to become a good one. And according to MacIntyre, people cannot persevere in a practice if they lack virtues of character without which they will simply "lose steam." It is, after all, very difficult to become excellent at what one has chosen to do. Among other things, observes MacIntyre,

> we have to learn to recognize what is due to whom; we have to be prepared to take whatever self-endangering risks are demanded along the way; and we have to listen carefully to what we are told about our own inadequacies and to reply with the same carefulness for the facts. In other words, we have to accept as necessary components of any practice with internal goods and standards of excellence the virtues of justice, courage, and honesty.[25]

Regarding the practice of healing, then, justice consists in fulfilling one's obligations to patients, colleagues, hospital authorities, the profession, and society in general; courage consists in providing whatever treatments one thinks are best for a patient, even if one is not absolutely certain that they will work; and honesty consists in realizing one's own limits as a health-care practitioner as well as the limits of others. As abstract as this may sound, anyone who has sincerely tried to meet all of her or his professional obligations well only to fall short, or even to fail miserably, knows whereof MacIntyre speaks.

Virtuous practitioners—just, courageous, and honest men and women—are a necessary condition for a practice's survival. However, they are not a sufficient condition. "No practice," proclaims MacIntyre, "can survive for any length of time unsustained by institutions."[26] But this is not to say that there are no differences between practices and institutions. Although we usually identify practices like teaching, business, and medicine with institutions like colleges, corporations, and hospitals, such identifications are to be resisted. Practices are characteristically concerned with internal goods—with the joy of healing, for example—and they are held together by the cement of human cooperation. In contrast, institutions are necessarily concerned with external goods like money, power, and status—such as a salary of $250,000 per annum—and they are energized by the fragmentary fires of human competition. Nevertheless, provided that "the ideals and the creativity of the practice" do not succumb to "the acquisitiveness of the institution,"[27] professors and deans, workers and managers, hospital administrators and health-care practitioners can help each other achieve their separate but still intersecting goals.

MacIntyre highlights not only the tensions between internal and external goods but also those among the multiple practices of any single agent. Health-care practitioners, for example, have duties over and beyond their professional responsibilities. They have familial duties, duties of friendship, duties as citizens, and so on. Only practically-wise health-care practitioners can judge which of these duties should take precedence over the other; and what enables them to do so is an awareness of the "traditions" of those people whom they identify as members of their communities. If we order our priorities correctly, says MacIntyre, not only will we feel at peace with ourselves, but our communities will admire and respect us as well.

Contemporary Sentiment Theory

Larry Blum, who also offers an alternative nonfeminist approach to ethics, is inspired more by the moral-sentiment theory of Hume than by the virtue theory of Aristotle. Like Hume, Blum believes that emotions play a crucial role in our moral development. Thus, he laments the fact that Kant and others in the deontological tradition tend to view the emotions as the enemy of reason—as that which hinders rather than helps our moral development.[28] Blum observes that Kantians are particularly suspicious of so-called altruistic emotions because they are generated by and directed toward specific people in specific situations. For example, we hear that Johnny, an appealing indigent child, will die without a bone marrow transplant, and so we work feverishly to raise the funds for his operation. What Kantians ask is whether we would work in an equally feverish fashion to raise funds for a crotchety, indigent adult in need of the same operation. As they see it, if we need to feel good about the people we help, we will often fail to do our duty. To act solely from altruistic feelings is, in Kantians' estimation, to act from inclination, a motivational force that, unlike steady reason, waxes and wanes depending on our moods. And unlike inclination, which pushes us in the direction of the appealing "Johnnys" of this world, reason instructs us that the lives of appealing children are no more valuable than the lives of crotchety adults. If one of them deserves our best efforts, then so does the other.

As much as Blum understands the appeal of an ethics built on the foundation of objective reason, he nonetheless insists with Aristotle that when the emotions are properly educated, they too can serve as reliable indices for human virtue and vice. Proper feelings of honor and shame, for example, enable us to be courageous (rather than cowardly or foolhardy) and self-respectful (rather than servile or arrogant). Moreover, there is a major difference between a raw emotion and an altruistic one. Whereas a raw emotion is little more than a visceral gut feeling, an altruistic emotion is a tendency to do good to others that has been reflectively cultivated for many years, beginning with our parents' admonition that we ought to think of other people's feelings.

Convinced that feelings have a major role to play in morality, Blum argues that far from undermining morality, feelings, especially altruistic emotions, usually enhance it. Indeed, Blum insists that such emotions are necessary components of morality. Consider the case of a cancer patient being consoled by a nurse. Much of the good that the patient will derive from this act of consolation is *the feeling* that the nurse really cares about her. If she senses that the nurse is only doing his duty in consoling her, it is hard to imagine the nurse's gesture being of any real consolation to her. This situation might explain why so many patients are dissatisfied with the quality of health care they receive, even when no amount of money or expertise is spared in their treatment. According to Blum's line of reasoning, unless health-care practitioners are emotionally well developed, they cannot provide their patients with the kind of humane care they require.

Existentialism

Alternative nonfeminist approaches to ethics are not confined to contemporary versions of Aristotle and Hume, however. So-called existentialist ethics emphasizes that human beings are free, meaning that "in the bright realm of values, we have no excuse behind us, nor justification before us."[29] We have no excuse *behind* us, because we alone are responsible for our choices. Not God, nor fate, nor the unconscious, nor some manner and fashion of external stimuli, but, rather, *we* are the motivating force behind our actions. More dramatically, we have no justification *before* us. Our values are valid only because we have chosen them as valuable, not strictly because they have good consequences. In short, our values cannot be confirmed as valuable by anyone else, human or divine. There are no principles, ideals, rules, virtues, or sentiments that make our choices right or wrong. We are our own source of moral value.

Individuals who are convinced that there is some God-like objective authority whom they can consult in making difficult moral choices are deceiving themselves, according to existentialist Jean-Paul Sartre.[30] Our fear of isolation causes us to seek affirmation for our ethical choices from other people; however, all this tactic gives us is a meaningless "security blanket." Human beings can try to shift the burden of moral authority from their shoulders, but the fact remains that what "happens" to them is the result of their own choices. In the existentialist picture of the human condition, we are tossed into difficult ethical dilemmas, forced to make independent choices, and left solely responsible for both the actions we choose and the justifications we develop for them.

However attractive we might find existentialism's celebration of human freedom (provided that we can bear the weight of its responsibility), critics claim that this approach to ethics would be dysfunctional in the world of medicine. To be sure, health-care practitioners and patients should be encouraged to take more responsibility for their decisions and actions; however, given the extreme vulnerability of some of these practitioners and patients, it seems cruel to leave them *no* excuses for their inability to control their own destiny. And chances are that the world of medicine would become utterly chaotic if Dr. Kevorkian, a total advocate of physician-assisted suicide, were assigned to Suite 1A; Dr. Quill, a cautious advocate of physician-assisted suicide, were assigned to Suite 2A; and a right-to-life physician, adamantly opposed to physician-assisted suicide, were assigned to Suite 3A. If each of these physicians sought to live according to her or his self-chosen values, one wonders how the *practice* of medicine could survive.

Communitarianism

In contrast to existentialists, so-called communitarians, such as Michael Sandel, Charles Taylor, Roberto Unger, and Michael Walzer, assert that ethics is not a matter of the lonely individual "willing" values into existence. On the contrary, ethics is a *group* project within the human community. It cannot be abstracted from the historical, social, and political forces that give rise to it. Thus, communitarian ethics is guided by individuals who realize that their self-identities are largely a product of their relationships to other people. Individuals cannot know who they are without making reference to their position in a community; nor can they decide what is right or wrong apart from this community. In order to know what is just, for example, we must ask our personal friends and professional colleagues what they mean by justice. If we wish to determine, for example, whether we have distributed scarce resources equitably, we need to take into account our community's reactions to our allocations. Largely negative reactions are a sign that one's own ideas of justice might be entirely idiosyncratic. Communities together, not individuals alone, decide what goods society owes to whom and in what measure.

Critics of communitarian ethics claim that it is so enamored of the status quo that it might further validate "business as usual" in the worlds of science and medicine. According to these critics, simply because a community believes that it is morally appropriate to give better health care to wealthy men than to indigent children does not mean that this allocation of scarce resources is just. Thus, if individuals protest this state of affairs, they should not automatically accept their community's condemnation as *deserved*. Perhaps the community is unjust. Communitarian ethics is, after all, only as good as the community it represents. An ethical system that has no room for the moral visionary who criticizes its standards is highly suspect. There must be some room for dissent in the moral world.

Pragmatism

Another alternative nonfeminist approach to ethics is so-called pragmatism, which combines elements of existentialism and communitarianism with the ideas of Aristotle, Kant, and Hume. Pragmatist thinkers such as Charles Pierce, Oliver Wendell Holmes, Jr., and John Dewey claim that pragmatism is neither simply deontological nor simply teleological, but both. In short, pragmatists explain and justify moral principles and rules in terms of their effectiveness in the world of actual experience. If a set of rules contributes to human happiness and perfection, and if most people are persuaded to follow these rules voluntarily, they are good rules. Otherwise they are not.

Of all the pragmatists, John Dewey (1859–1952) wrote the most about ethics. As he saw it, ethics is essentially an inquiry, like science. A moral dilemma is not a situation in which we are tempted to do what we know is wrong. Rather, it is a situation that confuses us: We do not *know* what we ought to do, but nonetheless we must *decide* what we ought to do. As in science, the role of theory in ethics is to help us sort through our confusion. We try to assess the consequences of our actions. Of course, we cannot simultaneously conceive of all the actions and consequences we might generate in any particular set of circumstances; that is, we cannot imagine all the ways in which we might make better or make worse the human condition by doing or not doing action x or y or z. Thus, the fallibility of science is also the fallibility of ethics. We do not have access to all the facts; and, paradoxically, the more facts to which we do have access, the more likely we will have to change our theories to explain them.

Dewey concluded that, because our ethics change in response to developments in our world, conflicts between ethical theories simply reflect different social needs at different times. For example, it is no accident that utilitarianism arose in the time and place it did. Moral inquiry brings people together to assess the biological, political, economic, cultural, and other facts that confront them, and to select the values that will enable them to interpret these facts in their quest to achieve integrity as individuals and as a community. Moral truth is not the property of any one individual. Rather, it is the result of an evolving process that requires people to collaborate in the ways that scientists collaborate. Faced with an unsettling problem, individuals need to propose a solution for it and then use this proposed solution, or "end-in-view,"[31] to guide their acquisition of information, reflections, experiments, and actions toward it. For Dewey and other pragmatists, then, the moral enterprise is the serious business of finding the social conditions under which individuals will flourish and then making sure that those conditions are realized.

A pragmatist approach to ethics has much to offer the world of contemporary medicine. After all, our era is one of rapid developments. In the process of solving one problem—locating the gene that causes Huntington's chorea, for example—we create another. Suddenly we are faced with questions like "Is it in this patient's best interest to know he has the gene for Huntington's years before any symptoms of it appear?" Evoking such principles as autonomy and beneficence will prove helpful in answering this question, as will the realization that someone must eventually take responsibility for either telling or not telling the patient the truth. But what will ultimately prove most useful, in the estimation of pragmatists, is for everyone involved in the decision-making process to share their different moral perspectives on the case. Only in this way will they be able to correct for one another's blind spots and together construct the *whole* picture of what is at stake when, for example, a physician decides to hide a patient's future from him.

Pragmatism is a plausible antidote for contemporary medicine's arrogance—as manifested, for example, in its tendency to view what it has to offer society as an unalloyed good. Recall William James's reflections on his negative perception of a clearing around a log cabin. James observed that the clearing—consisting of several tree stumps, pigpens, and muddy gardens—which to him was "a mere ugly picture on the retina" was to the land-clearers "a symbol redolent with moral memories and sang a very paean of duty, struggle and success."[32] Realizing how blind he had been to the land-clearers' reality, James eventually concluded that we should not pronounce "on the meaninglessness of forms of existence other than our own."[33] Our moral world will be much improved if we tolerate, respect, and even indulge those whom we perceive to be harmlessly happy in their own ways, however unintelligible such ways may be to us. As difficult as it might be for health-care practitioners to adopt a Jamesian attitude toward patients, failure to do so might reinforce, instead, an inappropriate, paternalistic attitude toward them.

Contextualism

Closely related to classical pragmatism is so-called contextualism. One of the chief exponents of contextualism, Robert L. Holmes, maintains that contextualism shares key features both with what he terms particularism (which holds that the rightness of acts depends solely on the situation in which they are performed) and with what he terms legalism (which holds that the rightness of acts is determined solely by rules, principles, or commandments).[34] However, unlike legalism and particularism, which are theories about *actual* rightness, contextualism is a theory about *actionable* rightness. All that a person can be expected to do is her or his best.

In Holmes's view, many elements populate a moral situation. To be sure, society's rules, practices, and customs are present in this situation, but so are the individual's roles, relationships, and personal recollections of previous moral judgments. No one element of this complex moral situation has absolute priority over the others. For example, even if we recognize principles such as autonomy, beneficence, nonmaleficence, and justice as morally binding in general, we still have to decide whether these principles are morally binding in a *particular* circumstance. In other words, it is we who must consider

> (1) whether a given principle applies, (2) what the principle requires in this particular case, (3) which takes precedence if it conflicts with another principle, (4) whether this case is an exception to the principle, or (5) whether this case shows that the principle is inadequate. To make such a decision is to act. And as with any other act, the decision may be right or wrong. But that determination cannot be made by appeal to a principle, because the situation that creates the need to make such a determination is one in which the relevance of principles is called into question.[35]

Thus, in order to determine whether or not we ought to respect an individual's autonomy, we need to consider what we will be required to do if, for example, we permit him to sell his kidney to the highest bidder. If something deep inside ourselves says, "No, I can't be party to this kind of sale," then we are left with no choice but to violate the principle of autonomy.

Holmes does not believe that it makes a real difference to the moral project whether a cognitive intuition or an affective emotion "tells" us not to follow the lead of a moral principle. He does think it is important, however, to recognize that we are constituted with something like a conscience that enables us to sense when something is, after all, just right or just wrong. The fact that Holmes emphasizes conscience does not mean that he is a relativist. By insisting that different moral judgments about the same conduct may be equally true, relativism leads us down different moral paths, some of which dead-end in moral isolation. In contrast, contextualism commits us to a high degree of consensus. When, for example, we judge one act as right, we must also judge any act like it as right. For the most part, we will be able to compare one action with another. But every once in a while, as William James has written, there will be an action that resists comparison: "The most characteristically and peculiarly moral judgements that a man is ever called on to make are in unprecedented cases and lonely emergencies, where no popular theoretical maxims can avail, and the hidden oracle alone can speak."[36] At other times, a situation is so distinctive that it defies categorization. All we can do is to "feel" our way through it.

Clearly, Holmes's version of contextualism offers the world of medicine many reassuring messages; but none are as reassuring as the message that all we are required to do is our personal best. Comments Holmes:

> [I]f humankind strives to understand the human situation complexly, and to follow the guidance of morality as steadfastly as it does science, moral judg-

> ments will eventually converge. The resultant moral beliefs and practices will be actionably rights; not for all *conceivable* rational beings, as Kant held, but for humans living in this world, interacting with one another and with other living things and the environment. We cannot say for certain those beliefs will also constitute what is actually right. If we cannot derive an "ought" from an "is," we cannot say conclusively that what is agreed to even by all people is right. But it is the best we can do. And we may, with as much confidence as we can achieve in this matter, postulate that it constitutes the actually right.[37]

Thus, although a physician may know that she should not dispense medication for free, Holmes's contextualism would allow her to take into consideration the special circumstances of an indigent person, for example, and "cheat" the hospital out of the sale of the medication.

Communicative Ethics

In its emphasis on human discussion and interaction, contextualism is closely related to communicative ethics. Developers of communicative ethics emphasize dialogue between diverse groups, dialogue that allows for honest discussion and values social responsibility. The goal of communicative ethics is not merely consensus but mutual critique. Among the thinkers who offer this type of approach to ethics are Jürgen Habermas and Richard Rorty. Although these thinkers are neither entirely "absolutistic" nor "relativistic" in their distinct but related approaches to ethics, Habermas is more likely to worry over the fact that unjust or prejudicial societal constructions may distort our conclusions about moral truths, whereas Rorty is more apt to dismiss the concept of a hard-and-fast moral truth and embrace unfettered discourse as the best route to moral knowledge.

A firm believer in communicative ethics, Habermas insists that people are the sole judges of their own interests, which are formed and discovered through dialogue. Habermas's discourse model for uncovering the best ethical perspective on any given moral situation demands both generality and reciprocity from its participants. All members of the community must be included, and each one must strive to put herself or himself into everyone else's shoes for the truest kind of communication to occur. If either empathy is neglected or certain individuals are shut out of the process, the mutual critique and eventual ethical consensus will be incomplete and thereby inferior. For this reason, Habermas views "the depoliticization of the mass of the population and the decline of the public realm as a political institution" as "components of a system of domination that tends to exclude practical questions from public discussion."[38] Not only does this situation block certain types of questions, it also makes it extremely difficult for people to remind one another that, when all is said and done, they share a lot of blood, sweat, tears, and toil in common. Habermas's strongest criticism against modern democratic government is that it fails to find "arrangements which can ground the presumption that the basic institutions of society and the basic political institutions would meet with the voluntary agreement of all those involved, if they could participate, as free and equal, in discursive will-formation."[39]

Before we endorse the ethical norms of a community, we must, says Habermas, determine whether those who have internalized them have genuinely accepted them. In order to make this determination, Habermas asks whether, under conditions of undistorted communication, everyone who is currently abiding by these norms would continue to embrace them as rational standards for appropriate human behavior. If the answer to this question is "no," we should, in his estimation, conclude that the members of the community in question have been tricked, mystified, or otherwise manipulated into internalizing its "ethical" norms.

Compared to Habermas, Richard Rorty adopts a more "free-style" approach to communicative ethics. Rorty holds that there is no true foundation for ethics—not God, pure reason, or the so-called conditions for ideal discourse. Rather, ethics is the product of a free and open exchange of ideas. It results from the kind of conversations that take place in liberal communities. According to Rorty, the Western world has come to the conclusion that cruelty is wrong, having gradually expanded the range of actions that it considers cruel and the number of people whom it forbids to be cruel.[40]

Rorty claims that we can provide neither *reasons* for why we hate cruelty nor *criteria* for distinguishing cruel from not-cruel action. He then suggests that the best way we might cope with this frustrating state of affairs is to become "liberal ironists"—that is, people who realize that even their most basic commitments are contingent.[41] According to philosopher Michael Roth, however, there are two basic objections to Rorty's understanding and articulation of the West's supposed moral development: "The first, from Michel Foucault, can be formulated as the ironic question: Do you really *believe* this self-congratulatory story about the 'development' of the West? The second, from Jürgen Habermas, can be formulated as a worried plea: Are you really going to offer no more legitimation to the development of the West in modernity than this mere *story*?"[42] According to Roth, these objections show that "Michel Foucault is an ironist who is unwilling to be a liberal, whereas Jürgen Habermas is a liberal who is unwilling to be an ironist."[43] In other words, Foucault fears that our "contingent" commitments will rapidly degenerate into efforts to control other people; and hence it is best that we not take ourselves too seriously. In contrast, Habermas fears that relativism will destroy us if we reduce ethics to poetry, narrative, or story-telling. We cannot give up on the idea that reason has a universal character. The notion of "undistorted communication" ensures that if different groups enter an ideal speech situation with the same problem, they will arrive at the same answer. Some things simply cannot be left to "contingency."

In response to critics like Foucault, Rorty insists that even if we cannot take credit for it, the story we have been telling in the West—one that emphasizes the wrongness of patterns of domination and subordination—is a *good* story. At least we *agree* that cruelty is wrong, even though we lapse into cruel behavior all too often. Rorty also has an answer for Habermas: Rather than looking for moral foundations that do not exist, we would better spend our time working together to combat cruelty. The more time and energy we spend on this project, the more united we will be. We can become one another's moral foundation.

In Rorty's view, contingency and commitment, irony and solidarity, are all compatible. What keeps them conjoined is conversation. Comments Rorty:

> [T]he ironist—the person who has doubts about his own final vocabulary, his own moral identity, and perhaps his own sanity—desperately needs to *talk* to other people, needs this with the same urgency as people need to make love. He needs to do so because only conversation enables him to handle these doubts, to keep himself together, to keep his web of beliefs and desires coherent enough to enable him to act.[44]

To be sure, Rorty's approach does not answer the objection "But what if the person with whom you are conversing thinks that cruelty is acceptable? Then what?" And, indeed, discussing matters of "right" and "wrong" with such a person would probably not help us develop a moral identity, no matter how long the conversation continued. Instead, it would probably just further confuse and confound us—essentially, by setting us on a moral wild-goose chase.

Whatever its limits, however, communicative ethics is an approach to moral reasoning that might still be able to serve the world of medicine exceedingly well. For example, faced with a "hard case" about which it needs consensus, an ethics committee would probably best be served by broadening its deliberations as much as possible. Its members should consult not only each other about the nature of the case at hand but all the key players as well, including the health-care practitioners, the patient's surrogates, and, if possible, the patient herself. Unless the committee directly encounters the individuals about whom it is deliberating, it will have great difficulty discussing them empathetically. For example, if all the members of an ethics committee are well educated, relatively wealthy professionals, they might not be able to understand why an indigent woman with AIDS "chose" to get pregnant and why she "refuses" to kick her cocaine habit. Absent some type of face-to-face encounter with the woman, such a committee might simply conclude that she is an "irresponsible" person who deserves to be punished.

Conclusion

Many of us probably agree with Dewey that ethical approaches change to meet the needs of the time. It is no coincidence that the three main alternative nonfeminist approaches to traditional ethics—existentialism, communitarianism, and pragmatism / contextualism / communicative ethics—have appeared in the late twentieth century. Our differences from one another in this age are very great and also more accentuated through global communication, news, and travel—so great, in fact, that at times we are tempted to think that either standing alone or immersing ourselves in a small group rich with traditions is the only way to proceed. But neither lonely isolation nor "groupthink" is ethically satisfying. If we have learned anything as citizens in this modern world, it is surely that there are a multitude of options for grounding moral philosophy, each promising to bring increased happiness and freedom to many people in its own distinct way.

To be sure, the fact that there are multiple views about ethics does not prove that they are all equally good. It simply complicates things a bit. Human beings will never stop "doing ethics"—that is, searching for the best way to harmonize one person's interests with those of others. Though it has always been clear that the path from self to others is full of potholes and pitfalls in our self-aware, multicultural world, we are repeatedly summoned to walk down this rough and rocky path. How, then, should we traverse it? It seems we are being led back toward some form of "democratic" communication in which we acknowledge the legitimacy of *at least considering* a variety of approaches and challenges to ethics. Because there are many theories, each with an accompanying critique, contemporary ethicists cannot disregard the competition, so to speak. Rather, they must talk with one another. And, indeed, the rules for this dialogue—who is to be included, upon what basis, and so on—are probably the main contribution of many alternative nonfeminist, late-twentieth-century moral theorists.

2

Feminist Approaches to Ethics

Since most feminist approaches to ethics resonate with one or more of the nonfeminist approaches to ethics discussed in the last chapter, we might well ask what makes a *feminist* approach to ethics distinctive. Although this question needs to be fully answered, for now let us simply agree that, to a greater or lesser degree, all feminist approaches to ethics are filtered through the lens of gender. The fact that feminists disagree about the ways in which and the degree to which culturally constructed concepts of "femininity" and "masculinity" contribute to women's subordination explains why we must speak of feminist ethics in the plural.

One way to categorize what is a very large array of feminist approaches to ethics is to distinguish between so-called feminine ethics and so-called feminist ethics. Philosopher Betty A. Sichel clarifies this distinction as follows:

> 'Feminine' at present refers to the search for women's unique voice and, most often, the advocacy of an ethics of care that includes nurturance, care, compassion, and networks of communication. 'Feminist' refers to those theorists, whether liberal or radical or other orientation, who argue against patriarchal domination, for equal rights, a just and fair distribution of scarce resources, etc.[1]

Agreeing with Sichel, philosopher Susan Sherwin claims that a "feminine" approach to ethics "consists of observations of how the traditional approaches to ethics fail to fit the moral expressions and intuitions of women,"[2] whereas a "feminist" approach to ethics "applies a specifically political perspective and offers suggestions for how ethics must be revised if it is to get at the patterns of dominance and oppression as they affect women."[3]

Although I have found the distinction between feminine and feminist approaches to ethics very useful in the past, I have become convinced that it is a distinction easily misunderstood. For this reason, I now prefer to contrast care-focused *feminist* approaches to ethics with power-focused *feminist* approaches to ethics. Whereas a care-focused feminist approach to ethics has as its primary task the rehabilitation of such culturally associated feminine values as compassion, empathy, sympathy, nurturance, and kindness, a power-focused feminist approach to ethics has as its first duty the elimination or modification of any system, structure, or set of norms that contributes to women's oppression. To the same degree that a care-focused feminist approach to ethics is aware that distorted forms of care can summon women to burn themselves out on behalf of others, a power-focused feminist approach to ethics realizes that distorted forms of power can lead women to cultivate a slew of Hobbesian vices.

Care-Focused Feminist Approaches to Ethics

The writings of Carol Gilligan and Nel Noddings comprise two widely recognized care-focused feminist approaches to ethics. In her pathbreaking book, *In a Different Voice*,[4] Gilligan offers an account of *women's* moral development that challenges Lawrence Kohlberg's account of *human beings'* moral development. According to Kohlberg, moral development is a six-stage, progressive process. Children's moral development, he says, begins with Stage One, "the punishment and obedience orientation"; this is a time when, to avoid the "stick" of punishment and/or to receive the "carrot" of reward, children do as they are told. Stage Two is "the instrumental relativist orientation." Based on a limited principle of reciprocity—"You scratch my back and I'll scratch yours"—children in this stage do what satisfies their own needs and occasionally the needs of others. Stage Three is "the interpersonal concordance or 'good boy–nice girl' orientation," when immature adolescents conform to prevailing mores simply because they seek the approval of other people. Stage Four is "the law and order orientation," when mature adolescents do their duty in order to be recognized as honorable as well as pleasant people. Stage Five is "the social contract legalistic orientation," when adults adopt an essentially utilitarian perspective according to which they are permitted considerable liberty provided that they refrain from harming other people. Finally, Stage Six is "the universal ethical principle orientation," when some, though by no means all, adults adopt an essentially Kantian perspective universal enough to serve as a critique of any conventional morality, including that of their own society. These individuals are no longer governed by self-interest, the opinion of others, or the rule of law but, rather, are motivated by self-legislated and self-imposed universal principles such as those of justice, reciprocity, and respect for the dignity of human beings as intrinsically valuable persons.[5]

Puzzled by the fact that women rarely climbed past the good boy–nice girl mark on Kohlberg's scale whereas men routinely ascended at least to the special-contract mark, Gilligan hypothesized that the deficiency lay not in women but in Kohlberg's scale. She claimed that his scale provided a way to measure *male* moral development rather than *human* moral development, and that if women were measured on a female-sensitive scale, they would prove just as morally developed as men. While studying how each of twenty-nine women decided whether it was right or wrong to have an abortion, Gilligan noted that, as a group, these women referred little to their rights and much to their relationships. She also noted that in the process of developing (or failing to develop) as moral agents, these women moved in and out of three understandings of the self-other relationship: (1) an overemphasis on self; (2) an overemphasis on the other; and (3) a proper emphasis on self in relation to the other.[6] On the basis of this and several other empirical studies of women's moral reasoning patterns, Gilligan gradually concluded that for a variety of cultural reasons, women typically utilize an ethics of care that stresses relationships and responsibilities, whereas men generally employ an ethics of justice that stresses rules and rights.

Even though Gilligan has conceded to her critics that not *all* women are care-focused and not *all* men are justice-focused, she has not entirely forsaken her gender-based claims over the years. For example, in one of her recent studies involving eighty educationally privileged North American adults and adolescents, Gilligan notes that although two-thirds of her men and women subjects raised considerations of both justice and care, they all tended to focus on one or the other of these two ethical perspectives. Of particular interest is her finding that whereas the women were just as likely to focus on justice as on care, only *one* man focused on care in preference to justice. For this reason, Gilligan concludes that even if justice has largely lost its connection to the "masculine" (i.e., men), care still retains its strong connection to the "feminine" (i.e., women).[7]

Even though Gilligan's ethics of care has been favorably received both by the general public and by many scholars, critics have raised several plausible objections against it. Over and beyond the criticism that justice and care are not strictly gender-correlated, these objections include the following: (1) The distinction between justice and care is not new to the age of feminism—in fact, it is simply a variation on the traditional distinction between justice and beneficence. (2) Justice and care are not so much two different approaches to morality as two complementary, equally necessary components of morality. (3) Justice and care are two different approaches to morality, but care is not as good an approach to morality as justice is—in fact, what Gilligan means by "care" might be little more than a "feminine" *personality* trait. (4) If justice and care are, after all, gender-correlated, it is in women's best interests that this correlation be broken. And (5) since justice and care, as Gilligan articulates them, seem to be linked to *political* descriptions of "man" the oppressor and "woman" the oppressed, valorizing care as normative for women only worsens the position of women.

Of all these objections to Gilligan's work, the fourth and fifth ones are potentially the most devastating. Taken together, these criticisms advise that even if care is a better value than justice, it would be an enormous mistake to identify women as the care-giving half of the human species. Continually associating women with caring promotes the idea that because women can care and have cared, they should always care—no matter the cost to themselves. Thus, in *Femininity and Domination*, philosopher Sandra Lee Bartky discusses whether women's experience of "feeding men's egos" and "tending men's wounds" ultimately disempowers or empowers women. She notes, for example, that the kind of emotional work practiced by flight attendants, most of whom are women, often leads "to self-estrangement, an inability to identify one's own emotional states, even to drug abuse or alcoholism."[8] Paying a person to be "relentlessly cheerful"[9]—to smile at even the most verbally abusive and unreasonably demanding passenger—means paying a person to feign a certain set of emotions. But a person can *pretend* to be happy for only so long before that person forgets how it feels to be *genuinely* or *authentically* happy.

Bartky admits that not all women experience their emotional work as draining or dispiriting. For example, the more intensely some wives care for their husbands, the better they claim to feel about themselves. They pride themselves on being the ones who keep their marriages going and who hold their families together. Nevertheless, in Bartky's estimation, such subjective feelings of empowerment are not the same as the objective reality of having power. As she sees it, women's androcentric emotional work tends to harm women far more than it benefits them; indeed, in some tragic instances, it actually destroys them. Bartky points to Teresa Stangl, wife of Fritz Stangl, who was kommandant of the Jewish extermination camp, Treblinka. Even though her husband's monstrous activities horrified her, she continued to "feed" and "tend" him dutifully, even lovingly. In the course of doing so, however, she destroyed her own soul: A person cannot remain silent about evil and expect to keep her goodness entirely intact. Because horror perpetrated by a loved one is still horror, no woman can afford to care unconditionally.[10]

Trying to avoid what Bartky summarizes as "the pitfalls and temptations of caregiving itself,"[11] Nel Noddings has written *Caring: A Feminine Approach to Ethics and Moral Education.*[12] In her book, Noddings notes that ethics is about personal relations defined as "a set of ordered pairs generated by some rule that describes the affect—or subjective experience—of the members."[13] There are, says Noddings, two parties in any relation: The first member is the "one-caring"; the second, the "cared-for." If the relation between these two parties is a good one, the one-caring is motivationally engrossed or displaced in the cared-for. She or he attends to the cared-for not only in thoughts, however, but also in deeds. When a caring relationship succeeds, the cared-for actively *receives* the caring thoughts and deeds of the one-caring, spontaneously sharing her or his aspirations, appraisals, and accomplishments with her or him. For Noddings, caring is not about feeling favorably disposed toward human beings in general; rather, it is about concrete interactions between particular persons.

Although Noddings's critics commend her for trying to provide a philosophical description of a caring relation, they fault her for focusing too much on successful acts of caring and not enough on failed acts of caring. Sometimes, after all, the cared-for does not *receive as gift* but *takes as entitlement* the affirming thoughts and sustaining actions of the one-caring. But Noddings, say her critics, does not really address lopsided relations in which the cared-for skillfully takes advantage of the one-caring, so much so that the one-caring settles for any sign that her or his thoughts and actions are appreciated.

To this objection, Noddings has replied that there does come a time when the one-caring is morally *permitted* to end an iniquitous relationship. Still, she indicates that even under exceptionally abusive circumstances, the one-caring is not morally *required* to withdraw support from the cared-for. For example, even though Noddings would permit an abused wife to leave her abusive husband, she suggests that, by "calling it quits" too hastily, the abused wife is in some way "ethically diminished."[14] Noddings observes that even though abusive husbands are to blame for the abuse they heap on their wives, not every abusive relationship has to terminate with a divorce decree, a prison sentence for the abuser, or an act of preemptive self-defense. In her estimation, provided that enough of the right kind of third parties intervene, some abusive relationships may be salvaged. Comments Noddings:

> Women in abusive relations need others to support them—to care for them. One of the best forms of support would be to surround the abusive husband with loving models who would not tolerate abuse in their presence and would strongly disapprove of it whenever it occurred in their absence. Such models could support and reeducate the woman as well, helping her to un-

derstand her own self-worth. Too often, everyone withdraws from both the abuser and the sufferer.[15]

Between the lines of Noddings's words, critics hear the voice of someone who hopes to overcome evil itself—to reconcile the irreconcilable. They fear that Noddings seeks the same grand reconciliation that Ivan rejects in Dostoyevsky's *The Brothers Karamazov* when he shrieks that he does not want to dwell in the kind of "heaven" where a cruelly murdered child, his mother, and his murderer embrace in a cosmic hug of forgiveness.[16] Like Ivan, Noddings's critics insist that some actions are so evil that they must not be forgiven. There is a *final* limit on caring.

Another thinker whose writings are compatible with these developing care-focused feminist approaches to ethics is Annette Baier. She has suggested that so-called care ethics should be reframed as an ethics of love and responsibility based on trust. For Baier, appropriately trusting relationships are the proper model for good human relationships in general. Although Baier believes that "appropriate trust" includes both men's "ethics of obligation" and women's "ethics of love," she concedes that it is easier for us to understand the relationship among trust, *love*, and feeling than that among trust, *obligation*, and reason. Although trusting someone is not the same as loving someone, unless people trust each other they will have enormous difficulty loving each other. Lack of trust is probably the common factor in most divorces and eroded friendships. Yet trust is also closely connected to obligation in the sense that "to recognize a set of obligations is to trust some group of persons to instill them, to demand that they be met, possibly to levy sanctions if they are not, and this is to trust persons with significant coercive power over others."[17]

With the introduction of the idea of coercive power, Baier moves her fundamentally care-focused feminist approach to ethics closer to a power-focused feminist approach to ethics, once again confirming that these two types of ethical approaches are not shy about stepping into each other's territory. Baier not only asks conceptual questions like "What is trust?" She also asks political questions like "Whom can we trust with coercive power? Ourselves? Others? No one? Why should we trust anyone?" Ethics has traditionally tended to look at moral obligations from the standpoint of those with the power: the legislators, the authorities, the experts. Thus, it has focused on punishing the rule-breakers: the renegers, the defaulters, the liars. In contrast, Baier inspects moral obligations from the perspective of those without power—namely, those who must trust the rule-makers, the people with power, not to harm them. "To trust," says Baier, "is to make oneself or let oneself be more vulnerable than one might have been to harm from others—to give them an opportunity to harm one, in the confidence that they will not take it, because they have no good reason to."[18]

In an attempt to show why trust relationships rather than contractual relations are the proper moral paradigm for good human relationships, Baier claims that the essence of trust is "reliance" on another person's "good will," knowing full well that the other person's "good will" is not absolutely dependable.[19] My spouse may betray me; my friends may desert me; my parents may abandon me; my colleagues may undermine me; and so on. Realizing that trust entails risks, we must ask ourselves why we should willingly make ourselves vulnerable. Baier answers that we need to trust others because we are not self-sufficient. Without the help of others, neither the production of things and ideas nor the reproduction of persons could proceed. Just as art, music, theater, literature, science, political debate, and economic exchange require more than one person for their existence and maintenance, so too do "life, health, reputation, our offspring and their well-being."[20]

Baier constructs a phenomenology of trust by describing *what* values we entrust to *whom*. Trust, she says, is a "three-place predicate": *A* trusts *B* with valued thing *C*. To appreciate the variety of forms trust can take, we need to look, for example, at the variety of ways in which *B* might disappoint *A*, or in which *A* might retaliate against *B*. The more carefully articulated and specified a relationship is, the easier it is to tell when trust has been violated. For example, if I promise to deliver your child's birthday cake on time and I fail to do so because I oversleep, you will probably conclude that I am untrustworthy. As it stands, however, most relationships are far less articulated and specified than those between cake-buyers and cake-deliverers. A young woman trusts her physician, for example, to keep confidential her gynecological history. Nevertheless, he may disclose some aspects of it on the grounds that doing so is in her best interests. Since the trust relationship between a physician and a patient is one that permits considerable discretion, the young woman will have to decide whether her physician has seriously, perhaps irrevocably, destroyed the trust between them, or whether he has only temporarily threatened it. There is, after all, a major difference between his discussing with several colleagues the medical risks of her going on the Pill and his discussing with her parents the nature and extent of her sexual activities. When trust (together with confidence) is destroyed, the physician-patient relationship dies with it; but when trust is merely threatened, "some tact and willingness to forgive on the part of the truster and some willingness on the part of the trusted both to be forgiven and to forgive unfair criticism"[21] may yet save the relationship.

Baier emphasizes that nonfeminist ethicists have not been much interested in analyzing "infant trust"—that is, the kind of natural and nonvoluntary trust that exists between unequals, especially intimates. Instead, they have analyzed "relations between more or less free and equal adult strangers, say, the members of an all-male club, with membership rules and rules for dealing with rule breakers and where the form of cooperation was restricted to insuring that each member could read his *Times* in peace and have no one step on his gouty toes."[22] Baier concludes that the preoccupation of nonfeminist ethicists with adult contractors or promise-makers (historically male) has had the consequence of relegating children and their mothers to the margins of morality. Moreover, it has seriously distorted the nature of trust as a moral phenomenon.

According to Baier, in order to understand what trust really is, we must look not to the kind of limited trust two (male) business partners have in each other but, rather, to the kind of total trust an infant has in his or her parents. Baier claims that infant trust is the most "primitive and basic"[23] form of human trust. Indeed, it is so fundamental that, without it, the human community could not survive let alone thrive: "The ultra-Hobbist child who fears or rejects the mother's breast, as if fearing poison from that source, can be taken as displaying innate distrust, and such newborns must be the exception in a surviving species."[24]

Baier's point in stressing infant trust is that, like it or not, we have to trust one another, for unless we operate on the assumption that most of us are trustworthy most of the time, we will become quite paranoid. This is not to say, however, that Baier espouses some theory of "blind trust." Like Gilligan and Noddings, who temper their feminist approaches to ethics with caveats about the perils of caring too much, Baier modulates her feminist approach to ethics with warnings about the dangers of trusting too much. Granted, we cannot construct a moral network if we are always looking over our shoulders for someone to stab us in the back; but we also cannot ignore warning scratches or pin pricks: the "compliment" that betrays its speaker's envy, the word of "concern" that reveals its speaker's contempt. Too much trust is as dangerous as too little trust, as Baier notes: "We should not assume that promiscuous trustworthiness is any more a virtue than is undiscriminating distrust. It is appropriate trustworthiness, appropriate trustingness, appropriate encouragement to trust, which will be virtues, as will be judicious untrustworthiness, selective refusal to trust, discriminating discouragement of trust."[25]

Because the oppression of women has in some measure been built upon their trust of untrustworthy men, women must cultivate the virtue of appropriate distrust as well as that of appropriate trust. Baier suggests that, even as an untempered nonfeminist ethic of care encourages exploitation, an unmodulated ethic of trust invites betrayal in patriarchal society. Until men learn to care about other people as intensely as women have, women should embrace the role of the one-caring selectively; and until women gain equal status with men, women should not assume that men will always honor their promises.

Closely related to Gilligan's, Noddings's, Baier's, and other care-focused feminist approaches to ethics are so-called maternal approaches to ethics. The writings of philosophers Sara Ruddick,[26] Virginia Held,[27] and Caroline Whitbeck,[28] for example, are care-focused to the degree that they celebrate the psychological traits and moral virtues that society associates with women who mother. Sharing many of Baier's sentiments, Ruddick, Held, and Whitbeck maintain that a moral paradigm built upon transactions between equally informed and equally powerful adults cannot adequately guide the bulk of our human relationships, which, after all, are mostly between unequals. Were ethics really gender-neutral, it would not favor paradigms like the contract model, which speak much more to men's experiences in the public world than to women's and children's experiences in the private world. When we relate to aging parents, young children, ailing siblings, and distraught friends, for example, we do not relate as if we were perfectly rational adults negotiating business deals. Nor should we. If any moral paradigm is able to guide our typically unequal relationships steadily, says Held, it is the model of an ideal mother-child relationship—or, more inclusively, an ideal mothering person–child relationship.[29]

Although Ruddick, Held, and Whitbeck have all developed insightful maternal approaches to ethics, Held has probably done the most to produce a detailed account of the moral differences between contractual and noncontractual relationships. As she sees it, the mothering person-child paradigm differs from the contract paradigm in at least six ways, each of which has implications about how we should relate to one another.

First, the relationship between a mothering person (who can just as readily be a man as a woman) and a child is not voluntary, especially from the standpoint of the child who has been called into an existence that she or he did not request, but also from the standpoint of the mothering person who might not have realized how demanding being a mother is. Nevertheless, most infants, upon reaching the age of reason, do not seek to divorce their parents; nor do most mothering parents seek to abandon their offspring the first night they cry and fuss until the wee hours of the morning. On the contrary, mothering persons and their children typically accept that their natural bonds to each other are essentially strings to which are attached important obligations, and that the full extent of these obligations cannot be known in advance but must be accommodated with wisdom and grace.

Second, the relationship between a mothering person and a child is typically permanent and nonreplaceable, in the sense that most mothering persons and children are either biologically related or legally related through some form of adoption or stepparenting. Thus, for better or worse, the once-separate lives of a mothering person and a child are either naturally or culturally intertwined in ways that are very difficult, sometimes even impossible, to escape. For this reason, all but the most pathological of mothering persons view their children not as reproductive or legal products that are as easily "sold" as they are "bought" but, rather, as unique personalities never again to be replicated in the annals of human history—not even through the anticipated technology of cloning.

Third, the relationship between a mothering person and a child is a relationship between unequals. In theory at least, contracts are made between equals and the equality at stake is that of equal rights. When people move out of the so-called state of nature into civil society, they relinquish some of their freedom to do as they please in exchange for certain guarantees such as the right to vote. And in an election, each citizen's vote counts as much as any other citizen's. In contrast, the kinds of relationships that exist in the family are not, as Held correctly insists, relationships between equals. Although each member of a family deserves respect and consideration, a decision whether to spend more money on a child's education than on an aged parent's health care involves much more than a discussion of who has a right to what. At stake is the family's spirit of cooperation, sense of solidarity, and capacity for love. Whether one's son has more of a *right* to the family's income than one's mother does not always matter—not, for example, if the only way to subsidize what many consider a luxury education for one's son (four years at Harvard) is by placing one's ailing mother in a low-quality nursing home.

Fourth, the relationship between a mothering person and a child is one based on positive rights (e.g., the right to be benefited) as well as on negative rights (e.g., the right not to be harmed). According to traditional political theory, so-called economic man treasures first and foremost his right not to be interfered with, to be left to his own devices. Yet, the right to be helped is probably as important as the right not to be hindered. Indeed, Held maintains that if society has the resources with which to benefit needy people, it has no excuse, let alone justification, for failing to do so.

Fifth, the relationship between a mothering person and a child constitutes a symbiotic whole: a community of two. The problem for economic man is how to build community. But if selves are utterly atomistic and fixated on their own individual gain, what can possibly motivate them to get together and to stay together? In contrast, the problem for mothering persons and children is how to achieve separation. They have community; what they need is individuality. "For the child," says Held, "the problem is to become gradually more independent. For the mothering person, the problem is to free oneself from an all-consuming involvement."[30]

Sixth, and finally, Held describes the relationship between the mothering person and the child as a "caring"/"relying" one.[31] Worried that he may not always be able to secure the so-called upper hand, economic man seeks to negotiate contracts that equalize the balance of power between himself and others. Were mothering persons to view themselves as always at war with their children, however, their children would suffer enormous harm. Fearful of losing their power over their children, mothering persons would be tempted to control them through force. As a result, all children would grow up the victims of physical, psychological, and sexual abuse, predisposed to do unto *their* children the violence that had been done unto them. The fact that abused children are still the exception rather than the rule in our society is a welcome sign that most mothering persons view their relationships with their children not in terms of strict domination and subordination but in terms of learning how to give and take.

Having drawn these six contrasts between the contract paradigm and the mothering person–child paradigm, Held argues that, morally speaking, it is better to live in a society guided by the latter—an ideal that views people as linked together rather than as chopped apart. Adding some power-focused points to her basically care-focused feminist approach to ethics, Held notes that, properly specified, many forms of power are moral. She specifically points out that "[t]he power of a mothering person to empower others, to foster transformative growth is a different sort of power than that of a stronger sword or dominant will. And the power of a child to call forth tenderness and care is perhaps more different still."[32] The only immoral type of power is that which permits one group of people (or one person) to oppress another group of people (or person)—as in relationships involving male domination and female subordination. In such relationships, the powerful dominator uses his power to foster dependence rather than growth, fear rather than confidence, and self-loathing rather than self-love.

Held's critique of noncontractual society confirms Baier's conception of the moral self. According to Baier, we must understand that we are not, first and foremost, "first persons"—independent "I's"—but rather "second persons"—interdependent "you's." In Baier's estimation, the "I" cannot think, or even exist, unless it is first, and perhaps always, a "you." Had our parents failed to relate to us as human persons, we would never have learned how to speak or to think. We would be like the "Wild Child of Aveyron," left as a babe to survive on his own in the forest. When finally rescued, the Wild Child—now nearing the age of a Wild Man—was indistinguishable from an animal. He had, in other words, no concept of himself as a *self,* and this because he had never been anyone's *other*. He could not meaningfully use the first-person singular pronoun "I" with reference to himself; nor could others convincingly use the third-person singular pronoun "he" with reference to him. In short, the Wild Child was not "recognizably human" because he had never been anyone's "you"—that is, anyone's *second person*.[33]

However appealing maternal approaches to ethics may be, some critics have claimed that no one human relationship, even a well-functioning mothering person–child relationship, either can or should serve as the moral paradigm for all human relationships. As they see it, any human relationship—whether one of husband-wife, parent-child, sibling-sibling, friend-friend, or ruler-subject—is simply too specific to provide a general model for how people should treat others in general. If it is misguided to urge unequals to relate as if they were equals, it is also misguided to urge equals to relate as if they were unequals.

Other critics have expressed similar reservations about maternal approaches to ethics, adding the feminist caveat that, currently, the mother-child relationship is a particularly problematic choice for a paradigm. According to these critics, associating maternal ways of thinking and acting with *women's* characteristic thought and action patterns risks reintroducing traditional gender roles at a time when women are just beginning to make significant strides educationally, professionally, and politically.[34] In their opinion, friendship is a better paradigm for fully human relationships than the mother-child relationship. Based more on need than desire, more on love than obligation, and more on trust than fear, friendship relationships, especially those involving shared projects as well as mutual emotional satisfaction and economic support, offer all that the mother-child relationship offers, and more. Like mother-child relationships, friendships are held together by tears, laughter, and sweat rather than by waivers, subpoenas, and depositions; but they are inherently less imbalanced than mother-child relationships. Friends are equals in the sense that, over time, they can give to each other approximately as much as they take from each other.[35] Rarely does the typical mother-child (or mothering person–child) relationship evolve into a friendship as such; for the most part, it remains instead, if only in very subtle ways, a relationship between unequals.

Power-Focused Feminist Approaches to Ethics

As I previously noted, unlike care-focused feminist approaches to ethics, power-focused feminist approaches to ethics ask questions about male domination and female subordination *before* they ask questions about good and evil, care and justice, or mothers and children. In an attempt to specify the kind of questions that feminist as opposed to nonfeminist ethicists typically ask, philosopher Alison M. Jaggar has claimed that to qualify as feminist, an approach to ethics, whether care-focused or power-focused, must critique the gender-biased character of most nonfeminist approaches to ethics. In particular, a power-focused feminist approach to ethics must fault nonfeminist ethicists for subordinating women to men by neglecting, downplaying, trivializing, or totally ignoring women's moral interests, issues, insights, and identities.[36]

Acutely aware of the ways in which nonfeminist ethicists have tended to dismiss women's morality as "second rate" or "lightweight," Jaggar urges feminist ethicists to develop power-focused approaches to ethics that begin "from the conviction that the subordination of women is morally wrong and that the moral experience of women is as worthy of respect as that of men."[37] In her view, regardless of what else a power-focused feminist ethicist aims to do, she or he is clearly required "(1) to articulate moral critiques of actions and practices that perpetuate women's subordination; (2) to prescribe morally justifiable ways of resisting such actions and practices; and (3) to envision morally desirable alternatives that will promote women's emancipation."[38] Although power-focused feminist ethicists should attend first and foremost to patterns of *male* domination and *female* subordination, Jaggar believes they should go on to address the immoralities caused by other patterns of human domination and subordination. Not only sexism but also classism, ethnocentrism, heterosexism, ableism, and so on are the enemies of feminist ethicists.

Among recent power-focused feminist approaches to ethics are so-called lesbian approaches to ethics, which view heterosexism in particular rather than sexism in general as the primary cause of women's subordination to men. Although these power-focused feminist approaches to ethics are deliberately directed to lesbian women, they also contain valuable lessons for heterosexual women. Consider, for example, the teachings of lesbian feminist Mary Daly. Like the nonfeminist ethicist Friedrich Nietzsche, Daly proposes a radical "transvaluation of values" that reverses the standard meaning of traditional moral concepts.[39]

Daly is Nietzschean in her insistence that when it comes to women, she whom the patriarch calls "evil" is in fact good, whereas she whom the patriarch calls "good" is in fact bad. If a woman is to escape the traps men have laid for her—if she is to assert her power, to be all that she can be—she must realize that it is not *good* for her to always sacrifice, deny, and deprive herself for the sake of the men and children in her life. What is actually good for a woman, observes Daly, is precisely what patriarchy identifies as *evil* for her—namely, becoming her own person.[40] Daly urges women to move from men's justice not to women's care but to Nemesis. She notes that "unlike 'justice,' which is depicted as a woman blindfolded and holding a sword and scales, Nemesis has her eyes open and uncovered—especially her Third Eye."[41] Nemesis is less concerned with punishing rule-breakers than with helping oppressed people overcome the causes of their oppression. Rather than contrasting "female" caring with "male" justice, then, Daly advances Nemesis as the appropriate foil for the kind of false justice that bolsters an oppressive status quo. The appropriate antidote for the kind of false justice that "is indeed *blind* to racism, sexism, war and poverty"[42] is not a caring born of sweet reasonability but, rather, a Nemesis born of "Rage."[43]

Continuing Daly's moral revolution, lesbian feminist Sarah Lucia Hoagland has developed a power-focused feminist approach to ethics that replaces the questions "Am I good?" and "Is this good?" with the question "Does this contribute to my self-creation, freedom and liberation?" Rejecting sexism in general and heterosexism in particular, Hoagland urges lesbian women to courageously and joyfully weave their own values, without insisting that heterosexual women, let alone men, follow their example.[44] In other words, as Hoagland sees it, a morality need not be applicable to all human beings in order to count as a bona fide morality.

Hoagland is considered to be misguided from the perspective of nonfeminist ethicists, who hold that unless one's own ethics can serve as everyone's ethics, it is a bogus ethics. Waving aside this criticism as entirely missing the point of lesbian approaches to ethics, lesbian feminist Marilyn Frye notes that the need to ask what *everyone* is permitted, required, or forbidden to do under certain sets of circumstances tends to arise only among people who have a stake "in being good and / or in others' being good."[45] Frye provides the example of a white / Christian / middle-class American who bases his conception of himself as a "judge, teacher / preacher, director, administrator, manager, and in this mode, as a decision maker, planner, policymaker, organizer"[46] upon his conviction that he is in the right—that he knows what is good for others as well as for himself. Thus, it does not strike him as authoritarian to prescribe universal, even absolute, rules of conduct. In fact, as he sees it, to fail to do so is to act in a less than rational manner; it is to succumb to the forces of tribalism, relativism, and irrationality.

Upon hearing the accusatory terms 'tribal,' 'relativist,' and 'irrational,' lesbian feminists like Hoagland and Frye do not flinch. Rather, these feminists clarify what kind of moral power they seek for lesbians. Clearly, they do not want the kind of moral power that has enabled small, elite groups to impose their self-serving visions of the "good" upon the masses. On the contrary, they want the kind of moral power that permits even the most vulnerable and imperiled individuals to make choices.

Hoagland claims that although a lesbian cannot always control the situations in which she finds herself, she is not necessarily doomed to fall victim to these situations. Telling the oppressed that they are total victims does not help them or excuse them, in Hoagland's estimation. It merely robs them of what little moral agency remains in their hands. Even when the oppressed cannot control situations, they can still *affect* them, says Hoagland: "In focusing on choice and moral agency, I mean to invoke lesbian ability to engage, to act in situations—that we move here now makes a difference. And I mean to suggest that whatever limits we face, our power—ability and agency—lies in choice."[47] For Hoagland, a power-focused *feminist* approach to ethics is not about some people making rules for other people to follow. Nor is it about some people sacrificing themselves on other people's behalf. Instead, says Hoagland, a power-focused *feminist* approach to ethics is about people making their own choices, no matter the constraints of their situation; it is about refusing either to dominate or to be dominated. Interestingly, Hoagland believes that one of the best ways to overcome the urge to dominate (or be dominated) is by practicing what María Lugones terms 'playfulness'. Playful people are imaginative people, cued to the possibilities that exist in others as well as themselves. They have the ability "to travel" in and out of the worlds of people who see reality differently than they do.[48] In Hoagland's estimation, playful people are powerful people because they are full of "adventure, curiosity, desire."[49] They have no interest in the boring game of domination and subordination. Thus, for them ethics ceases to be an instrument of restraint and constraint; it becomes instead a way for lesbians—and other playful souls—to empower each other with meaning.

Conclusion

Whether they are care-focused or power-focused, feminist approaches to ethics differ from nonfeminist approaches to ethics in that they are sensitive to women's moral concerns and to the ways in which being a member of a culturally disfavored gender—in this instance, the "feminine" or "female" gender—leads to women's disempowerment morally and personally as well as politically, economically, and socially. Because feminist ethicists focus on women—or, more abstractly, on gender—some nonfeminist ethicists have dismissed their work as being just as "sexist" as traditional Western ethics supposedly is.[50] These critics claim that if it is wrong to use a "male" perspective in developing an approach to ethics, it is equally wrong to use a "female" perspective. Likewise, if it is wrong to disguise men's preferences as human values, it is wrong to disguise women's preferences as human values. Either gender-free moral values exist or they do not. If they do exist, they belong equally to men and women. Finally, it is wrong, for example, to keep women on the moral defensive by reminding them where they fall on Kohlberg's scale, just as it is wrong to keep men on the moral defensive by focusing discussion on issues such as men's violence against women.

Feminist ethicists deny that the care-focused and power-focused approaches to ethics are sexist. For example, Alison Jaggar convincingly argues that feminist ethics is not a "simple inversion"[51] of the five most frequently raised feminist challenges to nonfeminist approaches to ethics—namely, their "(1) lack of concern for women's interests; (2) neglect of 'women's issues'; (3) denial of women's moral agency; (4) depreciation of 'feminine' values; and (5) devaluation of women's moral experiences."[52] As Jaggar sees it, the fact that feminist ethicists fault nonfeminist ethicists for not being concerned about women's interests does not mean that they wish to ignore men's interests. On the contrary, most feminist ethicists would be "morally outraged" [53] by any such suggestion. They would insist that ethics is concerned about everyone's interests.

Moreover, as a rule, most feminist ethicists would insist that when nonfeminist ethicists neglected such "women's issues" as the nonavailability of affordable child care and the dearth of safe as well as effective contraceptives, they actually neglected men's issues as well.[54] After all, childbearing and childrearing practices and policies affect men, too. Jaggar also insists that just because feminist ethicists wish to point out that women are moral agents capable of making genuinely moral decisions, it does not follow that feminist ethicists believe that women are morally perfect creatures or angels.[55] Neither is it the case that feminist ethicists believe each and every "feminine" value is superior to each and every "masculine" value or that all women, just because they are women, share precisely the same moral experiences. Rather, what all this means is that feminist ethicists want simply to refocus nonfeminist approaches to ethics using the eyes of women—or, once again, more abstractly—the lens of gender.

As we have seen, feminist ethicists, whether care-focused or power-focused, do not attempt to be neutral. They specify they are considering *women's* moral concerns, gladly acknowledging their focus and voluntarily opening themselves up to criticism. It is easier, after all, to criticize individuals or groups that reveal their heartfelt thoughts to others than to criticize an impartial, objective, neutral spectator whose very *lack of humanity*—of specificity and particularity—wards off any and all criticisms. *The fact that an approach to ethics is gendered does not necessarily mean it is sexist.* An approach to ethics becomes sexist only when it systematically excludes the interests, identities, issues, and values of one or the other of the two sexes, and feminist ethicists have no plans to do unto men what nonfeminist ethicists did unto women.

3

Nonfeminist Approaches to Bioethics

The rules, principles, ideals, sentiments, laws, and agreements that play a central role in nonfeminist *ethics* also figure strongly in nonfeminist *bioethics*. But this is not surprising given that medical ethics, from which bioethics has developed, is an attempt to apply general ethical theories to specific forms of conduct and moral judgment in the medical realm.[1] Thus, philosopher K. Danner Clouser is correct when he writes that medical ethics is

> a special kind of ethics only insofar as it relates to a particular realm of facts and concerns and not because it embodies or appeals to some special moral principles or methodology. . . . It consists of the same moral principles and rules that we would appeal to, and argue for, in ordinary circumstances. It is just that in medical ethics these familiar moral rules are being applied to situations peculiar to the medical world.[2]

Clouser bolsters his definition of medical ethics with some examples, including the rule "Do not kill." Although corporate executives and physicians share similar views about killing, murderous acts assume different contours in the worlds of business and medicine. For example, corporate executives need to ask themselves under what circumstances their knowing distribution of possibly harmful products to consumers amounts to the willful imperilment of consumers' lives. In contrast, physicians need to ask themselves under what circumstances their withholding or withdrawing possibly beneficial medical treatment from patients amounts to killing patients. Similarly, what amounts to deception, unfairness, coercion, and so on, will differ in the worlds of business and medicine simply because these worlds are so different. Concealing information from a competitor about a product is very different from withholding information from parents about their child's prognosis for recovery.

Medical ethics has a long history in the Western world. Indeed, in a recent discussion of its history, British theologian G. R. Dunstan reminds us that Chaucer's Doctour of Phisik—"a verray parfit praktisour"—invoked such ancient authorities as Hippocrates, Galen, Rhazis, Avicenna, Averroes, and Constantine to justify his interpretation of the *proper* practice of medicine. Apparently, the monks of the Christian world, along with the physicians of the Islamic world, passed down to Chaucer's "Doctour" the ancient Greek ethics as well as the science of medicine.[3] This tradition, generally referred to as the Hippocratic tradition, is reflected not only in Chaucer's medieval *Canterbury Tales* (1387) but also in Percival's nineteenth-century *Medical Ethics* (1803) and most twentieth-century versions of the American Medical Association's *Code of Ethics*. For nearly 2,500 years, the Hippocratic Oath ("First, Do No Harm") and the "deontological books" that elaborated upon it shaped physicians' practice. The Oath laid out such ethical duties as beneficence, nonmaleficence, and confidentiality for physicians, calling upon them to lead pure lives of virtue. The deontological books gave instructions in gentlemanly conduct and rules of etiquette. Together they constituted the "Gold Standard" for physicians' character and behavior. Armed with the virtue of practical wisdom, physicians sought to align their decisions with the spirit if not also the letter of their guild's Oath and books. They trusted themselves and one another to be good men as well as good physicians. Indeed, they regarded themselves as fraternity brothers with self-imposed rules governing their "demeanor, rebates for referrals, decorum in consultations, soliciting another's patient, rumor mongering about other doctors, advertising, and endless other behavioral possibilities within medicine."[4]

In Edmund Pellegrino's estimation, the Hippocratic tradition flourished for as long as it did largely because it developed in relatively homogeneous societies. Individuals seldom disagreed about the application of such terms as 'right' and 'wrong' or 'good' and 'bad'. However, as societies became more heterogeneous, and as people became more egalitarian and suspicious of powerful "in-groups," the Hippocratic tradition and its guild mentality began to crack. By the middle of the twentieth century, the stage was set for some major shocks to the Hippocratic tradition—indeed, to all of the West's major ethical traditions.[5] The events of the 1960s and 1970s were particularly cataclysmic—especially in the United States, which, according to Pellegrino, witnessed a decline in community-wide values, a heightened sense of ethnicity, and a distrust of authority and institutions of all kinds. Protest was the order of the day. Civil rights demonstrations, consumer movements, and feminist activism thrived. Many people no longer knew whom or what to believe; and as the public became more aware of the increasing specialization, fragmentation, institutionalization, and depersonalization of medicine, the average patient began to lose confidence in the medical establishment.[6]

Agreeing in the main with Pellegrino, philosopher Stephen Toulmin notes that other factors over and beyond our increased social heterogeneity contributed to the demise of the Hippocratic tradition. In particular, advances in science and technology began to complicate medical decisionmaking.[7] For example, artificial respirators could now keep alive patients who would previously have died. But because these tools of technology were capable of sustaining the breath of permanently comatose as well as temporarily unconscious patients, an increasing number of concerned citizens questioned whether a decision in favor of *more* life—especially if it transpired in a "vegetative" state—was necessarily one that accorded with Hippocrates' words, "First, Do No Harm." Thus, the stage was set for the birth of bioethics from the womb of medical ethics. No longer would the medical world's "ethics" be the exclusive concern of health-care practitioners. Henceforth, it would also be the concern of the general public.

Among all the events that led to bioethics' birth, philosopher Albert R. Jonsen singles out three. First, he discusses the 1962 establishment of a hospital ethics committee in Seattle, Washington—a committee that was constituted to resolve a particularly distressing problem of resource allocation. Because Seattle physicians had far more patients for whom renal dialysis was medically indicated than they had dialysis machines, they asked a group of laypersons to help decide which of several candidates should receive the scarce technology. Since all of the candidates could *medically* benefit from renal dialysis—indeed, it would save their lives—these laypersons relied upon largely *nonmedical* criteria to decide among the competing candidates. For example, they asked questions about the candidates' past or expected social contributions, finances, personalities, family dependents, and personal support systems. According to Jonsen, this event, more than any other he recalls, signaled bioethics' break from medical ethics, and this specifically because physicians had ceded some of their decisionmaking authority to a group of laypersons. In a very dramatic way, medical decisionmaking entered the public domain. It was no longer the prerogative and charge of health-care practitioners alone. Citizens became increasingly aware that the line between fact and value—between medical and nonmedical criteria—is one that is easily crossed and, therefore, that laypersons as well as health-care practitioners should have a voice in the world of medical decisionmaking.[8]

As Jonsen sees it, the second event that convinced the public that they should take an active role in bioethics was the publication of Dr. Henry Beecher's article exposing unethical design and conduct in twenty-two biomedical research studies. Although the public did not want to believe that medical researchers would in any way take advantage of or manipulate their human subjects, the revelation of the role of the U.S. Public Health Service in the Tuskegee syphilis experiment, for example, forced the public to admit that all was not morally well in the realm of science, technology, and medicine. The fact that government researchers let unsuspecting African-American men die of syphilis—men whose lives they could have saved—so shocked the U.S. citizenry that Congress established a National Commission for the Protection of Human Subjects of Biomedical and Behavior Research. Between 1974 and 1978 the members of this commission met and recommended several policies, many of which contributed to the articulation of bioethics' basic concerns—patient autonomy, informed consent, and risk-benefit trade-offs.[9]

The third event that Jonsen discusses as pivotal in bioethics' birth was Dr. Christian Barnard's 1967 transplantation of a brain-dead person's heart into a patient with terminal cardiac disease. Critics of the transplant questioned whether the heart donor had *really* been dead prior to the moment of transplant. Their concerns led to the Harvard Medical School's 1968 articulation of the criteria for brain death. According to Jonsen, these criteria were so well publicized that by 1975 the majority of the public had grasped the concept of brain death and largely, though not unanimously, had accepted it as the official standard for death.[10] Thus, when the courts finally permitted the family of Karen Ann Quinlan to have their permanently comatose daughter disconnected from a life-support system, relief was the general reaction.[11] From the standpoint of most U.S. citizens, the fruits of science, technology, and medicine were not unalloyed blessings, and new moral principles, rules, and ideals as well as new laws were needed in the medical realm.[12]

Jonsen's analysis of bioethics' growth continues into the 1980s and 1990s. For Jonsen, the ascendancy of bioethics is a public response to the political and social implications of developments in science, technology, and medicine. Bioethics is a mode of moral reasoning, a way of thinking about events that, in his estimation, is specifically geared toward protecting vulnerable individuals from abuse by the institutionalized systems and structures of power that support the practice of medicine.[13]

Significantly, most bioethicists accept Jonsen's views on bioethics in general, even if they seek to amend, modify, or otherwise improve on them. For example, K. Danner Clouser cautions that bioethics' supposedly *new* rules are not fundamentally different from the *old* rules of medical ethics and ethics; in short, they are "derived." "Morality," insists Clouser, "is not invented or legislated; at most it is 'discovered'; that is, it is an unpacking, explication, and articulation of our deepest intuitions about what we ought and ought not to do."[14] Stressing bioethics' applied nature, Clouser adds the caveat that "[b]ioethics appears to have no essences that would mark it off."[15] Many of the issues it considers are indeed related to concerns about the ever-increasing control of contemporary science, technology, and medicine over human beings' bodies, minds, and quality of life. Nevertheless, some issues preoccupying bioethics entail the *nonhuman* world (e.g., the "rights" of animals and even plants),[16] and yet others *predate* the scientific and technological revolution (e.g., human beings' general inability to accept their carnality and mortality).

One of the most controversial claims Clouser makes about bioethics is that "much of what is compressed under the umbrella of 'bioethics' is really concerned with public policy—that is, with the legislation, policies, and guidelines that should be enacted with respect to all these issues."[17] Clouser distinguishes between ethics on the one hand and bioethics and public policy on the other. For him, ethics is about "don'ts"—about not inflicting evil, not doing harm, and not violating individuals' rights; it is "primarily a system of restraints."[18] In contrast, bioethics and public policy are about "do's"—about prioritizing goods, benefiting persons, and doing what is best for the most people possible. Moreover, Clouser not only links the principles of autonomy and nonmaleficence to ethics, and the principles of justice and beneficence to bioethics and public policy, but he also insists that the former two principles are more fundamental than the latter two. Accordingly, he maintains that the kinds of weighings, balancings, trade-offs, and compromises that characterize policymaking are inappropriate when it comes to genuinely ethical deliberations about individuals' rights, especially their right not to be harmed.[19]

Whether or not Clouser's analysis is ultimately correct, it raises interesting questions about the nature and function of morality; the differences among private, professional, and public ethics; the cross-fertilization between ethics and bioethics; and the boundary line, if there is one, between ethics and politics. My own view is that Clouser's conception of ethics is flawed—that ethics, as well as bioethics and public policy, is about doing good as well as avoiding evil. As I see it, ethics is not only about the rights of individuals and their quest to develop themselves, but also about the responsibilities of individuals and their desire to relate to each other. Ethics encompasses more than just the rules that enable individuals to pursue their separate interests; it also comprises the ideals that enable individuals to cooperate toward the achievement of common purposes.

Dominant Nonfeminist Approaches to Bioethics

Deductivism

One of the most widely recognized dominant nonfeminist approaches to bioethics is so-called deductivism. According to David de Grazia, an ethical theory is deductivist when its theoretical structure is so well defined that, given knowledge of the pertinent facts, all justified moral judgments flow from that structure's basic premises. From the individual's point of view this derivation is rote and does not require her or him to engage in reflection. Comments de Grazia: "[O]nce the correct structure or theory has been identified, there is no need to appeal to intuitions in arriving at correct moral judgments—either in balancing conflicting principles or in making particular judgments."[20] Thus, deductivists approach ethics as if it were science, seeking to bring to the former the kind of precision that characterizes the latter. Indeed, Dr. Joan Gibson claims that there are striking procedural similarities between the giving of good reasons in science (so-called explanation) and the giving of good reasons in deductivist ethics (so-called moral justification). She ably summarizes these similarities as follows:

Science (As Explanation)	**Ethics (As Moral Justification)**
Theory	Theory
Law	Principle
Hypothesis	Rule
Observation	Moral Value Judgment
Why did the pencil fall when dropped?	Why should Mr. Jones's pacemaker *not* be deprogrammed?
Because of the hypothesis that all objects fall when dropped. Why?	Because of the rule that you should never do an act that will kill another person. Why?
Because of gravity (i.e., because objects with mass attract each other). Why?	Because of the principle of nonmaleficence (i.e., you should never do something that will cause another harm). Why?
Because of the theory of Newtonian Mechanics or General Relativity (which I will not try to describe here).	Because of the theory of (take your pick) Christianity, Judaism, Islam, Utilitarianism (and others which I will not try to describe here).[21]

Deductivists claim that their approach to ethics helps shield us from all sorts of subjective mischief: bias, prejudice, misperception, intuition, opinion, emotional reactions, and so forth. Provided that we can determine *the* "correct" ethical structure or theory—for example, utilitarianism or Kantianism or whatever—we will find it relatively easy to answer any question in bioethics. Thus, the problem for deductivists is to determine which ethical theory ought to guide our moral reasoning. Seeking the "magic set of rules" is the only genuine quest that deductivists conduct; for after the guiding moral corpus has been agreed upon, the answers to moral dilemmas are easily reached.

Among the deductivists who claim to have found *the* theory that ought to guide our moral reasoning is philosopher Bernard Gert. As he sees it, the primary function of morality is to provide us with the means to minimize the amount of evil we suffer.[22] Gert believes that if each of us were to obey ten simple rules of behavior, our own best interests would be well served. The rules are as follows: (1) Don't kill, (2) Don't cause pain, (3) Don't disable, (4) Don't deprive of freedom, (5) Don't deprive of pleasure, (6) Don't deceive, (7) Keep your promises, (8) Don't cheat, (9) Obey the law, and (10) Do your duty.[23]

Although Gert thinks that we would be even better off if we also followed what he identifies as moral ideals—for example, preserving life, relieving pain, and lessening disabilities—he insists that, strictly speaking, we are not morally required to follow these moral ideals. It is one thing to be obliged not to harm people and quite another to be obliged to benefit people. For example, it takes relatively little effort for a physician "not to kill" a patient, whereas a great deal of effort is required to heal a patient—especially if that patient is suffering from a serious disease.

Gert believes that his deductive theory of ethics is an improvement over those that preceded it. In his estimation, we can apply concrete moral rules to specific situations more easily than such abstract principles as the Categorical Imperative or the Principle of Utility. Rather than spending hours adding and subtracting utilitarian units of pleasure and pain or trying to determine whether the maxim guiding our act is universalizable as a law of nature, all we need to ask ourselves before we decide to disable someone is whether we are willing to have our violation publicized. As co-authors Gert and Clouser further explain,

> Although this [deductive theory of ethics] resembles Kant's Categorical Imperative, it is significantly different. It captures the impartiality that is an essential part of morality without leading to the absurdities that Kant's theory does. And, just as important, in determining the *kind* of action, it takes into consideration the action's foreseeable consequences that are the strongest feature of Utilitarianism—but without leading to the absurdities of Utilitarianism.[24]

But not everyone is as impressed with deductive systems of ethics as Gert and Clouser are. Critics of deductivism claim that what actually grounds most deductivist moral theories are basic intuitions or unproved assumptions shared by a relatively homogeneous group of people. Thus, deductivism is unlikely to be a useful moral system in an increasingly heterogeneous world where a decreasing number of people share the same values. For every person who embraces the Principle of Utility, there is someone who instead embraces the Categorical Imperative; and for everyone who follows Gert's ten basic moral rules, there is someone who views them as little more than Gert's moral hobbyhorses. Moreover, argue deductivism's critics, even if everyone agreed that we should judge the rightness or wrongness of our actions in terms of the Principle of Utility, or the Categorical Imperative, or Gert's moral rules, we would still be faced with the problem of "local interpretation." In other words, it is conceivable that, irrespective of their race, class, gender, ethnicity, and so forth, all rational agents could agree that Gert's moral rules are *the* moral rules for everyone and yet not come to the same decision about the morality of, say, abortion. Depending on how someone interprets the word 'kill' in the moral rule "Don't kill" and/or the word 'freedom' in the moral rule "Don't deprive of freedom," for example, she or he might just as easily forbid as permit abortion. In short, deductivism seems unable to deliver to bioethics the clear-cut simplicity it promises.

Inductivism (Casuistry)

Because deductivists cannot prove to everyone's satisfaction that a certain set of universal, hierarchically ordered principles, rules, and the like exist as *the* criteria for all rational persons' moral conduct, so-called inductivists urge us to admit that ethics does not come down from on high and impose its strictures upon us ready-made. Rather, ethics is the cumulative by-product of the contextual judgments we humans have made throughout history about what should or should not be done under certain sets of circumstances.

Casuistry is probably the best-developed inductivist approach to bioethical reasoning. Philosophers Albert Jonsen and Stephen Toulmin assert that the defining feature of casuistry is that it uses "the concrete circumstances of actual cases, and the specific maxims that people invoke in facing actual moral dilemmas"[25] rather than procedures of reasoning based on grand principles such as Mill's or Kant's, or sets of rules such as Gert's. Casuists claim that it is a mistake to start with general norms and reason down to particular cases, since general norms tend to operate like Procrustean beds that are able to accommodate only those facts that do not excessively burden their logic. Accordingly, inductivists accuse deductivists, who favor this kind of top-down reasoning, of selecting precisely those facts of a case that best fit their general norms. For this reason, casuists argue that induction (reasoning from particular cases to general norms about these cases)—including analogy (looking for similarities among particular cases)—is superior to deduction as a form of moral reasoning. Induction, they say, allows the particular facts of a case to speak loudly for themselves, permitting us to better see if these particularities justify exceptions and qualifications of the general norms that deductivists would have been only too eager to impose upon them.

Perhaps one of the best ways to understand how casuists reason is to focus on a specific cluster of cases. Casuists proceed from what they regard as an obviously wrong decision—for example, not operating on an otherwise healthy infant with an esophageal blockage—to less obvious cases—not operating on an infant with Down's syndrome, or an infant with Tay-Sachs disease, or an extremely low-birth-weight infant, each of whom has an esophageal blockage. Reasoning by way of analogy from the paradigm case whose resolution they are sure of to cases whose resolution they are not sure of, casuists will ask themselves in what ways unhealthy infants with esophageal blockages are like healthy infants with esophageal blockages. Depending on how much the former infants are like or unlike the latter infants, casuists would either recommend or not recommend surgery to open the esophageal blockage. For example, the fact that Down's syndrome infants are *like* healthy infants in that they can experience many of life's pleasures would incline casuists to conclude that it is wrong not to operate on a Down's syndrome infant who has an esophageal blockage. Similarly, the fact that infants with Tay-Sachs are *unlike* healthy infants and Down's syndrome infants in that they are destined for relatively short and extremely painful lives would incline casuists to conclude that not operating on an infant with Tay-Sachs is the most humane course of action possible. With respect to extremely low-birth-weight infants, however, casuists might find themselves at the limits of their wisdom. Because it is very difficult to predict the quality of life such infants will experience, casuists are uncertain whether such infants are more like infants with Down's syndrome or infants with Tay-Sachs. Thus, casuists might be very hesitant to take a firm stand on cases involving extremely low-birth-weight infants.

Because casuists keep moral reflection so close to the facts of cases, some critics suspect that casuistry rejects general norms or principles altogether. For example, philosopher Tom Beauchamp and theologian James Childress do not find in casuistry any reason to ever "give general rules authority over particular judgments."[26] To this criticism, philosopher Al Jonsen responds that casuistry does not reject principles or general norms altogether but, rather, uses them only when it makes sense to do so.[27] In some cases, particularly so-called paradigm cases, principles rule unequivocally. There is no question that the principle of beneficence was violated, for example, by the researchers who conducted the Tuskegee Syphilis experiment. It was simply maleficent for them not to give the African-American men enrolled in that experiment the proper treatment for syphilis when that treatment became available.[28] In other cases, however, it will not be clear whether the principle of beneficence has been violated. For example, a breast-cancer patient might beg to be enrolled in an experimental study that poses considerable risks to her but also the *chance* of some limited benefits. In such circumstances, casuists would immerse themselves in the facts of the patient's case, hoping to find within them the morally right answer to her request. And if they deal with the principle of beneficence at all, they would tend to use it as a rhetorical device through which to express their judgment that, after all, the breast-cancer patient should (should not) be granted her request.[29]

Principlists

Aware of the strengths as well as the weaknesses of both inductivism and deductivism, so-called principlists (many of whom describe themselves as "coherentists") urge us to move between particular judgments on the one hand and general norms on the other. As principlists see it, their primary task is to continually calibrate the balance between these two poles of moral decisionmaking so that they fit together and reinforce each other. Revealing what could be interpreted as a greater affinity to deductivism than to inductivism, however, principlists usually undertake this complex process of moral calibration by attending first to the general-norm pole of moral reasoning and then to the particular-judgment pole of moral reasoning (hence the name 'principlists').

From the standpoint of principlists, the principles of autonomy, beneficence, nonmaleficence, and justice are continually competing for our moral attention. We respond to these principles because each of them represents a cluster of crucial values embedded in our "common morality"—that is, the morality that pervades our culture. When we make a moral decision, we are asked to rationally determine which of these values we are bound to follow in a particular situation. To the degree that our decision meshes with the content of our common morality, as developed over decades or even centuries, we can be confident that it is right. However, since our common morality is not an *a priori* set of rigidly ranked absolute principles, true for all times and in all places, but is instead an evolving social institution, our decision might be right even if it departs somewhat from our common morality. After all, morality does not evolve by itself; rather, its progress depends on the wisdom and courage of individual moral agents to challenge it occasionally.

Among the thinkers who have developed principlist systems are Thomas Beauchamp and James Childress. In their estimation, four historically grounded, nonuniversal, co-equal principles govern bioethics: "(1) respect for autonomy (a norm of respecting the decision-making capacities of autonomous persons), (2) non-maleficence (a norm of avoiding causing harm), (3) beneficence (a group of norms for providing benefits and balancing benefits against risks and costs), and (4) justice (a group of norms for distributing benefits, risks, and costs fairly)."[30]

Beauchamp and Childress believe that most of us (at least, most of us in the United States) currently accept these principles as part of our common morality. Whereas the principles of beneficence and nonmaleficence hark back to the ancient Hippocratic injunction to act always in the best interests of the patient and, at the very least, to do no harm, the principles of autonomy and justice resonate not so much with the Hippocratic tradition as with fundamental American moral values. Beauchamp and Childress maintain that it is precisely because these principles are so familiar to us that we automatically rely on them to make judgments about what we should or should not do in particular situations. Although it troubles us when two or more principles conflict, largely because we are loyal to them all, we trust that our cognitive skills and powers of judgment will be able to adjudicate the dispute.

Interestingly, not all principlists agree with Beauchamp and Childress that the principles of autonomy, nonmaleficence, beneficence, and justice are, in the abstract, equal; and that, therefore, in cases of conflict, the winning principle cannot be declared in advance of our deliberations. Edmund Pellegrino, for example, argues that *beneficence* is the paramount principle in medical care. Health-care practitioners' eyes must remain focused on the patient's good or the practice of medicine will degenerate. Pellegrino does not believe that autonomy and justice should play just as large a role in health care as beneficence and its correlate, nonmaleficence, have traditionally played. He worries that too much autonomy is just as bad as too little autonomy, claiming that in the form of patients' rights and privacy, autonomy sometimes "override[s] good medical judgment, encourage[s)]moral detachment on the part of the physician, and even work[s] against the patient's best interests."[31] Pellegrino also worries that, as inequities in the distribution of health care widen and anxieties about the cost of health care increase, appeals to justice may require physicians "to become agents primarily of fiscal or social purposes rather than of the patient."[32]

In their book unsurprisingly entitled *For the Patients' Good: The Restoration of Beneficence in Health Care,* Pellegrino and his co-author David Thomasma argue that conflicts in bioethics are not conflicts among beneficence, nonmaleficence, autonomy, and justice but, rather, conflicts *within* the meaning of the patient's good.

Pellegrino and Thomasma believe that there are four components of the patient's total good. The patient's first good is her ultimate good—the vision, purpose, or being (e.g., God) that grounds the meaning of her existence. The patient's second good is her autonomy in general, the moral power that enables her to act as an independent decisionmaker. The patient's third good is manifested in the particular decisions she makes. Depending on her fundamental values, it is up to her as an autonomous person to decide what kind of medical treatment she desires. The patient's fourth good is a very special one. It flows from the fact that, as a result of admittedly unfortunate circumstances, the patient has an opportunity to develop a particularly intimate relationship with her physician. This bond has a long history and is rooted in the ends and goals of medicine: Can the healer make her or his patients well? If not, the healer should admit her or his limits and, for example, stop aggressive treatment. Of these four goods, the first, according to Pellegrino and Thomasma, is the one to which the other three must always defer.[33] Thus, for example, if a physician believes that a cervical-cancer patient should continue chemotherapy, but the patient does not want to submit to the treatment because *quantity* of life is not as important to her as *quality* of life, then the physician must defer to her wishes. In short, it is the patient's beliefs about what ultimately makes life worth living that must guide the physician's actions.

Despite the enormous appeal of principled approaches to bioethics, however, a variety of critics have challenged them. Perhaps because of its very popularity, Beauchamp and Childress's version of principlism has met with the most criticism. Not surprisingly, strict deductionists like Clouser and Gert fault Beauchamp and Childress for offering individuals what they regard as a mere potpourri of principles. They claim that Beauchamp and Childress simply borrow the principle of beneficence from Mill, the principle of autonomy from Kant, the principle of justice from Rawls, and the principle of nonmaleficence from Gert, and then present the resultant blend as if it were an integrated and unified theory, when nothing could be further from the truth.[34] They also claim that Beauchamp and Childress encourage moral agents to mix and match the principles of bioethics as they please, "as if one could sometimes be a Kantian and sometimes a Utilitarian and sometimes something else, without worrying whether the theory one is using is adequate or not."[35] In sum, Clouser and Gert reject Beauchamp and Childress's approach as well as other principlist approaches to bioethics because, in their estimation, they fail to provide moral agents with "a single, clear, coherent, and comprehensive decision procedure for arriving at answers."[36] According to Clouser and Gert, whenever two or more of a principlist's principles conflict, decisionmakers are left to their own intuitions. This state of affairs in turn pushes the principlist into the waiting arms of relativists, who are only too eager to exclaim that there is no "right" way to resolve a conflict between principles.

In response to such criticisms, principlists insist that their approach to ethics does provide adequate action-guides. They concede that conflicts among principles can generate excruciating moral dilemmas for physicians who are not sure, for example, whether they should withhold aggressive and costly medical treatment from an uninsured, imperiled newborn whose chances of leading a relatively normal life are uncertain and whose parents want to cease treatment. Nevertheless, insist the principlists, there is an order among the principles that govern such tragic cases—an order that is either set in advance (according to Pellegrino and Thomasma) or that will emerge in the process of deliberation (according to Beauchamp and Childress).

Pellegrino and Thomasma maintain that when principles conflict, beneficence must rule the day. Thus, in the case alluded to above, the *good* of the infant must remain paramount in treatment discussions. If physicians believe that they can provide effective treatment for the infant in ways that offer her or him more long-term benefits than burdens, then they should provide the treatment (beneficence). It matters not if the infant's parents *want* to withhold the treatment (autonomy). Nor does it matter if society wants to use the money, otherwise to be spent on this one infant, for prenatal care for thousands of imperiled fetuses (justice).

In contrast to Pellegrino and Thomasma, Beauchamp and Childress offer a different way to handle the above case—a way that depends not on automatically privileging the principle of beneficence but, rather, on developing W. D. Ross's rule for handling conflicts among principles. Ross had proposed that when conflicting principles suggest different courses of action, people should perform the action that yields "the best balance of right over wrong."[37] Beauchamp and Childress go a step further in suggesting that when we wish to reject one principle in favor of another principle, we must meet not one but five requirements:

1. Better reasons can be offered to act on the overriding norm than on the infringed norm (for example, typically if persons have a *right*, their interests deserve a special place when balancing those interests against the interests of persons who have no comparable right).
2. The moral objective justifying the infringement has a realistic prospect of achievement.
3. No morally preferable alternative actions can be substituted.
4. The form of infringement selected is the least possible, commensurate with achieving the primary goal of the action.
5. The agent seeks to minimize the negative effects of the infringement.[38]

Thus, if in the name of *justice*, a physician decides to violate both *beneficence* and *autonomy* by not performing the needed operation on the infant described above, she must be relatively certain that (1) the infant does not have a right to the operation, (2) the funds saved will in fact be used for prenatal care, (3) no private citizen is willing to underwrite the entire cost of the infant's care, and (4) nothing short of not performing the operation will secure the necessary funds for the prenatal care. Moreover, (5) the physician must try to make the infant as comfortable as possible throughout the process of dying, providing in addition as much emotional support to the infant's parents as possible.

Predictably, inductivists have different reasons than deductivists for challenging principlism. From the perspective of inductivists, principlists such as Pellegrino, Thomasma, Beauchamp, and Childress are to be commended to the extent that they leave agents a measure of moral space within which to exercise their own individual powers of judgment. Nonetheless, they are to be faulted either for privileging the role of principles in biomedical decisionmaking or for underestimating just how susceptible principles are to "interpretation"—that is, to distortion, manipulation, and the general vagaries of human communication.

In short, some inductivist critics of principlism claim that principles, far from being objective norms, are simply subjective preferences in disguise. Robert Holmes, for example, suggests that our choice of principles is simply the result of our personal moral predilections. Thus, Holmes charges that whatever a bioethicist claims about the universality or rationality of his principles, "what happens in practice is that [he] simply chooses a favorite theory and, with the unwitting help of fudge factors, arrives at a 'solution' that he knew to be intuitively acceptable in the first place."[39] According to Holmes, then, what we need in ethics is not so much people who are skilled at defending their self-chosen principles as people who are of "sensitive, caring, and compassionate character."[40] So long as the physician in the above case is a *good* person, we can trust her to make the right decision about the imperiled newborn even if she never alludes to a moral principle.

Ronald Green, another inductivist critic of principlism, worries not so much that moral agents are inclined to substitute their own pet principles for truly universal principles as that they are inclined to use principles unreflectively. He claims that principlists tend to charge into the ethical arena, rotely chanting the words 'autonomy', 'beneficence', 'justice', and 'nonmaleficence' without ever asking themselves (or others) exactly what 'autonomy', for example, means in the context of the particular situation that confronts them.[41] Is a person acting autonomously simply because she gets to refuse a treatment she does not want? What if the treatment she is refusing—say, an antidepressant—would enable her to get control of herself, to once again become the functional and happy person she used to be? In other words, as Green sees it, principlists are so taken with their principles that they forget that moral reasoning is not restricted to principles and theories and the like but also entails people's experiences, some of which do not mesh well with the rules and regulations that the experts have designated as reliable action-guides. Abraham should have followed his heart rather than his head when "God" (was it really God?) commanded him to sacrifice his son Isaac to him. Fathers should know better than to honor a law that requires them to kill their sons.

Along the same lines, but with an emphasis on somewhat different points, Carl Elliott observes that it is a mistake to epistemically privilege principles as a source of moral knowledge, for one simple reason: namely, that most people do not ordinarily make much, if any, use of abstract norms as they struggle with decisions about their own or loved ones' medical treatment. In other words, when asked to decide, for example, whether a transplant is warranted for an octogenarian, most of us would not immediately refer to the Principle of Utility, the Categorical Imperative, Gert's moral rules, or even the more fluid principles of autonomy, beneficence, nonmaleficence, and justice. On the contrary, most of us would perhaps tell anecdotes about the octogenarian in an attempt to determine whether she is a person who believes "for everything there is a season" or, instead, a person who believes "never say die." Similarly, rather than presenting rational arguments for and against operating on an imperiled newborn, carefully assessing them for completeness and soundness, most of us would use persuasive methods in the form of, say, reminding each other about how much the newborn's parents wanted a child or cautioning each other about how much pain the newborn is in.[42] Eventually, the necessary decisions would be made based on people's feelings as well as on their reasonings.

One way of expressing Elliott's challenge to principlism is to underscore the fact that, as he sees it, it makes little sense to waste precious time striving to conceive "tidy" moral theories, since our moral world is anything but tidy. Elliott admits, however, that it is difficult for us to resist the siren call of theories and principles. In the first place, objective moral structures and norms have a certain "psychological appeal." Most of us would be extremely distressed if, in the pursuit of brutal honesty about our foundationless moral realm, we were not permitted to impose any order on our moral intuitions. Second, moral theories and principles are actually quite useful. To be sure, they can overly simplify our moral world, but they still "capture and summarize the kind of intuitions that we (at least in the West) often come to when we think about such problems." Third, moral theories and principles have "rhetorical power." As such they are part and parcel of our persuasive tools.[43]

Despite the pull that moral theories and norms exert on us, Elliott's concluding advice is not to put all our faith in them. Indeed, as he sees it, if moral reasoning came to resemble "mathematical reasoning," we would not like the consequences. To be sure, if we all agreed that certain moral theories were absolutely true, we could also reach agreement about which actions were "right" and "wrong"; but we would pay a great price for this certitude. "Moral maturity" would, in Elliott's estimation, "simply be a matter of acquiring the mental skills to reason correctly."[44] As a result, we would allow to slip away from us what many of us regard as some of the most important features of morality: "The concept of conscientious objection would vanish; we would have no moral reformers and no civil disobedience. We would lose the notion of one's moral ideals being self-chosen, of making up one's own mind about a matter of moral discretion. Also gone would be the idea of moral maturity, which would be replaced by conformity to the moral consensus."[45]

Many principlists, but Beauchamp and Childress in particular, have responded to their inductivist critics by asserting that they are well aware that fallible and flawed human beings will be tempted to use principles to serve their own ends. For example, parents who do not want to be burdened by a very sickly child might argue that "beneficence" demands that their imperiled infant be allowed to die rather than be "subjected" to a series of costly operations. Nevertheless, the fact that human beings are imperfect creatures who are just as apt to misuse principles as to use them properly is not a reason to debunk the principles themselves.

Principlists also insist that their inductivist critics have paid insufficient attention to the ways in which principlism has *evolved* as a moral theory. For example, Beauchamp and Childress claim that their emphasis on principles, rules, obligations, and rights is not to be interpreted as a rejection of ethics' other elements. On the contrary, they themselves embrace these other elements as crucial to the project of ethics:

> Often what counts most in the moral life is not consistent adherence to principles and rules, but reliable character, moral good sense, and emotional responsiveness. Principles and rules cannot fully encompass what occurs when parents lovingly play with and nurture their children, or when physicians and nurses provide palliative care for a dying patient and comfort to the patient's distressed spouse. Our feelings and concern for others lead us to actions that cannot be reduced to the following of principles and rules.[46]

According to Beauchamp and Childress, then, the fact that principles are excellent tools to use in sorting through a moral dilemma does not mean that they are the *only* tools to use. Nor does it mean that principles are the most important ingredient in a person's moral life. On the contrary, Beauchamp and Childress believe that the key to being moral "is a developed character that provides the inner motivation and strength to do what is right and good."[47]

Specified Principlism

Interestingly, so-called specified principlists go even farther than Beauchamp and Childress do in mediating the tensions between deductivism and inductivism. For example, philosopher Henry Richardson claims that specification is the solution to the age-old problem of understanding the relation between general ethical norms and their application to real-life cases.[48] He believes that we should specify the general principles of bioethics until they are able to reach down to embrace the facts of a particular case and help us decide what it is we ought or ought not to do. To get his point across, Richardson uses the example of a lawyer, hired to defend an alleged rapist, who must decide whether to cross-examine a rape victim about her past sexual encounters in a way that would make an unfavorable impression on the jury. Since any simple application of general principles ("It is wrong for lawyers not to pursue their clients' interests by all means that are lawful" versus "It is wrong to defame clients' character by knowingly distorting their public reputation")[49] would call for contradictory courses of action, Richardson specifies *both* of these principles in a way that helps the prosecutor resolve his dilemma. He suggests that lawyers must pursue their clients' interests *ethically* as well as *legally*, and that, given the nature of the crime in question, it is not *prima facie* but *actually* unethical for a lawyer to knowingly present the victim of the rape as if she were a "whore" who had begged to be "banged."[50] Too much of this kind of bias against women is already operative in our society, and our system of justice ought not to exacerbate it. By appealing not only to general principles but also to their extended cultural specifications, the defense lawyer will be able to conclude that he is morally required to restrain himself in the cross-examination process.

Critics admit the usefulness of specification, but they question whether it is really an improvement over other intuitive approaches to ethical reasoning. After all, isn't the choice of how to specify a general moral principle simply a matter of intuition? In answering this question, Richardson notes that moral agents are not permitted to specify principles in any way whatsoever. There must be a definite rationale for ordering one's specifications of principles. According to Richardson, then, only those specifications of principles that are consistent with the whole set of general principles that intuition reveals as plausible are to be acknowledged as appropriate ones.[51] But is *consistency* the ultimate test of our morality? After all, one can be consistent in the use of any moral theory, regardless of its content. If the consistent set of principles on which Richardson builds morality is fundamentally flawed in its content, then specifying norms does not help us make better moral decisions. On the contrary, all it enables us to do is to better justify our bad moral decisions.

Alternative Nonfeminist Approaches to Bioethics

In the previous section of this chapter, I examined inductivism and principlism (especially specified principlism) as a mediation between deductivism and inductivism. Now I consider two very recent nonfeminist approaches to bioethics, both of which seem to depart from the dominant nonfeminist approaches discussed earlier in the chapter. Because nonfeminist approaches to bioethics are evolving so rapidly, however, it remains uncertain whether these two and other so-called alternative nonfeminist approaches to bioethics are replacements for or simply complements to dominant nonfeminist ones. What *is* currently clear is that these alternative nonfeminist approaches resist classification as "deductive," "inductive," or "principlist."

Bioethics of Care

Convinced that, at bottom, care is a precondition for the whole moral life, several nonfeminist bioethicists have recently explored the possibility of developing a nonfeminist bioethics of care that does not focus on gender-related or women-centered issues. According to theologian Warren Reich, 'care' has at least four meanings. First, it can mean anxiety, anguish, or mental suffering. Second, it can mean a basic concern for those persons, institutions, or ideas that truly matter to oneself. Third, it can mean "solicitous, responsible attention to tasks."[52] Finally, care can mean having a regard for and attending to the specific needs of a particular person. Reich claims that these four meanings of care share at least one element in common—namely, an attitude of "worry." As he explains: "One can scarcely be said to care about someone or something if one is not at least prepared to worry about him, her, or it. The truly caring health professional is one who worries about—is concerned about—his or her patients, especially the patients who cannot take care of themselves."[53]

Turning to history for inspiration, the thinkers who are developing nonfeminist bioethics of care have found that the ideal of care has had two *main* meanings in the context of health care. The first is taking care of the *sick* person—that is, delivering competent (skilled, technical, scientific, even state-of-the-art) treatment to the patient. The second is caring for or about the sick *person*—that is, manifesting deep concern for the patient as a unique individual. These two meanings of care surfaced in an early twentieth-century debate between Dr. Richard C. Cabot and Dr. Francis Peabody, both at Harvard. Cabot championed the idea that it is the job of physicians and nurses not to care for the whole person—we have social workers and ministers for that—but only to take care of the patient's body—that is, to use the tools of technology to restore the patient's body to health. In contrast, Peabody insisted that unless physicians take care of their patients as *persons*, they are apt to improperly diagnose and treat their patients. Peabody believed that physicians must be scientists, social workers, and ministers combined—men and women able to attend to the psychological, social, and spiritual as well as bodily needs of their patients.[54]

Interestingly, Peabody's 1927 call for a personally caring perspective in medicine fell on largely deaf ears until the 1960s and 1970s. By this time, as the result of scientific and technological advances in medicine, the test tube and the machine had come to dominate the practice of medicine. Increasingly fascinated with disease, physicians were now expressing disinterest in focusing on anything other than the patient's body. Insisting that physicians need to view medicine as both an art and a science in order to be truly helpful to patients, critics of reductionism in medicine urged physicians to treat their patients not as "kidneys" or "hearts" but as unique individuals enmeshed in intricate webs of personal and professional relationships.

Among these anti-reductionists was and remains Dr. Eric Cassell. As he sees it, the role of the physician is not simply to *cure*, say, a patient's heart disease, to repair her or his "ticker" in the same way that an auto mechanic repairs someone's auto engine. Rather, it is to *heal* the patient—that is, to make the patient *whole* again.[55] Cassell concedes that healing as opposed to merely curing a patient is no easy task: In order to develop a treatment plan that will not only ameliorate or eliminate the patient's disease but also restore the patient's sense of self, says Cassell, physicians must develop their emotional and aesthetic skills as well as their rational and scientific skills.[56] It is not enough for a physician to determine through a series of complex technological tests that "this woman has breast cancer." Indeed, it is also the physician's task to learn what "having breast cancer" means to *this* woman. Why does she feel as though her life is over when only a month ago she thought it was just beginning? Unless the physician cares enough to discover the true sources of the woman's depressive feelings, she or he will have trouble determining the *right* treatment for her—namely, a treatment capable of restoring her to wholeness even if it cannot quite restore her to wellness.

Although many physicians agree with Cassell that not only they but also all other health-care practitioners need to be more caring, an equal if not greater number continue to claim that curing, not healing, is physicians' primary responsibility. These later care-resistant physicians insist that they are scientists, not ministers, and that if anyone has a duty to dry patients' tears or to hold patients' hands, it is nurses, social workers, and hospital volunteers. Perhaps suspecting that most of these care-resistant physicians are men who do not wish to develop qualities culturally identified as "feminine," Warren Reich and Nancy Jecker suggest that bioethicists should develop a bioethics of care that relies on "the understanding of care that emerged earlier in human history"[57] instead of the understanding of care that recently surfaced in Gilligan's and Noddings' care-focused feminist approaches to ethics. If nonfeminist bioethicists take Reich and Jecker's advice to heart, however, their bioethics of care will serve as an alternative not only to dominant nonfeminist approaches to bioethics but also to care-focused feminist approaches to bioethics. Thus, feminist bioethicists cannot help but be concerned lest we come to the conclusion that no matter how important a value seems—say, the value of care—*at least* half of us are prepared to reject it merely because of its links to the "feminine."

Postmodern Bioethics

At the heart of postmodern bioethics is the denial that there are objective bioethical rules "out there" for philosophers or health-care practitioners to uncover. Postmodern bioethicists such as Tristram Engelhardt point to the fact that rational communication about moral issues is no longer possible in a world full of divergent views, nor is there any widely accepted moral authority.[58] Thus, Engelhardt levels heavy criticism at any ethics consultant who seeks to pass off his or her own bioethical vision as canonical for all persons. Engelhardt observes that standards in ethics and bioethics have been sought "in the content of moral thought (e.g., in intuitions), in the form of moral reasoning (e.g., in the idea of impartiality or rationality), or in some external objective reality (e.g., in the consequences of actions or the structure of reality)."[59] But none of these candidates for morality's foundation works, he argues, because "(1) an appeal to any particular moral content begs the question of the standards by which the content is selected, (2) an appeal to a formal structure provides no moral content and therefore no content-full moral guidance, and (3) an appeal to an external reality will show what is, not what ought to be or how what is should be judged."[60] In short, each of these three candidates for moral rightness presupposes exactly what it seeks to justify: a particular moral content. Though each of us may feel sure that we know right from wrong, discovering an objective basis for our beliefs is often quite difficult. For example, I "know" my intuitions are right because my community thinks they are right. I "know" I am rational because my community thinks I am rational. I "know" which consequences are good because my community says they are good. And I "know" what is natural because my community labels it so. The problem, then, is that my community is not someone else's community and vice versa. Therefore, when we disagree with each other about the rightness or wrongness of an action, we will not be able to appeal to *everyone's* intuitions, conception of rationality, notion of good consequences, or conception of natural acts. Instead, we will be forced to rely upon *our own* moral perceptions as filtered through the conventional principles of *our own* community.

Englehardt maintains that in a postmodern society, there are only two conventional principles that everyone can invoke irrespective of their "home base": the principle of permission and the principle of beneficence. The first of these is totally formal (i.e., without specific moral content). All the principle of permission tells us is that in a secular pluralistic society, authority for resolving moral disputes "can be derived only from the agreement of the participants, since it cannot be derived from rational argument or common belief. Therefore, permission or consent is the origin of authority, and respect of the right of participants to consent is the necessary condition for the possibility of a moral community."[61] Unfortunately (or perhaps fortunately), the principle of permission cannot get us very far in the moral realm. After all, no matter how secular or pluralistic our society is, morality must retain some content. Thus, we need the principle of beneficence. Morality cannot be morality unless it concerns itself with "the achievement of goods and the avoidance of harms."[62] Granted, my good might be your harm. Nevertheless, even in a secular, pluralistic society, we all have to be committed to pursuing good and avoiding harm in some way or another. This is what Engelhardt means when he recommends that we order our lives in terms of the principle of beneficence as well as the principle of permission.

Is postmodern medicine possible or, for that matter, desirable? According to Engelhardt, it is the only kind of medicine that is currently possible. Let there be Christian Scientist medicine, Jehovah's Witness medicine, Roman Catholic medicine, and so on, he says. Each of them carries moral weight because some community of believers endorses it as a bioethical system and is prepared to live by its values. Thus, it would seem that postmodern medicine is at least *possible*—that any number of like-minded bioethical communities could spring up and practice medicine as they saw fit, free from outside moral regulation. However, to say that postmodern medicine is possible is not necessarily to say that it is *desirable,* according to critics. Rightly or wrongly, most people would find it morally distressing for informed-consent procedures to be adhered to on the west side of town but not on the east side, or for assisted suicide to be practiced in northern but not southern cities. But should we interpret such moral discomfort as a sign that most people are hopelessly old-fashioned or, instead, as a sign that most people are not prepared to stand by idly as the practice of medicine becomes "balkanized" into a set of incompatible fiefdoms? Postmodernists have no persuasive answer to this question.

Conclusion

Clearly, nonfeminist *bioethics* faces the same question as that confronting nonfeminist *ethics*. Namely, which is the superior ethical approach: one that applies overarching rules and guidelines to all ethical problems, or one that grants ethical leeway to decisionmakers based on their assessment of a specific problem? To be sure, principlists and specified principlists have provided a promising answer to this crucial question. They believe it is the task of bioethicists to move between principles and cases, sensitively calibrating them to each other in a way that is loyal to the moral history from which they both emerge. Although principlists insist that this process of calibration is a *rational* one, inductivists, especially casuists, along with those developing alternative nonfeminist approaches to bioethics, stress that the idea of rationality, like all of our ideas, depends on culture for its ever-shifting meaning and, therefore, that we cannot eliminate moral intuitions from the realm of biomedicine.

This is a time for considerable self-reflection within the nonfeminist bioethics community. Although most nonfeminist bioethicists are unwilling to return to a strictly deductivist world in which principles, roles, and norms rule like absolute monarchs, they are equally unwilling to enter the brave new postmodern world. Principlism and inductivism are doing their best to serve as prudent means between the excesses of deductivism and the defects of postmodernism; yet both, perhaps having realized their limits, seem increasingly willing to open themselves to those developing alternative nonfeminist approaches to bioethics. Whether nonfeminist bioethics can also open itself fully to the insights of those developing feminist approaches to bioethics is less clear. (As noted above, Reich and Jecker counsel caution.) Thus, one way for nonfeminist bioethicists to read the next chapter is as an invitation to throw caution to the wind and join with feminist bioethicists in a collaborative effort to create a moral environment in which truly good medicine can be practiced.

4

Feminist Approaches to Bioethics

Given that feminist thought is a vast conceptual field in which many and diverse feminist politics, ontologies, epistemologies, and ethics energize each other, it is not surprising that feminist approaches to bioethics do not constitute a uniform lot. On the contrary, feminist bioethicists are in the process of sorting and sifting through the insights of feminist thought (especially feminist approaches to ethics) as well as through the insights of nonfeminist approaches to ethics and bioethics. Diversity rather than unity is the order of the day. Yet all feminist approaches to bioethics seem interested in asking the so-called woman or gender question, raising women's (and men's) consciousness about the subordinate status of women and eliminating gaps between feminist theory and feminist practice. For feminist bioethicists a question-posing, consciousness-raising session that does not conclude with a *program of action* aimed at overcoming gender inequities in the realms of medicine and science is morally incomplete.

In this chapter I seek to convey to readers some sense of the richness and diversity of the feminist thoughts upon which feminist bioethicists rely. Since feminists do not share a common politics, ontology, epistemology, and ethics, but only a question-posing, consciousness-raising, action-oriented methodology, there are about as many feminist approaches to bioethics as there are feminist bioethicists. This state of affairs might be changing, however. As I see it, many feminist bioethicists, apparently independent of one another and without any conspiracy of purpose, seem to be moving in the direction of eclectic politics, autokoenomous ontology, positional epistemology, and relational ethics—terms that I will fully explain later in the chapter. If what I am seeing is not imaginary, then, feminist bioethicists are in the process of creating a conceptual context that permits—indeed requires—the kind of consensus that facilitates the *achievement* of gender equity (and other related equities) in the realms of medicine and science in particular.

The claim that I have just made is, of course, more about the *future* of feminist approaches to bioethics than about the *present*. Nevertheless, it is a claim that I wish to defend here, beginning with a descriptive summary of the present state of feminist thought (politics, ontology, epistemology, and ethics) and ending with a sketch of feminist approaches to bioethics now and in the future. Whether my predictions about the future of feminist approaches to bioethics prove true or not, these approaches will continue to offer nonfeminist bioethics insights that it can no longer afford to ignore, trivialize, downgrade, or neglect.

Feminist Approaches to Politics

Feminists belong to a variety of schools of thought, each of which has its own politics. By feminist politics I mean the values that orient the members of a particular school of feminist thought—whether liberal, Marxist, radical, socialist, multicultural, global, ecofeminist, existentialist, psychoanalytic, cultural, or postmodern—toward the development of their own explanations of and solutions for women's continuing subordination to men. For feminists, politics is about iniquitous male-female power relationships. In particular, it is about analyzing the precise causes of gender oppression, articulating its moral wrongness, and offering remedies for its elimination.[1]

Liberal feminists' overall claim is that female subordination is rooted in a set of customary and legal restraints that block women's entrance and/or success in the public world. Excluded, as many women are, from the academy, the forum, the marketplace, and the operating room, their true potential goes unfulfilled. Only when society grants women the same educational and occupational opportunities it grants men will women become men's equals.[2] Because liberal feminists are revisionists, not revolutionaries, they propose reformist measures that expand opportunities for women within the so-called System. For example, they advocate affirmative-action and comparable-worth laws as well as laws that crack down on sexual harassers, rapists, and women-batterers.

In contrast, Marxist feminists believe that the System itself, not just the rules that privilege men over women in it, causes women's oppression. If all women—not just the relatively privileged or exceptional ones—are ever to be liberated, the capitalist system must be replaced by a socialist system under which everyone's economic needs are met. Only then will women have the power to seize the opportunities men have always seized.[3]

Radical feminists insist that neither women's economic position nor their lack of equal educational and occupational opportunities provides an adequate explanation for female subordination. Rather, women's reproductive roles and responsibilities, as well as what poet-philosopher Adrienne Rich has termed the "institution of compulsory heterosexuality,"[4] are the fundamental causes of women's oppression by men. For this reason, radical feminists demand an end to all laws that in any way restrict women's reproductive and sexual lives. Unless women become truly free to have or not have children, to love or not love men, they will remain men's subordinates.

Seeing wisdom in both the Marxist feminist and radical feminist approaches to the situation of male domination and female subordination, socialist feminists attempt to weave these separate streams of thought into a coherent whole. One such effort is made in *Woman's Estate,* where Juliet Mitchell argues that four structures *overdetermine* women's condition: production, reproduction, sexuality, and the socialization of children.[5] A woman's status and function in *all* of these structures must change if she is to be a man's equal. At the same time, as Mitchell notes in *Psychoanalysis and Feminism,* a woman's interior world, her psyche, must also be transformed; for unless a woman is convinced of her own value, no change in her exterior world can totally liberate her.[6]

Alison M. Jaggar develops these socialist feminist streams of thought in *Feminist Politics and Human Nature.* She uses the concept of alienation to explain how, under capitalism, everything and everyone that could be a source of women's integration as persons become a cause of their disintegration.[7] Women experience nature, work, other people, and even themselves not as allies to be embraced but as aliens to be resisted. Thus, Jaggar insists, unless we fundamentally alter society's structures—and with them women's self-image—women will remain both unhappy and unfree.

Multicultural feminists affirm the general thrust of socialist feminist thought, but they fault it to the degree that it remains inattentive to issues of race and ethnicity.[8] For example, in the United States the oppression of African-American women is different from that of white women. "White" popular culture does not praise the physical attractiveness of African-American women in a way that validates the natural arrangement of black facial features and bodies, but only insofar as they "look white" with straightened hair, very light brown skin, and thin figures. This is an example of the double oppression confronting African-American women: They are subject not only to gender discrimination in its many forms but to racial discrimination as well. This invidious combination invites generalizations about the inferiority of African-American women and other women of color. For example, although more white women than African-American women are on welfare, the dominant white society simply assumes that blacks are the "problem" and thus castigates African-American women, but not white women (unless they are poor), for being sexually and reproductively irresponsible.

Although global feminists do not disagree about the ways in which multicultural feminists amplify socialist feminist thought, they observe that even this enriched discussion of women's oppression remains incomplete. All too often, feminists focus in a nearly exclusive manner on the internal gender politics of their own nation. Thus, for example, U.S. feminists are not always aware of how extensively women in other countries are oppressed. While U.S. feminists struggle to formulate laws to prevent sexual harassment and date rape, thousands of women in Peru, Argentina, Chile, Uruguay, Bolivia, and Paraguay are being sexually tortured on account of their own, their fathers', or their husbands' political beliefs.[9] Similarly, while U.S. feminists debate the extent to which contraceptives ought to be funded by the government or distributed in public schools, women in many Asian and African countries have no access to contraception or family-planning services from any source.

Ecofeminists agree with global feminists that it is important for feminists to understand, for example, how women in affluent countries sometimes inadvertently contribute to the oppression of women in impoverished countries. When a wealthy U.S. woman seeks to adopt a Central American child, her desire might prompt profiteering middlemen to prey on pregnant Central American women, the poorest of whom are receptive to the argument that their children would be better off in the arms of wealthy U.S. women. What ecofeminists add to this analysis is that, in wanting to give her child the best of everything, an affluent woman might close her eyes to the ways in which the human desire for "more, more, more" can and does damage not only the less fortunate segments of the human community but also many members of the greater animal community and the environment in general. The bigger and "better" one's home is, the more natural resources and animal products must be used to maintain it.[10] Thus, ecofeminists urge women to frame their considerations of power relations between men and women globally rather than locally, since we are *all* involved as world citizens in everything from international trade to environmental responsibility.

In a departure from these increasingly inclusionary ways of understanding women's oppression, existentialist feminists stress how, in the final analysis, all selves are very lonely and fundamentally in conflict with others. Opposition, not relation, is the order of the day. For example, in her groundbreaking book *The Second Sex*, existentialist feminist Simone de Beauvoir notes that, from the beginning, man has named himself the Self and woman the Other.[11] If the Other is a threat to the Self, then woman is a threat to man; and if man wishes to remain free, he must subordinate woman to him. To be sure, woman is not the only designated "Other" who knows oppression; blacks know oppression by whites, and the poor know oppression by the rich. Nonetheless, woman's oppression is unique because, first, it "is not a contingent historical fact, an event in time which has sometimes been contested or reversed," but, rather, a state of affairs that has always existed; and, second, women have, to a marked degree, "internalized the alien point of view that man is the essential, woman the inessential."[12] Thus, according to de Beauvoir, women will always remain the "second sex" unless they become selves equal to men's selves.

Like existentialist feminists, psychoanalytic feminists look to the inner recesses of women's psyche for an explanation of women's oppression. Relying on Freudian concepts such as the pre-Oedipal stage and the Oedipus complex, psychoanalytic feminists believe that gender inequity is rooted in sexual differences traceable to infant or childhood experiences. According to standard psychoanalytic accounts, all infants are symbiotically attached to their mothers during the pre-Oedipal stage. But it is during the Oedipal stage that the mother-son symbiosis usually breaks once and for all. The boy gives up his close attachment to his mother in order to escape castration at the hands of his father. As the result of submitting his desires (the id) to the laws of society (the superego), the boy fully integrates into culture. Together with his father he will rule over woman, whose power is just as irrational as nature's. In contrast to the boy, the girl, who has no penis to lose, separates slowly from her mother. As a result, the girl's integration into culture is incomplete. She exists at the periphery or margin of culture, always to be ruled over and never to rule.[13]

Psychoanalytic feminists believe that the best way to rewrite the ending of the Oedipus drama is to promote dual parenting as well as dual careers for heterosexual couples. They theorize that if children were reared by men as well as by women, they would no longer view the values of authority, autonomy, and universalism as strictly male; and they would no longer view the values of love, dependence, and particularism as strictly female. Rather, they would view all of these values as human values—as values that men and women share in equal measure.[14]

Like psychoanalytic feminists, cultural feminists believe that men and women have differing sets of values. Women, they say, put a premium on creating and maintaining intense, intimate, and caring relationships with others, whereas men are more interested in asserting their individuality and controlling their own and others' destinies. Thus, cultural feminists reject what they perceive as a masculine chase for political power, corporate status, and medical expertise. Indeed, they argue, as long as our society's institutions are dominated by the male drive to control others, most women will be unable to survive, let alone thrive, in them. Cultural feminists wish to transform competitive institutional relations based on furthering each individual's interests into cooperative institutional relations based on achieving a common goal. They are convinced that women's ability to weave thick relational networks is the source of whatever power women *do* have in both the private and public realms. They admit, however, that within a patriarchal society, women's caring posture can mutate into a masochistic posture. Women who are convinced that their interests are not as important as men's or even children's interests may end up trading self-respect for servility. Thus, most cultural feminists take very seriously Sheila Mullett's advice that until gender equity is achieved, women must continually ask themselves whether the kind of caring in which they are engaged

1. fulfills the one caring;
2. calls upon the unique and particular individuality of the one caring;
3. is not produced by a person in a role because of gender, with one gender engaging in nurturing behavior and the other engaging in instrumental behavior;
4. is reciprocated with caring, and not merely with the satisfaction of seeing the ones cared-for flourishing and pursuing other projects; and
5. takes place within the framework of consciousness-raising practice and conversation.[15]

Finally, according to postmodern feminists, all attempts to provide a single explanation for women's oppression not only will fail but also should fail. They *will* fail because there is no one entity, "Woman," upon whom a label may be fixed. Women are individuals, each with a unique story to tell about a particular self. Moreover, any single explanation for "Woman's" oppression *should* fail from a feminist point of view, for it would be yet another instance of so-called phallogocentric thought: that is, the kind of "male thinking" that insists on telling as absolute truth *one* and *only* one story about reality.[16] Thus, in the estimation of postmodern feminists, women must reveal their differences to one another so that they can better resist the patriarchal tendency to congeal and cement thought into a rigid "truth" that always was, is, and forever will be.

Feminist Approaches to Ontology

Just as feminists do not restrict themselves to one politics (i.e., to a single explanation for what has caused or might yet resolve male domination and female subordination), they do not limit themselves to one ontology (i.e., to a single conception of the self and the self's relationships to others). Some feminists view the self as fully integrated, self-sufficient, and separate. For them, the self is basically independent from and, at times, even in opposition to others. In contrast, other feminists believe that the self is somewhat fragmented, always needy, and ever connected. For them the self is fundamentally dependent on others for its psychic identity and material existence. Still other feminists claim that the best way to understand ourselves is as selves who are neither independent nor dependent but always interdependent.

Among the feminists who stress the autonomy, rationality, and independence thesis is existentialist feminist Simone de Beauvoir. As noted above, she accepts the Sartrean view that the Self is fundamentally at odds with the Other: a lonely, separate being that must either control or be controlled. Thus, de Beauvoir and other existentialist feminists frequently describe human relations, particularly male-female sexual relations, as essentially conflictual. For them, the state of love is basically masochistic—the Self subordinates itself to the Other—whereas such states as hate, indifference, and erotic desire are essentially sadistic—the Self seeks to control the Other. Men and women, they argue, spend their lives either trapped in one of these two states of being (on the average men are supposedly more inclined toward sadism and women, toward masochism) or vacillating between them in perpetual torment.[17]

Postmodern feminists take de Beauvoir's understanding of Otherness and turn it on its head. Woman is still the Other, they say, but, rather than interpreting this condition as something to be rejected, they proclaim its advantages. They claim that the condition of Otherness enables women to stand back and criticize the norms, values, and practices that the dominant male culture (patriarchy) seeks to impose on everyone, particularly those who live on its periphery—in this case, women. Thus, Otherness, for all its associations with being excluded, shunned, rejected, unwanted, abandoned, and marginalized, has its advantages. It is a way of existing that allows for change and difference. Women are not unitary selves, essences to be defined and then ossified. On the contrary, they are ever-moving and continually evolving free spirits.

In her writings, Hélène Cixous aims to develop the postmodern feminist view of the *male* self as an unchanging, Paramedian self, totally satisfied with what it is, and of the *female* self as a changing, Heraclitean self, always seeking to be other than it currently is. According to Cixous, there are profound connections between male sexuality and masculine writing, on the one hand, and female sexuality and feminine writing, on the other, that reveal fundamental differences between male selves and female selves. Male sexuality, which centers on what Cixous called the "big dick," is ultimately boring in its pointedness and singularity.[18] Like male sexuality, masculine writing, usually termed phallocentric writing by Cixous, is also ultimately boring. Men, she says, write the same old things with their "little pocket signifier"—the trio of penis/phallus/pen.[19] Fearing that the multiplicity and chaos that exist outside their Symbolic Order might overwhelm them, men always write in black ink, carefully containing their thoughts in a sharply defined and rigidly imposed structure.

Unlike male sexuality and male writing, female sexuality and female writing are anything but boring in Cixous's estimation. She claims that for women both sexuality and writing are open and multiple, varied and rhythmic, full of pleasures and, perhaps more important, of possibilities. When a woman has sex, she lets her body go on an adventure; she permits her drives to take her on "trips, crossings, trudges"[20] so that she can experience "abrupt and gradual awakenings, discoveries of a zone at one time timorous and soon to be forthright."[21] Similarly, when a woman writes, she uses "white ink,"[22] letting her words flow freely where she wishes them to go.

Multicultural and global feminists share with postmodern feminists a view of the self as fragmented, or at least divided. However, for multicultural and global feminists the roots of this fragmentation are cultural and national rather than sexual and literary. In the United States, for example, a Hispanic woman is likely to experience herself as a self within her own family and friendship circle, but as "the other" outside of her home boundaries. Writing from the vantage point of an Argentinean woman who has lived in the United States for several years, philosopher María Lugones gives voice to what she means by "we" (namely, other Hispanic women) and "you" (namely, white/Anglo women). She writes that although Hispanics *have* to participate in the Anglo world, Anglos do not have to participate in the Hispanic world. An Anglo woman can go to a Hispanic neighborhood for a church festival, for example, and if she finds the rituals and music overwhelming, she can simply get in her car, drive home, and forget the evening. There is no way, however, that a Hispanic woman can escape Anglo culture so easily, for the dominant culture sets the basic parameters for her survival as one of its minority members.

What most concerns Lugones about the relations between Hispanic and Anglo women is the fact that Anglo women, especially Anglo feminist theorists, tend to miss the fact that cultural differences create a *different* experience for the Hispanic woman. Comments Lugones:

> But you [feminist theorists] theorize about women and we are women, so you understand yourselves to be theorizing about us and we understand you to be theorizing about us. Yet none of the feminist theories developed so far seem to me to help Hispanas in the articulation of our experience. We have a sense that in using them we are distorting our experiences. Most Hispanics cannot even understand the language used in these theories—and only in some cases the reason is that the Hispana cannot understand English. We do not recognize ourselves in these theories. They create in us a schizophrenic split between our concern for ourselves as women and ourselves as Hispanics, one that we do not feel otherwise. Thus they seem to us to force us to assimilate to some version of Anglo culture, however revised that version may be. They seem to ask that we leave our communities or that we become alienated so completely in them that we fall hollow.[23]

Global feminists also have a schizophrenic sense of self. They claim that European colonizers robbed the peoples of many developing nations not only of their land and resources but also of their self-identities. For example, prior to being overrun by white imperialists the peoples of Africa did not think of themselves first and foremost as "black." On the contrary, they thought of themselves as linguistically and culturally unique groups of people whose skin color, by no means identical throughout continental Africa, played only a small role in their self-definition. After they became colonial subjects, however, these peoples were told that who they were, *essentially*, was black. Worse, they were told that to be black was "bad," whereas to be white was "good." Thus, as Andree Nicola McLaughlin observes, "[t]hat which was "white" (or Anglo, male, Christian, wealthy) was extolled and infused with connotations of benevolence and superiority, while that which was not white (or not Anglo, female, non-Christian, poor) was debased and associated with malevolence and inferiority."[24]

To the extent that the peoples of Africa internalized the colonists' view of them as uncivilized barbarians, this artificially constructed and systematically imposed "self-conception" did violence to their original, positive self-conceptions. Worse yet, the longer the colonists remained in power, the more difficult it became for their "black" subjects not to aspire to "whiteness." Realizing that such an aspiration could destroy their peoples' souls, many indigenous African leaders rallied their kith and kin to rebel not only against white colonizers' armies but also against their *ideas*. But even when such rebellions were successful politically, they were not necessarily successful culturally. Once "colonized," a mind is almost never liberated.

Liberal feminists also advance a view of the self as separate from the other; but unlike existentialist, postmodernist, multicultural, and global feminists, they neither employ the language of alienation and fragmentation nor speak from the perspective of the other. On the contrary, they speak from the perspective of the *whole* self. In their desire to secure for women the same opportunities, occupations, rights, and privileges that men enjoy, liberal feminists, in the opinion of legal theorist Robin West, have effectively adopted the ontology of liberal legalism. According to this perspective on reality, the self's separation from the other is the necessary precondition for the self's freedom. However, the very separation that enables individuals to pursue their own unique vision of the good is also what makes them vulnerable. Given that human beings are all separate, their different goals sometimes conflict. And since the subsequent competition often leads to suffering, injury, or even death, "annihilation by the other" becomes "the official *harm* of liberal theory, just as autonomy is its official value."[25] Thus, liberal feminists navigate very cautiously through the public and professional worlds of business, medicine, law, the academy, and so on, ever alert to the harms that might befall them there—particularly those that men might inflict upon them.

In contrast to these feminist ontologies, each of which relies on some version of a separate, split, or even schizophrenic self, there are, as I indicated above, several feminist ontologies that view the self as intertwined with and/or constituted by the other. Just as the liberal concept of human nature is present in liberal feminist thought, the Marxist concept of human nature is present in Marxist and socialist feminist thought. In general, liberals believe that what distinguishes human beings from other animals is a specified set of abilities, such as the capacity for rationality and/or the use of language; a specified set of practices, such as religion, art, science; and a specified set of attitude and behavior patterns, such as competitiveness and the tendency to put self over other. Marxists, however, reject this liberal theory of human nature, claiming that what makes human beings more than mere animals is the fact that human beings produce their own means of subsistence. We are what we are, they say, because of what we do; we create ourselves in the process of intentionally, or consciously, transforming and manipulating nature.[26]

In his *Introduction to Marx and Engels*, Richard Schmitt cautions that the statement "Human beings create themselves" is not to be read as "Men and women, *individually*, make themselves what they are." Rather, it is to be read as "Men and women, through production, *collectively* create a society that, in turn, shapes them."[27] This emphasis on the so-called collective characterizes the Marxist view of history. For liberals, in contrast, the ideas, thoughts, and values of individuals account for change over time. For Marxists, including Marxist feminists, material forces—that is, the production and reproduction of social life—are the prime movers in history. In the course of articulating this doctrine of how change takes place over time, a doctrine usually termed historical materialism, Marx stated that "the mode of production of material life conditions the general process of social, political, and intellectual life. It is not the consciousness of men that determines their existence, but their social existence that determines their consciousness."[28]

Interestingly, psychoanalytic feminists also espouse a social view of the self; but as they see it, the self's conception of its relation to others is a product not of material forces but of psychological experiences. According to most psychoanalytic feminists, what boys and girls learn about their "proper" sexual identities as children (and, indeed, as infants) has long-term implications for the ways in which they will organize their public, professional, and personal lives as adult men and women. Psychoanalytic feminists maintain that the boy's separateness from his mother is the source of his inability to relate deeply to others—an inability that prepares him for work in the public sphere, which in turn values single-minded efficiency, a down-to-business attitude, and competitiveness. Similarly, the girl's oneness with her mother is the source of her capacity for relatedness, a capacity that is necessary for her role as nurturant wife and mother in the private sphere.[29] Ironically, it is precisely women's ability to connect to other people, especially to children, that causes everyone, including women, never to be quite satisfied with how women discharge their relational responsibilities. In particular, society expects women to be perfect mothers who raise perfect children. Although psychoanalytic feminists think society should not blame women for their children's faults, they concede that women's ability to relate to people in general and to children in particular, as wonderful as it is, can go awry.[30]

Like psychoanalytic feminists, radical and cultural feminists believe that "women are 'essentially connected,' not 'essentially separate,' from the rest of human life."[31] But unlike psychoanalytic feminists, the two latter groups provide a biological as opposed to psychological explanation of what constitutes this capacity for relatedness. For cultural and radical feminists, pregnancy, intercourse, and breast-feeding are some of the paradigmatic ways through which women connect to others. However, as legal theorist Robin West has pointed out, cultural and radical feminists disagree about whether women's connectedness is a blessing or a curse.[32]

Valorizing the traits and behaviors traditionally associated with women, cultural feminists praise women's capacities for sharing, nurturing, giving, sympathizing, empathizing, and, especially, connecting. They believe the fact that women menstruate, gestate, and lactate gives women a unique perspective on the meaning of human connection. For them, connection is not about separate individuals signing social contracts but, rather, about women literally using their bodies to link one generation to the other. In cultural feminists' estimation, relationships with family members and friends are so important to women that they view separation from others as the quintessential harm.[33]

Radical feminists point to a darker side of the connection thesis. They agree with cultural feminists that connection is women's fundamental reality, but they lament this state of affairs. They observe that women's connections set women up for exploitation and misery: "Invasion and intrusion, rather than intimacy, nurturance and care, is the unofficial story of women's subjective experience of connection."[34] Women are connected to others, most especially through the experiences of heterosexual intercourse and pregnancy. But when the sugarcoating is licked off, those connecting experiences taste of women's violation. This harm is unique to women; men cannot understand it. Whereas men fear annihilation, isolation, or disintegration of their fragile, artificially constructed communities, women fear occupation: "Both intercourse and pregnancy are literal, physical, material invasions and occupations of the body. The fetus, like the penis, literally occupies the body."[35] According to radical feminists, women actually crave individuation—the freedom to reject their connectedness, at both the ontological and political levels, so that they can pursue their own separate projects. But they dare not express this desire either to men or to those women who stress the positive dimensions of the connection thesis. Men might punish them for their *self*-assertions through violent retribution (rape) or emotional revenge (divorce or spinsterhood). And many women, including cultural feminists, might accuse them of rejecting the difference that, for all its riskiness, is also the source of women's special power: the female body.

Of all the feminist schools of thought that employ a relational view of the self, however, ecofeminists have the broadest and most demanding conception of the self's relationship to the other. According to ecofeminists, we are connected not only to one another, but also to the nonhuman world: animal and even vegetative. Unfortunately, we do not always acknowledge our responsibilities to other people, let alone those to the nonhuman world. As a result, we deplete the world's natural resources with our machines, pollute the world's environment with our toxic fumes, and threaten the world's very survival with our tools of total destruction. In so doing, we delude ourselves that we are enhancing ourselves by controlling nature. In point of fact, says ecofeminist Ynestra King, nature is already rebelling, and each day the human self is impoverished as yet another forest is "detreed" and yet another animal species is extinguished.[36] The only way not to destroy ourselves, insist the ecofeminists, is to strengthen our relationships to one another and to the nonhuman world.

Feminist Approaches to Epistemology

Just as there is no single feminist politics or ontology, there is no single feminist epistemology or common understanding of what constitutes true knowledge. Some feminists believe that only impartial spectators can attain true knowledge. Others agree that there is truth to be known but insist that only certain people with certain vested interests can hope to grasp it. Still other feminists deny that truth exists at all. Among the main feminist epistemologies that have been popular over the last quarter-century are rational-empirical epistemology, standpoint epistemology, and postmodern anti-epistemology.[37]

Primarily, or perhaps even exclusively, liberal feminists adopt a rational-empirical epistemology. Because liberal feminists define equality in terms of the "sameness" of all human beings, be they male or female, they tend to believe in objective, impartial, neutral, and universal standards of behavior. They maintain that these standards exist as ideals. In other words, when human beings let biases, prejudices, mistaken views, incorrect data, or unsound hypotheses interfere with their reasoning process, they make false judgments. In contrast, when human beings overcome these distortions in reasoning, they come to terms with reality.

For the most part, liberal feminists suspect that medicine and science, as currently practiced, are not objective and impartial but androcentric. However, they believe that this undesirable situation is far from unchangeable, since *facts*, as opposed to myths and stereotypes, about women's as well as men's minds and bodies are available. In order to access these facts, physicians and scientists need only listen to women's narratives attentively and take very seriously the physical and psychological complaints that women register. The physician or scientist's authority of expertise is no substitute for the authority of the patient's experience.

Note, for example, that several studies have shown significant differences between the ways in which medical professionals and women of menopausal or postmenopausal age (1) rank menopausal symptoms for frequency, severity, and causality, and (2) rate their treatment preferences (counseling, hormone replacement therapy, mood-altering medication, or no treatment). On the average, medical professionals judge the various symptoms to be more frequent and severe than their patients do. Even more interesting is the finding that medical professionals tend to use a psychogenic model, attributing symptoms to psychological causes, whereas women of menopausal or postmenopausal age tend to attribute their symptoms to somatic disease.[38] In other words, when a menopausal woman complains that she is having a "rough" time, her physician is more likely to view these complaints as the result of mental depression than the result of bodily pain. Feminists who wish to interpret reality through a rational-empirical grid describe this tendency as a bias. Indeed, all too many health-care practitioners, convinced that women's complaints about "female diseases" are only "in the head," tend to treat these complaints as signs of depression or, worse, as mere "bellyaching."

Significantly, unlike liberal feminists, most other feminists believe that it will take more than accurate facts and attentive ears to make medicine and science objective. Existentialist, multicultural, global, Marxist, socialist, cultural, radical, and ecofeminists all adopt some version of standpoint epistemology. Feminist standpoint epistemologists believe that the liberal feminists' quest for gender neutrality, for sameness with men, and for the articulation of impartial and objective "human" standards is misguided. They argue that it is a major error to assume that men's and women's interests are fundamentally the same, since the differences between men's and women's interests are quite apparent: "One cannot simply be 'human,'" says Susan Bordo. "Our language, intellectual history, and social forms are 'gendered'; there is no escape from this fact and from its consequences in our lives."[39]

It is the opinion of feminist standpoint epistemologists that some people—in this case, women—see things better than other people—in this case, men. There are many ways to elaborate this point, but radical and cultural feminists have done so in the greatest detail. Radical feminists are inclined toward a version of standpoint epistemology that describes women's privileged status as that of the "victim." They argue that because the victimizer has a vested interest in maintaining the status quo, his position functions to produce "distorted visions of the real regularities and underlying causal tendencies in social relations."[40] In contrast, because the victim has anything but a strong desire to maintain things as they are, her status as a victim enables her to see what is wrong about some human beings dominating other human beings. Thus, radical feminists point out, for example, that because nurses, most of whom are still women, are lower in the hospital hierarchy than physicians, most of whom are still men, they share with patients certain vulnerabilities from which physicians are normally insulated. For this reason, nurses are probably more motivated than physicians to criticize "accepted interpretations of reality" (in this case, appropriate medical care for patients) and to develop "new and less distorted ways of understanding the world."[41]

Like radical feminists, cultural feminists offer a version of standpoint theory, but it is one that privileges the vision of so-called carers. They argue that women's biologically given and/or socially constructed roles as life-givers and relationship-creators put women in a better position than men to understand what is really important in life—namely, relationships with particular people as opposed to obedience to rules and regulations. Thus, according to cultural feminists, it is because women see the world through caring eyes that nurses seek to make their patients as comfortable as possible. A carer cannot simply stand by and say "Them's the rules" as she watches a patient writhe in agony.

As persuasive as feminist standpoint epistemology is, critics have faulted it on several counts. First, they say, it seems to attribute to all women one essential nature—whether that of the *victim* or that of the *carer*—thereby downplaying the fact that not just gender but also a woman's class, race, ethnicity, religion, age, and so on affect her social status and/or psychological disposition. The word 'victim' may fit a black female orderly at a hospital, but not the white female administrator who runs it. Similarly, the word 'carer' may describe a nurse who always responds cheerfully to her patients' demands, but not a nurse who views her charges as disagreeable people she would rather not serve at all.

Second, dividing the world into female victims and male victimizers, or female carers and male noncarers, contributes to an adversarial framework that is certainly antithetical to feminist practice, if not also to feminist theory. Privileging anyone's point of view—even that of a woman—is a problem. It is an especially serious problem, moreover, when gender reform is misconstrued as the "conquest of the now-all-powerful enemy male"[42] rather than as the destruction of those *ideologies* about masculine and feminine gender roles that harm men as well as women.

In contrast to standpoint epistemology, which presumes that knowledge is attainable from certain privileged standpoints, postmodern anti-epistemology dictates that no "true" facts exist for anyone to discover, regardless of their standpoint. Medicine and science can never be objective. Postmodern feminists rebuke feminists who formulate general theories about women's subordinate status in society. In their estimation, feminist standpoint theorists simply mimic the kind of universalistic, absolutist, deductivist, phallogocentric thought that insists on telling as absolute truth one and only one story about reality. There is no truth, no integrated self, no transcending reality but, instead, only shifting, ephemeral, changing realities that evolve within our social contexts. "Woman" does not exist. Only individual women exist, and none of them are unified selves. Thus, according to feminist postmodernists, women have no *one* vantage point from which to criticize the practice of medicine, the ethics of science, or anything else. All that they can do is engage in guerrilla warfare, taking "potshots" at existing power structures and flouting oppressive norms as much as possible.

Feminist Approaches to Ethics

Given that feminists have such different politics, ontologies, and epistemologies, it is to be expected, as we observed in Chapter 2, that feminist approaches to ethics are also diverse. Psychoanalytic, cultural, and ecofeminists are particularly interested in developing care-focused approaches to ethics, based on the view that women's traditional virtues (e.g., compassion, empathy, sympathy) are absolutely essential to the moral project; indeed, they are the conditions of its possibility. These feminist schools of thought claim that women approach moral reasoning and moral life differently from men. They assert that this is so either because of men's and women's differing reproductive roles and responsibilities or because of the differing ways in which boys and girls are socialized. They also claim, however, that in order to become fully developed moral persons, both women and men must learn how to strike an appropriate balance between caring and justice. Like justice, caring can be taken to extremes, in their estimation. There are times when it is necessary to treat each individual differently, but there are also times when it is necessary to treat all individuals alike.

In contrast to psychoanalytic, cultural, and ecofeminists, most of the other feminists discussed in this chapter are concerned more with power-focused than with care-focused approaches to ethics. Indeed, Marxist, socialist, multicultural, global, existentialist, and postmodern feminists are far less interested in celebrating traditionally "female" virtues than in articulating the moral wrongness of gender oppression. They view fighting for gender equity in the public and private realms as women's foremost moral obligation. Indeed, for them, the fundamental ethical quest is to make certain that women are just as free and powerful as men and that women are treated with just as much respect and consideration as men are.[43]

Feminist Approaches to Methodology

Despite the fact that feminist approaches to politics, ontology, epistemology, and ethics embody such diverse claims, it seems that virtually all feminist thinkers share a common methodology. In one way or another, all feminist thinkers ask the so-called woman question in order to raise women's (and men's) consciousness about how gender oppression distorts and hinders women's personal and professional lives; and, in one way or another, they also engage in forms of practical reasoning aimed at moving gender-aware persons from thinking about gender oppression to doing something about eliminating it.

According to Katharine T. Bartlett, a question becomes a method when it is regularly asked,[44] and the so-called woman question has been regularly asked by feminists ever since Simone de Beauvoir raised it so forcefully in *The Second Sex*. Why, she asked, is man the Self and women the Other? Why can man think of himself without woman, whereas she cannot think of herself without man? Why is this man's world, not woman's world?[45] Elaborating on de Beauvoir's statement of the woman question, a variety of feminist thinkers have sharpened it into an analytical tool for the purpose of "identify[ing] the gender implications of rules and practices which might otherwise appear to be neutral or objective."[46] Contemporary feminists ask the woman question when they ask why women have been excluded from clinical research studies. They ask it when they ask why there are so few women chief corporate executives or why those who work in female-dominated occupations are generally paid far less than those who work in male-dominated occupations. They ask it when they ask why so many women but so few men fall prey to eating disorders like anorexia and bulimia. The ways to raise the woman question are many indeed—a fact that contemporary feminists interpret as a sign of how deeply gendered our society is, and of how easily we accept as "natural" the systems and structures of male domination and female subordination that we ourselves have constructed.

Asking the woman question helps feminists raise women's (and men's) consciousness about the subtle as well as blatant forms of gender oppression in our society. Most feminists agree with legal theorist Catharine A. MacKinnon that "[c]onsciousness-raising is the major technique of analysis, structure of organization, method of practice, and theory of social change of the women's movement."[47] Although MacKinnon is sympathetic to Marxist thought, she nonetheless strenuously objects to Marxists' critique of feminism as too inward directed, too focused on women's feelings and attitudes. Indeed, MacKinnon claims that true revolution begins in the psyches of individual persons. She elaborates this point as follows:

> In consciousness raising, often in groups, the impact of male dominance is concretely uncovered and analyzed through the collective speaking of women's experience, from the perspective of that experience. Because marxists tend to conceive of powerlessness, first and last, as concrete and externally imposed, they believe that it must be concretely and externally undone to be changed. Women's powerlessness has been found through consciousness raising to be both internalized and externally imposed, so that, for example, femininity is identity to women as well as desirability to men. The feminist concept of consciousness and its place in social order and change emerge from this practical analytic.[48]

In other words, MacKinnon believes that unless women radically change the way they *think*, especially about themselves, nothing very fundamental will change in the material world. Business will proceed as usual. Oppression will remain the order of the day. She reiterates this view particularly skillfully in her explanation of feminism's relationship to Marxism: "Feminism stands in relation to marxism as marxism does to classical political economy: its final conclusion and ultimate critique. Compared with marxism, the place of thought and things in methods and reality are reversed in a seizure of power that penetrates subject with object and theory with practice.[49]

Consciousness raising enables individual women to realize not only how gender oppression affects them negatively but also how their experiences of personal hurt are related to other women's. When Adrienne Rich wrote in *Of Woman Born* the following description of her pregnancy, she described both her own experience and that of many women in my generation (we are now in our late forties or early fifties):

> When I try to return to the body of the young woman of twenty-six, pregnant for the first time, who fled from the physical knowledge of her pregnancy and at the same time from her intellect and vocation, I realize that I was effectively alienated from my real body and my real spirit by the institution—not the fact—of motherhood. This institution—the foundation of human society as we know it—allowed me only certain views, certain expectations, whether embodied in the booklet in my obstetrician's waiting room, the novels I had read, my mother-in-law's approval, my memories of my own mother, the Sistine Madonna or she of the *Michelangelo Pieta*, the flashing notion that a woman pregnant is a woman calm in her fulfillment or, simply, a woman waiting.[50]

Had Rich not written these words, many women would have continued to think that only "odd" or "abnormal" women like themselves, rather than reasonable ones, find fault with the ways in which some members of the medical establishment handle women's pregnancies.

Although some women experience consciousness raising through inner reflection upon their circumstances, this process most often occurs in the course of discussions among women. Women who feel comfortable with and trusting of one another first voice their personal experiences and then begin to see how they fit into the systems and structures of male domination and female subordination. For example, at the college at which I teach, the Women's Issues Committee sponsors a book discussion group for a small group of women, both faculty and students. The group members choose a woman-centered book and then meet to discuss how they have personally dealt with the issues raised in the book—issues such as body image and eating disorders, sexual harassment, date rape, and so on. Hearing other women express their own concerns about an issue provides the crucial "I'm-not-alone-in-feeling-this-way" realization for many women. Consciousness raising is not without its perils, however. The problem of so-called false consciousness looms large. Not every woman leaves a consciousness-raising session convinced, for example, that cosmetic surgery is a tool of gender oppression. The question then becomes whether it is these women or the ones seeking to enlighten them who see reality as it *truly* is. As it stands, feminists are inclined to believe that it is they who have 20/20 moral vision and that any woman who professes to have had several face-lifts simply to please herself is deluding herself.

Yet, from the perspective of some feminists, there is a certain arrogance in being convinced of one's own "rightness." In their estimation, feminists must be willing to entertain the possibility that, like most people, their moral vision might be not 20/20 but somewhat myopic. Every once in a while, feminists' consciousness rather than that of their nonfeminist sisters may be the false one.

Feminist Approaches to Bioethics

As mentioned above, the question "Is there anything that all feminist approaches to bioethics can and should have in common?" has a future as well as a present answer. The *present* answer is that all feminist approaches to bioethics share a common methodology—namely, the methodology of feminist thought. The *future* answer is that one day these approaches might also share a philosophical framework flexible enough to accommodate a very wide range of feminist politics, ontologies, epistemologies, and ethics. Indeed, I would suggest that some feminist bioethicists have already begun to develop this framework. At least three of the book-length approaches to feminist bioethics now in print—Susan Sherwin's *No Longer Patient*, Mary Mahowald's *Women and Children in Health Care*, and Susan Wolf's collection, *Feminism & Bioethics*—go some distance toward explaining what it means to be an "eclectic," "autokoenomous," "positional," and "relational" feminist bioethicist.

In *No Longer Patient*, Sherwin states:

> I believe we must expect and welcome a certain degree of ambivalence and disagreement within feminist theorizing. Contemporary feminism cannot be reduced to a single, comprehensive, totalizing theory. I shall try, then, to use the minimal number of theoretical commitments in my analysis, in the hope that feminists and bioethicists of many different persuasions may find value in this study.[51]

Having made this point, Sherwin proceeds to view bioethical problems through the lens of what she terms *eclectic* feminism, a political framework that permits her to use two or more feminist politics simultaneously, each of them serving as a corrective for the other's myopic tendencies.

Mahowald also uses the lens of eclectic feminism to focus her bioethical reflections. In *Women and Children in Health Care*, she states that she is trying "to combine an emphasis on equality with a 'feminine' approach to issues in health care"[52] and that her "account of equality is consistent with a socialist or Marxist version of feminism because either version holds that equality is not a beginning point, but a communitarian ideal or goal."[53] Given that socialist feminism is frequently described as a combination of Marxist and radical feminist approaches to gender inequity, the eclecticism of Mahowald's feminist politics is manifest. Throughout her book, she explains how women's sexual roles and reproductive responsibilities (stressed by radical feminists) often combine with women's economic status (stressed by Marxist feminists) in ways that put women at a decided disadvantage compared to men. A woman's "choice" to be an egg donor or surrogate mother, for example, is not the precise analog of a man's choice to be a sperm donor.

In her introduction to *Feminism & Bioethics: Beyond Reproduction,* Susan Wolf searches for a definition of 'feminism' broad and inclusive enough to envelop as many self-identified feminists in its folds as possible. She settles upon the following "safe," short definition: "[F]eminist work takes gender and sex as centrally important analytic categories, seeks to understand their operation in the world, and strives to change the distribution and use of power to stop the oppression of women."[54] Clearly, Wolf's definition reflects the author's wish to respect and work with the considerable political differences among the *sixteen* feminist authors she chose to anthologize. To read *Feminism & Bioethics* is to realize just *how* eclectic feminist politics is.

Interestingly, Sherwin, Mahowald, and many of the authors in Wolf's collection seem drawn not only to eclecticism in feminist politics but also to so-called autokoenomy in feminist ontology. Just as eclecticism in politics permits feminist bioethicists to use two or more feminist politics to better focus their differing perceptions of male domination and female subordination in the realm of biomedicine, autokoenomy in ontology permits feminist bioethicists to use two or more feminist ontologies to better explain the paradox that consists in being a self whose individuality is necessarily constituted through relationships with others. Either by coincidence or by design, Sherwin, Mahowald, and many of the authors in Wolf's collection work within ontological frameworks that closely approximate what feminist philosopher Sarah Lucia Hoagland refers to as autokoenomy.[55]

Hoagland points out that unlike the term 'autonomy', which stems from the Greek words for self ('auto') and rule ('nomos'), the term 'autokoenomy' stems from the Greek words for self ('auto') and community ('koinonia'). Unlike the *autonomous* man who thinks that his self is entirely separable from others, then, the *autokoenomous* woman realizes that she is a self inextricably related to other selves. Since she views herself as largely the product of her relationships with other selves, the autokoenomous woman, when she chooses to do something for someone else, perceives her action as self-directed as well as other-directed. In other words, the autokoenomous woman realizes that in choosing a "good" for others, she is simultaneously choosing a "good" for herself. Her actions will cause a reaction in others who, in turn, will exert their will upon her.

In the same way that an eclectic framework in politics and an autokoenomous framework in ontology permits feminist bioethicists to mix and match feminist insights, I believe that so-called positionality in epistemology permits feminist bioethicists a degree of latitude in drawing the line between mere belief (appearance) and true knowledge (reality). According to Katharine T. Bartlett and other exponents of positionality, feminists need to overcome the limits of the kind of feminist standpoint epistemology discussed earlier.[56] Positionalists claim that although there is truth to be known, knowledge of this truth is always situational and partial, even if one possesses a feminist consciousness—a point with which Sherwin, Mahowald, and the authors anthologized by Wolf seem to agree. On the one hand, truth is *situated* in that it emerges from the roles and relationships an individual has. Thus, society, not just biology, shapes the meaning of aging, for example—whether it is viewed as a disintegrating process, a prelude to death, or an integrating experience during which the last and perhaps even the best chapters of one's life are written. On the other hand, truth is *partial* in that no one individual or group possesses it in entirety. Knowledge comes from facts and experiences, but since our facts and experiences are inevitably limited, our truths are never total. We are never objective enough because we can never see, hear, taste, smell, or touch enough. If I wish to secure a truth greater than my own, then I must talk to as many different kinds of people as possible. Everyone's knowledge, including feminist bioethicists' knowledge, is limited. My standpoint is close to that of many other feminist bioethicists, but I dare not cement my feet in it for fear that it will become an Archimedean standpoint obscuring realities that I need to see.

Conversing with others is something like a moral requirement for feminist bioethicists who adopt an eclectic framework for politics, an autokoenomous framework for ontology, and a positional framework for epistemology. Each feminist must be sensitive to the possibility that her perspective is offensive or hurtful to others. For example, my view that surrogate motherhood is a social arrangement best avoided by women is one that distresses many women who have either served as surrogate mothers or used surrogate mothers. In fact, my reservations about surrogate motherhood have complicated my friendships with two women who decided to use surrogate mothers and who are now the legal mothers of some very happy toddlers. Yet the fact that I must be sensitive to other, differing perspectives on surrogate motherhood does not mean that I have to abandon my own perspective; I must simply entertain some doubts about it from time to time. Bartlett makes a similar point:

> Although I must consider other points of view from the positional stance, I need not accept their truths as my own. Positionality is not a strategy of process and compromise that seeks to reconcile all competing interests. Rather, it imposes a twin obligation to make commitments based on the current truths and values that have emerged from methods of feminism, and to be open to previously unseen perspectives that might come to alter these commitments. As a practical matter, of course, I cannot do both simultaneously, evenly, and perpetually. Positionality, however, sets an ideal of self-critical commitment whereby I act, but consider the truths upon which I act subject to further refinement, amendment, and correction.[57]

Additionally, it seems to me, just as eclecticism leads to autokoenomy, and autokoenomy leads to positionality, all three of these frameworks lead to some version of so-called relational ethics. Like Sherwin, Mahowald, and the authors anthologized by Wolf, most feminist bioethicists appear to be steering a midcourse between an ethics of care and an ethics of power, each of which is relational in its own way. Whereas an ethics of power focuses on the macrocosmic relationship between the two genders, an ethics of care emphasizes microcosmic relationships—such as the relationship between a particular man and a particular woman. When an ethics of power and an ethics of care combine their moral perspectives, it becomes possible for feminist bioethicists to judge, for example, whether the relationship between a particular woman and her Alzheimer's-afflicted husband is freely chosen or socially coerced. On the one hand, if this woman cares for her husband day and night simply because society expects "good" women to totally subordinate their interests to those of men, her act of "caring" could border on masochism. On the other hand, if this woman attends to the needs of her ailing spouse because *she* chooses to do so and in ways that energize rather than enervate her spirit, then her act of caring serves as a self-empowering testament of her own love for her husband rather than as evidence of women's subordination to men.

Finally, and perhaps most important, it seems to me that an eclectic politics, an autokoenomous ontology, a positional epistemology, and a relational ethics invite feminist bioethicists to develop a feminist methodology in ways that may increase their ability to forge mutually agreeable public policies that actually reduce gender oppression in the world of biomedicine. As I see it, what Alison Jaggar terms "feminist practical dialogue"[58] provides the basis for this desirable methodological advance.

As Jaggar describes it, feminist practical dialogue typically begins not with the articulation of general moral rules or principles but, instead, with the creation of opportunities for participants to speak about their own moral experiences.[59] These bits of personal narrative are then molded together through a process of collective reflection, the goal of which is to transform the tendency of individual women to think about their past situations and actions as merely "personal." Feminist practical dialogue debunks this notion by giving individual women the opportunity to hear that their personal experiences of gender oppression are anything but "personal." On the contrary, they are "political"; they are a product of the large social systems and structures that maintain patterns of male domination and female subordination among us.

Jaggar cautions that feminist practical dialogue is not easy. On the contrary, she says, genuine dialogue is hard work; it has little, if anything, in common with gossiping or "coffee-clubbing." It takes more than good will. It takes effort, skill, and the practice of such virtues as responsibility, self-discipline, sensitivity, respect, and trust. It also assumes "that understanding between diverse people becomes possible only when those involved *care* for each other as specific individuals."[60] In this connection, Jaggar notes that in a much-cited article, María Lugones and Elizabeth Spelman propose that neither self-interest nor duty but friendship is the only appropriate motive for Anglo and Hispanic women to come together to iron out their differences. Lugones in particular writes that "[a] non-imperialist feminism requires that . . . you [Anglo feminists] follow us into our world out of friendship."[61] Once there, the task for Anglo and Hispanic women is to find ways of interacting that are respectful of each other's cultural differences, and yet courageous enough to articulate the gender-oppressive implications of these differences.

The most striking difference between feminist and nonfeminist versions of practical discourse is, in Jaggar's estimation, the nurturant nature of the former. She points out that speaking is not as important as listening in feminist practical dialogue. In other words, the goal of each woman is not to be thinking while others are speaking about how she will refute or interrupt them when they pause to take a breath—not to make sure that her own point of view is heard, let alone that it prevails—but, instead, to listen attentively to others' opinions in the hope of working with them to forge a consensus position on the issue being discussed.

A realist, Jaggar further cautions that, like any theory, feminist practical dialogue has its limitations in practical application. It sometimes fails to bring about the consensus it so urgently seeks. The goal of consensus may also open the dialogue process to abuse by those who would "screen" participants for agreement on a particular moral issue so that consensus is likely from the start. Furthermore, the *ideals* upon which feminist practical discourse are based—for example, equal respect and consideration for persons—may be compromised by cultural limitations. Some women, especially those from non-Western cultures, may find feminist practical discourse alien if it violates their conventions of discourse regarding, for instance, self-disclosure, eye contact, forms of address, and direct disagreement. Other women may be unable to participate in feminist practical discourse because the very means of discourse are unavailable to them. In other words, their inability to engage in dialogue may result from speaking a language other than that of the discourse group, from physical challenges, from mental illness, or from a history of abuse that renders them unable to trust and communicate with others.[62] Nevertheless, provided that those who participate in feminist discourse continually remind one another of its limitations, in Jaggar's view this method of conversation holds out at least the hope of true consensus—a coming together of minds, made all the more precious by their diversity.

Conclusion

By developing an eclectic, autokoenomous, positional, and relational philosophical framework in which they can practice feminist practical dialogue, feminist bioethicists are empowering one another to achieve consensus on the issues that have divided them in the past. In Part 2 of this book, we will see how differently *feminist* as opposed to *nonfeminist* bioethicists have approached issues related to the old and new reproductive and genetic technologies. We will also discover how vociferously feminist bioethicists have disagreed *among themselves* about whether these technologies harm or benefit women. Finally, we will come to understand that precisely because of some of *feminism's* recent philosophical advances, *feminist bioethicists* are now in a position to use their differences to recommend procreative policies that will permit the widest variety as well as the greatest number of women to control their interconnected reproductive and genetic destinies.

Part Two

Practical Applications

5

Nonfeminist and Feminist Perspectives on Contraception and Sterilization

A powerful way to control one's reproductive destiny is to decide not to procreate. Of course, not procreating requires more than wishing not to do so. In order not to procreate, individuals must either abstain from sexual intercourse or find some way to block the consequences of sexual intercourse: pregnancy and the subsequent birth of a child. For centuries, individuals who desired sexual intercourse but not children used a variety of contraceptives that included plugging the cervical opening with wool, jumping up and down after sexual intercourse, cleaning the vagina to rid it of semen, or swallowing a "magic" drink, such as the water in which blacksmiths cool red-hot metals.[1]

Beginning in the late nineteenth century, these crude means of birth control were gradually replaced by more effective and safer methods of preventing pregnancy or birth. Realizing that these new methods actually worked, an increasing number of individuals began to use them. As a result, nonfeminist bioethicists became quite interested in topics related to the "rightness" or, alternatively, "wrongness" of separating sex from procreation—of preventing births that might otherwise have occurred. Interestingly, these nonfeminist bioethicists rarely focused on how the reproduction-controlling technologies of contraception and sterilization affected the interests of women in particular; instead, they emphasized the mysterious status of persons who *might* have been called into existence.

Not surprisingly, feminists have faulted nonfeminist bioethicists for downplaying, or even ignoring, the ways in which gender differences shape one's moral assessments of contraception and sterilization. They claim that unless bioethicists ask the "woman question," their moral analysis of these two reproduction-controlling technologies will be flawed. As previously noted, however, asking how a principle, policy, or practice affects women's health and well-being does not necessarily result in provision of the same answer by all feminists. Depending on whether issues of choice, control, or connection are paramount in a feminist's mind, she might express views about contraception and sterilization to which other feminists will take exception. Generally, this expression of difference is to be affirmed. Diversity is a sign of the richness and vitality of feminist thought. Only when this challenging diversity prevents feminists from developing at least some mutually agreeable principles, practices, and policies for contraception and sterilization does it become a problem—one problem that can be overcome, however, through reliance on some version of the consensus-enabling philosophical framework I sketched out at the end of Chapter 4.

Nonfeminist Bioethical Perspectives on Contraception

Despite the fact that contraception is standard practice nearly worldwide, nonfeminist bioethicists continue to debate its morality. The most prominent opponents of contraceptive use—both voluntary and involuntary—belong to the tradition of natural law. For centuries, natural-law thinkers debated whether procreation is *the* purpose or simply *a* purpose of sexual intercourse. Initially, the majority stressed the procreative function of human sexuality. For example, the thirteenth-century theologian St. Bonaventure claimed that marital relations are morally right only "if motivated solely by the desire to have children."[2] But because most married couples confessed that, for them, sexual intercourse was more often a matter of pleasure than of procreation, natural-law thinkers gradually modified their initial thesis that sex is for procreation *only*.

Currently, most natural-law thinkers concede that marriage has two aims: (1) a conceptual aim, directed toward procreating, and (2) a relational aim, directed toward bringing husbands and wives together in a network of pleasure and love.[3] Nevertheless, they emphasize that the conceptual aim of marriage is primary, whereas the relational aim is secondary: Each and every act of sexual intercourse must, in principle, remain open to the transmission of life. Thus, natural-law thinkers typically forbid all forms of birth control that deliberately frustrate conception.

They permit only those "natural forms of birth control that work with, rather than against, the natural reproductive cycle."[4] Chief among these modes of birth control is the so-called rhythm method, which entails intentional abstinence from sex during periods when pregnancy is most likely to result.

Aside from the natural-law thinkers described above, however, most nonfeminist bioethicists support at least the *voluntary* use of "unnatural" as well as "natural" contraceptives. They claim that if individuals are not ready, willing, or able to be parents, they have not only the *right* but the *duty* to use contraceptives. Most nonfeminist bioethicists also endorse the use of contraceptives for the purpose of population control. They reason that the mere fact that individuals want large families and have the means to raise several children does not mean that they should do so. On the contrary, they say, individuals have a moral responsibility to restrain their procreative desires if their societies lack, for instance, the natural resources to support a large population. Not all nonfeminist bioethicists agree, however, that individuals in countries *without* population problems owe individuals in countries *with* population problems such a moral debt. They claim that spatial (geographical) and temporal (cross-generational) factors limit our moral responsibilities. As they see it, we do not owe people in distant lands what we owe our neighbors. Nor do we owe our possible great-great-great grandchildren what we owe our actual children.

With respect to *involuntary* family-planning and/or population control, nonfeminist bioethicists espouse a much greater variety of positions. Proponents of involuntary contraception claim that, under certain circumstances, it is morally justified for a society to take at least some of the following steps to limit its population:

1. *Social structure adjustment:* For example, encouraging women to find employment outside the home or raising the minimum legal age for marriage, thus remotely affecting reproductive choices by affecting the context in which reproductive choices are made.
2. *Positive incentives:* Providing financial rewards for the practice of contraception, for not having children, etc.
3. *Negative incentives:* Inflicting financial penalties on those who have children or on those who have more than a certain number of children.
4. *Involuntary fertility controls:* For example, the compulsory sterilization of individuals after they have had a certain number of children, compulsory abortion in the case of mothers who already have had a certain number of children, or even the wide-scale control of fertility through the addition of a fertility-control agent to the water supply.[5]

Opponents of involuntary contraception argue strenuously against not only the fourth and most coercive of these measures but also against the second and third ones. They claim that all incentive programs, but especially those involving negative incentives, cause people to make reproductive decisions they would not otherwise make. Insisting that people are more likely to act against their own best-reasoned interests when a threatened punishment is severe, opponents of involuntary contraception point to China's one-child family policy with particular horror. In the early 1980s, Chinese government officials decided to monitor the fertility of approximately 340 million Chinese women, going so far as to track their menstrual cycles. They also decided to punish more-than-one-child couples and to reward one-child-only couples. Whereas a variety of economic sanctions were levied against the former, the latter were given pay raises of up to 40 percent, extended maternity leave, and better housing.[6] In 1995 a new generation of Chinese government officials stepped up the effort to decrease the size of China's population. They posted signs warning women to report every three months to a local clinic for a pregnancy test or else face a steep fine. In addition, these officials urged women with one child either to be sterilized or to accept an intrauterine device. Failure to comply with such urgings proved to be no small matter in some rural outposts. After blasting into rubble the home of a family with *three* children, government dynamiters in the village of Xiaoxi warned shocked villagers that: "[t]hose who do not obey the family planning police will be those who lose their fortunes."[7] Although most incentive programs are not as draconian as China's, opponents of such programs argue that similar pressures are at work in all of them, rendering them morally suspect.

In recent years, nonfeminist bioethicists have focused less on the difference between voluntary and involuntary contraception and more on the quality of the informed-consent procedures that purportedly accompany the voluntary use of contraceptives. In general, they urge obstetricians and gynecologists to provide their patients with the kind of information, advice, and assurances that, for example, Dr. Robert Hatcher considers appropriate. As he sees it, obstetricians and gynecologists should (1) discuss the risks as well as the benefits of any recommended contraceptive with the patient and, if possible, the patient's partner; (2) explain how the recommended contraceptive works, urging the patient to ask questions and taking the time to answer them; (3) present alternatives to the recommended contraceptive (including abstinence from sexual relations and the use of no contraceptive whatsoever); (4) encourage the patient to report any problems she has with the recommended contraceptive and to discontinue its use if she finds that it does not suit her specific needs; and (5) ascertain that the patient has understood items 1 through 4, requesting her to repeat in her own words, if necessary, the gist of the communicated information.[8] Although some health-care practitioners insist that it is impossible to meet these five requirements perfectly, most nonfeminist bioethicists respond that, in general, a good-faith effort will yield satisfactory results. In other words, if all other strategies fail, health-care practitioners can rely on legal standards to assess the adequacy of the contraceptive information they provide to their patients. In particular, they can simply ask themselves whether they have disclosed to their patients the kind of information that (1) responsible health-care practitioners ordinarily would disclose to patients and/or (2) reasonable patients ordinarily would need and want to know.

Since it is not clear whether minors are generally capable of giving their informed consent to medical treatment, nonfeminist bioethicists often debate just how liberally adolescents' legal right to obtain and use contraceptives should be interpreted. In *Carey v. Population Services International* (1977), lawyers for the state of New York argued before the Supreme Court that a state may refuse minors access to harmful, or merely offensively displayed, *nonprescription* contraceptives. The minors' lawyers countered that there is no evidence either that nonprescription contraceptives are harmful or that minors find public displays of them offensive. (Whether they find it embarrassing to purchase them is another question.)[9] Agreeing with the minors' lawyers, the Court held that the state's reasons for restricting minors' access to nonprescription contraceptives were uncompelling and that, absent *compelling* reasons to limit minors' access to these contraceptives, personal autonomy over contraceptive choice remains the standard for minors as well as for adults.

After the *Carey* decision came down, nonfeminist bioethicists found themselves divided. Those who wished to limit adolescents' access to contraceptives urged concerned parents to lobby either for parental consent laws that make a minor's receipt of contraceptive services conditional on parental agreement or for parental notification laws that require parents simply to be informed that their children are receiving such services. Among the first governmental agencies to propose a parental notification regulation was the U.S. Department of Health and Human Services (USDHHS). In 1982, the USDHHS mandated that publicly funded family-planning clinics notify parents or guardians within ten days from the time their children receive prescription drugs or devices from them. Exceptions to this regulation could be made, but only when there was evidence that parents or guardians might physically harm a minor on account of her use of contraceptives. The USDHHS defended its proposed regulation as one that would break down "Berlin Walls" between parents and children, permit parents to protect their children from the harmful side effects of some contraceptives, and deter teenagers from having sex.[10]

Those nonfeminist bioethicists who wished to expand adolescents' access to contraceptives countered that the USDHHS's proposed regulation was misguided. They claimed that parental notification rules lead not so much to improved parent-child communication as to parent-child conflict. Fearing disapproval or worse, many teenagers decide not to discuss contraception with their parents, and either go without or try to get birth control some other way. As a result, parental notification rules ironically contribute to an *increase* in teen pregnancy rates, since sexually active teens often remain sexually active whether or not they have access to contraceptives.[11]

Currently, the United States has the highest teen pregnancy rate (96 per 1,000) among industrialized countries.[12] Many of these pregnancies are terminated. In fact, 39 percent end in abortions and approximately 13 percent end in miscarriages. The ones that do come to term are often fraught with problems. Because many teens are children themselves, they tend to give birth to malnourished, low-birth-weight, or very premature babies, approximately 20 percent of whom will die before reaching their first birthday.[13] Some of these unfortunate consequences could be avoided if pregnant teens routinely received adequate prenatal care. However, many teens cannot afford, or do not know where to obtain, proper prenatal care, and still more simply do not want to admit to others that they are pregnant in the early stages of pregnancy when prenatal care is particularly crucial. Given these stark realities, opponents of parental notification regulations regard such rules as part of the problem rather than part of the solution. They insist that it is better that teens use contraceptives than that teens get pregnant.

Nonfeminist bioethicists take different sides about who should be *required* to use contraceptives as well as about who should be *permitted* to use them (i.e., only adults or minors as well). In particular, they disagree about the scope of developmentally disabled individuals' right to procreate or not procreate. Those who favor limiting the reproductive freedom of such individuals claim that parenting is hard work for everyone, but especially for those who lack the basic skills it requires; and as a result, when developmentally disabled individuals have children, their family members, their friends, or the state often find themselves burdened with extra parental responsibilities. In addition to claiming that there are other-directed reasons for limiting the reproductive freedom of developmentally disabled individuals, proponents of this limitation claim that it serves the best interests of the developmentally disabled individuals themselves. Being required to use contraceptives, they argue, is preferable to being (1) compulsorily sterilized; (2) prevented from engaging in any sexual relations whatsoever; (3) traumatized by a pregnancy, the process of which one might not be able to understand; or (4) burdened by an infant for whom one cannot take responsibility.

In contrast to those nonfeminist bioethicists who favor restricting the procreative liberty of developmentally disabled individuals, those who oppose restricting it stress that not all such individuals are equally disabled. They point out that unlike *severely* developmentally disabled people, *mildly* developmentally disabled people can become exemplary parents with a minimum amount of supervision and assistance. Although intelligence generally facilitates the development of good parenting skills, it is not nearly as important as the ability to nurture and love a child. Therefore, to restrict *mildly* developmentally disabled individuals' right to procreate, simply because they are somewhat mentally challenged, is to discriminate against them in a grievous way.

Another issue debated by nonfeminist bioethicists is whether individuals who receive state subsidies for raising their children should be required, or at least urged, to use contraceptives. On one side of this debate is a group of nonfeminist bioethicists who insist that the right to procreate is limited, and that individuals have no right to bring children into the world if they lack the means to take care of them. From their standpoint, long-lasting contraceptives such as Norplant are more than just effective means of personal birth control: They are acceptable instruments of social policy. These nonfeminist bioethicists thus support legislative bills mandating the use of Norplant, for example, to limit the pregnancies of women on welfare. Politicians in favor of this measure claim that they have turned to Norplant "out of desperation" to control birth rates among the poor.[14]

On the other side of this debate is a group of nonfeminist bioethicists who claim that it is unfair for government to limit some women's procreative liberty just because circumstances—for example, a lack of marketable job skills—have required them to go on welfare. For a woman who scarcely has the means to feed her children, a $500 incentive payment to use Norplant can be a heavy government hand on the scales of "choice." Real choice would consist in providing her with the funds she needs to develop marketable job skills—skills that would help push her off the welfare rolls. Moreover, in the estimation of philosopher Arthur Caplan, inducing indigent women to use Norplant may ultimately be one step on a whole staircase of state-sponsored measures to cut welfare costs through control of reproduction: "I can see us mandating the genetic testing of embryos and fetuses. . . . If we're willing to put Norplant into a 16-year-old today to contain costs, then why couldn't there be a government official saying you can't be a parent because you're likely to create a kid whose needs will cost society too much?"[15]

A final matter about which nonfeminist bioethicists disagree is whether the state may punish child abusers and/or child neglectors by offering them a choice between serving time in prison, on the one hand, or using contraceptives, especially long-lasting contraceptives like Norplant, on the other. Some nonfeminist bioethicists view such proposals as more than fair since the alleged abusers or neglectors escape imprisonment. Other nonfeminist bioethicists dismiss such proposals as coercive "bandage" solutions. Whatever caused the abusive or neglectful parent to be abusive or neglectful remains untreated, they argue. And since contraceptives are not without risks, some individuals who choose contraception over prison might risk their health or even their lives in order to secure their freedom.

Nonfeminist Bioethical Perspectives on Sterilization

For nonfeminist bioethicists, sterilization (i.e., tubal ligation or vasectomy) raises approximately the same set of bioethical considerations as does contraception, the primary difference being sterilization's relative permanence. Although most nonfeminist bioethicists outside the natural-law tradition support *voluntary* sterilization for purposes of either family planning or population control, few of them support *involuntary* sterilization unless it is intended to serve the best interests of the person who is forcibly being deprived of his or her ability to procreate. In this connection, consider the 1980 court case in which the physician and parents of Lee Ann Grady, a nineteen-year-old woman with Down's syndrome, sought to have her sterilized. When the hospital refused to sterilize Lee Ann without court approval, lawyers seeking such approval described her condition as follows:

> She is the oldest of three children, lives at home with them and her parents, and has never been institutionalized. Her IQ is in the "upper 20's to upper 30's range." She can converse, count to some extent, and recognize letters of the alphabet. She can dress and bathe herself. Her life expectancy and physical maturation are normal; however, her mental deficiency has prevented the normal emotional and social development of sexuality. If she becomes pregnant, she will not understand her condition, and she will not be capable of caring for a baby alone.[16]

Lee Ann's parents believed not only that it would be in their daughter's best interest to live in a group home for developmentally disabled adults, but also that it would be in her best interest to be sterilized before this move. In this way, they could be assured that, should their daughter engage in sex, she would not face a frightening pregnancy or, worse, burdensome motherhood.

Lee Ann's case led to the landmark decision *In the Matter of Lee Ann Grady* (1981).[17] In deciding this case, the court had three options. First, it could hold that only legally competent persons may exercise the right to procreate and, therefore, that legally incompetent persons—persons who lack decisionmaking power—cannot request to be sterilized. Second, it could hold that only parents or court-appointed guardians of legally incompetent persons may make such momentous decisions for their charges. Third, it could hold that only the court may decide for persons like Lee Ann whether sterilization is in their best interests. Fearing that not all parents and physicians would be as well intentioned as Lee Ann's parents and physicians, however, the court followed through on the third option.[18]

Even though most nonfeminist bioethicists support the *Grady* decision, few of them support involuntary sterilization for eugenic purposes (i.e., for purposes of procreating people with "superior" traits). In the first place, most nonfeminist bioethicists claim that forcing people with "inferior" genes to be sterilized does not necessarily make scientific sense, given the lack of certainty as to whether one gene or another is "inferior." For example, the gene that causes sickle cell anemia also protects the carrier from malaria. In addition, geneticists and psychologists are not always in agreement about the relative contributions of "nature versus nurture." Sterilizing someone with a supposedly "bad personality gene," only to discover that environmental factors had caused his disorder, is certainly the wrong solution to a societal health hazard.

Second, most nonfeminist bioethicists fear that mainstream society might use a program of involuntary sterilization for eugenic purposes to bolster certain political agendas. They argue that a terrifying "slippery slope" effect might begin. Initially, they warn, there would be a push to prevent so-called genetically defective people from procreating, but inevitably that push would be extended to prevent all allegedly "undesirable" or "dangerous" people from procreating. Of course, the people whom mainstream society labels "dangerous" may simply be high-spirited revolutionaries or committed social reformers who are threatening to upset an oppressive status quo. And the people whom it labels "undesirable" (e.g., the homeless) may simply be individuals who, because they live on the margins of society, assault the sensibilities of those who occupy its center. After a while, moreover, mainstream society would forget that "dangerousness" and "undesirability" are not genetic traits but social labels, and a very pernicious type of eugenics would become the order of the day.

Third, most nonfeminist bioethicists are reluctant to permit the state to determine when a life with a genetic disorder is a life not worth living. On the contrary, they argue, it is the prerogative of individual citizens to decide how worthwhile their lives are. The fact that a person suffers from a genetic disorder such as Down's syndrome does not preclude her or him from leading a happy and productive life.

For all the above reasons, most nonfeminist bioethicists insist that the less the state involves itself in programs of involuntary sterilization, the better for individual citizens. In particular, most nonfeminist bioethicists reject using involuntary sterilization as a punishment for crime. They note with regret the chapter of U.S. history that ended in the landmark Supreme Court decision *Skinner v. Oklahoma* (1942).[19] Oklahoma had a law that permitted the sterilization of "habitual criminals"—that is, persons convicted of at least three felonies involving moral turpitude (significantly, white-collar crimes such as embezzlement or political transgression were deliberately excluded from the list of targeted felonies).[20] Meanwhile, after being convicted on one count of chicken-stealing and two counts of committing robbery with a firearm, Jack Skinner was ordered by the state to be sterilized for eugenic reasons. The Oklahoma supreme court upheld the sterilization order even though no *scientific* evidence existed to prove, for example, that the children of criminals are genetically programmed to become criminals themselves. Later, the U.S. Supreme Court struck down the Oklahoma supreme court's decision on the grounds of discrimination. It noted that the state of Oklahoma had treated its criminal population with an "unequal hand," since it targeted for sterilization those people convicted of grand larceny but not those convicted of embezzlement.[21] In reaction to laws and cases such as the one just described, most nonfeminist bioethicists continue to emphasize the bias underlying many involuntary sterilization proposals, including recent suggestions to make the payment of welfare benefits contingent upon indigent women "choosing" to be sterilized.[22]

Feminist Bioethical Perspectives on Contraception and Sterilization

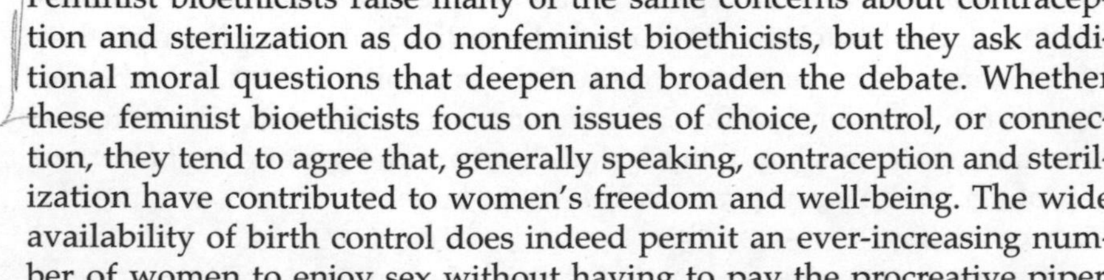

Feminist bioethicists raise many of the same concerns about contraception and sterilization as do nonfeminist bioethicists, but they ask additional moral questions that deepen and broaden the debate. Whether these feminist bioethicists focus on issues of choice, control, or connection, they tend to agree that, generally speaking, contraception and sterilization have contributed to women's freedom and well-being. The wide availability of birth control does indeed permit an ever-increasing number of women to enjoy sex without having to pay the procreative piper, and to time their pregnancies to coincide with their willingness and ability to parent a child alone or with the help of others. In short, contraception and sterilization afford many women approximately the same opportunities men have always had: to pursue a career, say, without worrying about getting pregnant and thus being forced to drop out of school or quit a job.

Granted, not all women's experiences with contraception and sterilization have been altogether positive. Feminist bioethicists note that the history of contraceptives, for example, is a tale not only of scientists developing increasingly safer and more effective means of birth control but also of women being used as nonconsenting research subjects. The first oral contraceptives that came on the market were far stronger than necessary and had many unpleasant and even harmful side effects. The fact that today's oral contraceptives contain as little as 4 percent of the progestogen and 20 percent of the estrogen found in the original formulations suggests that, in the past, many women were unknowingly exposed to unnecessarily high doses of these hormones.[23]

As women became increasingly aware that some oral contraceptives could be hazardous to their health, they began to ask their physicians more questions about the relative risks and benefits they faced. Although the physicians responded by stressing that, in their experience, the only "harms" oral-contraceptive women typically experienced were headaches, weight gain, and exacerbated acne, they conceded that some of these women—particularly if they were obese, over thirty-five years of age, had high blood pressure, or smoked—had suffered such serious side effects as blood clots and heart attacks. The same physicians also admitted that, although scientists continued to debate the issue, there was some evidence of a link between using certain oral contraceptives and developing liver, breast, or cervical cancer.[24]

Interestingly, knowing more about the risk of oral contraceptives did not stop most women from using them. By the mid-1970s, a majority of U.S. women had decided that the benefits of these contraceptives far outweighed their risks.[25] Among those who disagreed, many turned to the intrauterine device (IUD) for protection against unwanted pregnancies. According to this latter group, the IUD had the advantage of being not only free of "risky" hormones but also "forgettable" once inserted.

In the United States, women's romance with intrauterine devices ended when a heated controversy broke out about one type of IUD, the Dalkon Shield. Shaped like a crab, with little spines and a multifilament tailspring to maximize the opportunity for monitoring its position in the uterus, the Dalkon Shield was initially hailed as a new, improved IUD. Unfortunately, the Dalkon Shield's crab-like qualities also made it difficult and painful to insert, wear, and remove; and its filamentous string facilitated the passing of infectious bacteria into the uterus. Indeed, studies showed that Dalkon Shield users were at much higher risk for pelvic inflammatory disease (PID) and septic abortions than were women who wore other IUDs available on the market.[26] Over the years, 14 deaths, 223 septic abortions, and thousands of PID cases, many of them resulting in infertility, were reported to the Food and Drug Administration (FDA) by Dalkon Shield victims or their survivors. Eventually, more than 300,000 claims were filed in a class-action suit against the A. H. Robins company, the manufacturer of the Dalkon Shield, alleging that the company had continued marketing the device even after becoming aware of its dangers. After paying out $378.3 million in 9,230 lawsuits, A. H. Robins filed for bankruptcy in 1985.[27]

Put on the alert by this event, feminists, particularly the National Women's Health Network, became very vigilant as other pharmaceutical companies brought new contraceptives to the market. They insisted that all contraceptives be subject to rigorous clinical testing before entering the U.S. market, and that U.S. researchers avoid the use of women as "guinea-pigs" in less-developed nations, where research practices are relatively unregulated.[28] Although U.S. researchers did not stop their studies in less-developed countries, U.S. pharmaceutical companies were slowed in their efforts to market several contraceptives in the United States, including the controversial injectable Depo-Provera.

In 1967 the Upjohn Company applied to the FDA for permission to sell Depo-Provera as a contraceptive. Upon making this application, Upjohn began the seven-year dog tests and ten-year monkey studies then required by the FDA. Although most of these studies produced favorable results, a few of them showed that large doses of Depo-Provera caused breast cancer in beagles and endometrial cancer in rhesus monkeys. Nevertheless, the FDA decided to permit Upjohn to market Depo-Provera in the United States, but with very stringent restrictions. For the most part, feminists responded angrily to this decision. They alleged that the pharmaceutical lobby had pressured the FDA into adopting a course of action that might prove detrimental to women's health. So vociferous was the feminist protest that in 1978 the FDA decided to ban even the limited marketing of Depo-Provera it had previously approved. Upjohn appealed this decision, offering to do yet more cancer studies, this time outside the United States.

The company picked New Zealand as its research base, giving two reasons for its choice: First, many women there were already using Depo-Provera; and, second, the social and ethnic compositions of New Zealand and the United States were assumed to be roughly equivalent. Feminists retorted that most of the New Zealand women using Depo-Provera were Polynesian, not white. In addition, they claimed that Upjohn chose New Zealand simply to take advantage of its very permissive attitude toward pharmaceutical research—an attitude manifested, for example, in the general reluctance of this country to permit citizens to sue such companies for damages. More troubling to some feminists was the fact that Upjohn limited its studies to Depo-Provera's possible *carcinogenic* effects, as if its already established harmful side effects (e.g., bleeding, infertility, depression, permanent weight gain, and sexual turnoff) did not also threaten women's health.[29] Eventually, Upjohn's researchers (together with some independent researchers) convinced the FDA that Depo-Provera was not carcinogenic—certainly not carcinogenic enough to warrant a ban on its sale. As a result, in 1992 the FDA finally permitted Upjohn to market Depo-Provera in the United States without special restrictions. This time, however, most feminists accepted the FDA's ruling. Apparently, they had been persuaded that Depo-Provera did not put women at serious risk for cancer, and that its side effects were no worse than those of many other hormonally based contraceptives favored by American women.

As concerned as feminists are about the safety of contraceptives, they are even more worried about women's lack of control over their use. For example, unlike many older means of birth control (condoms, spermicides, and even the rhythm method), newer methods almost always require the skilled services of physicians or other health-care practitioners. Physicians must prescribe oral contraceptives; and physicians or other skilled health-care practitioners must insert IUDs, inject Depo-Provera, or implant Norplant in women's bodies. Of all these new contraceptives, Norplant is probably under physicians' control or supervision the most, because it requires surgery. A physician injects the woman with a local anesthetic, makes a quarter-inch incision in her upper arm, and inserts six matchstick-thin rods, each containing the synthetic hormone levonorgestrel. Once inserted, the rods prevent pregnancy for up to five years. Their removal also requires surgery.

For some feminists, the fact that women must rely on physicians or other skilled health-care practitioners to get access to a full range of contraceptives means that women are becoming increasingly dependent on the medical establishment for their reproductive freedom. And, unfortunately, not all health-care practitioners are feminists. A physician might refuse to give a woman the contraceptive of her choice on the grounds, for example, that it will permit her to engage in promiscuous sex. Or a physician might push a woman to use a contraceptive that she or he regards as highly effective, but whose side effects the *woman* finds quite burdensome. Feminists claim that such abuses of power occur throughout the world, but that they are particularly serious in countries less developed than the United States. In some of these less-developed countries, what matters is not what women want but what men want. For example, in some African nations physicians refuse to remove Norplant from a woman unless her *husband*, intent on producing heirs, asks them to do so. The fact that the woman cannot tolerate Norplant's side effects (heavy bleeding, blinding headaches, acne, acute depression) does not, in and of itself, motivate them to remove the irritant.[30]

Fear of this degree of control over women's bodies is quite reasonable, in feminists' estimation. It is precisely the effectiveness and relative permanence of Norplant, Depo-Provera, and the IUD that tempts some health-care practitioners and politicians to force them on certain women. For example, because some physicians believe that some women cannot manage their reproductive choices well, they refuse to offer them any contraceptive options other than Norplant, Depo-Provera, or the IUD.[31] Similarly, and as noted earlier, some legislators who do not value individual women's reproductive freedom very highly may view Norplant as a means to bring down the teenage pregnancy rate and to limit the number of children born to welfare mothers.[32] Thus, they try to pass laws that introduce incentives—either positive or negative—to get certain women to use long-acting contraceptives.

Although feminists agree that it is wrong for the state to hinge public assistance payments (so-called welfare) on a low-income woman's agreement to use long-lasting contraceptives, they disagree among themselves as to whether it is also wrong for the state to pay "bonuses" to welfare recipients who agree to use them.[33] In an attempt to show that, unlike negative incentive programs, positive ones might be in women's best interests, philosopher Bonnie Steinbock raises the following question: "Are Norplant bonus programs in general coercive? Or are they a logical extension of other kinds of incentive programs, such as those that offer incentives for welfare recipients to stay in school?"[34] In particular, Steinbock notes that proponents of Norplant bonus policies see no difference between bonus policies aimed at getting the poor to curb their fecundity and tax-break policies aimed at getting the rich to give to charity. Both policies intend to promote "socially responsible" ways of behaving. Against this line of reasoning, opponents of Norplant bonus policies protest that there are major differences between using monetary incentives to get rich people to give to charity and using them to get poor people not to procreate. They claim, first, that the state should not try to save money by paying citizens not to procreate—thereby implying that its citizens' most fundamental rights are for sale; and second, that because women on welfare are particularly needy, they are generally unable to say "no" to extra money, even when saying "no" deprives them of the opportunity to procreate a child they would very much like to have.

Steinbock finds both of these arguments against Norplant bonus policies unpersuasive. She contends that even if the state's primary motivation for developing these programs is to save itself money by reducing the number of children on welfare, not having more children than one can support is also in the best interests of women on welfare: Unburdened by excessive parental responsibilities, women on welfare would be in a better position to improve their standard of living. Steinbock also stresses that the kinds of financial incentives the state offers women are generally so modest that it is difficult to believe that a woman who truly wished to procreate would feel she had no choice other than to accept the additional money.[35]

Whatever feminists' ultimate position on state-mandated Norplant bonus policies might be, they are generally agreed that long-acting contraceptives like Norplant have a *potential* for coercive use. For this reason alone, some feminists urge women to use only those means of birth control over which they have the greatest control—namely, diaphragms, cervical caps, spermicides, sponges, and especially the new "female condoms" or vaginal pouches.[36] Though not as reliable as oral contraceptives, IUDs, implants, and injectables, the latter birth control methods are quite effective. In addition, they tend not to have risky side effects, and, unlike hormonal contraceptives, they afford some protection against HIV and certain sexually transmitted diseases (STDs). Finally, a subset of these birth control methods—spermicides, sponges, and female condoms—can be purchased over the counter.

In contrast to feminists who rue the day Norplant entered the contraceptive market are those who believe that, just because long-acting contraceptives have a *potential* for coercive use does not mean that women will be unable to control their use. After all, there is much that is attractive about Norplant, Depo-Provera, and the like. Because of their effectiveness and relative permanence, injectables and implants are particularly useful ways for many women to control their fertility. Thus, it concerns this group of feminists that some of the women who want to use Norplant cannot afford it (Norplant typically retails in the United States for about $365, plus sizable fees for insertion, counseling, checkups, and removal).[37] In their estimation, pharmaceutical companies and health-care delivery systems should price their contraceptives and services as reasonably as possible, perhaps on a sliding scale based on a woman's income. If profits need to be made for research and development, they should be made elsewhere than in the procreative arena. Moreover, physicians, physicians' assistants, and nurse practitioners should make it one of their priorities to serve women in rural areas and inner cities.

To be sure, if researchers were to develop a variety of safe and effective contraceptives over which women had control, feminists would no longer need to debate women's use of contraceptives among themselves.[38] Regrettably, however, neither the private nor the public sector seems particularly interested in doing so for U.S. women. Private-sector spokespersons argue that it is against their best interests to spend money developing contraceptives that *feminists* might then fault as not being good enough. This is how one pharmaceutical executive defended his company's recent decision to abandon contraceptive research and development in favor of other kinds of health-care research and development:

> Look, you must bear in mind that there were billion-dollar single entities out there, like Tagamet for ulcers. Immunotherapy drugs. Cardiovascular drugs. In those fields you don't have to be 100 percent effective, you can be 70 percent effective. Your side effects don't have to be zero, they can be 20 percent and still not be unacceptable. You don't have a sea of bad publicity endangering your other drugs, and your researchers can get Nobel Prizes.[39]

The thoughts of this pharmaceutical executive are not at all atypical. Only Ortho Pharmaceutical Corporation, a Johnson & Johnson subsidiary with an estimated profit margin of 36 percent from an extensive line of birth control products, has a significant contraceptive research and development program.[40] Moreover, it was the Population Council, an international nonprofit organization, rather than a pharmaceutical firm that brought Norplant to the U.S. market—and it struggled long and hard to do so. The Population Council was burdened not only by litigation fears and political pressures but also by the FDA's rigorous testing standards. At first, the council objected that it could not assume the financial costs of the seven-year dog tests and ten-year monkey studies demanded by the FDA before it approves a new drug. Only after the FDA hinted that it might be willing to relax some of its regulations in Norplant's case did the Population Council proceed with its research and development program. Even with reduced test and study requirements, however, it took nearly four years for the Population Council to complete its application for FDA approval—entailing 19,000 pages of data on 55,000 Norplant users in 46 countries and thousands of others in U.S. clinical trials.[41] As a result of this experience, Dr. C. Wayne Bardin, the Population Council's director for biomedical research, stated that relying on nonprofit, private organizations for contraceptive research and development "is good only if you are opposed to contraception. This way of doing things will certainly keep contraceptives off the market."[42]

In contrast to the *private* sector's reasons for steering clear of contraceptive research and development, the *public* sector's reasons have more to do with inflammatory politics than with finances and bureaucratic red tape. In response to political pressures from the influential National Right to Life Committee, which views anything that interferes with the development of a fertilized egg after implantation as a type of abortion, the federal government spends very little money on reproductive research. For example, the National Institutes of Health have an annual budget of $10 billion, $2 billion of which goes to cancer research and $1 billion of which goes to AIDS research. Only $15 *million* is earmarked for contraceptive research.[43] As a result of such underfunding, U.S. women have far fewer contraceptive choices than women in some European countries. Comments Dr. Luigi Mastroianni: "While we in the United States make do with the same range of options available 30 years ago, in some European countries people can choose among contraceptives, and a variety of pills, IUD's and sterilization techniques not available here."[44]

Many feminists worry that because U.S. women have relatively little access to a variety of affordable, safe, and effective contraceptives, all too many of them are "choosing" sterilization as their method of birth control. In 1980, of all U.S. women using birth control, 29.5 percent had tubal ligations. And if vasectomies are included in the calculations, the number of U.S. women relying either indirectly or directly on some type of sterilization tops 42 percent.[45] Although most women who get sterilized are in their thirties and forties, a growing number of women in their twenties now view sterilization as their best birth control option.

In an effort to ascertain that adult women's choice to be sterilized is indeed voluntary, feminists recommend that health-care practitioners thoroughly discuss with women their other birth control options. Realizing that, in the past, they may have overemphasized the risks of using IUDs, oral contraceptives, injectables, and implants, many feminists currently underscore the benefits of using reversible, long-lasting contraceptives while downplaying sterilization. Thus, these feminists urge physicians and nurses to remind couples seeking sterilization that although they think they have had as many children as they want, this may prove not to be the case. If one or more of their children die, a sterilized couple may rue the day they said "no" to more children. Feminists also urge health-care practitioners to counsel couples about another sad possibility—namely, that their relationship could end through death or divorce. In the event of remarriage, a sterilized man or woman might regret not being able to have children with his or her new spouse.

Feminists' reservations about sterilization partly arise from the procedure's long history of abuse in the United States, beginning in the late nineteenth century and officially ending as late as the 1960s when most state eugenic laws were declared unconstitutional.[46] These laws generally targeted developmentally disabled individuals, and they worked in tandem with sterilization programs focused on indigent African-American women in particular. Regrettably, advantaged women, who throughout most of this century have been white, well-to-do, and unchallenged by exceptional physical or mental limitations, did not always appreciate how their interests differed from those of developmentally disabled or socioeconomically disadvantaged women, especially women of color. Convinced that, so far as they were concerned, sterilization was safer, more effective, and less bothersome than any other contraceptive on the market, advantaged women fought against policies that made it difficult for them to be sterilized. One such policy was the so-called rule of 120, which precluded sterilization of a woman unless her age times the number of her living children equaled 120 or more.[47] What advantaged women did not initially realize, however, was that their gain in reproductive freedom would work against the interests of indigent African-American women, whom many physicians were only too eager to rush into the operating room for tubal ligations.

When feminists realized, for example, that in some southern states sterilizations of indigent African-American women were so common that physicians and others routinely and irreverently referred to them as "Mississippi appendectomies,"[48] they were determined to press not for totally permissive sterilization laws but, instead, for those specifying informed-consent procedures, counseling requirements, and waiting periods. Yet, although the efforts of these feminists resulted in better sterilization laws, sterilization abuse remains a reality for some U.S. women.[49] For example, welfare mothers are still likely to be *directly* counseled to have hysterectomies or tubal ligations immediately after delivering a child. Many feminists view such advice as a pressure tactic that is used on women who do not always understand the permanence of sterilization or have access to other reliable and affordable means of contraception.[50] As difficult as it is for feminists to develop good contraception and sterilization policies for adult women, they find it even more difficult to strike an appropriate balance between protecting teen-aged women from harm and letting them make their own reproductive choices. For example, it concerns feminists not only that so many women in their thirties and forties are using sterilization as a last-resort means of safe and effective birth control, but also that a large number of teens and women in their twenties are following suit.[51] In contrast to older women, younger ones, especially teens, are not always mature enough to appreciate the fact that, although sterilization might increase their freedom to engage in sex without "consequences" now, it might later limit their freedom to have a child. Indeed, what strikes a woman as a very important "good" when she is a teen might strike her as a significant "bad" when she turns thirty or forty. Feminists also emphasize that many of the welfare mothers whom the state "encourages" to become sterilized are teens. In their estimation, it is particularly problematic to pressure these young women into prematurely forsaking their childbearing capacities. After all, teenagers are just on the verge of adulthood, and their economic and social situations might yet improve enough to permit them to properly parent children later in life.

Feminists also wish to protect teens from traumatic and unnecessary abortions. They suspect that one reason for the very high rate of teen pregnancy in the United States (95.2 per 1,000 compared with 39 in Canada, 46 in England and Wales, 29 in Sweden, and 13 in the Netherlands)[52] is that unlike teens in other Western industrialized countries, U.S. teens are relatively uneducated about contraceptives, many of which they also cannot afford or obtain.[53] Since all too many teen pregnancies end in abortion, if not in miscarriage or the birth of an imperiled infant, many feminists urge that parents and educators provide young women and men with better sex education—namely, the kind of sex education that presents reproductive as well as sexual matters candidly and thoroughly to teens. Teens need to know that they always have the right and sometimes even the duty to say "no" to sex. Equally important, they need to know how to protect themselves from sexually transmitted diseases and unwanted pregnancies in the event that they say "yes." Feminists believe that, ideally, parents should help their children make wise reproductive and sexual choices. But because parents and children do not always share the same values, and because some parents are either unable or unwilling to discuss sexual matters with their children, most feminists support school-based sex-education courses.

Feminists' recommendations to provide teens with more information about birth control have not met with universal approval, however. Currently, many U.S. parents (approximately half of whom are women) want their children to learn about birth control not at school but, instead, in the privacy of their own homes, especially if they sense that their children's values are beginning to diverge from their own fundamental commitments. As some parents see it, sex education, especially when coupled with access to school clinics, invites teens to engage in "immoral" sex—that is, sex outside of marriage. Thus, they reason, the less the schools say about sex, the better: Let parents teach their children about sex. They also reason that the less access teens have to birth control, the better. Teens, they believe, will avoid sex so as to avoid pregnancy.[54]

To the above arguments, feminists typically respond that teens probably learn more about sex and contraception from their friends, television, and magazines than they do from either their teachers or their parents, and what they learn can be very confusing. What is more, as noted above, many teens are inclined to engage in sex whether or not they are protected from pregnancy. Thus, according to feminists, if U.S. parents really want what is best for their children, they should work with educators to develop sex-education curricula that provide teens with the kind of information they need to make wise decisions about engaging (or not engaging) in sex and using (or not using) contraceptives. The information should be forthright, medically accurate, and complete. Specifically, in order to emphasize the overall importance of proper sex education, feminists urge schools to establish an "opt-out" mechanism rather than an "opt-in" mechanism. In other words, sex-education classes should be considered mandatory unless *students* exempt themselves on account of strong religious or personal beliefs.

In addition to recommending the development of first-rate, mandatory sex-education programs in schools, most feminists press educators to establish health centers at which teens can be confidentially given (or purchase) the reproduction-controlling technologies about which they have learned. When concerned parents lobby for parental consent or notification policies, feminists remind them that statistical evidence increasingly suggests that adolescents will have sex whether or not they have access to birth control. They then ask the parents to focus on what sorts of policies are most likely to serve their children's best interests—those that prevent unwanted pregnancies or those that result in unwanted pregnancies?

Conclusion

Among the remaining issues that continue to concern feminists about the reproduction-controlling technologies of contraception and sterilization are those involving relationships between men and women. Does using contraceptives or being sterilized bring men and women closer together or further apart? Whose responsibility is it to use contraceptives? To be sterilized? Because contraception and sterilization make sex without procreation possible, these reproduction-controlling technologies have supposedly led to new sexual rights and reproductive responsibilities for both men and women. According to many feminists, however, these new responsibilities and rights are being distributed asymmetrically between women and men. Women receive more reproductive responsibilities and fewer sexual rights, whereas men receive more sexual rights and fewer reproductive responsibilities.

With respect to women's sexual rights, many feminists wonder whether contraception and sterilization have really increased women's ability to make uncoerced choices about when to have sex, with whom, and under what circumstances. With the widespread availability of contraceptives and sterilization has come the presumption that women are more available for sexual intercourse than ever before. No longer can a woman discourage a man from making sexual advances with the chilling caveat "I might get pregnant." As a result, some men, especially if they are in a close heterosexual relationship, are inclined—again, more than ever before—to view "sex-on-demand" as a right of theirs. Similarly, with respect to women's reproductive responsibilities, many feminists suspect that far from decreasing women's procreative burdens, the widespread availability of contraception and sterilization has added to them. They point out, first, that despite the risks and unpleasant side effects that accompany the use of oral contraceptives, the IUD, and the new implants and injectables, many men fail or refuse to use condoms on the grounds that an unwanted pregnancy is "the woman's problem." Second, because many men still have the false belief that a vasectomy will lessen their virility or sexual potency,[55] they expect their wives to be the ones to "volunteer" for sterilization. But, over and beyond the fact that a vasectomy is minor surgery whereas a tubal ligation is major surgery, what these men fail to consider is that many *women* also approach sterilization ambivalently. Some women fear that sterilization will "desex" them; others fear that they will no longer be "real" women if unable to procreate.

Although it concerns feminists that men are not always willing to assume their fair share of the birth control burden on the grounds that an unwanted pregnancy is "the woman's problem," it concerns them even more that some women, particularly those who also regard themselves as feminists, claim that in the final analysis birth control probably is the woman's responsibility. For instance, feminist Mary Ann O'Loughlin expresses considerable concern about some of feminist Carol Gilligan's views on birth control. She notes that *In a Different Voice*, Gilligan claims that if a woman gets pregnant, "the onus of responsibility" should fall on her.[56] As evidence for her view that Gilligan blames the woman, far more than the man, for having unprotected sex, O'Loughlin cites Gilligan's assessment of Betty, a sixteen-year-old girl she interviewed during her study of moral decisionmaking and abortion. In her notes on Betty, Gilligan writes as follows:

> Betty begins by saying that the second pregnancy, like the first, was not her fault. Feeling both helpless and powerless to obtain contraception for herself, because she did not have any money and she believed she needed her parents' permission, she also felt powerless to deal with her boyfriend's continuing harassment. In the end, she gave in to his assurance that he knew what he was doing and would not get her pregnant, influenced by her belief that if she refused, he would break up with her. Since she has asked both him and her mother for contraception without success [her mother had refused because she believed the pill caused cancer], Betty explains that she became pregnant because no one was willing to help her.[57]

According to O'Loughlin, Gilligan proceeds to interpret Betty's remarks negatively—namely, as evidence of the young woman's unwillingness to accept responsibility (i.e., blame) for getting pregnant. For this reason, Gilligan considers it a sign that Betty has matured morally when, one year later, she accepts responsibility (i.e., blame) for not having used birth control.[58]

Reflecting on Gilligan's assessment of Betty, O'Loughlin comments that Betty should not view herself as the only, or even the primary, person to be blamed for the unwanted pregnancy. After all, Betty's boyfriend had assured her that he would not get her pregnant. Moreover, he had pressured Betty to have sex with him, so much so that she felt she had to say "yes" in order to preserve her relationship with him. According to O'Loughlin, then, because Gilligan puts too much stock in women's ability to make "free" choices, she fails to realize that Betty's real problem is not moral immaturity but her problematic relationship with a morally irresponsible man who bullied her into having unprotected sex.

O'Loughlin insists that it is a mistake to so readily let off the moral hook those men who fail or refuse to use birth control. She points out that although Betty's boyfriend urged her to go on the Pill, he failed to help her gain access to this mode of birth control. Since he was the one who wanted so much to have sex, this is the least he could have done; and, if he had no means of helping her get the Pill, he should have used a condom. After all, condoms do not require a physician's prescription, and they are quite inexpensive. Thus, O'Loughlin concludes, Betty should not blame *herself* for getting pregnant, since the net effect of this outcome is to exempt from equal blame "a sexually harassing, irresponsible male."[59]

Some feminists agree that O'Loughlin is right to argue that men *should* be as responsible about birth control as women are. However, other feminists claim that Gilligan's position is not totally unreasonable: Until men *actually* assume equal responsibility with women for birth control, women seem to have little choice other than continuing to shoulder this responsibility themselves. Still other feminists reaffirm what seems to be O'Loughlin's major point—namely, that by making sure she's "protected" just in case her partner is not, a woman plays into the traditional notion that if a woman gets pregnant she has only herself to blame (as if two people—a woman and a man—were not required to bring about a pregnancy). For this reason, these latter feminists conclude that men, no less than women, are morally obligated to protect themselves from unwanted pregnancies (the baby is the "man's problem just as much as the woman's); and that if definite health risks are associated with available contraceptives, these risks should be shared between the male and female partners. Indeed, feminist Mary Mahowald goes so far as to suggest that, at present, men may be *more* obligated than women to use contraceptives. Comments Mahowald:

> From an egalitarian perspective, responsibility for contraception should be shared by sexual partners in a manner that respects the values and preferences of each, and the disproportionate burdens and benefits that pregnancy involves for each. It may be argued, for example, that men have a stronger obligation to practice (accept the burden of) contraception because the burden of pregnancy falls on women rather than men. If pregnancy is seen as a benefit mainly to women, the opposite claim could legitimately be made.[60]

Even if Mahowald is wrong—that is, even if men do not have a stronger obligation to practice contraception than women do—most feminists still think that it is time for society to shift the burden of responsibility for contraception off of women and onto both sexes, particularly if researchers can develop safe and effective contraceptives and sterilization procedures for both. Better contraceptives, including less invasive and less permanent types of sterilization, would indeed ease the burden of birth control for women. Regrettably, as noted earlier, pharmaceutical companies are loath to develop such products because of the high costs they incur by doing so. In this connection, scientist James Knight and philosopher Joan Callahan have noted that

> [o]ne possible solution to the problem of decreased interest in new birth control product development by pharmaceutical companies is for the government to subsidize their involvement in new product research and development (either directly or through tax incentives) and to provide them with indemnity against litigation for product failure when a product has been responsibly tested.[61]

Were this the decade of the 1960s or 1970s, most feminists would probably be opposed to shielding pharmaceutical companies from lawsuits. Where there is money to be made, they would argue, there is always the temptation to produce a product that is not entirely safe—another Dalkon Shield, for example. But now that we are well into the 1990s, what women (and men) have to fear is that overly strict and cautious government regulations will impede basically satisfactory means of birth control from reaching the market.

Undoubtedly, pharmaceutical companies are no more eager to develop contraceptives for men than for women, even though considerable progress has already been made in the area of male contraceptives. For example, the Chinese, for some time now, have used gossypol, a yellowish, phenolic compound derived from cottonseed oil, as a male contraceptive. This drug blocks the action of the lactate dehydrogenase X enzyme, found only in sperm or testicular cells. By blocking this enzyme, gossypol hinders sperm maturation and mobility. However, the drug, which is 99.89 percent effective and very inexpensive to make, has several disadvantages. It causes potassium deficiencies, hair discoloration, and listlessness, and it seems to be particularly problematic for men with subclinical varicose veins in the testicles.[62] Moreover, it appears to cause impotence and, in some instances, permanent infertility.[63]

In the United States, researchers have focused on male contraceptives that inhibit the development of sperm. One of the products they have developed so far is "belly jelly," a salve that is rubbed on the abdomen or the chest of a man immediately before intercourse. The combination of testosterone and estradiol in the cream is able to stop fertility without depleting the male libido. The trouble with belly jelly, however, is that it can bring about increased male characteristics in the female partner of the user. In fact, it often causes hair to sprout on the inner thighs or the upper lip of women who come in contact with it. Until a solution to this problem is discovered, belly jelly will remain unmarketable.[64]

Even if better male as well as female contraceptives can be developed, men will have to be persuaded that they have at least as much responsibility to practice birth control as women do. Although condoms are not 100 percent effective, they are very safe and have the advantage of protecting against certain sexually transmitted diseases including AIDS. And using a condom imposes very little hardship on a man—certainly less of a hardship on a man than taking an oral contraceptive imposes on a woman. What is more, if men as well as women were to use contraceptives, women would be spared not only some of the risks associated with contraceptive use but also some of the social embarrassments. Indeed, as feminist writer Anne Woodhouse has pointed out, our society continues to associate birth control with female promiscuity to such a degree that young, unmarried women often refuse to use contraceptives for fear that men will get the wrong idea about their sexual availability.[65] But if men felt as responsible for contraception as women do, chances are that society's attitudes about the relationship between birth control and female promiscuity would change. In all likelihood, the use of birth control would come to signal not sexual promiscuity but sexual responsibility, attesting to the fact that a man and a woman have carefully considered the possible consequences of their engaging in sexual intercourse.

To be sure, not all men will respond well to the above criticisms, but some will and others already have. In the meantime, as feminists have noted, parents and educators must teach children that birth control is just as much the responsibility of men as of women. And sexual partners need to discuss what means of contraception or sterilization is most likely to equalize their procreative rights and responsibilities. There is no one "feminist" means of birth control. For instance, it makes sense for a man to start using a condom if his one and only sexual partner can no longer tolerate the side effects of her contraceptives, but not if she is an entirely satisfied IUD user who does not like the "feel" of a condom in her body. Similarly, it makes sense for a husband to have a vasectomy so that his wife can be spared a tubal ligation, but not if his wife can have a tubal ligation during the course of some other surgical procedure. Properly handled, birth control decisions can be powerful bonding experiences for men and women. Certainly, they can provide women with increased respect for those men who are willing to acknowledge that they, too, consider it unfair that women should always be the ones who must put their bodies at risk so as not to bring into the world any more children than can be reared properly and loved fully.

6

Nonfeminist and Feminist Perspectives on Abortion

The moral problems associated with abortion are in many ways similar to those associated with contraception and sterilization. Abortion is, after all, a means of birth control. The crucial difference is, of course, that abortion does not prevent conception; it eliminates the fetus once it is conceived. As we shall see in this chapter, not only are there major differences between nonfeminist and feminist approaches to abortion, there are surprising differences among *feminist* approaches to abortion. All of these differences challenge our society to find ways to better balance women's and fetuses' interests, ways that account more adequately for the connections as well as boundaries between women and the possible lives only they can bring into actual existence.

Nonfeminist Bioethical Perspectives on Abortion

The questions that nonfeminist bioethicists have most often raised about abortion are twofold: (1) What is the moral status of the fetus? And (2) *if* the fetus is a person from either the moment of conception or sometime during its gestation, is its right to life always or only sometimes more weighty than the pregnant woman's procreative rights and/or rights to bodily integrity? To ask about the moral status of the fetus is to ask not simply when it starts to *live* but when it becomes a *person*.[1] The question "When during gestation does 'human life' begin?" says philosopher Frederick Jaffe, needs to be restated as the question "When does a fetus become a 'person' who merits protection equal to or greater than the woman in whose body it would cease to exist?"[2] In giving their answer to

Jaffe's "restated" question, so-called extreme conservatives claim that virtually everyone agrees that a newborn infant is a person. They then add a second claim: namely, that working backward in time from birth, there is no "magic moment" at which the developing fetus suddenly became a person—for example, while it was in the birth canal, or with the first contraction. In effect, extreme conservatives argue that there is no morally significant difference between any one moment in a fetus's gestation and any other moment. Fetal development, like child development, is simply the gradual and continuous development of the *person* who came into existence at the moment of conception and who is born nine months later. Comments John T. Noonan, Jr.: "At conception the new being receives the genetic code. It is this genetic information which determines his characteristics, which is the biological carrier of the possibility of human wisdom, which makes him a self-evolving being. A being with a human genetic code is man."[3]

Whatever the ultimate truth or validity of the extreme conservative position on personhood may be, it has serious moral and legal consequences. If developing members of the human species are persons from the moment of their conception onward, and if it is wrong to kill a person without adequate justification, then it is morally wrong to abort a fetus. Although some extreme conservatives accept self-defense as an adequate justification for killing and therefore permit abortion to save the mother's life, others forbid even this exception. They argue that since fetuses are not aggressors but simply innocent victims, their mothers lack the moral justification for killing them even in self-defense.

Unlike extreme conservatives, all so-called moderate conservatives permit abortion not only to save the mother's life. They also permit abortions that terminate pregnancies caused by rape or incest, although their justifications for these exceptions to the "no-abortion" rule are far from compelling ones. After all, a fetus that results from rape or incest would seem, *as a fetus*, to have the same moral status as a fetus conceived during sexual intercourse between happily married persons. Therefore, if moderate conservatives believe it is permissible to kill a fetus in order to spare its mother grave psychological trauma, they should probably make exceptions to the "no-abortion" rule not only for rape and incest victims but also for women who cannot bear the idea of carrying to term a fetus with a severe genetic disease, or a fetus they cannot afford to rear.

Although some moderate conservatives are inclined to make these further concessions to the "no-abortion" rule, most try to hold the line at rape and incest. But no matter how they distinguish between a morally justified abortion and a morally unjustified one, moderate conservatives are disinclined to judge, in an equally harsh fashion, all women who terminate their pregnancies. Noting how the law ranks killings according to the level of intentionality that accompanies them (e.g., first-degree murder, second-degree murder, voluntary manslaughter, and involuntary manslaughter), they point out that ours is a culture in which not every killing is considered as morally blameworthy as every other killing. Thus, most moderate conservatives believe that aborting a genetically diseased fetus that one cannot afford to rear is much more excusable than aborting a healthy fetus because one would *prefer* to postpone motherhood for a year.

In contrast to extreme and moderate conservatives, so-called extreme liberals claim that fetuses are not human persons during any moment of their gestation. At most they are human life in the same way that pieces of human tissue or organs are human life. Extreme liberals begin their argument with the premise that the ovum is part of a woman's body; it is one of her reproductive cells. Working forward in time from conception, they add a second premise: namely, that there is no "magic moment" in the development of a member of the human species, not even the moment of birth, when it becomes a person—that is, an entity that manifests consciousness, reasoning, self-motivated activity, the capacity to communicate, and the presence of a self-concept.[4] Personhood, then, occurs only some time after birth, most clearly after the age of two.

Whatever the ultimate truth or validity of the extreme liberal view on personhood may be, like its conservative counterpart it has dramatic moral and legal consequences. If the fetus at any stage of development is merely a part of the woman's body, and if the woman has the right to do whatever she wants with her body, then all abortions are justified. Morally, there would seem to be no difference between aborting a first-trimester fetus because the woman cannot sustain a life-imperiling pregnancy and aborting a third-trimester fetus because the woman has a sudden urge to squeeze into a slinky evening gown. *If* the only right at stake is the *woman's* right to physical autonomy or bodily integrity, then abortion on demand is her moral as well as legal right.

Claiming that extreme liberals are wrong to deny a *moral* difference between a one-hour-old conceptus and an eight-month-old fetus, so-called moderate liberals insist that as the fetus develops, its incipient right to life increases. The right to life is not an all-or-nothing matter with respect to a fetus. On the contrary, the fetus's right to life grows in strength as the fetus gradually manifests the characteristics associated with being a human person. Thus, moderate liberals balance the fetus's growing right to life against both the women's right to bodily integrity and her right to procreate or not procreate. Not all, but only some, abortions are morally justifiable choices for women.

In their attempts to distinguish between morally justified and morally unjustified abortions, moderate liberals have sought to identify the moment at which the fetus makes the transition to personhood. They often cite viability, the point at which a fetus is able to exist independently of a woman's body, as the "magic moment" at which the fetus becomes a person. But viability has proved to be an unsatisfactory criterion for personhood. First, it is not clear that the ability to exist independently of someone else's body is what makes one a person. Siamese twins are regarded as two separate persons; yet, if surgery is out of the question and the twins share a heart, for example, each of their "existences" is dependent on the other's body. Second, the point of viability is not fixed. When the Supreme Court handed down its 1973 *Roe v. Wade* decision, it noted that "viability is usually placed at about seven months (28 weeks) but may occur earlier, even at 24 weeks."[5] As a result of technological improvements in neonatal care since 1973, however, the point of viability is now routinely set at twenty-four weeks, with survival occasionally possible at twenty-three weeks. To be sure, as philosopher Daniel Callahan has pointed out, "the age of viability will not necessarily continue to drop. The physiological obstacles to further advances, most notably the immaturity of fetal lungs, mean that 22 to 23 weeks may be the immediately foreseeable limit."[6] However, scientists have overcome limits greater than this one. If they develop an artificial placenta, functionally equivalent to a woman's womb, all fetuses, including *very* young ones, would be able to survive outside a woman's womb. Therefore, any fetus would be "viable" from the moment of conception, and the moderate liberal position on abortion would become virtually identical to the conservative one.

Suspecting that viability is, after all, an unsatisfactory criterion for marking the inception of personhood, many moderate liberals conclude that personhood has to do not with *accidental* matters such as an entity's location or its ability to live independently but, rather, with *essential* matters such as whether it is a genetically distinct, unique individual with the capacity for rationality. According to Thomas A. Shannon and Allan B. Wolter, a fertilized egg must undergo three processes before it can be said to be a person. First, the fertilized egg has to become genetically distinct; that is, it must add to the genetic information within its chromosomes such supplementary genetic information as is found in the maternal mitochondria and in the maternal or paternal genetic messages conveyed through RNA or protein signals.[7] Next, the genetically distinct fertilized egg, now about a week old and implanted in the womb, has to become a unique individual, singular rather than plural in number. This occurs around the third week of embryonic development during a stage termed gastrulation, after which the cells of the genetically distinct fertilized egg are no longer totipotent (i.e., each capable of forming an entire organism on its own).[8] Finally, the genetically distinct, uniquely individual fertilized egg has to develop the *capacity* for rationality, a capacity that will emerge only when its nervous system is integrated enough to support the possibility of rational activity. Such integration can be marked at one of two points: (1) at organogenesis, the appearance of all major systems of the body, occurring around the eighth week of gestation; or (2) at the development of the thalamus, which permits the full integration of the nervous system, occurring around the twentieth week of gestation.

Depending on whether moderate liberals view organogenesis or the development of the thalamus as the moment after which a genetically distinct, uniquely individual fertilized egg attains the capacity for rationality and therefore personhood, they will be inclined to morally permit a lesser or greater range of abortions. If "brain birth" occurs at eight weeks, then only first-trimester abortions are permissible. But if "brain birth" occurs at twenty weeks, then most second-trimester as well as all first-trimester abortions are permissible. Since 91 percent of abortions take place prior to the twelfth week of pregnancy, the second of these two views of personhood would permit the vast majority of abortions.[9]

Feminist Bioethical Perspectives on Abortion

Most feminists believe that the abortion debate should center not on the question of whether fetuses are the moral equivalent of adult persons but, rather, on the fact that fertilized eggs develop into infants inside the wombs of women. As feminist commentator Ellen Willis observes:

> Pregnancy and birth are active processes in which a woman's body shelters, nourishes, and expels a new life; for nine months she is immersed in the most intimate possible relationship with another being. The growing fetus makes considerable demands on her physical and emotional resources, culminating in the cataclysmic experience of birth. And childbearing has unpredictable consequences; it always entails some risk of injury or death.[10]

A mother herself, Willis observes that as a result of her experiences during pregnancy and childbirth, she became convinced that the key question in the abortion debate should be "Can it be moral, under any circumstances, to make a woman bear a child against her will?"[11] If women are ever to have the same degree of autonomy as men do, says Willis, they must have the power to say "no" to potential life.

Recently, as in years past, many feminists have claimed that the fetus's right to life must be weighed against women's rights to bodily integrity and privacy. Those who emphasize the latter rely on the kinds of arguments that philosopher Judith Jarvis Thomson has made. As Thomson sees it, "Having a right to life does not guarantee having either a right to be given the use of or a right to be allowed continued use of another person's body—even if one needs it for life itself."[12] Given her understanding of what the right to life does and does not include, Thomson has little difficulty justifying abortion in those cases where a woman will die unless she aborts the fetus. But because the right to self-defense is a right that virtually every nonfeminist ethical system accepts, Thomson wonders why the natural-law tradition forbids abortion even when the mother's life is at stake. What she forgets is that natural-law theorists invoke the principle of self-defense only against so-called non-innocent aggressors. Because they believe the fetus is innocent—it does not, after all, *deliberately* invade the womb of the woman in which it gestates—and because they also believe that all persons, including not-yet-born persons, have an equal right to life, natural-law theorists reason that the life of a fetus and that of the woman are of equal value. When only one of these two persons can live, we must not intervene. "Nature" must decide the matter.

Although Thomson agrees that the fetus is innocent, and although she concedes that both the fetus and the woman who gestates it have a right to life, she insists that when the fetus's life comes into conflict with that of its gestator, the woman's right to life overrides that of the fetus. Thomson bases her judgment on the observation "that the mother and the unborn child are not like two tenants in a small house which has, by an unfortunate mistake, been rented to both: The mother *owns* the house."[13] Thomson argues that possessing the right to life does not automatically give one person the right to *use* another person's body in order to keep on living. For instance, a man who needs to use a set of healthy kidneys in order to go on living cannot justifiably kidnap a woman and plug himself into that woman's kidneys for even a short period of time. Analogously, the fetus has no right to use the body of the woman who gestates it, even if it cannot survive outside of that woman's body.[14]

Thomson admits that her analogy is imperfect. It fits cases of unwanted pregnancy after rape or the use of faulty contraceptives far better than cases of unwanted pregnancy after voluntary intercourse. If a woman invites a strange man to use her kidneys for a specified number of months, during which time a personal relationship develops between them, she may come to *owe* that man continuing access to her body even though he has no *right* to use her body. A sudden decision on her part to break the personal relationship she initiated by inviting him to use her body would seem *prima facie* wrong, even if such a rupture does not constitute a violation of the dependent person's *rights*. Analogously, if a woman becomes pregnant because she wants to have a child, it would seem *prima facie* wrong for her to abort the fetus—especially if she has been hosting it for several months.[15]

Assuming that Thomson is correct—that the right to life does not include the right to use someone else's body to support that life—and even assuming (as Thomson does not) that *all* fetal *extractions* are therefore justifiable, unnecessary fetal *extinctions* would not necessarily also be justified. Nevertheless, when a woman seeks an abortion, fetal extinction rather than mere fetal extraction is probably her goal. She simply does not want to procreate—to bring another life into the world—at that time. In this connection, some feminists claim that it is more important to stress women's rights to *privacy* (to procreate or not) than women's right to *bodily integrity*.

Among those feminists who have reflected on whether a woman's right to procreate entitles her to the death of the fetus, even in cases where it survives the abortion procedure, is philosopher Christine Overall. She presents and evaluates four arguments, each of which supports the view "that failure to observe the wishes of the biological mother with respect to the death of the fetus is morally wrong."[16] The first argument in favor of killing the fetus is that keeping a fetus alive against the wishes of its biological mother violates that woman's reproductive autonomy. Overall notes that although it is easy enough to relieve the biological mother of any *social* obligations to her fetus, it is not possible to erase the biological mother's *genetic* connections to her fetus. But Overall further observes that, since some biological mothers want to break their genetic as well as social links to their fetuses, anything less than the death of their fetuses would fail to satisfy them.

The second argument in favor of killing the fetus is that "saving the fetus against the mother's will would be like compelling her to donate organs, blood, or gametes against her will."[17] Although Overall believes that unlike organs, blood, or gametes, fetuses have a life of their own, she remains adamantly opposed to efforts aimed at "rescuing" fetuses from abortion.[18] In her estimation, it is up to the pregnant woman to decide whether, when, and how to remove the fetus from her body. She claims that forcing a woman to submit to whatever abortion procedure is most likely to preserve the life of a second-trimester fetus, for example, is "comparable to a compulsory organ 'donation' in which the patient chooses organ removal but does not agree to the subsequent salvaging and use of the organ."[19]

The third argument in favor of killing the fetus is that "by virtue of her physical relationship to it, the biological mother is the most appropriate person—perhaps the only one—to decide the disposition of the fetus."[20] Overall supports this argument totally with respect to not-yet-born fetuses, but only partially with respect to born fetuses, including those who survive the abortion procedure. To the extent that the latter fetuses are like premature infants, she believes, their biological mothers have an obligation to take their interests, including their interests in living and being adopted, into account.

The fourth and final argument in favor of killing the fetus is that "deliberately withholding the determination of the disposition of the fetus from the biological mother is yet another example of the takeover of reproduction from women."[21] In this connection, philosopher Anne Donchin asks:

> [I]f extrauterine gestation were to become an established practice, would not many women be pressured to adopt it—"for the good of their baby?"
>
> Though abortion may count as a harm to the fetus, laboratory gestation would as well—not only to particular "unwanted" fetuses but to *all* future fetuses. For, within the prevailing social framework, once the practice was established, it is unlikely that only intentionally aborted fetuses would be nourished in laboratories. Any other fetus considered "at risk" for any reason would count as a potential beneficiary of laboratory observation and intervention.[22]

Overall agrees with Donchin that legal and medical encroachments on women's reproductive autonomy *during pregnancy* must be resisted at all costs. No one should be permitted to invade a woman's womb to "rescue" her fetus; and, within the limits of good medical practice, no one but the pregnant woman should be permitted to decide what kind of abortion she will have.[23] Moreover, in the event that her fetus survives the abortion procedure, it is up to the woman to decide what is in its best interests. This is not to say, however, that she has an absolute right to demand that it be killed. Rather, the point is that, like the mother of a premature infant with severe health problems, the mother of an equally imperiled infant that survives the abortion procedure has the *prima facie* right to decide what is in the infant's best interests—for example, aggressive or simply palliative medical treatment.[24]

Overall's argument that the *mother* of an imperiled infant who survives abortion should decide her or his fate strikes critics as counterintuitive. They point out that when a parent does not want a child, there is good reason to think that the parent does not have the child's best interests at heart. Thus, in the case of the imperiled infant who survives abortion, they insist that not the mother but someone else who *wants* the child—perhaps the father—should decide what is in the child's best interests.

In order to understand better why Overall and other feminists think that the mother has the *prima facie* right to determine what is in her born fetus's best interests, it is helpful to review Alison Jaggar's justification for the claim that, in a patriarchal society, a woman should have the sole legal right to decide whether, in her own case, an abortion should be performed. Instead of appealing to women's privacy rights, bodily integrity rights, or pursuit of happiness rights, Jaggar appeals to two fundamental principles: (1) The right to life for a human being "means the right to a full human life and to what ever means are necessary to achieve this," and (2) "decisions should be made by those, and only by those, who are importantly affected by them."[25] Jaggar reasons that unless an individual or a group is prepared to rear to adulthood the fetus they saved from abortion, he, she, or they have no moral grounds for compelling a woman to continue a pregnancy she wishes to terminate. Since she is the one who will probably have the responsibility to rear the infant to adulthood if it is born, the decision to have or not have the infant is hers.

But what about the father? Shouldn't he have some say in the abortion decision? What if he is willing to raise the infant to adulthood? To these questions Jaggar would respond that we must focus not on the *individual man* who wants to have *his* baby but on the fact that pregnancy generally affects women in ways that it cannot possibly affect men, and also on the fact that, in this culture, "motherhood" is generally a more burdensome institution than "fatherhood." As Jaggar explains:

> Biology, law, and social conditioning work together to ensure that most women's lives are totally changed as the result of the birth of a child while men can choose how much they wish to be involved. It is for this reason that the potential mother rather than the potential father should have the ultimate responsibility for deciding whether or not an abortion should be performed. If conventions regarding the degree of parental responsibility assumed by the mother and by the father were to change or if the law prescribing paternal child support were to be enforced more rigorously, then perhaps the father should be required to share with the mother in making the decision. (He could never take over the decision completely, of course, because it is not his body which is involved.) But in the present social situation, the right of a woman to decide if she should abort is not limited by any right of the father.[26]

Jaggar further notes that if the *father* has no right to interfere with a woman's decision to abort, then certainly *physicians* and other health-care practitioners have no right to interfere with her decision since they will play no role in rearing the child to adulthood.

What complicates Jaggar's analysis is the fact that, although she does not think physicians and other health-care professionals are entitled to *interfere* with a woman's abortion decision, neither does she think they are required to *implement* a woman's abortion decision. In response to some feminists' objection that if substantial numbers of physicians and health-care practitioners refused to perform abortions for reasons of conscience, women's ability to exercise their abortion rights would be severely limited, Jaggar observes that such a problem would be, at worst, a short-term one:

> In practice, if there is a difficulty in finding the medical staff prepared to perform abortions, this is an indication that medical practitioners should be drawn from a broader spectrum of the population. Specifically they should

include more women. People are not generally slow in recognizing their rights and, if each woman has a right to choose whether or not she should abort, then female staff are unlikely to have moral qualms about helping her to exercise that right.[27]

Jaggar's hypothesis—that as more women become obstetricians and gynecologists, more rather than fewer physicians will be willing to perform abortions—is a plausible one. But plausibilities do not always generate certainties. The fact that a physician is a *woman* does not necessarily mean that she will be willing to perform or assist in abortions. On the contrary, there is considerable evidence that the majority of obstetricians and gynecologists in private practice, irrespective of gender, avoid the abortion issue by referring most of their abortion patients to clinics or teaching hospitals.[28] Moreover, at many medical schools, abortion procedures are given scant attention or not taught at all;[29] and for political reasons, most hospitals avoid performing anything but medically necessary abortions. In fact, nationwide, only 10.1 percent of abortions are performed in hospitals, with another 3.8 percent done in physicians' offices. The remaining 86.1 percent are performed in clinics.[30]

Until relatively recently most abortion clinics were well staffed; but when extremists in the pro-life movement began to bomb abortion clinics and to take sometimes fatal shots at those working within,[31] staff members began to resign. As a result, an increasing number of largely unstaffed abortion clinics shut their doors and women's access to abortion diminished dramatically. The situation, say feminists, is very dire. In Duluth, Minnesota, for example, a clinic that serves forty-two counties relies on the services of one seventy-eight-year-old physician who flies in once a week.[32] No matter how hard he tries to help all the women who need his services, this physician is forced to send away more women than he can treat.

As many feminists have observed, tactics such as harassing women who seek abortions and terrorizing physicians and others who assist at them pose just as great a threat to women's abortion rights as do past and present challenges to *Roe v. Wade* (1973). In this Supreme Court decision on abortion rights, the Justices articulated the scope of women's privacy rights as follows:

1. During the first trimester of pregnancy, states may not enact laws to interfere with a woman's *and* physician's abortion decision.
2. During the second trimester of pregnancy, states may enact laws, but only in such instances as to preserve and protect maternal health.
3. During the third trimester of pregnancy, states may enact laws to protect the viable fetus, but only if such laws make exceptions for

those instances in which the woman's life or health (physical or mental) are at risk.

4. States may not enact laws requiring all abortions to be performed in accredited hospitals, or to be approved by hospital committee or a second medical opinion, or to be performed only on state residents.[33]

No sooner was the *Roe* decision announced than anti-abortion forces mounted their opposition to it. The legal means by which anti-abortionists have traditionally sought to limit women's choice not to procreate include public-funding restrictions on abortion procedures, third-party consent or notification requirements for abortions, and procedural requirements for abortions.

With respect to the first of these legal strategies—public funding restrictions—anti-abortionists have gained some important victories. In *Maher v. Roe* (1977) and *Beal v. Roe* (1977), the Supreme Court ruled that the fact that a state may not enact laws to interfere with women's first-trimester abortions does not mean that it must fund medically unnecessary abortions for indigent women.[34] Virtually all feminists objected to the Court's ruling for two main reasons. First, and foremost, such funding restrictions discriminate against indigent women. Unlike a rich woman, who can pay for her supposedly medically unnecessary abortion out of pocket, a poor woman cannot. Second, such terms as 'medically necessary abortion' and 'medically unnecessary abortion' are susceptible to a wide variety of interpretations. By 'medically necessary abortion' a legislator may mean an abortion performed to end a pregnancy that is literally endangering a woman's life. In contrast, by 'medically necessary abortion' a physician may mean an abortion performed for any of the following reasons: (1) the fact that the pregnant woman has phlebitis, varicose veins, cancer, diabetes, myoma of the uterus, urinary tract infections, intrauterine device in utero, ulcerative colitis, previous cesarean sections, anemia, malnutrition, and obesity; (2) the fact that the woman is under stress; (3) the fact that the woman's pregnancy is the result of rape or incest; (4) the fact that the woman is an adolescent; (5) the fact that the fetus is defective; or (6) the fact that the woman is emotionally compromised.[35] Given the disparity between some legislators' and some physicians' respective interpretations of the term 'medically necessary', risk-aversive physicians, fearful of violating the law, might classify as 'medically *unnecessary*' those abortions they would otherwise classify as 'medically *necessary*'—that is, as being in the best overall health interests of the women who have requested them.

Despite feminists' efforts to secure public funds for indigent women's medically unnecessary abortions, anti-abortionists have had considerable success limiting abortion coverage under the Medicaid program. Only Hawaii, New Mexico, New York, and Washington voluntarily cover abortions for indigent women for non-life-endangering health reasons. Eleven other states do the same, but under court order. Maryland, North Carolina, Wisconsin, Virginia, Iowa, Pennsylvania, and Wyoming have more restrictive limits in that they limit abortion coverage to life endangerment, rape, and incest. The final thirty states technically allow coverage only in cases of life endangerment; in practice, however, they fund abortions in cases of rape and incest.[36] Faced with this state of affairs, feminists have launched a full-scale search both for physicians willing to classify a wide range of abortions as medically necessary and for private agencies and individual philanthropists willing to subsidize abortions for indigent women. Although this search has been fruitful, feminists believe that it is no substitute for state provision of funds for indigent women needing abortions. The fact that eighteen- and nineteen-year-olds have an abortion rate twice as high as the national average, that unmarried women account for about 80 percent of all abortions, that women in families whose income is under $11,000 are four times more likely to have an abortion than those whose family income is $25,000 or more, and that women of color are nearly twice as likely as white women to have an abortion suggests that the women most inclined to seek abortions are precisely those who do not have the funds to provide adequately for a child or an additional child.[37] In the estimation of many feminists, these women *want* to act responsibly, and it is wrong for the state to add to the difficulty of their decision by denying them the funds they need to exercise their abortion "right."

The second way that anti-abortionists have sought to limit women's procreative choices is through so-called third-party consent or notification provisions, which invite the intervention either of parents or of spouses into the abortion decision. Proponents of such legislation argue that since the abortion decision is so difficult to make, it is in the best interests of women to involve their parents or husbands in the process. Opponents argue that parents and spouses do not always have the same interests as their daughters and wives do. Fearing her relatives' possibly negative reaction, a woman might attempt to end her own pregnancy or appeal to a less than medically competent person for an abortion. Alternatively, she might run away from home or undergo a pregnancy she does not want simply in order to maintain her familial relationships.

So far, the Supreme Court has not upheld either *spousal* consent or *spousal* notification laws.[38] However, it has upheld both *parental* consent and *parental* notification laws, generally with the proviso that the state provide a judicial bypass procedure should the adolescent girl be unable or unwilling to involve her parents. The Court has justified its ruling largely on the grounds that, unlike adult women, adolescent girls are not always capable of giving their informed consent to an abortion. Currently, thirty-six states have parental consent and/or notification laws, although only twenty-five enforce them. Thirteen other states have no such laws. The remaining state, Connecticut, requires a young woman to receive counseling that includes a discussion about involving her parents.[39] Although advocates of consent and notification laws usually describe them in terms that sound supportive of women, feminists view these measures as yet another attempt to whittle away women's access to abortion, starting with the most vulnerable participants—young and frightened girls.

The third way that anti-abortionists have sought to limit women's abortion rights is by requiring women seeking abortions and the healthcare practitioners assisting at them to jump through a series of bureaucratic hoops. Feminists believe that anti-abortionists have invoked the concept of informed consent not so much to increase women's knowledge about abortion as to make the abortion decision more difficult for women. In Ohio, for example, anti-abortionists developed legislation in the past that required physicians to recite to their clients a litany of state-approved recommendations discouraging abortion and to delay the abortion procedure at least twenty-four hours after the recitation.[40] Similarly, in Pennsylvania, and also in the past, anti-abortionists developed legislation that required abortion providers to give the following sort of information to women seeking abortions:

> the name of the physician who would perform the abortion, the probable gestational age of the fetus, a description of the medical risks associated with the procedure and with carrying the fetus to term, and an offer of material to review regarding the probable anatomical and physiological characteristics of the unborn child at two-week gestational increments from fertilization to full term, including any relevant information on the possibility of the unborn child's survival.[41]

When feminists countered that the above-mentioned legislation constituted not use but misuse of the doctrine of informed consent, they scored a victory against it. The Supreme Court ruled in *Akron v. Akron Center for Reproductive Health* (1983)[42] that a state must remain neutral with regard to a woman's choice between childbirth and abortion. In other words, a state cannot provide women with information entirely biased in the direction of birth or, alternatively, abortion. In the related case of *Thornburgh v. American College of Obstetricians and Gynecologists* (1986), Justice Blackmun underscored this point. He wrote that, far from helping a woman make an autonomous decision about whether to have an abortion, counseling biased in the direction of condemning abortion would only "confuse and punish" a women considering abortion.[43] Thus, the legislation in both Pennsylvania and Ohio was declared unconstitutional.

However, for reasons that seem more political than logical, and to the consternation of feminists, the Supreme Court has recently reversed itself with respect to the importance of neutral abortion counseling. In *Planned Parenthood v. Casey* (1992), a Pennsylvania case, the Supreme Court ruled that a state may "enact persuasive measures which favor childbirth over abortion," provided that those measures do not impose an "undue burden" on a woman's right to choose abortion.[44] Henceforward, unless it can be *proven* that information over and beyond that which outlines abortion's health risks constitutes an *undue* burden on women seeking abortions—and here I refer to state-sponsored material that includes pictures of fetuses at two-week gestational intervals and lists alternatives to abortion; information about the availability of public assistance for medical expenses associated with prenatal care, delivery, and neonatal care; and advice to the woman that the father of the child is liable to assist in the support of her child—women in Pennsylvania and other like-minded states will receive such information. The question then becomes whether all women, most women, few women, or no women *want* this kind of information. Does the doctrine of informed consent require that people receive information that they do not want—information that they view, for example, as extraneous, obnoxious, or anxiety-producing?

By way of consolation, feminists tell themselves that even though states will now be able to disseminate more "pro-life" material at *abortion* clinics, they will not be able to ban information about abortion from a *family-planning* clinic simply because it receives federal money such as so-called Title-X funds. Feminists consider it a victory that the "gag rule," enacted during President George Bush's administration, is no longer the order of the day. This rule, which the Supreme Court upheld in *Rust v. Sullivan* (1991), required anyone working in one of 4,000 federally funded family-planning clinics to conceal from their patients any information about their right to abortion.[45]

In arguing against the gag rule, feminists observed that it is one matter to proclaim that federally funded family-planning clinics must not perform or advocate abortions and quite another to insist that clinic physicians may not even explain the abortion option to their pregnant patients or refer them to physicians outside the clinic who perform abortions, even when their patients request such referrals. To silence clinic physicians, feminists maintained, is to violate physicians' First Amendment right to free speech and to interfere with their practice of medicine by making full informed consent virtually impossible. Defenders of the gag rule countered that it was intended not to inhibit free speech or the practice of good medicine but, instead, to promote the government's "value judgment favoring childbirth over abortion."[46] If a clinic did not share this value judgment, it could refuse federal monies and provide as much abortion information as it chose. Had it not been for the election of pro-choice William Clinton to the White House in 1992, the gag rule might still be in effect. However, Clinton and his administration found persuasive the feminist argument that the gag rule erodes not only the doctrine of informed consent but also trusting relationships between women and health-care practitioners. In one of his first acts after taking office in 1993, Clinton removed the gag rule by executive order.[47]

Over and beyond their increasingly successful efforts to impose heavy informed-consent requirements on women seeking abortion, anti-abortionists have attempted to impose regulations aimed at slowing down or otherwise making difficult the implementation of a woman's abortion decision. Initially, anti-abortionists did not have much success in regulating the time, place, or method of second- and third-trimester abortions. For example, in three 1983 decisions, the Supreme Court ruled that states may not require that all second- or third-trimester abortions be performed in hospitals. The Court also struck down regulations that required not only a twenty-four-hour waiting period between the signing of the abortion consent form and the abortion itself but also blanket restrictions on the method of abortion that could be used after viability.[48] Of late, however, the Court seems to have turned a more attentive ear to anti-abortionists' arguments—at least, those on behalf of waiting periods. Indeed, in the *Casey* (1992)[49] decision alluded to above, the Court decided that waiting periods are constitutional provided that they do not impose an undue burden on women.[50]

In reaction to *Casey*, most feminists have responded that, almost without exception, waiting periods do constitute a significant barrier to many women's ability to exercise their abortion rights. In this connection, Janet Benshoof notes:

> A woman seeking an abortion will have to make two visits to a clinic instead of one. Because of scheduling difficulties and the limited availability of abortion providers most women in Pennsylvania will have to endure 48-hour to 2-week delays before they can obtain the health care they seek. Since women will be forced to travel to clinics twice, and many will have to pay for accommodations, perhaps lose 2 days of wages, and pay for child care, this requirement will effectively preclude many low-income women and women living in rural areas from obtaining abortions. Among American women seeking abortions, 27% must travel at least 80 km to reach a provider, 18% travel between 80 and 160 km, and 9% travel more than 160 km.[51]

Other feminists add that, even if a woman lives close to an abortion clinic, she is unlikely to be well served by a waiting period during which she is invited to reconsider a decision she has probably already considered many times. If society wishes to protect the best interests of women and not simply to give them more grief, then the best way to guarantee that a woman makes a wise abortion decision is for her physician simply to follow standard informed-consent procedures, including a discussion of the risks and benefits and all of the alternatives to abortion (including the alternative of continuing her pregnancy) and then to implement her decision when *she* says she is ready to do so.

Feminists are worried that the *Casey* decision will encourage anti-abortionists to seek other restrictions on abortion—for example, regulation of the method of abortion used after the point of viability, provided that this measure does not unduly burden women. To be sure, a *blanket* restriction on the method of abortion used after viability would be unconstitutional, since it would put physicians in the untenable position of being unable to serve the best interests of their patients (i.e., the *women* seeking abortions) on a case-by-case basis. Among the procedures for second-trimester abortions are the prostaglandin method, saline amniocentesis, and intact dilation and evacuation. The first of these methods relies on the use of hormones called prostaglandins to induce labor. The negative side effects of this relatively costly procedure include gastrointestinal symptoms and cervical lacerations. Moreover, the procedure leaves open the possibility for birth of a live, viable fetus. In the saline amniocentesis procedure, the physician withdraws a small amount of amniotic fluid and replaces it with a saline solution that effectively kills the fetus within the uterus. Labor is then induced and the woman delivers a dead fetus. Though less expensive than the prostaglandin method, saline amniocentesis is not without its own negative side effects, including intravascular clotting, myometrial necrosis, and cerebral edema. Finally, there is the method of intact dilation and evacuation, which does not require the woman to undergo labor. It involves partially extracting a fetus, legs first, through the birth canal; cutting an incision in the barely visible skull base; and then draining the contents of the skull. Supposedly, this technique is somewhat safer for the woman than either the prostaglandin method or saline amniocentesis.

Concerned about her or his patient's well-being, a physician might choose intact dilation and evacuation over both the prostaglandin method and saline amniocentesis. In justifying this decision to others, the physician would note that the intact dilation and evacuation procedure is not only the safest of the three abortion methods but also one that, like saline amniocentesis, assuredly results in the death of the fetus. To this justification, however, anti-abortionists would probably respond that intact dilation and evacuation and saline amniocentesis are not really *much* safer than the prostaglandin method, inasmuch as the latter, from their point of view, has the *advantage* of giving a viable fetus the chance to live. In their estimation, the psychological trauma of going through a prostaglandin abortion, without knowing whether the fetus will be born alive or dead, does not constitute an *undue* burden on a woman's health. Whatever anxiety and distress the woman suffers is slight, they say, compared to a viable fetus's loss of life.

Feminists believe that at least three questions need to be answered to determine whether regulating the method of abortion after the point of viability unconstitutionally limits women's procreative rights. First, who is to decide whether a fetus has attained viability—the attending physician in the good-faith exercise of her or his medical judgment, or a prosecutor and jury in the course of a criminal proceeding? Second, precisely what constitutes an undue burden on a woman's health or life? Is it not possible that forcing a woman to submit to an abortion procedure (such as the prostaglandin method) that mimics a normal delivery is enough to cause her grave psychological trauma? Third, as discussed much earlier, are women's procreative rights restricted to fetal extraction, or do they also encompass fetal extinction? If women are entitled to fetal extraction only, then it would seem that when a woman's health or life is not compromised, physicians should use the abortion technique that *maximizes* the fetus's survival prospects—namely, the prostaglandin method. However, if women are also entitled to fetal extinction (a much more controversial "entitlement," to say the least), it would seem that physicians should use those abortion techniques that ensure the fetus's death—namely, saline amniocentesis or, in those countries where it is legally permitted, intact dilation and evacuation.[52]

In addition to worrying that anti-abortionists might redouble their efforts to regulate the timing and method of abortion, many feminists are concerned that anti-abortionists might renew their efforts to regulate the place of abortion. In the past, anti-abortionists argued that hospitals have a right to refuse to perform certain kinds of medical procedures, and that reasons of institutional conscience as well as fiscal reasons are adequate justification for such refusals. Opponents of this point of view objected that it is one thing to say that no *individual* should be coerced, held liable, or discriminated against in any manner because of a conscientious refusal to perform, accommodate, or assist in an abortion, but quite another to say that no *institution* should be legally required to offer abortion services. Only individuals have consciences. Nevertheless, the courts have been sympathetic to the argument that *private, sectarian* hospitals (e.g., Roman Catholic hospitals) may refuse to offer abortion services for religious reasons. More recently, courts—including the Supreme Court—have supported the view that *public* hospitals, clinics, or other tax-supported facilities are under no constitutional requirement to perform *elective* abortions. Thus, in *Webster v. Reproductive Health Services* (1989), the Supreme Court upheld a Missouri law that restricted abortion in three ways:

1. Public employees, including physicians, nurses, technicians, or other health-care providers, are forbidden to perform or assist in performing an abortion, except when necessary to save a woman's life.
2. Public hospitals, clinics, or other tax-supported facilities cannot be used to perform abortions not necessary to save a woman's life, even if no public funds are involved.
3. Physicians are required to perform tests to determine the viability of a fetus, if they have reason to believe the woman has been pregnant for at least twenty weeks.[53]

Presumably, a Missouri woman who wants an elective abortion can still secure one at a *private*, nonsectarian hospital or clinic, but because many of these hospitals and clinics receive public money or have contractual arrangements with state or local governments, they might also fall under the *Webster* ruling. Although the Supreme Court ruled in *Turnock v. Ragsdale* (1992) that a state may not require abortion clinics to maintain the same standards as full-care hospitals,[54] a state may still set high standards for abortion clinics. Depending on how high these standards are set, however, many private abortion facilities might be forced to close their doors, with the result that an increasing number of women would find it extremely difficult to secure an abortion.

As concerned as feminists are about funding restrictions, notification and consent laws, and regulations about the time, place, or method of abortion, their major worry is that as a result of developments in neonatology, which have pushed back the point of fetal viability from twenty-eight to twenty-three weeks, the Supreme Court might indeed reject what Chief Justice Rehnquist has termed the "rigid trimester analysis of *Roe v. Wade*."[55] As he and others see it, what should count in the abortion decision is *fetal viability* whenever this moment occurs—whether in the first, second, or third trimester of pregnancy. Following this reasoning, if states were previously permitted to ban or restrict medically unnecessary, third-trimester abortions on the grounds that the fetus is viable at approximately *twenty-eight* weeks, they should now be permitted to ban or restrict medically unnecessary, second-trimester abortions on the grounds that the fetus is viable at approximately *twenty-three* weeks.[56]

Even though the technological means to support fetuses younger than twenty-three weeks old outside of the womb will not be available in the near future, feminists urge women to seek their abortions as early as possible in their pregnancies and to consider using abortifacients such as RU-486. Sometimes called the "abortion pill," RU-486 was developed by a French pharmaceutical company, Roussel-UCLAF, and has been marketed to physicians in France since 1988. French women who wish to use RU-486 go to an authorized clinic for a pregnancy test and counseling, after which they wait one week before receiving RU-486. When the week is up, they go back to the clinic where they receive an appropriate dosage of RU-486. What some people do not realize is that two days after a woman swallows the abortifacient, she returns to the clinic for either an injection or oral dosage of contraction-inducing prostaglandin, which generally takes four hours to work. During this period of time, she is monitored for hemorrhaging, which occurs among 4 to 5 percent of the women who use RU-486. If the embryo is not expelled in what the clinic considers a reasonable length of time, the woman is sent home to wait for the expulsion there. To ensure that the abortion is complete, the woman returns to the clinic for a final checkup two weeks after the supposed expulsion of the fetus. Only about 2 percent of the women who use RU-486 fail to have a complete chemical abortion and require a surgical one instead.[57]

Many feminists favor drugs such as RU-486 because there is good evidence that, if administered properly, RU-486 is safer and also less traumatic than surgically invasive forms of abortion. In addition, RU-486 makes abortion accessible to more women—especially rural women who may live great distances from abortion clinics or hospitals—and it is less expensive than most other forms of abortion. Finally, RU-486 has the potential of being used in private, thereby increasing women's overall control over the abortion process. Indeed, French users of RU-486 are reported to "feel in control, conscious that they are doing this to themselves, not just as a patient, and they like that."[58]

RU-486 had a very difficult time gaining entry into the United States. Roussel-UCLAF believed it was "suicidal" to release its drug in a country with an exceptionally strong anti-abortion movement.[59] In fact, Roussel was so concerned about political pressure that it withdrew RU-486 from the *French* market after some European anti-abortionists began to protest its use. However, when the French government, which owns 36 percent of Roussel, declared that RU-486 was "the moral property of women,"[60] Roussel promptly returned RU-486 to the French market. Later, when Roussel realized that by limiting the drug to France it was inviting foreign competitors to duplicate and then market RU-486, Roussel decided to market the drug in "politically safe" countries such as England and Sweden. Yet it held firm in its decision not to enter the U.S. market. Not until the nonprofit Population Council agreed to negotiate on behalf of Roussel with both the U.S. Food and Drug Administration and U.S. anti-abortion activists did Roussel reverse its decision to avoid the U.S. market.

Currently, the Population Council is testing RU-486 on 2,100 U.S. volunteers. The first volunteer described her experience as follows:

> Everyone was really excited on Wednesday, when I was given the first dose of medication. I made a joke that we should have a ribbon-cutting ceremony. They kept telling me I was making history.
>
> I was very nauseous in a couple of hours. I threw up constantly for three days. I went to work. Luckily, there's a restroom in my department. I moved a little slower. Usually I'm very upbeat but I wasn't for those three days. It was like food poisoning. I couldn't keep anything down.
>
> I went in on Friday and took the second dose of medication. After 15 minutes there was a tiny bit of cramping, but less than menstrual cramps. After two hours the cramps got stronger, and I started using a heating pad on my belly. I went to the restroom. When I started to stand up, it was like a faucet turned on. There was a steady stream of blood. I passed a golfball-size blood clot that scared me. I thought maybe it was the fetus.
>
> The cramps stayed steady. In the last 15 minutes of my appointment, I was doubled over. The bleeding was very heavy, heavier than a period. My mom drove me home. By this time, I was bleeding severely, and I had diarrhea. It reminded me of the way you bleed after you give birth. Maybe a woman that hasn't given birth might be a little more distressed.
>
> I aborted at 6:30 on Friday night. I heard it fall into the toilet. It looked like a blood clot. I cried when I knew it had passed—partly from relief, partly from sadness. I knew it was over.[61]

If the experience of this woman is at all typical, opponents of RU-486 need not worry that its availability will encourage a careless and morally unreflective use of the drug to terminate pregnancy.

Many feminists suspect that RU-486's most vociferous opponents resent the drug simply because it affords women who want an abortion "the opportunity for greater privacy and more control."[62] Specifically, use of RU-486 permits women to escape the condemning eyes, shouting voices, and life-threatening bullets of the anti-abortionists who routinely show up at the doors of abortion clinics. While feminists applaud the potential of RU-486 to remove stigmatization and danger from a woman's choice to have an abortion, anti-abortionists are naturally incensed over the fact that RU-486 keeps the abortion decision hidden from public scrutiny. Evil not seen is, in their estimation, evil not challenged.

Interestingly, not all feminists think that making abortions widely available necessarily increases women's control over their reproductive destiny. For example, Anne M. Maloney argues that the availability of abortion actually limits the choice of those women who want to keep their babies but are not in a position to do so economically and/or socially. Instead of providing these women with the support systems and structures they need to rear their children to adulthood, Maloney argues, pro-choice society implies that the responsible thing for them to do is have an abortion. Maloney further claims that as a "feminist for life," she wants society to value women and their power to give and nurture life:

> As long as abortion exists as a cheap and easy solution, this society will remain a dream. Abortion exists because it's a man's world. If men got pregnant, they would demand health care, living wages, family leaves, child care. They would demand that society value their ability to give and sustain life. But abortion? Having one's body forcibly violated, being told that the price of success is such constant violation? Forget it. Men would never stand for it. It's time for women to stop standing for it, too.[63]

Another feminist who argues that U.S. abortion laws do not necessarily increase women's control over reproduction is legal theorist Catharine A. MacKinnon. She claims that it is a mistake for women to defend their right to abortion on the basis of their right to privacy. As she sees it, the right to privacy works far better for men than for women since it helps men keep women hidden, subjected, and dominated in the so-called personal realm. It is in this realm that men get women pregnant and then tell them to "handle" the situation by getting an abortion. Comments MacKinnon:

> The meaning of abortion in the context of a sexual critique of gender inequality is its promise to women of sex with men on the same terms as promised to men—that is, "without consequences." Under conditions in which women do not control access to our sexuality, this facilitates women's heterosexual availability. In other words, under conditions of gender inequality, sexual liberation in this sense does not free women, it frees male sexual aggression. The availability of abortion thus removes the one remaining legitimized reason that women have had for refusing sex besides the headache. As Andrea Dworkin puts it, analyzing male ideology on abortion: "Getting laid was at stake." The Playboy Foundation has supported abortion rights from day one; it continues to, even with shrinking disposable funds, on a level of priority comparable to its opposition to censorship.[64]

In short, according to MacKinnon, women must understand that their right to abortion is dependent not on their having more privacy but on their having more equality with men.[65]

One of MacKinnon's interpreters, philosopher Russell McIntyre, restates her view on abortion rights very strongly—indeed, as implying that "the *only* way in which a woman can truly compete equally with men in this society is if she is truly equal both in opportunity and protection under the law. . . . Because women—and not men—get pregnant and have to interrupt their lives (personal and private) to be mothers, they have unequal opportunities unless women are as free as men not to be under the burden of an unplanned or unwanted pregnancy."[66] If the law truly viewed women's abortion rights as a matter of equality rather than of privacy, says McIntyre, it would have to permit women to terminate their pregnancies at *any* point in time and for *any* reason.[67] Realizing that this liberal interpretation of women's abortion rights entirely undermines any claim to life that a fetus might have, McIntyre adds that women should have their abortions as soon as possible—ideally, before the fetus is viable. In his estimation, there is no need for a woman to flaunt her abortion rights by deliberately timing her abortion as late as possible in her pregnancy.

Matters of equality between the races as well as the sexes have manifested themselves in some African-American feminists' discussions of abortion. For example, Beverly Smith has speculated that permissive abortion laws do not increase the range of real choice for African-American women who would like to give birth to their children but dare not because they are unhealthy (HIV-infected, cocaine-addicted, etc.) or poor (AFDC benefits are paltry at best). In addition, many African-American women fear that were they to carry their pregnancies to term and put their children up for adoption, good homes would not be found for them.[68] Finally, some African-American women and other women of color fear that "white society," including its supposedly "pro-life" segments, actually *wants* women of color (especially unhealthy and poor ones) to have abortions. They note that many pro-life supporters also support limiting or cutting welfare benefits for women with dependent children—despite the fact that such limits and cuts would probably push even more poor women in the direction of abortion. For this reason, observes philosopher Alison Jaggar, "[a] real choice about abortion requires that a woman should be able to opt to have her child, as well as to abort it. This means that the full right to life of the child must be guaranteed, either by community aid to the mother who wishes to raise it herself, or by the provision of alternative arrangements that do not put the child who is not raised by its own mother at any significant disadvantage."[69] Thus, the abortion "choice" is more complex than many people take it to be. We must remember that circumstances such as poor health and poverty stultify many choices for women, this one no less than others.

From a feminist perspective, issues of connection are just as important as issues of choice and control in the abortion debate. After listening to twenty-nine women recount their abortion decisions, Carol Gilligan concluded in *In a Different Voice* that no matter what their age, social class, marital status, or ethnic background, all of these women seemingly shared a concept of self different from the one typically expressed by men in moral-reasoning studies. Whereas the women in her study tended to view the self as an interdependent being whose identity hinges on relationships to others, the men whom Gilligan had queried in other studies tended to view the self as an autonomous, separate being. According to Gilligan, these gender-based differences in self-perception account for variations in women's versus men's style of moral reasoning.

In an attempt to further explicate what she means by "women's style" of moral reasoning as opposed to "men's style," Gilligan points to one of moral psychologist Lawrence Kohlberg's well-known hypothetical cases, in this instance involving a man named Heinz who cannot afford the drug his dying wife desperately needs to survive. Should he steal the drug or not? Gilligan claims that when boys are asked the "Heinz question," they typically approach it abstractly, as if they were solving a math problem. For example, a boy named Jake solves Heinz's dilemma by weighing the rights of the pharmacist to receive payment for his property against the rights of Heinz's wife to live: "A human life is worth more than money, and if the druggist only makes $1,000, he is still going to live, but if Heinz doesn't steal the drug, his wife is going to die."[70] In contrast, according to Gilligan, when girls are asked the "Heinz question," they typically approach it contextually, as if they were resolving a human relations problem. For example, a girl named Amy urges Heinz to arrange a "heart-to-heart" talk with the druggist. She reasons that if the druggist knew that Heinz's wife will otherwise die, he would willingly give the drug to Heinz.[71]

From the foregoing it would seem that, in making an abortion decision, men are more inclined to set women's rights to privacy and bodily integrity against fetuses' right to life, whereas women are more inclined to reflect on how their having (or not having) an abortion might affect the quality of their human relationships. As it happens, Gilligan's abortion study (which focused only on women) suggests that women do make moral decisions in terms of their understanding of the relative importance of their interests versus the interests of others close to them. Thus, says Gilligan, depending on how morally developed a woman is, she will have a better or worse understanding of whose interests should take priority. The better a woman's understanding of her relationships to others, the better her moral decisions will be on any matter, including abortion.

Elaborating her view, Gilligan claims that a woman's moral development typically moves her through three levels: (1) an overly egocentric or selfish position, (2) an overly altruistic or self-sacrificial position, and (3) a balanced position in which her interests count as much as anyone else's. At level (1), where moral sensibility is the least well developed, a woman's care is directed completely inward. She feels scared and vulnerable, in need of affection and approval. For example, the women in Gilligan's abortion study who felt alone in the world, helpless, and uncared for saw a baby as someone who would care for them, who would give *them* some love. However, as these women struggled through their abortion decisions, many came to describe as "selfish" the decision to bear a child when they lacked the material and psychological resources to care for him or her. In Gilligan's estimation, a woman able to arrive at this kind of conclusion has reached level (2) of moral development.

It is at level (2) that a woman shifts from self-centeredness to other-directedness. She becomes the stereotypical nurturant woman, who subordinates her wants and needs to those of other people. This is the kind of woman who, in Gilligan's study, permits her lover, husband, parents, and/or social group to determine her abortion decision. From Gilligan's standpoint, however, it is a mistake for a woman to try to be overly other-directed, for she will eventually resent the very persons she is trying to accommodate. She will come to wonder why *their* having their way about her having or not having a baby is more important than *her* having her way. Rather than letting themselves come to hate the people they started out loving, overly other-directed women are thus urged to push beyond level (2) of moral development to level (3), where they can learn to care for themselves as well as for others.

At level (3), the decision to abort becomes a complex choice that the woman must make about how best to care for the fetus, herself, and anyone else likely to be directly affected by her decision. One of the women in Gilligan's study explained her abortion decision as just such a choice: "I would not be doing myself or the child or the world any kind of favor having this child. I don't need to pay off my imaginary debts to the world through this child, and I don't think that it is right to bring a child into the world and use it for that purpose."[72] Thus, in Gilligan's view, a woman attains full moral stature when she stops vacillating between egoism and altruism, and instead recognizes the falseness of this polarity. When a woman finally chooses to have an abortion, she has fully evaluated the depth both of her connection to others *and* of their connection to her. The best decision, then, is one that permits a woman to balance her commitment to herself against her commitment to others, realizing that although connections to others are very valuable and must be protected, she does not necessarily have to sacrifice her interests for those of her fetus.

Like Gilligan, Nel Noddings defends abortion on a "relational" basis. In order to understand Noddings's views on abortion, however, we must review some aspects of her care-focused feminist approach to ethics. Recall that, according to Noddings, ethics is about particular relations, whereby "a 'relation' means a set of ordered pairs generated by some rule that describes the affect—or subjective experience—of the members."[73] There are two parties in any relation: The first is the "one-caring"; the second is the "cared-for." In the ideal, the one-caring is motivationally engrossed in the cared-for. She makes it a point to attend to the cared-for in deeds as well as in thoughts.[74] In turn, the cared-for actively receives the attentions of the one-caring—ideally, sharing his aspirations, appraisals, and accomplishments with her. For Noddings, then, caring is not simply a matter of feeling favorably disposed toward humankind in general, of being concerned about people with whom one has no concrete connections. Rather, real care requires *actually* doing something for specific individuals; it cannot be accomplished through good intentions alone.

Noddings uses her relational framework to discuss abortion, which she regards as a pregnant woman's decision to end her relationship with the fetus. Noddings maintains that the more abstract an analysis of abortion is—that is, the more it is phrased in terms of the fetus's right to life versus the woman's right to privacy—the less likely it is to help a woman make a morally correct abortion decision. Thus, she suggests, we approach the abortion dilemma not with the language of *rights* but with the language of *relations*. We must question all of our values, including the ones that seem most basic to our identity—for example, the idea that competent adults are the standard for personhood. According to traditional ethics, rationality is what makes a human being a *person*—that is, a *special* kind of human being. As Noddings sees it, however, what makes a human being a person is neither rationality nor even the capacity for rationality but, rather, the fact that she or he is able to respond to others' caring feelings.[75]

This perspective, says Noddings, requires that we address abortion in a new way. Women are permitted to abort their fetuses not because their fetuses lack rationality but because their fetuses cannot respond to others' caring feelings in typically human ways.[76] Noddings claims that a woman who has a first-trimester abortion ought not *feel* any differently about the fate of her fetus than a woman who miscarries early on in her pregnancy. In both cases the appropriate emotional response is not the intense grief adults feel when a young child dies but the kind of disappointment adults feel when a possibility evaporates. "We do not," claims Noddings, "hold funerals for lost embryos."[77] Until a fetus develops enough to respond to caring feelings, it is not a person, and no parent-child *relationship* can be said to exist at this point.

Noddings does not agree that the fact that miscarriages are *unintentional*, whereas abortions are *intentional*, changes the significance of a fetus's death. Whether the death is unplanned or planned does not matter, since the early fetus does not have a "response-based claim" on its parent(s).[78] Thus, we should not seek to justify abortion by appealing to the principle of double effect, whereby the pregnant woman seeks simply fetal extraction, of which the regrettable side effect is fetal extinction. If fetal extraction rather than fetal extinction were indeed the essential aim of abortion, the abortion controversy would end with the development of an artificial placenta. As already noted, however, most women who seek abortions do so not simply to avoid serving as fetal containers but mainly to avoid becoming biological parents. More than anything, says Noddings, these women "do not want a person to exist who, by its genetic make-up, will have a response-based claim on them."[79] Choosing an abortion means choosing to end a relationship before it has really begun.

Yet another feminist who has offered an essentially relational argument in defense of abortion is philosopher Susan Sherwin. She notes that feminist analyses of abortion, unlike nonfeminist ones, regard "the effects of unwanted pregnancies on the lives of women individually and collectively as the central element in the moral examination of abortion."[80] Although anti-abortionists sometimes claim that women decide to have abortions for trivial reasons, Sherwin stresses that in fact most women who choose abortion do so for substantial reasons related to their physical and/or psychological health, to their ability to rear a child, or to their fetus's health status. Were abortion suddenly made illegal, many of these women would be prompted to seek out illegal, sometimes life-threatening abortions (an action one would not resort to in order to solve a "trivial" problem).

Another difference between feminist and nonfeminist approaches to abortion, says Sherwin, is that the former stress that the abortion decision ultimately belongs to the woman, for two reasons. First, the woman, not the man, is the fetus's gestator. Second, usually only the woman is properly situated to weigh all the relevant factors operative in an abortion decision—especially the needs and interests of everyone to whom she is related.

The reasons that justify one woman's decision to have an abortion, Sherwin adds, may not justify another woman's decision. To be sure, women will sometimes make a "wrong" abortion decision, but no more frequently than will other people whose lives are far less affected by it. Thus, the fact that some pregnant women might "wrongly" abort (or fail to abort) their fetuses does not mean that the decision should be wrested from them.

Feminist accounts of abortion, unlike nonfeminist ones, also stress the role played in pregnancy by sexual coercion, as well as by the lack of safe, effective, inexpensive, and accessible contraceptives. Feminists reject the view that unwanted pregnancies are usually the result of irresponsible women choosing to have sex without any thought of its procreative consequences. They point out that many women feel they are in no position to deny their partners sex because of the existence (or threat) of violence in their relationship. Having unprotected sex becomes more understandable when the woman who engages in it is trying to avoid a beating. Moreover, young women may be taken in by older, more experienced boyfriends who promise to "pull out" or assure them that they "can't get pregnant the first time." Given the great social pressure to "hang on to your man," these women may give in to sex on *his* terms—that is, without a condom. Feminists stress not only that it takes two to tango, as the saying goes, but also that the relationship between a man and a woman may be distorted by unequal power dynamics.

Finally, feminist as opposed to nonfeminist accounts of abortion do not stress the "personhood" of fetuses to the point of reducing the women who carry these fetal individuals to "passive hosts whose only significant role is to refrain from aborting or harming their fetuses."[81] It bothers Sherwin that there is a growing tendency among some legal and medical authorities to view women as the enemies of the fetuses they carry—as heartless types who show inadequate concern for their fetuses' well-being. In recent years some pregnant women have been forced to undergo cesarean sections against their better judgment; others have been imprisoned for drug abuse or other socially unacceptable behavior likely to damage their fetuses. In the future, fetuses might be "protected" against their mothers in even more restrictive ways. Sherwin reports that one Australian legislator recently proposed a bill that would make women liable to prosecution "if they are found to have smoked during pregnancy, eaten unhealthy foods, or taken any other action which can be shown to have adversely affected the development of the fetus."[82]

Sherwin notes that unless feminists more adequately explain the woman-fetus relationship, the already-existing anti-abortionist explanation of this relationship will prevail. Agreeing with Sherwin, feminist Rosalind Pollack Petchesky claims that anti-abortion activists stress, as much as possible, that the fetus is a self, independent of its mother. Indeed, they often use images of a highly developed fetus within the uterus in an attempt to force public recognition of the "independent" status of fetal life. Petchesky comments that such photographs represent "the foetus as primary and autonomous, the women as absent or peripheral."[83]

Convinced that it is wrong to give the public the impression that fetuses are little persons whose interests are fundamentally at odds with the interests of the women who "house" them, Sherwin claims that a truer understanding of pregnancy sees the pregnant woman and her fetus "as a biological and social unit."[84] On this view, fetuses are morally significant not because they possess some abstract quality such as independent selfhood but, rather, because they are related to the human community *in* and *through* the bodies of the women who gestate them. Sherwin further comments that

> [p]ersonhood is a social category, not an isolated state. Persons are members of a community and they should be valued in their concrete, discrete, and

> different states as specific individuals, not merely as conceptually undifferentiated entities. To be a morally significant category, personhood must involve personality as well as biological integrity. It is not sufficient to consider persons simply as Kantian atoms of rationality, because persons are embodied, conscious beings with particular social histories.[85]

Sherwin concedes that if an entity needs to be in relation to others in order to be a person, fetuses are, indeed, in a vulnerable position. They are entirely dependent upon their gestators for any connections they might have to the larger human community. Nevertheless, says Sherwin, because of where the fetus is located (and whether society likes it or not), "the responsibility and privilege of determining a fetus's specific social status and value must rest with the woman carrying it."[86] It is the woman who must decide whether her relationship with the fetus is valuable enough *to her* to warrant her developing it. Should she decide that this relationship is less valuable to her than some of her other relationships, her health, or her life plans, she has the right and, in some instances, the responsibility to end her relationship to the fetus by aborting it.

Conclusion

There is a growing sentiment among many feminists that the time may have come for feminists to work with *nonfeminists of good will*—that is, with those nonfeminists who value the lives of women as much as they value the lives of fetuses. It makes little sense for women to fight among themselves when they could instead be seeking areas of agreement, cooperation, and consensus. Since feminists agree with nonfeminists of good will that no woman should have to "choose" an abortion because the state refuses to provide her with needed services and support (e.g., prenatal care, welfare, maternity leave, day care), feminists support policies aimed at increasing funds to meet the medical, economic, and social needs of women and their children. In other words, precisely because feminists are *pro-choice*, they wish to facilitate and then support women's decision to continue *or* to terminate their pregnancies.

To be sure, the sore point between feminists and nonfeminists of good will concerns not whether and how to support women who wish to continue their pregnancies but whether and how to support women who wish to terminate their pregnancies. Given that both feminists and nonfeminists have a wide variety of opinions about the moral status of the person, however, many feminists believe that nonfeminists of good will might yet join them in forging an abortion policy that both respects women's privacy and bodily integrity *and* recognizes the fetus's gradual growth toward personhood *during* the process of its gestation.

Forging a consensus policy on abortion might begin with the reminder that the *need* for abortions could indeed be reduced not only by providing generous subsidies to women who wish to carry their children to term but also by providing excellent means of birth control to all women, especially teen-aged women and girls. Realizing that no program of contraception is likely to be 100 percent effective, however, many feminists seem increasingly willing to accept a time frame for abortion that restricts women's ability to have very late abortions but facilitates their ability to have early abortions. Since many nonfeminists believe that it is a conceptual mistake to attribute personhood to fetuses before implantation, gastrulation (at eight weeks), or organogenesis (at twenty weeks), compromise-seeking feminists think that these nonfeminists might support policies—for example, those sanctioning easy access to so-called morning-after pills or to drugs like RU-486—that permit women to have the *early* abortions they apparently prefer (only 3.7 percent of U.S. women who have abortions do so after the sixteen-week stage).[87] Indeed, compromise-seeking feminists think that most of these nonfeminists might even support policies permitting women to have a surgical abortion for any reason before organogenesis.

In return for a no-restriction policy on abortion prior to the twentieth week of gestation, compromise-seeking feminists seem prepared to accept some restrictions on abortion after twenty weeks. Although abortions after this point would still be permitted for *therapeutic* reasons (e.g., when the continuation of the pregnancy seriously endangers the woman's life or health, or when there is a strong possibility that the unborn child is suffering from a serious disease or condition considered incurable at the time of diagnosis), abortions would not be permitted for *nontherapeutic* reasons (e.g., when a healthy woman simply decides in the seventh month of her pregnancy that she does not want to be a mother after all). Given that *very* few women really "demand" a late abortion for nontherapeutic reasons, however, compromise-seeking feminists see little wisdom in insisting that *all* women should *always* have the *absolute* right to abort their fetuses. The price of such extremism in the cause of women's procreative liberty is not only the escalation of clinic protests and bombings but also the lost ability of feminists and nonfeminists of good will to work together on behalf of most women.

Whatever kind of consensus policy on abortion is achieved by feminists and non-feminists of good will, however, it is vital that they come to appreciate each other's goodness. Pro-choice advocates need to remember that the first "anti-abortionists" were not politically motivated groups (and certainly not terrorists) but service groups who wanted to help unwed mothers. Currently, there are at least 3,000 emergency pregnancy centers in the United States, 20 percent of which offer not merely counseling and emergency funds to pregnant women but also hospital coverage, housing, job training, and postnatal care. Such services give disadvantaged women the opportunity to choose to continue their pregnancies, a choice that is no less important than its opposite. Likewise, opponents of abortion need to realize that pro-choice supporters are not selfish, heartless baby-killers. On the contrary, many feminists who are pro-choice describe themselves as "conflicted" when it comes to the topic of abortion. As they see it, the abortion decision is frequently a very difficult one to make. As a woman goes about deciding whether to end her pregnancy, she is less likely to be thinking about her *right* to choose than about the *life* that, for a variety of reasons, she is unwilling, unready, or unable to bring into the world. There is simply too much that is special about women's capacity for gestation and birth, for transforming potential life into actual life, to relinquish it without anguish. Many feminists concede, however, that they have not always felt safe enough to voice their genuine ambivalence about abortion. As a result of having always to *fight* for gender equity, feminists have resorted to the protective, defensive, and isolating language of *rights*, concealing from others, if not also from themselves, their deep feelings of *responsibility* toward the actual *and* potential people to whom they are intimately related.[88]

The actual people to whom feminist as well as nonfeminist women are related include, of course, men; and no discussion of abortion is complete without asking how much or how little men should be involved in the abortion decision. Carol Gilligan's study on abortion has been faulted for precisely the fact that she did not interview the twenty-nine men who had obviously played a role in the pregnancies of the twenty-nine women she did interview. What were these men's attitudes toward their girlfriends' and wives' abortion decisions? Were the men more or less inclined than the women to choose abortion over pregnancy? Did they view the women's abortion decisions as ones that should have been made jointly with them? Finally, did they support or abandon the women during the abortion procedure or continuing pregnancy? From what the women had to say about them, it seems that most of the men abandoned the women either right before or right after the unwanted pregnancy was made known to them. Their attitudes toward their wives' and girlfriends' abortions were often coercive, taking the form of demands that the pregnancies be terminated. For at least some of the women, then, the lack of support from their partners was the main reason they chose not to continue their pregnancies.

For a variety of reasons, including the ones just mentioned, men's role in the abortion decision is controversial. Pro-choice advocates fear that if any concession is made in the direction of men having a moral right to participate in women's abortion decisions, then spousal notification and consent laws will become the order of the day. Nevertheless, because procreation is an activity that involves men as well as women, many feminists willingly concede that, *ideally*, men and women should make abortion as well as contraception and sterilization decisions together.

In a 1990 study reported in *Time* magazine, parents were asked what advice they would give their teenage daughter if she became pregnant. Of those who responded, 14 percent said, "Marry the father"; 22 percent said, "Raise the child alone"; 15 percent said, "Give the child up for adoption"' and 11 percent said, "Get an abortion." Asked what advice they would give their teenage son if he impregnated someone, the same parents replied as follows: 20 percent said, "Marry the mother"; 7 percent said, "Help pay for an abortion"; 52 percent said, "Help pay for medical expenses and child support"; and 1 percent said, "Try to get out of the situation."[89] Clearly, the parents wanted their sons to act responsibly; only 1 percent of them encouraged their sons to view pregnancy as the "girl's problem." But let us assume for a moment that the girl wants the baby but the boy does not. If she goes ahead with the pregnancy, she will be choosing fatherhood for him. To be sure, he helped choose motherhood for her when they engaged in unprotected sexual intercourse. If he had wanted to guard against fatherhood, he could have used a contraceptive, urged her to use one, or simply refrained from sexual intercourse. Likewise, if the girl had wanted to guard against motherhood, she could have used a contraceptive, urged him to use one, or simply refrained from sexual intercourse. At this point, however, the girl is pregnant; and if she chooses to be a mother, the boy will become a father, whether or not he wants to be. Similarly, if the girl chooses not to be a mother, the boy cannot become a father, even if he very much wants to be. Although few feminists would want the state to empower this boy to force the girl to carry the fetus to term, there are many feminists who have some sympathy for him—who can see their own son in his place.

In the final analysis, because the fetus is within the woman's womb the decision regarding abortion is most properly hers. Whether she or anyone else likes it or not, in choosing for herself she will choose for others. We have been so busy debating the abortion decision that we have failed to pay adequate attention to the ways in which this decision, more than any other, reveals how the act of procreation makes men and women interdependent. If a man and a woman are not committed enough to each other to regard themselves as a "we," loving and responsible enough to make the abortion decision together, then the way for them to avoid mutual disappointment, anger, and even hate is to practice birth control or to refrain from sexual intercourse.

7

Nonfeminist and Feminist Perspectives on Artificial Insemination and In-Vitro Fertilization

Many Americans probably would not recognize the name of Louise Brown, the first child conceived in a petri dish. She may not be well known, but her birth in 1978 signaled a new age in reproductive technology.[1] For the first time ever, human beings were able to procreate a child outside of its mother's womb. As we will discover, the bioethical consequences of this event have been vast and far-reaching. In the last two chapters we reflected on some major reproduction-*controlling* technologies: contraception, sterilization, and abortion. In this chapter we consider two major reproduction-*aiding* technologies: artificial insemination, or AI (increasingly referred to as donor insemination, or DI) and in-vitro fertilization (IVF).[2] Just as nonfeminist bioethicists have varying perspectives on these technologies, so too do feminists. Issues of choice, control, and connection pervade feminists' differing analyses of so-called assisted reproduction. Working toward a common feminist policy on the reproduction-aiding technologies is no less difficult than achieving some measure of feminist consensus on the reproduction-controlling technologies.

Nonfeminist Bioethical Perspectives on Fertility and Infertility

Given that the population of the world continues to grow at an alarming rate, it seems difficult to believe that anyone has much trouble procreating. Yet many people do. Approximately 13.5 percent of American couples are infertile.[3] The term 'infertility' is used in reference to couples who fail to achieve pregnancy within one year of unprotected intercourse. There are two broad categories of infertility: *Primary infertility* is diagnosed when a couple has never successfully conceived, whereas *secondary infertility* is diagnosed when a couple has successfully conceived at least once.[4] Although a couple's reproductive difficulties may rest with only one of the partners, very often they rest with both of them or between them, as in cases of reproductive incompatibility (whereby each member of the couple is able to beget children with a different partner but, for some reason, not with the existing partner). As more physicians choose to specialize in infertility services, more infertility clinics are opening their doors. Significantly, the growing supply of infertility specialists and infertility clinics shows no sign of outstripping the demand for them. On the contrary, this demand seems to be expanding rapidly, as evidenced by the fact that the "infertility business" now exceeds the billion-dollar mark. Between 1968 and 1983, the number of couples seeking infertility services rose from about 600,000 to 2 million. At present, about 1 million couples seek infertility services annually, and each year general practitioners, obstetrician-gynecologists, and urologists see anywhere from 110,000 to 160,000 new cases.[5]

Infertility rates vary with age and socioeconomic class. In general, older women have higher rates of infertility than younger women, due largely to the biological effects of aging. However, over the last quarter-century the infertility rate of women aged twenty to twenty-four has swelled from 4 to 11 percent. The increase can be explained by rising rates of gonorrhea and other sexually transmitted diseases, which, if left untreated, can cause infertility; greater use of intrauterine devices, the filaments of which can lead infectious bacteria into the fallopian tubes at an accelerated rate; and increased environmental dangers. In addition, African-American women and poor women suffer from infertility problems more than white and middle-class women do, largely because many of them do not receive adequate preventive health care.[6]

Nonfeminist bioethicists have often debated whether infertility is a disease or simply a regrettable human limitation that causes many couples to experience guilt, disappointment, depression, low self-esteem, and often marital conflict. Those who believe that infertility is a human limitation, not a disease, observe that infertile people are just as healthy and vigorous as fertile people. They also note that if infertility were a disease, artificial insemination and in-vitro fertilization would not count as cures for it: Although these technologies enable many infertile people to have children, they leave them as infertile as ever.[7] In contrast, those who do regard infertility as a disease argue that although infertility neither threatens life nor causes physical pain or discomfort, it does prevent affected persons from functioning normally—that is, from reproducing. They also point out that physicians are often content to treat diseases in lieu of being able to cure them. Thus, in the same way that insulin is a treatment but not a cure for diabetes, AI and IVF are treatments but not cures for infertility.[8]

Whether infertility is considered a limitation or a disease is a matter of some consequence. If infertility is viewed as "just one of those things," then infertile people should focus on the advantages as opposed to the disadvantages of a childless marriage, or they should consider adoption, foster parenting, or working with children as meaningful options. In contrast, if infertility is viewed as a disease or disablement, then infertile couples should take advantage of all the reproduction-aiding technologies now available. At present, the disease or disablement view of infertility is the dominant one, inasmuch as infertile people are increasingly seeing it as a medical problem that can be remedied.

As this chapter makes clear, nonfeminist bioethicists have reacted both positively and negatively to so-called assisted reproduction. On the one hand, most of them concede that AI and IVF permit individuals to have the children they could not have otherwise. On the other hand, most of them also express concern that the reproduction-aiding technologies are enabling individuals to break the lines between biological and social parenting before society has had the time to assess collectively the likely ethical, legal, and social consequences of such a breakage. Accordingly, nonfeminist bioethicists have expressed a range of views on assisted reproduction, some decidedly less enthusiastic than others.

Nonfeminist Bioethical Perspectives on Artificial Insemination

There are two types of artificial insemination: artificial insemination by husband (AIH), in which the sperm donor is the woman's husband or male partner; and artificial insemination by donor (AID), in which the sperm donor is a man other than the woman's husband or male partner. AIH is the preferred method of treatment when the husband's sperm cells are normal and able to fertilize the egg but the sperm count is low. And AID is indicated when the husband's sperm count is so low that pooling his sperm is not of much use, where there is an Rh incompatibility, or when the husband suffers from a serious hereditary genetic disorder. At present, artificial insemination is the most widely used mode of assisted reproduction in the United States. In fact, the Office of Technology Assessment (OTA) recently reported that, in 1987 alone, 172,000 women had artificial inseminations and 65,000 babies resulted.[9]

With few exceptions, nonfeminist bioethicists have no objections to AIH.[10] When they do oppose the use of artificial insemination, they tend to focus on AID. Critics of AID fear, first, that using this means to procreate might jeopardize good marital and parental relationships. They note that some infertile couples choose AID over adoption, reasoning that they will be able to love a child who is genetically related to at least one of them (the wife) more easily than a child who is genetically related to neither of them. But things do not always work out as planned. When a couple has a child by AID, the mother is the child's begetter, bearer, and rearer; the father is only the child's rearer. For couples who are convinced that parenthood consists essentially in the rearing of a child, this asymmetry does not present a problem; but for couples who have mixed feelings about what makes one a "real" parent, the asymmetry can generate serious difficulties.[11] For example, one father whose wife had conceived their son through AID confessed to his psychologist that he had hoped his wife would deliver a girl, inasmuch as "a son would highlight my loss because he wouldn't be a small version of me."[12] Such reactions are not atypical. Many psychologists report that one of AID's long-term negative effects is the fact that husbands sometimes become passive and distant from their children and wives sometimes become assertive about being their child's *primary* parent—that is, *the* parent in charge.[13]

Second, critics of AID claim that children conceived by means of this procedure often suffer psychologically. Judging it best to hide the AID "secret," some physicians still advise patients against telling their children that their social fathers are not their biological fathers. Regardless of what precautions are taken, however, such secrets do not always remain secure. Some AID children, upon suddenly discovering the circumstances of their conception, are reportedly traumatized. As Suzanne Rubin, an AID child herself, writes: "No one considers how the child feels when she finds that her natural father was a $25 cup of sperm. The fantasies revolve around what the donor was thinking while he was filling the cup. There is no passion, no human contact in such a union; just cold calculation and manipulation of another person's life."[14] Clearly distressed by the circumstances of her conception, Rubin concludes that healthy family relationships cannot be built on a "foundation of deliberate lies" and that the people who suffer the most in AID families are the children, some of whom never learn to cope with the anonymous sperm donor in their background.

Third, critics of AID speculate that sperm donors might eventually regret their decision to donate or sell their gametes, either because they find themselves pursued by a genetically related child who threatens to disrupt their own family life or because they are haunted by thoughts of having a genetic child whom they cannot contact. The presence of unwanted connections to a child or the lack of wanted connections can be a source of great suffering for a sperm donor, especially if his motivation for donation had simply been to help an infertile couple in need.

Fourth, critics of AID worry that couples might want to use the procedure for unacceptable eugenic purposes—that is, not simply to avoid passing on some genetic disease or disorder besetting the husband but, rather, to gain access to "superior" donor genes. Not only is such a quest morally questionable, in these critics' estimation, it is also pragmatically misguided since AID does not guarantee its recipients "superior" genes.[15] Screening of sperm donors remains uneven. Although responsible clinics and physicians test possible sperm donors stringently for genetic and sexually transmitted diseases (so much so, in fact, that they reject anywhere from 85 to 95 percent of them), less responsible clinics and physicians screen sperm donors haphazardly or not at all. Much the same can be said about sperm banks. The more meticulous ones do provide so-called quality sperm to couples; but often the less careful ones negligently or recklessly sell inadequately screened sperm.[16]

Fifth, critics of AID note that as a result of the availability of this procedure, many infertile couples drop their plans to adopt a child in the belief that it is preferable to rear a child to whom at least one parent is genetically related. These critics object that it is a mistake to think that genetic connection is a necessary let alone sufficient condition for strong parent-child bonds. An adopted child is just as much one's own child as a child conceived by means of AID, so couples should be urged to choose adoption over AID.

Sixth, and finally, critics of AID note that since this procedure is available to single women, lesbian couples, and unmarried heterosexual couples, it permits the creation of a wide variety of unorthodox family structures. According to these critics, it is not in the best interests of a child to be born to an "atypical" family. To bolster their position they refer to such reports as that of the Warnock Commission in Great Britain, which concluded that "the interests of the child dictate that it should be born into a home where there is a loving, stable, heterosexual relationship and that, therefore, the deliberate creation of a child for a woman who is not a partner in such a relationship is morally wrong."[17] AID's critics insist that it is particularly deleterious for children to be *deliberately* conceived and raised exclusively by women. In their estimation, children without a regular male presence in their lives are likely to develop a distorted view of sexuality and procreation.[18]

AID's advocates insist, first, that the critics have greatly exaggerated its possibly negative consequences. They claim, first, that the kind of husband-wife conflicts some couples experience subsequent to the birth of their AID child are no worse than those that ordinarily accompany the assumption of parental responsibilities and can usually be resolved in a few sessions of counseling. Moreover, to the degree that parents who use AID are honest with each other and with their children, these conflicts can be kept to a minimum. Increasingly, there is no need for parents to lie to their children about the complex way in which they were procreated. If parents speak about their use of AID matter-of-factly, and describe it as a common procedure, their children will come to view their AID origin positively. Comments one daughter conceived through AID:

> Knowing about my AID origin did nothing to alter my feelings for my family. Instead I felt grateful for the trouble they had taken to give me life. And they had given me such a strong set of roots, a rich and colorful heritage, a sense of being loved. With their adventure in biology, my parents had opened up the fairly rigid culture they had brought with them to this country. The secret knowledge of my "differentness" and my sister's may have helped our parents accept ... the few deviations from their norms that we argued for.[19]

Second, AID's advocates doubt that AID is particularly harmful to sperm donors. For the most part, they say, sperm donors sell their sperm without any regrets about lost opportunities for "fatherhood." On the contrary, most leave the sperm bank happy to have made a few dollars by contributing to the well-being of an infertile couple. Any harm that does come to sperm donors is usually the result of breaches of confidentiality. But the problem of leaked information is not insurmountable. Indeed, a proper balance can be struck between AID children's interest in knowing their genetic heritage and most sperm donors' interest in remaining anonymous. For instance, laws can give AID children access to *nonidentifying* information about their genetic fathers (e.g., their medical histories) without giving AID children access to *identifying* information (e.g., their names or photographs).

Third, AID's advocates insist that, as things stand, most couples who use AID do not ordinarily request "genetically superior" donors. In fact, few of them express any interest at all in using sperm from sperm banks like the Hermann J. Muller Repository for Germinal Choice in California, which about fifteen years ago began collecting the sperm of Nobel Prize–winning men for the purpose of inseminating only the most fit of women.[20] Instead, most couples ask only that they be matched with a person of the same race, ethnicity, body type, or intellect as the husband. In the estimation of AID advocates, such requests are morally defensible. They simply permit the couple to procreate a child who resembles the child they would have procreated had the man been fertile.

Fourth, AID's advocates stress that it is unfair to condemn *infertile* couples who want a genetically related child as "selfish." After all, most *fertile* couples also prefer genetically related children to adopted children. And pressuring people to adopt is not necessarily in the best interests of the child, who might thereafter be viewed as "second-best."[21] In addition, because pregnancy and childbirth are special experiences that help create intense parent-child (especially mother-child) bonds, AID's advocates claim that critics reason wrongly when they present the decision to adopt a child as always morally superior to the decision to have a child by AID.

Fifth, AID's advocates claim that one of AID's moral advantages is precisely that it permits the creation of so-called alternative family structures. They see the inclusion of homosexual parents within the meaning of family as a move toward greater equality in a society where lesbians and gay men suffer from prejudice and discrimination. They also see value in affirming the deliberate decision of some women to become single parents, inasmuch as this decision goes some distance toward correcting the social misconception that, without a man, a woman cannot successfully raise a happy and socially adjusted child. In short, AID's advocates claim that what children need is not a particular kind of family structure (e.g., the nuclear family structure) but any loving, stable home environment.

Finally, AID's advocates note that technological developments in AIH might substantially lessen the need for AID. Some infertility clinics have already reported considerable success with a technique called intracytoplasmic injection (ICI). During this procedure, physicians remove an egg from the woman's ovary and directly inject a single sperm from her husband into it. Other infertility clinics have reported success with so-called zona drilling. Apparently, some men's sperm are simply unable to penetrate the egg's surface. In order to make penetration possible, physicians "drill" the egg's surface, softening it in ways that facilitate the sperm's entry into the interior of the egg cell.[22] Clearly, these techniques, along with other related ones, have the potential to help thousands of men unable to father a child because of very low sperm counts.[23]

Feminist Bioethical Perspectives on Artificial Insemination

In general, feminists agree that artificial insemination and, for that matter, most other reproduction-aiding technologies increase women's procreative options. If they have any basic disagreement at all about the use of these technologies, it centers on the question of whether women's right to use them should be almost absolute or considerably restricted. Philosopher Christine Overall, for one, accepts the view that "reproductive rights are derived from the central importance of reproduction in an individual's life and are limited only by a capacity to participate meaningfully and an ability to accept or transfer rearing responsibilities."[24] She also accepts the standard distinction between a weak sense of one's reproductive rights and a strong one.

Supposedly, the *weak* sense of the right to procreate implies an obligation on the part of the state not to interfere with anyone's reproductive freedom through, say, forced sterilization or contraception programs, or through racist or eugenic marriage laws. In addition, it implies an obligation on the part of the state not to limit women's reproductive freedom by requiring women to have cesarean sections in the supposed best interests of their fetuses, or by insisting that women give birth in hospitals attended by obstetrical technologists rather than at home attended by nurse midwives, family members, and friends.

In contrast to the weak sense of the right to procreate, the *strong* sense of this right implies an obligation on the part of the state not only to avoid interfering with procreation but also to facilitate it. So interpreted, the strong sense of the right to procreate presumably entitles all individuals to access "all available forms of reproductive products, technologies, and labor, including the gametes of other women and men, the gestational services of women, and the full range of procreative techniques including *in vitro* fertilization, gamete intrafallopian transfer, uterine lavage, . . . embryo freezing, and sex preselection."[25]

Some feminists believe it is vital for women that the right to reproduce be affirmed in its strong as well as its weak sense. As they see it, unless the right to reproduce is total, only certain women (and men) will be given access to gamete donors, for example; and the fortunate recipients will probably be heterosexual, married, economically well-to-do, and racially privileged.[26] This state of affairs is fundamentally unfair, insist many feminists. The fact that certain people do not want to marry someone of the opposite sex or engage in heterosexual intercourse does not mean that they should be deprived of having children genetically related to them.

Other feminists, however, believe it might be a mistake to interpret the right to reproduce in the strong sense specifically. For example, feminist Maura Ryan takes exception to law professor John Robertson's exceptionally strong interpretation of the right to reproduce, according to which "[t]he right of married persons to use noncoital and collaborative means of conception to overcome infertility must extend to any purpose, including selecting the gender or genetic characteristics of the child or transferring the burden of gestation to another."[27]

In Ryan's view, if the strong sense of the right to reproduce does in fact include what Robertson says it does, then children are little more than commodities that adults can "order" or "purchase" in accordance with their specific parental desires.[28] Worse, a strong interpretation of the right to reproduce leads to the incoherent position that having a genetic connection to one's children is both very important and not important at all. For the infertile couple who wants to use AID, for example, the genetic connection to the child is supposedly all-important, whereas for the sperm donor this type of connection is supposedly unimportant. What worries Ryan most about a strong interpretation of the right to procreate, however, is that it automatically privileges the *wants* of individuals over the *needs* of their communities. Thus, she claims that feminists, at least,

> need to ask whether we should support the right of individuals to go to any length to acquire the type of child they want when there are so many children already living who are not being taken care of. And, recognizing that collaborative reproduction ordinarily has as its object a white child, we need as well to examine the kind of racial attitudes being perpetrated.[29]

In short, the mere desire to procreate does not imply the strong right to do so, as if an infertile woman could simply demand that a fertile woman give her the eggs without which she cannot reproduce.[30]

Clearly, Ryan's concerns about the strong sense of the right to procreate are not idle speculations. Considerable evidence now exists for what some critics initially dismissed as "paranoia" on the part of some feminists who, like Gena Corea, sought to expose what they viewed as the unethical practice of "snatching" eggs from unsuspecting women.[31] A case in point is the scandal uncovered in 1995 at the University of California Irvine's Center of Reproductive Health. Unapproved egg "transfers" involving at least thirty women were made between 1988 and 1992,[32] and there is some suspicion that such practices were not confined to the state of California.

As might be expected, similar concerns have arisen about the retrieval and use of men's sperm. For example, in 1984 a French woman named Corinne Parplaix sued a sperm bank to release her dead husband's sperm cells to her even though he had left no specific instructions as to what he wanted done with them. The state prosecutor argued that Mrs. Parplaix had no more right to her dead husband's sperm than to his feet or ears. Mrs. Parplaix's lawyer countered that Mr. Parplaix knew he was dying of cancer when he deposited his sperm. By so doing, he implied a contract with his wife, a contract to bear his child after his death. The court agreed with Mrs. Parplaix's lawyer. When apprised of the decision, Mrs. Parplaix said: "I'll call him Thomas. . . . He'll be a pianist. That's what his father wanted."[33]

More recently, some women have requested that physicians retrieve sperm from their near-dead or dead husbands. When the Northeast Organ Procurement Organization asked more than fifty other organ procurement organizations if they had been requested to recover sperm from organ donors, more than 80 percent of these organizations reported that they had. In seven of the reported forty-six cases, sperm retrieval was attempted. Only three of these succeeded, and none of the procurement organizations knows whether any of the three widows actually became pregnant or had a child. However, the procurement organizations that gave the widows the sperm of their dead husbands have realized that they are probably on shaky legal ground. It is not clear, for example, that a widow has a right to claim her deceased husband's sperm, especially if there is reason to think he did not want any offspring, including ones born posthumously. In this connection, Maggie Gallagher of the Center for Social Thought, a conservative think tank, has commented: "It really does violate the principle of reproductive choice. A man can't tell his wife she can't have an abortion, and a woman can't tell her husband he can't have a vasectomy. I question making a man a father when he has never indicated he would want to be a father under these circumstances."[34] Yet, despite the soundness of Gallagher's reasoning, many feminists would suggest that widows are ordinarily good interpreters of their deceased husband's desires. For example, Pam Mareska, widowed shortly after her marriage, insisted that her deceased husband, Manny, very much wanted to have children. Since Manny Maresca's family agreed with his widow's judgment, his physicians removed Manny's sperm cells from his body. Pam Maresca then stored them in a sperm bank for her future use. Although Pam Maresca has not ruled out marrying again, she insists that "it will have to be someone special enough to accept Manny's child."[35]

As risky as it is to interpret the right to procreate too strongly, some feminists caution that it is probably just as risky—if not more so—to interpret this right too weakly. There is, after all, much evidence indicating that legal and medical authorities have inappropriately restricted access to AID and other reproduction-aiding technologies. In the past, U.S. courts refused to legally recognize the alternative families that AID enabled. In fact, some courts not only classified AID as adulterous but also branded AID children as illegitimate. Traditionally, the law regarded the genetic father, not the social father, as the child's "real" father; and any child begotten through a man other than a woman's husband was considered illegitimate. It mattered not if the woman's husband, the child's social father, viewed the child as his own.

In the United States, a legal trend toward ruling that, under certain circumstances, the social father is no less a father than the genetic father began in 1948. In a New York divorce case, *Strnad v. Strnad,* a woman sued to limit her ex-husband's right to visit their child who had been conceived through AID *with his consent*. Although the court did not explicitly rule that the child was legitimate, it held that the ex-husband, though not the genetic father of the child, was "entitled to the same rights as those acquired by a foster parent who has adopted a child, if not the same rights as those to which a natural parent under the circumstances would be entitled."[36] Later, in a 1968 California case, *People v. Sorenson*, a woman sued her ex-husband for child support. He refused to support the child on the grounds that the child was not his, even though he had consented to his ex-wife's use of AID. The supreme court of California ruled against the man. It held that since he had consented to his wife's insemination by donor, the child was his in the eyes of the law.[37]

Although decades have passed since the *Sorenson* case, no comprehensive federal statute governing AID has been written. However, several states have enacted a variety of laws to regulate certain aspects of AID. Despite the variations in these laws, most states agree that both partners must consent to AID; and that if they both consent, the child born to them is legitimate. Some states go further than this, explicitly stating that the sperm donor is not the legal father of the child. Other legal or quasi-legal attempts to regulate the practice of AID include requirements for (1) documenting the consent of sperm recipients and/or their spouses or partners to AID; (2) keeping the personal identity of sperm donors confidential; (3) limiting the number of times any one man can serve as a sperm donor in a certain geographical area; (4) regulating the quality of sperm used in AID; and (5) confining the performance of AID to an authorized or licensed person, generally a physician.[38]

In addition to legal authorities, health-care practitioners have sought to regulate AID in a variety of ways. Recently, reputable clinics have begun to screen donor sperm rigorously and to expand informed-consent procedures to include discussions of possible legal problems associated with AID (such as breaches of confidentiality or attempts by the sperm donor to enter his genetic child's life) as well as possible medical risks.[39] What feminists find troubling are not such measures themselves but the tendency of some physicians to restrict access to AID to "childworthy," married infertile couples.[40] Apparently, these physicians believe that since *they* are the ones who enable people to have children they could not have otherwise, it is their responsibility not to use their medical skills "to create children who will suffer from their poor start in life."[41] Convinced that children need to be raised by a man and a woman who are married to each other and have all that it takes emotionally, physically, and financially to rear children to adulthood, these physicians routinely turn away single persons, lesbian couples, unmarried heterosexual couples, and married couples whom they perceive as unstable.

Generally speaking, feminists view as flawed the reasoning of those who would restrict AID to "childworthy," married heterosexual couples. They doubt not only that physicians are particularly good assessors of "childworthiness" but also that children need two (and only two) parents—one male, the other female—in order to thrive. On the contrary, they note, there is growing evidence that children fare well in any kind of family structure, including those headed by single parents, provided that their primary caregiver(s) treat them responsibly and *lovingly*.[42] Observing that it is not the number or gender of a child's parents that makes the difference in a child's life but, rather, the quality of the parent-child relationship, most feminists insist that physicians should provide AID not only to married heterosexual couples but also to unmarried ones and to single women—be they heterosexual or lesbian. The fact that a woman chooses not to marry a man or to have sex with a man is no reason, in and of itself, to deny her the opportunity to have children of her own if she is physically, emotionally, and financially able to do so. If physicians want to restrict access to AID only to people who are "good parenting material," then they should subject *all* persons who wish to use AID to the same level of *objective* scrutiny. In this connection, feminist philosopher Mary Mahowald has reported that she personally knows at least one infertility specialist who declines to perform AID unless the person(s) who request it obtain an evaluation of "competence" for parenthood from a recognized expert. Mahowald has no objections to this physician's policy per se, although she worries that the officials in charge of the evaluations might be subtly biased in the direction of married, heterosexual couples.[43]

Frustrated by legal and medical impediments to obtaining AID, some feminists urge women to take control of the situation. After all, a woman can achieve pregnancy through casual intercourse—the proverbial "one-night stand." However, casual intercourse is anything *but* casual for lesbians or for women who believe that sex outside of a meaningful, long-term relationship is wrong or at least distasteful. Moreover, it might take multiple "one-night stands" for a woman to get pregnant, during which a woman may be exposed to sexually transmitted diseases or the HIV virus. Thus, although casual intercourse can be an effective way to get pregnant, it is not a method that feminists are eager to endorse. Instead, feminists have organized themselves into groups committed to finding a more independent and fulfilling way for women to get pregnant.

Self-insemination is a reproductive possibility that many feminists laud as being quite liberating not only from the control of the medical profession but also from that of men in general. In the early 1980s a group of lesbian feminists in London established the Feminist Self Insemination Group.[44] Using homosexual men as donors, these women inseminated themselves with every manner and fashion of syringe, including turkey basters. Says one member of the Feminist Self Insemination Group: "'Doing it ourselves' [is] . . . one of the roads to getting in charge of our reproductive capacities."[45] In addition to putting reproduction entirely within the control of women, self-insemination is inexpensive since the women who use it typically rely on altruistic males to provide them with sperm. Being able to inseminate oneself is therefore a boon not only to lesbians rejected by the medical establishment but also to those women who cannot afford the cost of AID (typically from $400 to $600 per cycle).[46] It is also a boon to those women who do not wish to involve an unfamiliar physician in what they consider a private matter, as private as the act of sex itself.

Yet for all its advantages, self-insemination has enough disadvantages to arouse some feminists' concern. Even if a woman is able to find a man willing to give her his sperm cells, she cannot be sure of their quality or safety, since she has no way to screen them for genetic defects or diseases, sexually transmitted diseases, or the HIV virus. Relying on physician-controlled AID has the advantage of removing many of these concerns since most physicians use frozen sperm from a sperm bank. And most of the nation's 138 sperm banks follow the safety guidelines of the American Fertility Society and the American Association of Tissue Banks. These guidelines (1) advise that potential sperm donors complete a medical history and undergo an extensive physical exam; (2) disqualify gay men, drug users, and men with multiple sex partners as well as men over fifty and men with low-quality or sluggish sperm; and (3) recommend appropriate genetic testing as well as screening for HIV, hepatitis B, gonorrhea, syphilis, and chlamydia. So rigorous are these guidelines that some sperm banks are forced to reject about 80–85 percent of potential donors.[47]

Granted, women who choose physician-controlled AID are not always shielded from unsafe or otherwise undesirable sperm. A minority of physicians still use fresh sperm. They claim that there is no need to screen their donors since they either know the donors personally or the donors belong to a "reliable" group: medical students, for example. Moreover, although some of these physicians inform their patients that they use fresh sperm, others do not. In one notorious case, two fertility doctors at Mount Sinai Medical Center inseminated dozens of women with fresh sperm that had been illegally sold to them by two hospital employees over a two-year period but had not been frozen and quarantined as New York state law requires.[48] Luckily, the sperm was found not to be carrying any diseases; however, many women were exposed to *possible* infection from HIV and STDs. Another physician in Vienna, Virginia, who inseminated more than seventy women at his infertility clinic with his own fresh sperm, told his patients that he used carefully screened donor sperm.[49] Fortunately, such shocking stories are rare: Physician-controlled AID generally proceeds safely and ethically for all those involved.

Perhaps the greatest risk faced by women who decide to self-inseminate (or even to use physician-controlled AID) is the possibility not of using unsafe sperm but of using a donor who will later demand access to his genetically related child. Feminist Gena Corea has cautioned that, according to U.S. law, the parental rights of sperm donors disappear or appear depending on the marital status of the woman. If a man donates his sperm to a married woman, his status shrivels to that of an anonymous "semen source" who supplies a bodily fluid; but if he donates his sperm to an unmarried woman, his status quickly swells "to that of a father with rights over his issue."[50]

Several court cases support Corea's observations. In 1977, a man gave some of his sperm to a woman friend who, after she was nearly three months pregnant, broke off all relations with him. When the child was born, the sperm donor sued for visitation rights. A New Jersey court not only granted him visitation rights but also declared him the child's legal father.[51] Significantly, the U.S. Supreme Court supported New Jersey's ruling. In another case, it ruled that, under certain circumstances, a sperm donor has a constitutional right to claim fatherhood. Apparently, state laws according to which sperm donors have no legal rights to a child produced through artificial insemination do not necessarily apply to sperm donors who have been in relatively long-term relationships with the recipients of their sperm. In the case considered by the U.S. Supreme Court, a man named McIntyre claimed to have been friends with a lesbian woman for more than thirteen years. Unable to adopt a child, he donated sperm to the woman, who supposedly agreed to his playing an active role in the child's life. Then, however, McIntyre and the woman had a falling out. After the child was born, she blocked McIntyre's access to the child, claiming she had never regarded him as anything more than a sperm donor. McIntyre filed a paternity-rights suit against the woman. Although a lower Oregon court dismissed his suit, an Oregon appeals court reversed the decision, ruling that "the due-process clause can afford no different protection to [McIntyre] as the biological father because the child was conceived by artificial insemination rather than by sexual intercourse."[52] As a result of this ruling, McIntyre was given the right to try to prove that the lesbian woman had originally agreed to let him act as the social father of the child. Although this decision probably does not affect the 20,000 *married* women who use a sperm donor in any given year, it probably does affect the 1,500 *unmarried* women who use a sperm donor in any given year. Unless an unmarried woman can prove she was not in a long-term relationship with the sperm donor, he might be in a position to establish himself as the child's legal father.

Over and beyond the legal risks incurred by single women who use AID, lesbian women who do so put their partners (when they have partners) at special legal risk. Suppose two lesbians in a relationship decide to have a child. If their relationship breaks up, the woman who is not biologically related to the child has no legal rights to the child. Under such circumstances, some judges empathize with the lesbian "co-parent," even though there is little they can do legally to ameliorate her situation. For example, after denying a lesbian co-parent the right to visit the eight-year-old girl who was conceived by her former lover and partner, California Judge Dana Henry urged his state to reform the law "in order to adequately deal with the increasing number of children of homosexual couples."[53] Other judges have gone even further, in one instance granting parental visitation rights to the lesbian co-parent of a child. In general, the lawyers who represent lesbian co-parents argue that a person becomes a "de facto" parent to the degree that she (or he) provides longtime physical and psychological nurture to a child. Should such arguments gain wide social acceptance, they will have consequences not only for the estimated 10,000 children now being reared by lesbians but also for the thousands of children now being reared by gay men and stepparents.[54]

Having realized that women's "choice" to use AID will remain limited unless legal authorities and medical practitioners make it possible for all women and/or couples to gain access to safe, affordable sperm, some feminists urge that women take complete control over the practice of AID now. Toward this goal, some enterprising feminists have already established their own sperm banks. The Sperm Bank of California (T.S.B.C.), located in Berkeley, is one such establishment. T.S.B.C. not only carefully screens the sperm cells that are deposited there but also provides sperm to any woman, regardless of her marital status, sexual preference, or physical disability. T.S.B.C. also permits sperm recipients to examine a catalogue of donor information and to select their own donor on the basis of this information. Finally, since 1983, T.S.B.C. has asked donors if they wish to list themselves as "yes donors"—that is, donors who are willing to disclose identifying information about themselves to future offspring. T.S.B.C. releases "yes-donors'" information to offspring who petition the bank in writing after they are at least eighteen years old. It does not, however, release identifying information to the donor concerning the recipient of his sperm or any child born as the result of his contribution.[55]

The rather open policies of The Sperm Bank of California invite feminists (as well as nonfeminists) to reconsider not only current U.S. laws that specify the rights and responsibilities of sperm donors and recipients, respectively, but also U.S. policies regarding both anonymous and commercial sperm donation. As noted earlier, the identity of sperm donors is kept secret, and most sperm donors are paid for their gametes (in the range of $50 per ejaculation).[56] As also noted earlier, these policies have been affirmed as serving *men's* best interests. Indeed, as Glanville Williams, a British law professor, points out, the reasons for donor anonymity are twofold: "to protect the *donor*'s reputation" and "to eliminate the risk of the wife transferring her affections to the *donor*."[57] In addition to these reasons, protecting the sperm donor from an unwanted financial or personal relationship with his biological child is typically cited in support of anonymity.[58]

Recently, a variety of psychologists and counselors have challenged the assumption that an anonymous policy (if not also a commercial policy) is actually in *men's* best interests. Some recent studies show that, more often than not, sperm donors want to know whether they "fathered" a child. Moreover, many sperm donors seem willing to share not only nonidentifying but even identifying information about themselves with recipients and children. For example, psychologist Patricia P. Mahlstedt discovered that nearly all of the seventy-two sperm donors in her study were inclined to pass on significant medical and personal background information about themselves to their recipients, and 60 percent were also willing to be contacted by their potential offspring when they (the offspring) reached age eighteen.[59] Mahlstedt's empirical research is bolstered in some interesting ways by the popular media. In an episode of the television show "St. Elsewhere," one of the physicians donates sperm to the hospital's infertility program. Through a complicated chain of events, he discovers the identity of his sperm recipient and follows her pregnancy obsessively. Eventually, he assigns himself to her case, at which point he begins to act like an expectant father. The pregnant woman's husband is bewildered by the physician's inappropriate behavior and asks the chief of residents to remove him from his wife's case. As a result, the physician nearly has a nervous breakdown, protesting that the woman is carrying his child and that he has a right to be involved in his child's life.

Given studies such as Mahlstedt's and media representations such as the "St. Elsewhere" episode, a more open policy of sperm donation might indeed be in the best interests of sperm donors. Whether or not this proves to be the case, however, the question remains for feminists: Would a more open policy or the current commercial and anonymous policy of sperm donation serve *women's* best interests?

Feminists who support the current policy argue, first, that *commercialism* serves women's best interests. Because it is neither desirable nor feasible for all women to secure sperm noncommercially (i.e., from altruistic male friends, acquaintances, or contacts), women need to have a way of securing sperm commercially for a fair market price. Second, the same feminists insist that, like commercialism, *anonymity* serves women's best interests because it insulates them and their children from the intrusions of uninvited "genetic fathers." Better that sperm donors know nothing about their recipients' or children's identity than that they make nuisances of themselves. Moreover, it is up to the sperm donors' genetic children to decide whether they wish to give any identifying personal information about themselves to their genetic fathers. (Interestingly, most feminists who favor an anonymous sperm donation policy regard sperm donors' right to privacy as less weighty than AID children's right to known their genetic fathers. They claim that AID children, like adopted children, should have access to nonidentifying medical information about their genetic fathers at any time and to identifying personal information about them upon reaching the age of majority. As it stands, however, the trend is to provide only nonidentifying medical information to children conceived through AID. Unless a donor is a "yes-donor" or voluntarily chooses to disclose his identity upon his genetic child's request, the child will remain in the dark as to his identity.)[60]

The feminist case for a commercial *and* anonymous sperm donation policy is countered by equally cogent feminist cases for sperm donation policies that are (1) noncommercial and anonymous or (2) noncommercial and open. Feminists who support noncommercial and anonymous policies regard as exemplary the policy developed by a network of twenty sperm banks in France known as CECOS (Centre d'etude et de conservation du sperme.) The guiding idea behind CECOS is that of "a gift from one couple to another." Potential donors must be married and have fathered at least one child of their own. In addition, they must have their wives' consent and cannot receive compensation for donating their sperm. The recipient couples must also be married (or in a long-term monogamous relationship) and need to have been referred to the CECOS bank for a medically proven *male* infertility problem (or for a genetically determined condition that the husband does not wish to transmit to his offspring). Finally, both donors and recipients must agree to psychological counseling, the primary purpose of which is to permit all parties to explore their feelings about this form of collaborative reproduction. Although CECOS keeps accurate records on donors and recipients, anonymity is guaranteed to all parties.[61]

Some feminists think that although the CECOS policy is a good one, it does not go far enough. They favor an open as well as noncommercial policy that includes not only infertile heterosexual couples in marriage or marriage-like relationships but also lesbian couples and single women wishing to raise children on their own. These feminists believe that if genetic connection is as important as people generally claim it is, and if men as well as women should take on full childrearing responsibilities for the sake of the child, then everyone involved in collaborative reproduction should play a more or less active role in their children's lives.

Among the family structures that meet with the approval of feminists who support open as well as noncommercial policies of sperm donation are those that bring together lesbian women and gay men to co-parent children they have conceived through AID. In one case of lesbian co-parenting, a lesbian couple, Nancy and Amy, formed a family that included Nancy's genetic child Sarah and Sarah's genetic father Doug. All three adults expressed satisfaction with the arrangement, which produced a very well-adjusted child. Indeed, Sarah's only recorded worry about the future was that she might not be able to find a "Daddy" and an "Amy" for the child she herself hopes to have someday.[62] To be sure, feminist advocates of open family structures like this one are well aware that when such families break up, a particularly great toll is taken. In the event that Nancy and Doug's relationship ruptures, Doug might sue Nancy for custody of Sarah; or if Nancy and Amy split up, Nancy could keep Amy from seeing Sarah. In addition, if both Nancy and Doug were to die, their wish that Amy should have custody of Sarah could be challenged in court by grandparents or even the state. Nevertheless, feminist advocates of such open family structures claim that the solution to these problems is not to forbid lesbians to form families or to keep sperm donors out of their genetic children's lives but, rather, to delineate the respective legal rights and responsibilities of genetic, gestational, and social parents more clearly and more fairly.

Of course, there is less inclination to invite the sperm donor to join the family when AID is used by a woman in a traditional heterosexual marriage. After all, the woman's husband usually desires to be the child's one and only social father. Therefore, if the main reason to admit the sperm donor into the family is to provide the AID child not so much with a genetic reference point as with a loving social father or male figure, then such admission seems unnecessary. If the AID child already has a stable and loving social father, she or he will probably feel little, if any, need to establish a close social relationship with his or her genetic father. Under such circumstances, a brief meeting between the genetic father and his genetic child might satisfy any curiosity they have about each other.

Nonfeminist Bioethical Perspectives on In-Vitro Fertilization

The term 'test-tube baby' conjures up all sorts of Faustian and Frankensteinian images, but these do not appropriately reflect the realities of in-vitro fertilization. The phrase 'in-vitro fertilization' (literally, fertilization in glass) ordinarily denotes any fertilization procedure that occurs outside the human body. The process of IVF begins when a woman's ovaries are stimulated with fertility drugs to produce multiple eggs, which the physician then retrieves through one of two means: laparoscopy or transvaginal ultrasound-directed oocyte retrieval (TUDOR). In the case of laparoscopy, the physician makes a small incision near the navel of the woman and inserts the laparoscope, a slender fiberoptic tube with a light and an optical system at the end. After pinpointing the eggs within the ovaries, the physician retrieves them with a long hollow needle fed through the laparoscope. The needle is inserted through the vaginal wall, rather than through the abdomen as in the TUDOR procedure, and ultrasonography guides the physician's retrieval of the eggs. After retrieval, each egg is placed in a separate glass dish and combined with sperm from the woman's partner or a donor. Those eggs that are successfully fertilized are inserted in the woman's uterus when they have divided to form between four and sixteen cells.[63]

Among the concerns about IVF that have most preoccupied nonfeminist bioethicists is the so-called moral status of the early embryo, increasingly referred to as the pre-embryo. The basic positions on the moral status of the pre-embryo are similar to those discussed in connection with abortion: (1) The pre-embryo is a human person from the moment of fertilization. (2) The pre-embryo becomes a human person at some later point during gestation. Or (3) human persons are only those already born and capable of rationality.

So-called full-protectionists espouse the first view of the pre-embryo. They believe that because the pre-embryo is a member of *homo sapiens*, and because it has the *future capacity* for sentience, self-consciousness, the ability to communicate, and rationality, it is a human person—albeit a potential one. Thus, if it is wrong to kill a human person, it is also wrong to "kill" an "unused" pre-embryo—by discarding it, for example.

Critics of the full-protectionist position believe that it leads to absurdities. If it is wrong to destroy any potential person, even a two-, four-, eight-, or sixteen-cell blastocyst, they argue, then it is wrong even to practice birth control—that is, to prevent the union of the egg and sperm. In this connection, philosopher Peter Singer raises the following consideration: "If the potential of the embryo is so crucial, why do all sides agree that they would not object to disposing of the egg and the sperm before they have been combined? An egg and a drop of seminal fluid, viewed collectively, also have the potential to develop into a mature human being."[64] By extension, say critics of full-protectionism, if techniques such as cloning (the production of offspring genetically identical to their parents from somatic cells) were developed, all of our cells would have the capacity for personhood. Under such a set of circumstances, they insist, even staunch full-protectionists would probably forsake the principle of potentiality in order to avoid the absurd consequence of equating the sloughing of one's cells with committing murder.

Because the principle of potentiality can be taken to the above extremes, so-called modified-protectionists and nonprotectionists distinguish between pre-embryos and human persons. Scientist Clifford Grobstein claims that the major difference between "human materials" such as cells, tissues, and organs, on the one hand, and "human beings or persons," on the other, is that only the latter are sentient. Since he holds that sentience (especially the capacity to experience pain) is a necessary condition for having interests or holding rights, Grobstein makes the further claim that until "human materials" attain sentience, they are without interests or rights.[65] Although physician-philosopher Leon Kass, like most other modified protectionists, and all nonprotectionists accept Grobstein's claim, they quickly add that the fact that pre-embryos are devoid of interests or rights does not give us permission to treat them disrespectfully. Flushing an eight-cell pre-embryo down the drain may not be the equivalent of homicide, observes Kass, but neither is it a trivial matter solely between a physician and his plumber.[66]

In the early days of IVF, full-protectionists debated modified-protectionists and nonprotectionists heatedly about the proper way to handle so-called surplus embryos—namely, those that women declined to host in their wombs (usually out of a fear of multiple births). Although modified-protectionists and nonprotectionists saw nothing immoral in couples' requests that their surplus embryos be discarded, full-protectionists claimed that such discards constituted ex utero abortions. They insisted that women should accept all of the embryos into their wombs rather than throw any of them away: Better to risk a multiple birth than to deprive any one child of life.

With the development of cryopreservation techniques has come a partial solution to the "discard" problem. Couples now have the option of freezing their surplus embryos for their later use. To be sure, embryo-freezing techniques do not totally resolve the surplus pre-embryo debate. Some critics view cryopreservation as unjustified human experimentation; others note that couples do not always use the embryos that have been frozen for their use. Perhaps they decide not to procreate after all, or they are fortunate enough to bear a child the first time they use IVF. In that event, unless another woman or couple requests to "adopt" their unused pre-embryos *and* the original couple permits them to do so, the pre-embryos will probably decay or be discarded.

A resolution to the "spare-embryo" problem more acceptable to full-protectionists is to substitute a technique called gamete intrafallopian tube transfer (GIFT) for the IVF procedure. In the case of GIFT, the egg that has been removed from the woman is not fertilized in vitro. Instead, a woman's eggs and her partner's sperm are placed directly into her fallopian tubes. If fertilization takes place, it does so as it would in a normal pregnancy. However, if the pregnancy is unsuccessful, the whole GIFT procedure, including the laparoscopy or TUDOR, must be repeated, since no pre-embryos would have been frozen to accommodate a failed pregnancy. Full-protectionists maintain that it is better to expose women to the statistically small risks associated with additional laparoscopies or TUDORs than to freeze pre-embryos that might later be discarded. Modified-protectionists and nonprotectionists disagree. They claim that since an eight-cell blastocyst has nothing akin to the interests or rights possessed by an adult woman, the woman should not be exposed to unnecessary extra surgeries. Better to freeze a pre-embryo and later discard it than to subject a woman to extra inconvenience and pain.

Because their beliefs about the personhood of pre-embryos are so divergent, nonfeminist bioethicists will undoubtedly continue to debate the moral permissibility of discarding pre-embryos. The only technological development likely to put an end to their debate would be the development of egg-freezing techniques. If such techniques were perfected, clinicians would simply remove the maximum number of available eggs from a woman, fertilize only as many as she is willing to receive into her womb, and freeze the remaining unfertilized eggs for later use, should that prove necessary. Since eggs have the same neutral moral status as sperm cells, discarding unused eggs should not offend the sensibilities of full-protectionists.

Clearly, embryo-freezing techniques have failed to resolve some of our long-standing moral problems. If anything, they have created new ones. In the first place, freezing pre-embryos sets the stage for inheritance and custody disputes. For example, in 1981 Mario and Elsa Rios entered an IVF program in Melbourne, Australia. Physicians there retrieved and fertilized with donor sperm several of Mrs. Rios's eggs. One of the fertilized eggs was placed in Mrs. Rios's womb. The two remaining fertilized eggs were frozen for possible future use. When Mrs. Rios miscarried, she told her physicians that she was not ready to have one or both of the frozen embryos inserted into her womb. She and her husband then left for a vacation trip, which ended tragically in their death. Questions were immediately raised about the legal status of the "orphaned" frozen pre-embryos. Did they have a right to inherit a share of the Rios's considerable estate? And who, after all, had the right to determine the frozen pre-embryos' future? The Rios's grown son, Michael, who had filed for guardianship? The sperm donor (assuming that his identity had been recorded somewhere)? Some right-to-life group willing to provide a surrogate mother for the frozen pre-embryos?[67] Ultimately, the state of Victoria assumed responsibility for this decision, ruling that the pre-embryos should not be discarded but, instead, should be anonymously donated to a woman unable to produce her own eggs.[68]

Whether any woman bore a child from the Rios's frozen pre-embryos is not known. What is known, however, is that nonfeminist bioethicists immediately disagreed among themselves as to whether "orphaned" frozen pre-embryos had a "right to life"—that is, a right to be gestated in the womb of a surrogate mother. Predictably, full-protectionists insisted that since frozen pre-embryos are persons, they have the same moral status and rights as orphaned (or otherwise abandoned) children. Rather than being discarded, they argued, unused frozen pre-embryos should be put up for adoption. In contrast, modified-protectionists and nonprotectionists claimed that since frozen pre-embryos are not persons but rather nonsentient beings, they have no rights. Couples should simply leave instructions concerning the disposition of the pre-embryos—in their wills, for example. Among their options would be disposal of the pre-embryos, donation of them to another couple, or use of them for research purposes.

Sometimes, as in the Rios case, the genetic parents of one or more frozen pre-embryos die, but this is a rare event. It is far more likely that a frozen embryo will become the object of a custody dispute than an inheritance dispute. In a widely discussed Tennessee divorce case, *Davis v. Davis* (1989), a couple had no prior agreement about the disposition of their seven frozen pre-embryos in the event of divorce. As it happened, the couple did divorce and the wife insisted that the pre-embryos be available to her for thawing and placement in her womb or the womb of a surrogate mother. Meanwhile, the husband strenuously objected to the idea of being burdened by children from a failed marriage. The trial judge awarded custody of the pre-embryos to the wife on the grounds that it was in their best interests. After all, only she could give them life in her womb, whereas in the husband's sole possession, they could only remain frozen. When the husband appealed this decision, the Tennessee supreme court ruled that the couple should have joint custody over them. It also ruled that, absent a prior agreement about the disposition of the pre-embryos in the event of divorce, a person's right (in this case the *husband's* right) to "procreational autonomy" outweighed the state's "at best slight" interest in "the potential life embodied by these four- to eight-cell pre-embryos."[69] The court added that if one member of a couple does not want to be a parent, his or her wishes outweigh the other's interest in using the pre-embryos, unless the other cannot become a parent in any other way (presumably including adoption). Subsequently, the wife carried her appeal to the U.S. Supreme Court, where the state court ruling was allowed to stand. Finally, in June 1993, the husband's wishes were honored, and the pre-embryos were destroyed.

Although some nonfeminist bioethicists claim that it is wrong to deliberately create pre-embryos that might fall victim to the kinds of conflicts described above, most of them believe that the benefit of life, in and of itself, far outweighs the harms that children *might* experience as the result of having been "disputed over" as pre-embryos. They also point out that, since many children who have been procreated "naturally" are the subject of equally unpleasant inheritance and custody disputes, it is not clear that deliberately created pre-embryos are entitled to special protection simply because they have been produced "artificially."

In addition to concerns about the moral status of the pre-embryo, some nonfeminist bioethicists have expressed concerns about IVF's effects on family relationships. In general, these nonfeminist bioethicists do not object to IVF when the gametes that are used come from the couple who plan to rear the child. They do object, however, when a couple uses the gametes of one or more "third parties" to conceive the child. As in the case of artificial insemination, critics of "third-party" IVF maintain that whenever a gamete donor enters the picture, there is a possibility for human discord. For example, the social parent who lacks a genetic connection to the child may not feel as close to her or him as does the parent who has such a connection; or, upon reaching adulthood, the child conceived through IVF might demand to know who his or her "real" (i.e., biological) parents are. Critics of "third-party" IVF insist that unless parents view themselves as biologically as well as socially related to their children, they will not be motivated to undergo the kinds of sacrifices that parents often have to make for their children. As in the case of AID, critics of "third-party" IVF think that it is morally wrong to *deliberately* construct familial relationships that have the potential to explode in unpleasant and even harmful ways. Therefore, they conclude, breaking the connections among begetting, bearing, and rearing children would be a serious mistake. In this context, nonfeminist bioethicist Leon Kass claims that even when IVF does not involve third parties and is confined to a husband and wife, it constitutes an assault on the biological foundations of the human family. Although Kass would not morally prohibit the use of IVF by married couples, he views IVF and, for that matter, AID as a threat to the "wisdom in that mystery of nature which joins the pleasure of sex, the communication of love, and the desire for children in the very activity by which we continue the chain of human existence."[70]

Advocates of IVF, including versions of the procedure that involve the use of donated gametes and embryos, doubt that families formed through assisted reproduction necessarily experience more worrisome marital and family tensions than do other types of families. On the contrary, they believe that it is more difficult to create a harmonious family when the father and mother both have children from previous marriages than when the father and mother have used the genetic material of an anonymous donor or, as will later be discussed, the womb of a surrogate mother to help procreate their child. Defenders of IVF also insist that there is nothing inherently wrong with breaking the connections among begetting, bearing, and rearing children, and that, in any event, relatively few people would choose to break these connections unnecessarily. When it is necessary, they argue, it is better to create a nontraditional family than to leave a couple without the child they yearn to have.

Nonfeminist bioethicists have also voiced concerns about the so-called experimental nature of some new reproductive technologies, especially the high-priced ones. In discussing just how risky or beneficial IVF is, and whether it is necessarily wise to develop such a costly way to treat infertility, nonfeminist bioethicists have focused on such topics as the need for clinical IVF research; the need for and adequacy of prior laboratory research, including animal research, on IVF and embryo transfer; the risks of clinical IVF research to the potential products of IVF; informed consent by participants in clinical IVF research; liability or compensation for IVF-research-related injury; potential long-term social consequences of clinical IVF research; appropriate allocation of research and clinical resources to IVF research; and appropriate institutional frameworks for the provision of advice on or monitoring of clinical IVF research.[71]

Since full-protectionists believe that pre-embryos are persons with rights, they object that laboratory research on pre-embryos is morally unacceptable because it in no way serves their interests.[72] Modified-protectionists and nonprotectionists do not share this view. Since they believe that pre-embryos have no interests, most modified-protectionists and nonprotectionists support laboratory research on pre-embryos, including the use of teratogens or mutagens on them. Leroy Walters argues that, provided the information we seek "cannot reasonably be acquired in any other way,"[73] this type of laboratory research on pre-embryos is justified to the degree that it contributes "to our understanding of fertilization, contraception, the origin of chromosomal abnormalities, and even the mechanisms by which cells become malignant."[74] In contrast, full-protectionists find it morally repugnant to create what they view as a human person, experiment on it in a variety of ways, and then destroy it. Nonfeminist theologian Bernard Häring sums up the opinion of full-protectionists as follows: "The very possibility that we may be faced with a human person in the full sense constitutes, in my opinion, an absolute veto against this type of experimentation."[75]

Since modified-protectionists and nonprotectionists have relatively few concerns about research on nonsentient human material—that is, pre-embryos—they have focused most of their attention on the interests and rights of the couples who use IVF. They maintain that such couples (or individuals) should enter an IVF program only if they have judged that the risks of the program are reasonable ones for them to assume. According to philosopher Joel Feinberg, several factors affect the reasonability of a risk assumption: the degree of probability that harm to oneself will result from a given course of action; the seriousness of the harm being risked; the degree of probability that the goal inclining one to shoulder the risk will, in fact, result from the course of action; the value or importance of achieving the goal—that is, just how worthwhile it is to oneself; and the necessity of the risk—that is, the availability or absence of alternative, less risky means to the desired goal.[76] Thus, a couple (or individual) should be informed about all the risks that IVF (or one of its variations) poses before consenting to the procedure. Given that at least the female member of an infertile couple will probably experience considerable pain and discomfort throughout an IVF program and that there is only a 10 percent chance that the infertile couple will actually bring home a child (after repeated hospital visits, an average time expenditure of four and a half years, and a cash expenditure of approximately $25,000), a decision to use IVF may well be unreasonable for some infertile couples.[77] Conversely, other infertile couples—for example, those who want a baby genetically related to them more than anything else in life—might decide that, for them, using IVF is a reasonable option, well worth their effort, time, and expense.

Since IVF is so costly and does not necessarily result in the birth of a child, many nonfeminist bioethicists object to the expenditure of already-scarce research dollars for its further development. Convinced that too much money is being spent on IVF research, political scientist Robert Blank argues that society should fund research for treatments that prevent infertility rather than continue to build up the lucrative (but often unsuccessful) "fertility business."[78] Nonfeminist bioethicists who disagree with Blank counter that it is unrealistic to hope that infertility will be totally eradicated anytime soon. The poor success rates of IVF lead these nonfeminist bioethicists to exactly the opposite conclusion about funding—that further research is the route to cheaper IVF procedures with better results in the future. They also point out that IVF research may lead to the discovery of ways to prevent or correct infertility in the first place, a goal that they support in addition to furthering the use of clinical IVF. In their view, investment in IVF research now will not only help infertile couples have children but also ensure greater access to "new and improved" IVF in the future.

Clearly, then, there are many bioethical issues to be considered when medicine and technology are used, as in the case of IVF, to supersede "nature's limitations." The debate about the ethics of research involving pre-embryos is, of course, intimately tied to nonfeminist bioethicists' view of the moral status of the pre-embryo. However, when it comes to questions about how IVF affects *families*, we can no longer rely on the traditional protectionist-versus-nonprotectionist dispute to frame our views. Nonfeminist bioethicists each bring their own conception of a "proper" family into the clinic or research lab and, to varying degrees, superimpose it upon their work. Thus, nonfeminist bioethicists need to ask themselves whether their view of alternative families or that of the people who will be living in them should prevail.

Feminist Bioethical Perspectives on In-Vitro Fertilization

Although there is no uniform feminist position regarding in-vitro fertilization, it is accurate to say that, unlike nonfeminist bioethicists, feminists rarely discuss the moral status of the pre-embryo. Instead, both feminist critics and feminist advocates of IVF worry that the women who participate in IVF programs are not always as aware of IVF's risks as they are of its benefits. Thus, they urge health-care practitioners to be honest about the *true* success rates of IVF. They also insist that health-care practitioners be as candid as possible about the physical and psychological risks of IVF. If a woman wishes to use IVF to attempt to become pregnant, she should realize just how long and arduous the process is. Feminists Gena Corea and Susan Ince note that a woman typically has to submit to at least two IVF cycles, each of which lasts approximately two weeks. First, as an outpatient, the woman is monitored for her daily plasma levels and cervical mucus and undergoes ultrasound examinations to determine her ovarian progress. Then, as an inpatient, she becomes the object of hormonal assays and the collection of eggs through laparoscopy. Finally, *if* egg collection and fertilization are successful, clinicians will transfer one or more of the pre-embryos into her womb. If any stage along the way—egg collection, egg fertilization, or pre-embryo transfer—is unsuccessful (and if additional frozen pre-embryos are not available), the whole process must be performed again. Each time the woman goes through an IVF cycle, she is subjected to several risks, including the following ones: "the adverse affects of hormones such as Clomid, which are usually taken in large, concentrated doses to stimulate hyperovulation; repeated anesthesia and surgery to extract eggs; the heightened risk of ectopic pregnancy (when the fertilized egg implants outside the uterus); the development of ovarian cysts and menstrual difficulties; and the early start of menopause and an increased risk of some forms of cancer."[79] Attempts to reduce such risks have not been very successful. For example, unlike laparoscopy, which is a relatively painful egg-extracting technique, transvaginal ultrasound-directed oocyte retrieval is, in theory, so painless that it precludes the need for general anesthesia. Nevertheless, many women claim that, in their experience of it, the TUDOR process was very painful—so much so that they had to ask for general anesthesia during it.[80]

Equally as taxing as the physical risks of IVF are its psychological risks, in feminists' estimation. Philosopher Mary Anne Warren notes that these include "the emotional ups and downs inherent in the cycle of hope and disappointment; the disruption of work and, often, personal relationships; and the humiliation and depersonalization that may result from the submission to painful and embarrassing invasions of their bodies."[81] Indeed, many women in IVF programs become highly preoccupied by all the things that can, and very often do, go wrong. A woman's eggs may not be retrievable; or if retrievable, her eggs may be of poor quality. Fertilization may not occur in the petri dish; and even if it does, the pre-embryo may fail to implant in her womb. In one study of IVF patients, all the women reported that the two-week waiting period after the transfer of the pre-embryo into their wombs was nearly intolerable. One woman said: "You sit . . . and pray and pray. . . . And when it doesn't work, that's when you curse everybody. You feel depressed. You're not worth anything."[82]

Feminists are also concerned about the well-being of egg donors, who assume many of the same risks that IVF enrollees do, but without receiving the same benefit: namely, a much-wanted child. Instead, egg donors receive financial compensation for their eggs.[83] Thus, feminists urge health-care practitioners to make certain that egg donors thoroughly comprehend the risks involved in egg retrieval. They have praised one clinic in particular not only for verbally communicating the risks of serving as an egg donor but also for showing prospective egg donors videos. One such video details TUDOR (the procedure by which their eggs are removed), thus underscoring that fact that egg donation is painful enough to require the administration of a general anesthetic.[84]

As serious as IVF's risks are, however, its feminist advocates nonetheless insist that it is up to the egg recipients and egg donors to decide whether they are risks worth taking. Each woman, they insist, should decide for herself just how much *she* wants a child or just how much *she* wants to help another woman have a child. Feminist critics of IVF counter that just because a woman knows cognitively what IVF's risks and benefits are, she is not necessarily emotionally able to make a fully voluntary decision to use or not to use IVF. As they see it, Western society teaches women that their "fulfillment" depends on their mothering a child, preferably a child that is flesh of their flesh.[85] To the degree that a woman is convinced that being a genetic and gestational as well as social mother is the sine qua non for her success as a human being, she will "want" to use virtually any reproduction-aiding technology to achieve her maternal goal. Thus, as Gena Corea comments, "[t]he propaganda . . . that women are nothing unless they bear children, that if they are infertile, they lose their most basic identity as women . . . has a coercive power. It conditions a woman's choices as well as her *motivations* to choose. Her most heartfelt desire, the pregnancy for which she so desperately yearns, has been—to varying degrees—conditioned."[86]

Feminist critics of IVF also worry that, simply owing to IVF's availability, society will pressure infertile women who are currently happy without children to "do something" about their childlessness. Likewise, they are concerned that society will pressure fertile women to help out their infertile "sisters"—by providing them with the eggs they so desperately need, for example. Corea points out that, in contrast to sperm donation, egg donation has historically relied on *known* as opposed to *anonymous* donors. Given that it is considerably inconvenient, uncomfortable, risky, and even painful to serve as an egg donor, clinicians initially required that their patients use female relatives or friends as egg donors. But when it became evident that some of these "donors" felt there was no way to say "no" to their loved ones, most clinicians reconsidered their open and noncommercial egg-donation policy and moved in the direction of an anonymous and commercial one.[87] They reasoned that anonymous egg donors would be able to sell their eggs without feeling obligated to do so. They also reasoned that so long as sperm donors were being paid for their gametes, egg donors should be paid for theirs.

Although some feminist critics of IVF applaud the switch to an anonymous and commercial policy of egg donation, others view it as a matter of replacing one evil with another. They contend that many egg donors "choose" to be egg donors simply because they are financially strapped and in serious need of the $750 to $3,000 they can collect for their eggs, or because they feel obligated to do a good deed.[88] Although most infertility clinics report that their anonymous egg donors are mature women able to assess what personal risks are entailed in their act of generosity, many of the same clinics also concede that some of their donors are burdened by heavy emotional baggage.[89] And, indeed, several recent empirical studies have confirmed that a statistically significant number of anonymous volunteers, perhaps as many as one-third, are either excessive risk-takers or the survivors of a major reproductive loss (abortion, miscarriage, giving up a child for adoption).[90] Thus, feminist critics of IVF conclude that a sizable percentage of egg donors might not be acting in their own best interests, and that such women should be discouraged from serving as egg donors. They are particularly concerned about "super donors" (who sell their eggs routinely), since these women are exposed to a level of medical risk that the average IVF patient escapes.[91] As bad as it is to take advantage of vulnerable persons, it is even worse to do so when they are exposed to considerable personal risk.

Of all the debates that IVF's feminist critics and feminist advocates have waged, none are greater than those concerning the ways that IVF and other reproduction-aiding technologies affect the childbearing experience itself. According to feminist philosopher Mary O'Brien, even though women's exclusive ability to bear children has been a source of oppression for women, it has also been a source of power—one that men have not been able to share. Thus, the experience and meaning of natural reproduction is very different for women than for men. In the first place, women experience procreation as a continuous process. For them, the spatial and temporal continuity between the egg and the resulting child is unbroken in natural reproduction, since the entire process of conception and gestation takes place inside their bodies. For men, in contrast, the spatial and temporal continuity between the sperm and the resulting child is broken in natural reproduction, since the entire process of conception and gestation takes place outside their bodies. Second, women, not men, have necessarily performed the fundamental *labor* of natural reproduction—pregnancy and birth. Without women, life could not go on. It is women who have the *individual* power to determine whether a *particular* child will be born, as well as the *collective* power to determine whether the human species will continue.[92] Third, prior to the introduction of DNA testing for paternity, women could know for certain in natural reproduction whether the children born to them were genetically related to them, whereas men could not know for certain that their female partners' genetic children were also their genetic children. For men, there was always the possibility that their female partners had been raped or had committed adultery.

Conclusion

Clearly, women have the advantage in natural reproduction; yet, according to some feminist critics of IVF, it is precisely this advantage that has compelled men to try to control women's sexual lives and reproductive capacities. Men have done so in the "privacy" of their homes by bullying, badgering, and even beating their wives and girlfriends. They have also used the courts, executive offices, and legislatures to control women's sexual and reproductive freedom. Finally, and in particularly effective ways, men have used medical authorities to limit women's reproductive freedom. In the past, health-care practitioners—most of whom have been men—sought to subject menstruation, pregnancy, delivery, lactation, and menopause to their control. And, in the view of feminist critics of IVF, reproduction-controlling and reproduction-aiding technologies have provided the same health-care practitioners with the means to consolidate their control over women's reproductive powers. So concerned is Gena Corea about society's drift in the direction of assisted reproduction that she urges women to ask themselves the following questions:

> Why are men focusing all this technology on woman's generative organs—the source of her reproductive power? Why are they collecting our eggs?

> Why do they seek to freeze them? Why do men want to control the production of human beings? Why do they talk so often about producing "perfect" babies?
>
> Why are they splitting the functions of motherhood into smaller parts? Does that reduce the power of the mother and her claim to the child? ("I only gave the egg. I am not the real mother." "I only loaned my uterus. I am not the real mother." "I only raised the child. I am not the real mother").[93]

Corea's questions have prompted feminist critics of IVF to speculate that *men* intend to make women's experience of reproduction just as "alienated" as their own is. As soon as a woman's eggs are removed from her body, or as soon as she decides to use another woman's eggs, the stage is set for her to experience the reproductive process as a discontinuous one. Absent DNA testing, a woman who uses IVF cannot be certain that the child she births is genetically related to her. After all, the lab can always make a mistake. Someone else's eggs may be labeled with her name by mistake or by design. In the future, moreover, women may be disconnected from their genetic progeny in an even more radical way, according to feminist critics of IVF. Should researchers develop an artificial placenta, for instance, women would no longer have the sole power to gestate and to give birth. Feminist Robyn Rowland is sufficiently concerned about this possible development that she asks us to imagine a world in which only a few superovulating women are allowed to exist, a world in which eggs are taken from women, frozen, and fertilized in vitro for transfer into artificial placentas. Rowland concedes that the replacement of women's childbearing capacity by male-controlled technology would remove some of women's biological burdens. But it would also leave women "without a product" with which "to bargain": "For the history of 'mankind' women have been seen in terms of their value as childbearers. We have to ask, if that last power is taken and controlled by men, what role is envisaged for women in the new world?"[94]

Corea, Rowland, and other feminist critics of IVF also suspect that removing the fetus from a woman's womb might facilitate full-scale genetic manipulation, a concern that I will discuss at length in the next chapter and only touch upon now. Gena Corea notes that an increasing number of IVF clinical and laboratory researchers are eager to develop screening techniques to eliminate genetically defective pre-embryos.[95] Although eliminating birth defects may sound like a wonderful scientific advancement, Corea cautions that even if genetic manipulation starts out benevolently, it may not end benevolently. As Corea sees it, the stage is now being set for laws and medical practices that would prohibit women not only from conceiving or birthing "defective babies" but also from exposing fetuses to their own "defective intrauterine environments."[96] Whatever the right to procreate will mean in the future, Corea warns, it will not mean the right of a couple to conceive and bring to term a severely or even moderately disabled child for whose support society as a whole will in some measure be responsible. Indeed, philosopher Joseph Fletcher has already asserted that "the right to conceive and bear children has to stop short of knowingly making crippled children."[97] Told that they are victimizing their offspring and the whole of society by using their defective eggs and/or sperm, a shamed couple will probably willingly accept donor gametes. But however "responsible" this decision may seem, feminists worry about the long-term social implications of the ideology of human perfectibility. In their view, if people are no longer willing (or even able) to accept unconditionally the imperfect children born to them—to love these children just as they are—the human species will be morally worse for this new intolerance.

Feminists who advocate IVF disagree with its feminist critics who predict dire consequences such as the replacement of women by artificial placentas. They assert that, with sufficient safeguards, women can use IVF without being exploited. In fact, they see in IVF a valuable affirmation of the genetic connection, at least when a couple uses their own gametes. When one woman needs another woman's eggs to experience pregnancy—perhaps the most intimate of all human connecting experiences—the relationship subsequently formed need not be viewed as one woman exploiting another woman but simply as one woman helping another.

8

Feminist and Nonfeminist Perspectives on Surrogacy

Surrogacy, often referred to as contracted motherhood or gestational motherhood, ordinarily comes into play when the female member of a married couple is infertile or, if fertile, unable or unwilling to carry a child to term.[1] If the woman has no eggs, she and her husband may decide to seek the services of a so-called partial surrogate. In cases of partial surrogacy, the surrogate mother agrees (1) to be artificially inseminated with the sperm of a man who is not her husband; (2) to carry the subsequent pregnancy to term for a fee (commercial surrogacy) or out of generosity (gift surrogacy); and (3) to relinquish the resulting child to the man and his wife to rear. Conversely, if the woman has eggs but is unable or unwilling to carry a child to term, she and her husband may decide to seek the services of a so-called full surrogate. In cases of full surrogacy, the surrogate mother is not genetically related to the child she carries but, instead, gestates the in-vitro fertilized embryo of the couple who has commissioned her services.[2]

Nonfeminist Bioethical Perspectives on Surrogacy

The Nonfeminist Moral Case Against Surrogacy

Most nonfeminist opponents of surrogacy base their arguments on either natural-law or Kantian considerations. Natural-law opponents of surrogacy view it as an attempt to defy the laws of nature. They reason that, insofar as it is morally wrong to try to prevent procreation "artificially" (e.g., by using the Pill, an IUD, or Norplant), it is also morally wrong to try to cause procreation "artificially" (e.g. by using AID, IVF, or a surrogate mother's services). If a couple have sexual intercourse, they must be ready and willing to accept the responsibilities of parenthood, for the natural end of sexual intercourse is to bring new life into the world. Similarly, if a couple are unable to procreate, they must accept the fact that they cannot have a child genetically related to them. For an infertile couple to procreate without having sexual intercourse is no less a violation of nature's laws than for a fertile couple to have sexual intercourse without being ready and willing to procreate.

According to natural-law thinker Leon Kass (previously also identified as a nonfeminist bioethicist), couples who use gamete donors and / or surrogate mothers threaten the institutions of marriage and the family.[3] In his view, the creation of babies in laboratories, especially if it involves the use of donor gametes, spoils or degrades one of the most beautiful experiences a man and a woman can have—namely, weaving a continuous line from their mutual act of sexual intercourse, to the union of their genetic material, to the embryonic development and birthing of their child, and, finally, to the rearing of that child.

As bad as it is to introduce an anonymous gamete donor into the marital relationship, Kass suggests, it is far worse to introduce a known surrogate mother into it. Unlike a gamete donor, the surrogate is not a peripheral presence in the couple's life but, rather, a central, unavoidable entity for at least the duration of the pregnancy. How will the woman, who together with her husband commissioned the surrogate mother, feel if she notices her husband's attentions gravitating toward the surrogate mother? Or how will she feel several years into the childrearing process, if her husband suddenly refers to their child as not *really* her child but his and the surrogate mother's child? Worse, how will she feel if her child one day asks her who his *real* mother is? "Was it the woman who supplied me with twenty-three chromosomes and gestated me for nine months, or is it you, the woman who reared me for eighteen years? Do I have one real mother or two real mothers, only one of whom is married to my father? Or is it the case that although I have a real father, I have *no* real mother?"

Kantian opponents of surrogacy base their arguments on the second version of Kant's Categorical Imperative, according to which no person should ever be reduced to an object or thing for another person's use. Kantians claim that each person is as valuable as any other person, and that each of us has an absolute duty to respect all persons, including our own selves. To respect persons is to treat them as unconditionally valuable human beings who have their own unique plans of action; to disrespect persons is to treat them as conditionally valuable things—that is, as instruments or tools who have no value in and of themselves. When I treat someone as a mere means, I ignore or trivialize his or her fundamental interests in freedom and well-being in order to secure or maintain my own. Similarly, when I treat myself as a mere means, I show little or no regard for my own fundamental interests in freedom and well-being.[4]

In this connection, Kantian opponents of surrogacy insist that, as a rule, commissioning couples care little or nothing about the interests of the women whose services they contract. Such couples, they insist, limit the surrogate mother's freedom, stipulating what she may eat or drink, prescribing with whom she may have sex and when, and forbidding her to abort or not abort depending on the condition of the fetus. In addition, they jeopardize the surrogate's well-being, requiring her to give up the child no matter how much she loves it. In short, Kantian opponents of surrogacy maintain that commissioning couples treat the surrogate mother like a mere thing: a reproductive container, a human incubator, a hired womb—to be used and then dismissed as an intruder in their lives.

Kantians are no less critical of surrogate mothers than they are of the couples who commission their services. In particular, they claim that the surrogate mother reduces herself to an object in order to improve her financial status, or to enhance her self-image as a "giver," or to increase the happiness of the infertile couple for whom childlessness is an intolerable state of affairs. In order to satisfy these inclinations, some more noble than others, the surrogate mother sells or inappropriately gives away "services" that self-respecting persons safeguard for those to whom they supposedly belong—for example, a spouse. Thus, Kantians argue that when a prostitute sells her sexual services to a patron or gives them to a man to whom she is not married, she becomes his plaything, his instrument of desire fulfillment. Similarly, they argue that when a surrogate mother sells or gives her reproductive services to a commissioning couple, she becomes the couple's incubator, their instrument of desire fulfillment. What is more, the surrogate mother, like the prostitute, sells what a person cannot sell without becoming alienated from the deepest grounds of his or her being. One adamant opponent of surrogacy makes the point that when commissioning couple William and Elizabeth Stern paid surrogate mother Mary Beth Whitehead, they were paying her "to experience maternal love, the forced cessation of that love, and a whole range of feelings in the process that are not ordinarily put up for sale."[5] What the Sterns were buying and what Whitehead was selling was supposedly not only Baby M but also Mary Beth Whitehead's emotions, and the "transaction fell through because neither buyer nor seller had a grasp of the commodity in the first place."[6]

Although Kantian opponents of surrogacy could and sometimes do fault the commissioning couple for treating the intended child as a mere means to meeting their "need" for happiness, they reserve their harshest words of condemnation for the surrogate mother. In their view, when a woman agrees to procreate a child with the intention to abdicate personal responsibility for it, she treats the child more like a thing than a person. Herbert Krimmel makes a similar point when he states: "The procreator should desire the child for its own sake, and not as a means to attaining some other end. Even though one of the ends may be stated altruistically as an attempt to bring happiness to an infertile couple, the child is still being used by the surrogate. She creates it not because she desires it, but because she desires something from it."[7] According to Kantians, then, for anyone to bring a child to term with *no* desire for a personal relationship with him or her—"I'm *just* an incubator carrying someone else's baby"—is to change the way children in general are viewed. They become commodities—to be bought and sold, taken and given.

The Nonfeminist Moral Case for Surrogacy

Before offering their positive case for surrogacy, nonfeminist advocates of surrogacy seek to rebut some of the main natural-law and Kantian arguments against it. First, they note that if the line between the "natural" and the "artificial" separates moral from immoral practices, then natural-law theorists should also forbid intravenous feeding, for example. Yet, inconsistently, natural-law theorists do not condemn physicians who feed sick persons intravenously on the grounds that the natural way for people to eat is to ingest their food orally. The fact that nourishment is the essential goal of eating does not mean that it is wrong, under all circumstances, for persons to get nourishment without ingesting their food orally. Analogously, the fact that procreation is the essential goal of sexual intercourse does not mean that it is wrong, under all circumstances, for persons to procreate without sexual intercourse.

Second, nonfeminist advocates of surrogacy observe that a surrogate mother does not necessarily jeopardize the marital relationship of the couple who hire her. She intrudes on them only as much as they permit her to. These advocates also observe that the situation of a child who is collaboratively reproduced by a commissioning couple and a surrogate mother is not that much different from the situation of a child who is adopted. In both instances the child might have questions about the identity of his or her biological mother, and in both instances the child's psychological well-being will largely depend on how sensitively the rearing parents respond to his or her questions.

Third, nonfeminist advocates of surrogacy insist that it is not necessarily disrespectful of persons. For every commissioning couple who cares nothing about the surrogate mother's interests there is a commissioning couple who is highly solicitous about the surrogate mother's freedom and well-being. Indeed, in some cases, commissioning couples even agree to give the surrogate mother a role in rearing their collaboratively reproduced child, including joint or limited custody, visitation, or child support.[8] To say that such couples are treating the surrogate mother merely as a reproductive vessel is to fly in the face of reality.

Fourth, nonfeminist advocates of surrogacy doubt that all or even most surrogate mothers treat themselves disrespectfully. They claim that when a woman sells her sexual or reproductive services, she does not lose control over her personhood any more than does the athlete who sells his muscle power to a football team or the teacher who sells her intellectual power to a university. Although prostitutes and surrogate mothers accept certain limits on their freedom and take certain risks, they do so in exchange for money; and, provided that they receive fair payment for the sexual or reproductive services they render, they are no more deserving of condemnation than are the people who sell their brawn or brain services for money.[9] Moreover, even if it is true that prostitutes and surrogate mothers sell their spiritual emotions together with their physical services, such sales do not necessarily threaten their personhood. All kinds of workers sell emotional labor, the kind of labor that Arlie Hochschild defines as "the management of feeling to create a publicly observable facial and bodily display."[10] According to this definition, flight attendants, development officers, and sympathetic psychiatrists are selling their emotions, and yet society does not view these professionals as striking a Faustian bargain in which they exchange the essence of their souls for cash.

Finally, nonfeminist advocates of surrogacy insist that the motivations of an infertile couple who commission the services of a surrogate mother are not really different from the motivations of a fertile couple who can procreate without the assistance of a surrogate mother. In both cases, the people who intend to rear the child very much desire the child for its own sake.

Having addressed each of the specific natural-law and Kantian arguments against surrogacy, nonfeminist advocates of this practice use a combination of utilitarian and contractarian reasoning to construct a positive case on its behalf. First, they argue that the aggregate benefits of surrogacy far outweigh its harms. At the same time, they admit that surrogacy is not without risks. Surrogate mothers assume the same kind of risks that all pregnant women do (e.g., fatigue, nausea, weight gain, discomfort, skin stretching, insomnia, altered or suspended sexual activity, miscarriage, cesarean section, and labor pains). In addition, they risk bonding with a child whom they might be forced to relinquish, or being *forced* to assume parental responsibilities for a child they never intended to rear, or simply not being paid for their services. Similarly, commissioning couples risk falling prey to blackmailing surrogate mothers who threaten abortion unless their fee is substantially increased, or to reneging surrogate mothers who suddenly protest that they cannot go through with the "deal." Finally, the children who are produced as the result of surrogacy arrangements are at some physical and psychological risk. Depending on how vested a surrogate mother is in the welfare of the fetus she carries, she may or may not take proper care of her body during pregnancy. If she drinks, smokes, or takes drugs, the child may be born in far worse condition than it would have been born otherwise. Moreover, like many adopted children, many children born to surrogate mothers will wonder why their birth mothers relinquished them for other people to love and rear. Far worse than this type of psychological harm, however, would be the feelings of rejection experienced by the child who, due to some physical or mental defect, is wanted neither by the commissioning couple nor by the surrogate mother.

Having honestly acknowledged the possible harms of surrogacy, nonfeminist advocates claim that its benefits to the surrogate mother are clear. Like sperm and egg donors, surrogate mothers have the option to sell or give away their reproductive services to people who need them. They also get an opportunity to do something worthwhile; indeed, many surrogate mothers report that there is nothing quite so wonderful as being able to give the "gift of life" to a commissioning couple.[11] Even clearer than surrogacy's benefits to surrogate mothers, claim these advocates, are surrogacy's benefits to commissioning couples. Anyone who has ever known an infertile couple who have tried virtually everything to have a child can imagine how happy that couple must feel when they are at last able to hold their child in their arms. Clearest of all, the advocates insist, are surrogacy's benefits to collaboratively reproduced children. Since so many people went through such trouble to bring them into the world, these children know they are "excruciatingly wanted" children[12]—precisely the kind of children who will be loved.

In weighing surrogacy's harms against its benefits, nonfeminist advocates note that most of the harms associated with surrogate motherhood can be eliminated or at least substantially ameliorated with clear legal remedies, adequate medical screening, and sensitive psychological counseling. Lawyer John A. Robertson suggests that until regulatory legislation is passed, surrogate brokers should make sure the women they recruit are well informed and counseled about both the risks and the benefits of surrogacy. Surrogate brokers, he recommends, should emphasize how "disappointing and difficult" surrogacy can be for some women. They should also make it clear to the women they recruit that their primary allegiance as surrogate brokers is to the commissioning couple, not the surrogate mother. Finally, Robertson insists that for the benefit of the surrogate mother as well as the commissioning couple, surrogate brokers should screen prospective surrogates for psychological and physical problems.[13] If all these precautions are taken, Robertson claims confidently, few surrogacy arrangements will go amiss.

Nonfeminist advocates of surrogacy bolster their utilitarian arguments with contractarian arguments. Not surprisingly, Robertson is among the main articulators of the latter. In this connection, he describes surrogacy as a form of "collaborative reproduction"—that is, reproduction that requires more than the energies, efforts, and endowments of one married couple.[14] Throughout the ages, according to Robertson, collaborative reproduction has assumed many forms, inasmuch as "children have often been reared by genetically unrelated stepparents, wet nurses, nannies, babysitters, and other surrogates.[15]

What distinguishes current forms of collaborative reproduction from past forms, says Robertson, is that we now have the possibility of breaking the line not only between bearing and rearing a child (as in adoption) but also between begetting and bearing a child. Another distinction is that the surrogates of the past—at least the wet nurses, nannies, and babysitters—made no legal, and perhaps no moral, claims on their charges. For example, when their charges reached school age, nannies did not insist on their right to remain in a relationship with them. Speculating that, just because the nannies of old made no parental claims, it does not follow that today's surrogate mothers should follow suit, Robertson claims that any full-blown defense of surrogacy as collaborative reproduction should spell out the proper parental rights and responsibilities of each and every collaborator.

In addition to pointing out that surrogacy is simply one way for more than two people to share in the process of procreation, Robertson highlights its contractual nature. To the degree that surrogacy involves the noncoerced exercise of free choice and does not pose substantial harm to the consenting parties, it is morally justified, he believes. Indeed, as he sees it, "[t]he morality of surrogate mothering depends on how the duties and responsibilities of the role are carried out, rather than on the mere fact that a couple produces a child with the aid of a collaborator."[16] Provided that the commissioning couple and the surrogate mother enter into and conclude their negotiations freely, and provided that these negotiations result in a fair contract, there is no reason to raise more moral concerns about a surrogacy arrangement than about, say, a freely chosen and fair private adoption arrangement.

Faced with the objection that surrogacy is an unjust practice because only rich, infertile couples can afford to pay a surrogate mother her $10,000 fee plus $15,000 worth of associated expenses, Robertson replies that limited accessibility is not unjust to poor, infertile couples because it does not leave them worse off than they were before.[17] To argue that rich, infertile couples should not be allowed to employ surrogate mothers because poor, infertile couples cannot afford them is like arguing that rich, sick people should not be allowed to spend their money on artificial hearts since poor, sick people cannot afford them. Justice, implies Robertson, does not have as one of its axioms the rule that if everyone cannot have something, then no one can. Admittedly, he concedes, a state of affairs in which the parental dreams of the rich but not the poor can come true is less than ideal. Nonetheless, the solution to this dilemma is not that the state should outlaw surrogacy but, rather, that the state should determine whether it has the responsibility to subsidize surrogacy so that poor as well as rich infertile couples can make use of it.

Nonfeminist Legal Remedies for Surrogacy

Among the legal remedies that nonfeminist bioethicists have suggested for surrogacy are the following: (1) nonenforcement of surrogacy contracts, (2) criminalization of commercial surrogacy, (3) enforcement of surrogacy contracts, and (4) consideration of surrogacy as a form of adoption. Opponents of surrogacy support either remedy (1) or remedy (2), whereas advocates of surrogacy endorse either remedy (3) or remedy (4).

Refusal to Enforce Surrogacy Contracts

In the original Baby M case, District Judge Harvey R. Sorkow ruled that it was in Baby M's best interests to enforce the terms of the contract that commissioning couple William and Elizabeth Stern had made with surrogate mother Mary Beth Whitehead to gestate their child for $10,000. But in overturning Judge Sorkow's decision, the New Jersey supreme court ruled that contracts for surrogate mothers are against public policy. This decision was in keeping with the view of some nonfeminist opponents of surrogacy: Since these contracts supposedly lead to the exploitation of financially needy women and the selling of babies,[18] the state, in enforcing them, would significantly harm some of its most vulnerable citizens.

To say that a surrogacy contract is unenforceable is to say that if the contract is breached by either the surrogate mother or the commissioning couple, the state would leave the parties as it finds them. It would not help them resolve their dispute. Thus, for example, if the commissioning couple fail to pay the surrogate mother her fee, the state would not help her collect it. Or if the commissioning couple refuse to take the child from the surrogate mother, the state would not force them to do so. Instead, the state would require the surrogate mother either to maintain her parental relationship with the child or to put the child up to adoption. In the former case, she may be entitled to child support from the genetic father; and, in the latter case, she may be entitled to his financial assistance.[19] Alternatively, if the surrogate mother refuses to take care of her health during the pregnancy, or if she threatens to abort or actually does abort the fetus, the commissioning couple would not be able to sue her for damages. Moreover, if the surrogate mother refuses to give the child to the commissioning couple, they would not be able to secure custody of the child based on the *contract* they made with the surrogate mother. To be sure, they might be able to secure full or joint custody based on their *genetic* relationship to the child. However, should a court rule that, genetics not withstanding, it is in the best interests of the child to be in the full custody of its birth mother, the commissioning couple would have to content themselves with whatever visitation rights the court awards them.[20]

Criminalization of Surrogacy Arrangements

Other nonfeminist opponents of surrogacy maintain that if it is a crime to exploit financially needy women and to sell babies, then it is not enough for the state to refuse to enforce surrogacy contracts; it must take the further step of criminalizing the making of such arrangements. In general, those who support a ban on at least commercial surrogacy favor statutes such as the United Kingdom's Surrogacy Arrangements Act. Passed by the House of Lords, this statute imposes criminal sanctions not on those who provide or utilize surrogacy services but, rather, on those who serve as the "middlemen" in commercial surrogacy negotiations. Accordingly, lawyers, physicians, and social workers are subject to fines and/or imprisonment if they "(a) initiate or take part in any negotiations with a view to the making of a surrogacy arrangement, (b) offer or agree to negotiate the making of a surrogacy arrangement, or (c) compile any information with a view to its ease in making, or negotiating the making of, surrogacy arrangements."[21] In addition, publishers, directors, and managers of newspapers, periodicals, and telecommunications systems are subject to fines and/or imprisonment if they accept advertisements reading "wombs for hire" or "couple willing to pay royalty for host womb."[22]

The authors of the Surrogacy Arrangements Act justified it largely on the basis of the principle of legal moralism, according to which a person's liberty may be restricted to prevent immoral conduct on his or her part. They proclaimed in the manner of Kant that

> [e]ven in compelling medical circumstances the danger of exploitation of one human being by another appears to the majority of us far to outweigh the potential benefits, in almost every case. That people would treat others as a means to their own ends, however desirable the consequences, must always

> be liable to moral objection. Such treatment of one person by another becomes positively exploitative when financial interests are involved.[23]

Though not inclined to criminalize behavior because it violates a widely held *moral* principle, several U.S. states have nonetheless banned or proposed to ban surrogacy on the grounds that, whether immoral or not, it is harmful. Among these states is Michigan, which passed a law making it a felony to serve as a "surrogate broker"—the penalty being a maximum $50,000 fine and five-year imprisonment.[24]

Enforcing Surrogacy Agreements Via Contract Law

Unconvinced that surrogacy exploits financially needy women or that it is a form of baby selling, many nonfeminist advocates of surrogacy have urged the state to view disputes between surrogate mothers and commissioning couples simply as breaches of contract. The surrogate mother can breach her agreement with the commissioning couple (1) by failing to abort or not to abort the fetus at their instruction; (2) by negligently, recklessly, knowingly, or purposely harming the fetus; or (3) by refusing to give up the child at birth. Conversely, the commissioning couple can breach their agreement with the surrogate mother (1) by failing to pay her the agreed-on fee, (2) by failing to honor their agreement to let her share in the child's rearing, or (3) by refusing to accept the child upon its birth. Regardless of which party breaches their mutual agreement, however, supporters of the contract approach to surrogacy believe that either a specific performance remedy or a damages remedy can adequately address such breaches.

A specific performance remedy forces the parties to a contract to fulfill its terms in an effort to eliminate the kind of uncertainty that characterizes informal human arrangements. Uncertainty is always difficult for human beings to handle, particularly when their most precious dreams are at stake. For a commissioning couple it is agonizing to wait nine months for a child without knowing whether the surrogate mother will finally relinquish her or him to them, just as it is agonizing for a surrogate mother to gestate a child for nine months without knowing whether the commissioning couple will accept the child upon "delivery."

Significantly, specific performance is not ordinarily the preferred way to enforce personal service contracts. For example, if a comedian refuses to come on stage and perform his act, no court is going to force him to do so. Under such circumstances, the comedian is unlikely to be very funny. Analogously, a commissioning couple would achieve less than optimal results if they try to force a surrogate mother to have an abortion, to *not* have an abortion, and/or to follow a list of onerous medical instructions. As supporters of the contract approach point out, however, because children are separable from their surrogate mothers in a way that comedians' funniness is not separable from comedians, specific performance might still be effectively used to force a balking surrogate mother to relinquish the child she agreed to gestate for the commissioning couple. Since she has contributed at most the same amount of genetic material as the genetic father has, and since genetic fathers "unwillingly deprived of access to their children suffer from feelings of regret and self-betrayal akin to those that contracted mothers feel when similarly deprived,"[25] the promises the surrogate mother knowingly and willingly made to the contracting couple arguably outweigh her interests in raising the child she was contracted only to gestate. Similarly, because children are indeed separable from their surrogate mothers, balking commissioning couples can be forced to take the child for whom they contracted—provided, of course, that it is indeed theirs. (One very unfortunate surrogacy dispute involved the birth of a retarded child. The man whose sperm was supposedly used in the artificial insemination insisted that he could not be the genetic father. The surrogate mother, in disagreement, insisted that she had followed all the stipulations of the surrogacy contract and should not be expected to assume parental responsibilities for the child. Eventually, blood tests established that the genetic father of the child was the surrogate mother's husband; and although her pregnancy resulted from conditions caused by the surrogacy arrangement, she and her husband were assigned parental responsibilities for the child.)[26]

Some supporters of the contract approach doubt that specific performance is the appropriate remedy for breach of a surrogacy arrangement. As they see it, this remedy does little to prevent or address the harms that hurt people most—namely, being deprived of the opportunity to play a parental role in the life of a child with whom one has bonded, or being forced to play a parental role in the life of a child one never intended to rear, or being the child no one wants.

For the foregoing reason, these advocates of surrogacy support a damages approach to prevent or address breaches of contract. A damages remedy permits parties to a surrogacy contract either to honor the contract, on the one hand, or to breach the contract and compensate the aggrieved party with a cash settlement, on the other. The argument for this remedy is that it avoids situations that most humane persons want to avoid—namely, forcing a surrogate mother to have or not have an abortion or to accept unwanted medical treatment, pulling a baby out of a surrogate mother's arms, or giving a baby to a commissioning couple who no longer desire to rear him or her. Presumably, the fact that they would have to pay out considerable monetary damages deters parties to a surrogacy contract from violating its terms on a whim. Were a damages approach to surrogacy contracts adopted, either abortion or failure to surrender the child could give rise to tort claims for intentional emotional distress or outrageous conduct, or for wrongful death.[27] Birth defects arising from negligent maternal care could also pose issues of liability. Negligence might be the result of a failure of the surrogate mother to seek proper medical supervision as contracted, or of the failure to properly limit physical activities. With respect to the commissioning couple, their failure to pay the surrogate mother's expenses and fee would be easily resolvable through damages. Moreover, in the event that the commissioning couple refused to accept the child after birth, the surrogate mother could sue the sperm donor for child support or for the costs associated with putting up a child for adoption.

Critics of the damages approach claim that this means of enforcing surrogacy contracts lacks several practical advantages. Since surrogate mothers are generally less wealthy than commissioning couples, they would have difficulty paying the damages assessed against them; and, even if they are able to pay these damages, the money would not adequately compensate the commissioning couple for the loss of the child whom they planned to rear. Likewise, money would not adequately compensate a surrogate mother who is left to rear a child she never intended to parent. For that matter, it is not clear just how theoretically sound the damages approach is. If pregnant women have the right to bodily integrity, including the right to engage in a wide range of activities, to seek or refuse medical treatment, and to abort or not abort their fetuses, then commissioning couples may lose more suits than they win against surrogate mothers. Their surrogacy contracts would simply be ruled null and void.

Assimilating Surrogacy Arrangements into Adoption Law

Owing to the weaknesses of the contract approach, some nonfeminist supporters of surrogacy favor adoption as a way of regulating it. In their view, since there is little difference between making arrangements to adopt a mother's baby shortly after she knows she has conceived and making arrangements to adopt a surrogate mother's baby shortly before it has been conceived, the same rules that govern adoption could also govern surrogacy arrangements.[28] Current adoption rules permit payment, but only for the pregnant women's reasonable medical expenses. They also provide for a "change of heart" period. The adopting couple may pull out of the negotiations at any time before or, lately, even after the adoption papers are signed;[29] and the biological mother has several days, weeks, or even months to decide whether she really wants to relinquish her child.[30]

According to its supporters, an adoption approach to surrogacy harmonizes with the long-standing legal view that the woman who gives birth to a child is the child's mother. In this connection, lawyer George Annas argues that whether or not the surrogate mother is genetically related to the child she bears, the state should recognize her as the child's legal mother, for several reasons. First, she is definitely present at the birth. Second, her identity is easy to determine. Third, she is there to care for the child.[31] Unless it can be proven that a surrogate mother is truly unfit, he says, she should be awarded sole custody of the child. In Annas's estimation, such a policy is in the child's best interest, since it leaves no question as to who is the custodial parent of the child. (Incidentally, Annas also recommends that if the surrogate mother has a husband, he should be regarded as the child's legal father.)

To the objection that to give custodial advantage to the surrogate mother is unfair to the commissioning couple, supporters of the adoption approach reply that the disappointment of the couple would be no greater than that sustained by prospective adoptive parents when a biological mother decides to keep her child after all. From the very beginning of the adoption negotiations, prospective adoptive parents know that if the birth mother decides to end these proceedings, they will have to go home to an empty nursery. Thus, provided that a commissioning couple knows from the outset that the surrogate mother has the right to void the contract they made with her, no injustice is done to them.

To the further objection that the adoption and surrogacy cases are nonanalogous because at least one and possibly both members of the commissioning couple is/are the genetic parent(s) of the child, supporters of the adoption approach reply that genetic linkage is not the determining criterion for parenthood. In their estimation, the fact that a man's sperm or a woman's egg constitutes 50 percent of the genetic material necessary for conception does not make her or him half-owner of any resultant child. Children are not possessions; rather, they are beings with whom relationships can be forged, and at birth the only direct relationship a child has is with the woman who has gestated her or him. All that genetic linkage gives a man or a woman, then, is the limited right to establish a relationship with a particular child, provided that it is in the best interests of the child that such a relationship be forged.

Feminist Bioethical Perspectives on Surrogacy

The Feminist Case Against Surrogacy

Feminist opponents of surrogacy, especially commercial surrogacy, are particularly concerned about the degree to which surrogacy creates harmful relationships among women. As they see it, commercial surrogacy drives wedges between economically privileged women and economically disadvantaged women. Relatively rich women hire relatively poor women to meet their reproductive needs, adding childbearing services to the childrearing services that economically disadvantaged women have traditionally provided to economically privileged women. Equally destructive are the rifts that surrogacy, whether commercial or altruistic, creates between childbegetters, childbearers, and childrearers. According to Gena Corea, reproduction is being segmented as if it were simply a form of production. Perhaps in the future, she cautions, no one woman will beget, bear, and rear a child. Rather, genetically superior women will beget embryos in vitro; strong-bodied women will carry these test-tube babies to term; and sweet-tempered women will rear these newborns from infancy to adulthood.[32]

Another deep concern of feminist opponents of surrogacy is that it may be setting the stage for the commodification of children. Over the years, they fear, acquiring a baby could come to be viewed as no more special than acquiring an equally costly purchase—say, a new car. Parents' love for their children would no longer be unconditional; rather, it would depend on whether their children were "good" products. In the worst-case scenario, parents might trade in their "defective models" for the "perfect models" that science and technology have to offer. Such a view of children is particularly distressing to those feminists who believe that human relationships are not something one simply takes or leaves depending on one's preferences. In this connection, philosophers Hilde and James Nelson argue that when parents bring a child into existence, they "create a vulnerability."[33] Having created a person with a set of basic needs, one parent, for example, may not let another parent, however willing, assume full responsibility for rearing that person. Not one but both parents owe a "debt . . . *to the child*."[34] It may be okay with Mom if Dad does not spend any time with Junior, but it may not be okay with Junior if Dad absents himself from his life. Similarly, even if the commissioning couple is only too happy to assume full parental responsibility for the child, it is still the surrogate mother's job to help rear her child unless she is unable to do so. It makes no difference if the surrogate mother believes that the commissioning couple will meet her child's needs, for, as the Nelsons explain, the surrogate mother "herself is the only person she can bring to *perform* the required services."[35] One parent is not necessarily as good as another and certainly is not the same as another.

In addition to asserting that surrogacy leads to harmful relationships among women and/or between parents and children, feminist opponents of surrogacy typically argue that when a woman consents to sell her reproductive services to an infertile couple, her consent is more often the product of economic coercion than of free choice. These feminists note that most surrogate mothers, like most prostitutes, are much poorer than the people to whom they sell their services. Unable to get a decent job, a woman may be driven to sell her body if it is the only thing she has that anyone seems to value enough to buy. But to say that a woman "chooses" to do this, claim feminist opponents of surrogacy, is to say that when a woman is forced to choose between being poor and being exploited, she may choose being exploited as the lesser of the two evils. Although some surrogacy agencies refuse to accept indigent women into their program,[36] others actually prefer poor women—for the reason that unemployed women or women on welfare, especially if they are single mothers, are highly unlikely to forsake their surrogacy fee in order to add yet another child to their family.[37] John Stehura, president of the Bionetics Foundation, Inc., an agency that contracts mothers, has even suggested that a surrogate mother can never be poor enough. Since the going rate for surrogate mothers is high even by middle-class American standards, he has urged the surrogacy industry to move either to poverty-stricken parts of the United States, where women are willing to gestate fetuses for one-half the standard fee, or to the Third World, where women are willing to do so for one-tenth the standard fee.[38]

Although many feminist opponents of surrogacy object only to commercial surrogacy, a significant number also take issue with altruistic or gift surrogacy. These latter forms of surrogacy, they insist, involve what philosopher Uma Narayan terms "gender-role exploitation," whereby "the very aspects of 'femininity' used to glorify motherhood—views of women as loving, nurturing, and self-sacrificing—also seem to be deeply involved in motivating women to be surrogates."[39] Indeed, because only women can be gestational mothers, surrogacy often becomes a "compassion trap" for women.[40] Frequently, the call for surrogate mothers is accompanied by images of desperately lonely, tragically unfulfilled infertile couples. Generous women are implored to step forward to give the gift of life to these unfortunate couples, and the fact that approximately one-third of all the women who answer this appeal have either had an abortion or given up a child for adoption strengthens many feminists' suspicion that the desire to assuage past grief is often what grounds a woman's "choice" to be a surrogate mother.[41]

The Feminist Case for Surrogacy

In contrast to feminist critics of surrogacy, feminist advocates defend it on two grounds. First, they claim that, to the degree women's liberation depends on women having the same educational, political, and economic opportunities and rights as men, women should be permitted to use whatever reproductive technologies they need in order to live as men's equals. Preventing a woman from working for payment as a surrogate mother, or from hiring a surrogate mother, violates her reproductive freedom just as much as does preventing her from using birth control or from having an abortion.

Second, feminist advocates of surrogacy note that it is just as likely to unite women as to divide them. For every surrogacy arrangement that fails, they insist, there are dozens that succeed. Reports of surrogate mothers living in close proximity to the couples who commissioned their services and rearing with them the child they collaboratively reproduced are not altogether unusual.[42] Such good news bolsters the claim that surrogacy can be viewed not as a male-manipulated specialization and segmentation of the female reproductive process but as a matter of women getting together to bring new life into the world. As in the case of the postmenopausal South African mother who carried her daughter's in-vitro fetus to term, the two women achieved something that neither of them could have achieved alone.[43]

Feminist advocates of surrogacy reason about mothering in much the same way that Marge Piercy does in her science-fiction novel *Woman on the Edge of Time*.[44] Piercy sets her utopian tale within the story of a multiply disadvantaged woman named Connie Ramos. Connie is a middle-aged, lower-class Chicana with a history of what society describes as mental illness and violent behavior. She has been trying desperately to support herself and her daughter, Angelina, on a pittance. One day, when Connie is near the point of exhaustion, she loses her temper and hits Angelina too hard. As a result of this outburst, Connie is judged an unfit mother and her daughter is taken away from her. Depressed and despondent, but also very angry, Connie is committed by her family to a mental hospital, where she is selected as a human research subject for brain-control experiments. Just when things could get no worse, Connie is transported by a woman named Luciente to a future world called Mattapoisett, where women are not defined in terms of reproductive functions and in which both men and women delight in rearing children.

What makes Piercy's future world plausible is artificial reproduction. In Mattapoisett, babies are born from what is termed the brooder. Eggs are fertilized in vitro with male sperm in a way that preserves a full range of racial, ethnic, and personality types, and then gestated within an artificial placenta. Unable to comprehend why Mattapoisett women have rejected the experience that meant the most to her—namely, the physical gestating, birthing, and nursing of a child—Connie is initially repelled. She see the embryos in the brooder as being "all in a sluggish row . . . like fish in the aquarium."[45] Not only does she regard these embryos as less than human, she also pities each one of them for not having a mother willing to carry him or her to term.

Eventually, Connie learns from Luciente that the people of Mattapoisett did not easily give up biological reproduction for technological reproduction. They did so only when they realized that the loss of biological reproduction was the price that had to be paid for the elimination of sexism as well as racism and classism:

> It was part of women's long revolution. When we were breaking all the old hierarchies. Finally there was that one thing we have to give up too, the only power we have had, in return for no power for anyone. The original production: the power to give birth. Cause as long as we were biologically enchained, we'd never be equal. And males never would be humanized to be loving and tender. So we all become mothers. Every child has three. To break the nuclear bonding.[46]

Thus, as a result of women's relinquishment of their exclusive power to give birth, the original paradigm for power relations is destroyed and everyone in Mattapoisett is in a position to reconstitute human relationships in ways that defy the hierarchical ideas of better-worse, higher-lower, stronger-weaker, and, especially, dominant-submissive.

In Mattapoisett individuals possess neither private property nor their own genetic children. And the children themselves are viewed not as the possessions of their biological mothers and fathers to be brought into this world in their parents' image and likeness and reared according to their idiosyncratic values but, rather, as precious human resources for the entire community, to be treasured on account of their uniqueness. Moreover, each child is reared by three "co-mothers" (one man and two women, or two men and one woman), who in turn are assisted by "kidbinders," a group of individuals who excel at mothering. In short, childbearing and childrearing are communal efforts, with each child moving between large-group experiences at child-care centers and small-group experiences in the separate dwellings of each of her or his co-mothers. Initially, Connie doubts that Mattapoisett's system for begetting, bearing, and rearing children is all it claims to be; she wonders whether co-mothers and kidbinders *really* love the children they are rearing. Eventually, however, she decides that technological reproduction is superior to biological reproduction since it results in a type of mothering that is genuinely unselfish because it is totally shared.

Feminist advocates of surrogacy maintain that this arrangement could easily develop into a paradigm not only for collaborative reproduction but also for collaborative parenting. In the ideal, the commissioning couple and the surrogate mother would know and like each other well before they decided to have a child together. Falling short of this ideal, the commissioning couple and the surrogate mother could forge agreements spelling out their respective parental rights and responsibilities subsequent to their child's birth. They could intentionally decide to create a new kind of family.

Feminist Legal Remedies for Surrogacy

Nonenforcement of Surrogacy Arrangements

Although most feminists seconded the New Jersey supreme court's concerns about surrogacy, few feminists support a "hands-off" policy with respect to surrogacy arrangements. Nonfeminist opponents as well as advocates of surrogacy believe that the state must do something to regulate surrogacy if it decides not to criminalize this practice. Absent some form of state monitoring, they argue, profit-making surrogacy agencies will be tempted to do whatever they can to provide their paying clients with an "ideal" surrogate mother as quickly as possible lest they take their business somewhere else. Their tendency, then, will be to minimize the risks and exaggerate the benefits of surrogacy. Little effort will be made to secure true informed consent from the surrogate mother or to remind her that her rights to privacy and bodily integrity entitle her to refuse medical treatments as well as to terminate the pregnancy. Similarly, little effort will be made to prepare either the surrogate mother or the commissioning couple for the kind of trauma they might experience, if, for example, the surrogate mother refuses to relinquish the child.

Currently, states that do not enforce surrogacy contracts handle disputes between commissioning couples and surrogate mothers as custody disputes. And since U.S. courts typically award custody to those adults most likely to serve the "best interests" of the child, the mere fact that the surrogate mother has agreed to relinquish the child at birth is often used as evidence that she is not suited to rear her child. Indeed, in the famous Whitehead/Stern dispute over Baby M, Judge Sorkow observed that the day surrogate mother Mary Beth Whitehead signed her name on the dotted line, she proved her "unfitness" as a mother.[47] Moreover, even if such evidence of "unfitness" was not permitted in a court of law, the surrogate mother would probably still fare worse in a custody dispute than the commissioning couple would. U.S. courts generally give custody to the parent(s) who can provide the child with a higher economic standard of living. Thus, the fact that surrogate mothers are typically poorer than the couples who commission for their services provides courts with the reason they need to make their Solomonic decision. Finally, in cases where the surrogate mother is not genetically related to the child she gestated, U.S. courts are unlikely to view her gestational relationship to the child as a more significant basis for parental claims than the commissioning couple's genetic and intentional relationship to the child.

For all these reasons, as well as the one cited by Uma Narayan that it may be in children's best interests to maintain relationships with all their parents—genetic, gestational, and social[48]—it may be necessary to reform custody law so that it does not automatically favor the claims of commissioning couples over those of surrogate mothers. In the view of most feminists, only to the extent that such reforms are made will nonenforcement come close to being the correct response to a failed surrogacy agreement. The question then becomes whether it is truly in the best interests of children for them to be in the joint custody of *all* of their parents. If each of them is child-centered enough to overcome her or his desire to be the children's *chief* or *main* parent, then all will go well. However, if the parents are basically unable to cooperate in their children's rearing, it becomes difficult to argue that the courts have done children a favor by giving them more rather than fewer parents.

Criminalization of Surrogacy If It Is Commercial in Nature

Some feminists believe that criminalization is the appropriate legal remedy for surrogacy, but only in cases of so-called commercial surrogacy. From their standpoint, there are good reasons to believe that commercial surrogacy harms women (and children) egregiously enough that the law should ban it.

Conversely, those feminists who are opposed to criminalizing surrogacy even in its commercial form provide several arguments for not doing so. In the first place, they claim, it is not fair to punish the agencies that bring surrogate mothers and commissioning couples together without also punishing the surrogate mothers and commissioning couples themselves. Uma Narayan makes a similar point: that if surrogacy is harmful enough to merit criminalization, then everyone who participates in it is a criminal. She views as extremely weak the arguments offered in defense of exempting commissioning couples and surrogate mothers from criminal penalties:

> It should not matter that, in Mary Gibson's words, parents "act in response to personal vulnerability, pain and desperation": such factors are not usually grounds for refraining from punishing those culpable of premeditated criminal conduct. The argument that criminal penalties should not apply to parents because it is not in the best interests of the child is equally problematic, since the effects on children of having parents incarcerated are not usually grounds for withholding criminal penalties on parents.[49]

Feminists opposed to criminalizing commercial surrogacy also think it is unfair to target commercial surrogacy without also targeting gift or altruistic surrogacy. Just because a surrogate mother refuses monetary compensation for her services from a friend or relative, it does not follow that she has not been exploited. Indeed, according to Narayan, families are not necessarily havens in an otherwise heartless world. She observes that cases like that of Alejandra Muñoz confirm that family members can be even more exploitative than surrogate brokers. Muñoz's relatives told her that the embryo she conceived would be flushed into the womb of an infertile cousin. When this failed to happen, Muñoz wanted to terminate the pregnancy, but her infertile cousin's family threatened to expose her as an illegal alien and forcibly confined her to the family home until she gave birth.[50]

Finally, feminists opposed to criminalizing surrogacy, whether in its altruistic or commercial form, suspect that a ban on it may be unconstitutional. If the equal protection clause, the due process clause, and the right to privacy protect infertile as well as fertile couples' procreative rights, then it would seem that infertile couples have a right to use surrogate mothers' services if the only way they can have a child genetically related to them is through this means.[51]

Enforcing Surrogacy Through Contract Law

Many feminist advocates of surrogacy believe that the so-called contract approach is the one most likely to further women's interests in becoming men's equals. In fact, they stress that surrogacy contracts are an excellent way "to illustrate that childbearing and childrearing are two quite distinct human functions and that childrearing need and should not be assigned exclusively to the woman who bears a child."[52] Just because a woman gives birth to a child, it does not follow that she is necessarily the most willing, able, and ready person to rear that child. Provided that she makes sure someone else assumes partial or full responsibility for rearing the child, she does nothing morally wrong by sharing or forsaking her parental rights to rear the child herself.

Feminist advocates of surrogacy contracts insist that it is misguided to view surrogacy as a form of baby-selling. Instead, they insist, it is a form of collaborative reproduction in which the woman who agrees to gestate the child gives or sells her reproductive services to a married couple (or, less frequently, to an unmarried couple or individual) who plan to assume full parental responsibilities for rearing the child. Since the law ordinarily regards the woman who gives birth to a child as the child's mother, the surrogate mother gives up her "parental right to have a relationship with the child,"[53] and the woman, who alone or together with her spouse plans to rear the child, must adopt him or her. The man, who alone or together with his spouse plans to rear the child, must also adopt the child, but only if he is not the genetic father.

Feminist advocates of surrogacy contracts also claim that if people are free to sell or give their gametes to others, they should be equally free to sell or give their gestational services to others. If an infertile couple needs the gestational services of a surrogate mother who requires a fee for her services, then it would seem that the state must permit commercial as well as altruistic surrogacy since, as John Robertson has noted, "paying surrogates . . . is probably necessary if infertile couples are to obtain surrogacy services."[54] Moreover, according to Carmel Shalev, banning the sale of procreative services is likely to "reactivate and reinforce the state's power to define what constitutes legitimate and illegitimate reproduction," whereas allowing payment is likely to "recognize a woman's legal authority to make decisions regarding the exercise of her reproductive capacity."[55]

Whether a surrogacy arrangement is commercial or altruistic, feminist advocates of surrogacy contracts caution that not every surrogacy contract is valid or in women's best interests as childbearers. In their estimation, surrogate mothers are not bound by the terms of exploitative contracts that violate women's rights to privacy and bodily integrity. On the contrary, any contract presented to a surrogate mother for her signature must be worded so as to ensure that she is free (1) to engage in self-chosen activities during pregnancy, (2) to refuse or accept proposed medical treatments during pregnancy and delivery, and (3) to continue or terminate the pregnancy. Moreover, the surrogate mother should not be liable for damages or subject to a lawsuit in the event that the fetus is spontaneously aborted, is delivered stillborn, or is born with defects.[56] Finally, the surrogate mother should be offered a fair fee for her services. Feminist Laura Purdy notes that the standard $10,000 fee paid to surrogate mothers is so small as to be exploitative. She argues that the risks, discomforts, and responsibilities borne by surrogate mothers are worth at least twice as much.[57]

Realizing that surrogacy contracts are indeed weighty ones to sign, feminist advocates of such contracts stress the crucial nature of informed consent. Physicians and psychologists, they insist, should clearly outline to prospective surrogate mothers and commissioning couples all of the physical and psychological risks that attend surrogacy. In particular, they should make certain that the prospective surrogate mother has not been pressured into selling or giving her services to a commissioning couple, since it is the surrogate mother—not the commissioning couple—who puts her health and even life at risk.

Yet for all the importance of informed consent, feminist lawyer Lori Andrews observes that too much of it can be as bad as too little. She notes, for example, that several years ago the city of Akron, Ohio, passed an ordinance requiring physicians to inform women seeking abortions that the fetus is sentient (able to feel pain) and that the abortion procedure is often dangerous.[58] "Speculative" and, in this case, misleading information caused numerous women to change their abortion decisions from "yes" to "no." What concerns Andrews is that, fearing liability suits or worse, some physicians and psychologists will exaggerate the risks that attend surrogacy—especially the risk of having to give up a child one wants to keep. In Andrews's view, it is a mistake to assume that a woman has great difficulty giving up a child to someone else, especially if she deliberately became pregnant in order to provide someone else with a child. Moreover, even if some surrogate mothers do find it heart-wrenching to relinquish the children they have gestated for others, it is in the best interests of women *in general* that they be required to do so. In Andrews's estimation, to permit a surrogate mother to renege on her contract is to perpetuate the notion that women are, after all, ruled by their hormones rather than by their brains. By the same token, according to Marjorie Schultz, women would be portrayed as unjust, compared to men. Specifically, Schultz argues that any biological relationship the surrogate mother has to the child is offset by the intentional relationship the commissioning couple have to the child:

> To ignore the significance of deliberation, purpose and expectation—the capacity to envision and shape the future through intentional choice—is to disregard one of the most distinctive traits that makes us human. It is to disregard crucial differences in moral meaning and responsibility. To disregard such intention with reference to so intimate and significant an activity as prevention and child-rearing is deeply shocking.[59]

In sum, feminist supporters of surrogacy contracts believe that mind should rule over matter, mental intention over biological connection. They also claim that their view is the one actually favored by the general public, including most women. For example, during the Baby M court proceedings, many commentators noted that, for the most part, women as well as men had no sympathy for Mary Beth Whitehead, the surrogate mother. "A deal's a deal!" they said. "She signed the contract, didn't she? She knew what she was doing."[60]Apparently, these people sided with the commissioning couple, whose emotional turmoil and good intentions seemed more compelling to them than those of the surrogate mother herself.

Assimilating Surrogacy into Adoption Law

Some feminist supporters believe that it is best to view surrogacy not as a contractual arrangement but as a form of adoption. In their estimation, it is a mistake to perceive the bonds that some surrogate mothers forge with the fetus during pregnancy as *merely* biological or hormonal. They cite with approval Iris Young's view of pregnancy. According to Young, pregnancy may appear to observers to be "a time of waiting and watching, when nothing happens," but for the pregnant woman "pregnancy has a temporality of movement, growth and change. . . . The pregnant woman experiences herself as a source and participant in a creative process. Though she does not plan and direct it, neither does it merely wash over her; rather, she *is* the process, this change."[61] If it is a mistake to ignore the role of the mind in the procreative process, so too is it a mistake to discount the role of the body. For this reason, feminists who view surrogacy as a form of adoption criticize feminist supporters of surrogacy contracts for speaking as if the relationship between a mother's body and the fetus growing in it was no more "intrinsic" than that between an artificial womb and the fetus that might develop in it.[62] Indeed, claim these adoption advocates, for every surrogate mother who maintains that throughout her whole pregnancy she viewed herself merely as a fetal container, there is a surrogate mother more like the one described by writer Anne Taylor Fleming:

> She had meant to be unfazed, meant to make her parents and friends proud of her generosity, meant to make the couple she had the baby for like her so much that "afterwards" she would be part of their extended family and could watch her son grow up. But none of it, not one piece of that, had come out the right way. Her parents were not particularly proud. The couple did not want her around. And she was not unattached from her son and clearly never would be.[63]

Feminists who view surrogacy as a form of adoption concede that the rules and regulations governing adoption would have to be modified in order to accommodate the unique features of a surrogacy arrangement. However, these adjustments, they insist, would be minimal. As in private adoptions, the surrogate mother would be paid only reasonable medical expenses and the surrogate mother would have a period of time after birth in which to decide whether she really wished to hand over the child to the commissioning couple. Significantly, feminists who view surrogacy as a form of adoption believe that this change-of-heart period should be granted not only to surrogate mothers carrying children who are genetically related to them but also to those carrying children who are *not* genetically related to them. In their estimation, it is the surrogate mother's gestational connection to the child that grounds her parental rights to and responsibilities for the child: What makes a woman a *real* mother is first and foremost not her *genetic* but her *gestational* connection to that child.[64]

Because emphasizing the gestational connection as the source of parental claims is such a radical departure from the traditional legal emphasis on the genetic connection as the source of such claims, feminists who view surrogacy as a form of adoption argue that it is a mistake to stress the genetic connection as the primary factor in determining parental rights and duties. For example, Sara Ann Ketchum notes, first, that as soon as scientists develop gene-splicing and chromosome-splicing techniques, it will be possible to procreate children with enormously complex genetic backgrounds. Who, then, asks Ketchum, will count as the genetic parents of each child? Only the donors who contributed the most genes or chromosomes to the child? Or also those donors who contributed just one less gene or chromosome than the highest donors? Or *all* the donors, no matter how many or how few genes or chromosomes they contributed to the child? After all, had even one gene or chromosome been different, the child in question would not be the same child. Under these circumstances, then, the gestational relationship seems especially significant. Second, says Ketchum, our intuitions suggest that at least in the case of rape, it is implausible to regard genetic connection as conferring parental rights. Third, as some feminists (e.g., Mary O'Brien) insist, men valorize *genetic* fatherhood because there is no such experience as gestational fatherhood. Fourth, notes Ketchum, to identify genetic connection as the essential criterion for parenthood is to suggest that this abstract relationship with a child is more important than such concrete relationships as gestation and child care. Fifth, and finally, observes Ketchum, to stress genetic connection as the essential criterion for parenthood is to imply that adoptive parents are not *real* parents.[65] Bolstering Ketchum's arguments in favor of privileging gestational connection, lawyer George Annas maintains that there are at least two moral reasons why the woman who gestates a child rather than the couple who commissions her services should be legally presumed to have primary parental rights to rear that child. In the first place, because it is the gestational mother and not the commissioning couple who assumes the major responsibility for bringing a new life into the world, she deserves to maintain her relationship with the child unless there is evidence of child abuse on her part.[66] Second, because the gestational mother "will of necessity be present at birth and immediately thereafter to care for the child," designating her the legal or "natural" mother of the child is more likely to protect the child's interests than any alternative arrangement.[67] What makes a person a parent, therefore, is the degree to which that person has shown that her or his commitment to a child is more than a matter of either mere genetic connection or mere intention.

Feminist critics of the adoption approach agree with its supporters that it is wrong to trivialize the gestational connection, as California Judge Parslow did when he equated gestating an embryo with providing daycare or "nanny" services for it.[68] Nonetheless, they insist, it is wrong for feminists to dismiss as entirely irrelevant adults' genetic and/or intentional connections to a child, for at least three reasons. First, many women as well as many men derive comfort from their genealogy—from the fact that they belong to a family who share a physical identity that stretches back toward the past and forward toward the future. Seeing one's physical characteristics reflected in one's children provides a sense of corporeal immortality—a sense that part of one's material as well as psychic identity will live on in a new and different form. Second, when a couple commissions the services of a surrogate mother, their intentions to rear the child are more than *mere* intentions. The fact that they cannot show a "physical" commitment to their future child does not mean their commitment to the child is less serious than that of the surrogate mother. Many commissioning couples start buying baby furniture and baby clothes in advance; some even set up savings accounts for their future children. But all of them spend many hours each day musing about life with these children. Third, and most significantly, the kind of care the gestational mother has provided the child in utero can be readily supplemented and gradually replaced by other caring acts of parental commitment. Although commissioning couples cannot breastfeed the new child, they can bottle-feed, diaper, caress, and comfort him or her. Once the child is born, the gestational mother's nine months of labor can be matched minute for minute by the commissioning couple.

In addition to claiming that it is misguided to automatically privilege gestational connections over genetic and intentional connections, feminist critics of the adoption approach to surrogacy claim that it might not be in women's best interests to overemphasize the importance of the gestational connection. On the one hand, if women want men to spend as much time caring for children as women generally do, then it is probably a mistake to repeatedly remind men that women have a connection to infants that is totally unavailable to men—indeed, a connection that makes men "second-class" parents until sometime after a child's birth. By stressing the importance of the gestational connection, some feminists do convey the impression that women are, by nature, the primary parents of children. On the other hand, feminist critics of the adoption approach to surrogacy caution that it may be *politically* inadvisable for women to emphasize the specialness of the gestational relationship. Lately, national attention has focused on a wide range of issues arising from actions taken by women during pregnancy that may have harmful consequences for their children. Among these issues are (1) medical interventions (such as refusal of a recommended cesarean section or insulin treatment for gestational diabetes), (2) innovative therapies (such as fetal surgery), (3) prenatal diagnosis, and (4) lifestyle concerns (such as alcohol or cocaine use during pregnancy). Since many people already believe that pregnant women have a moral responsibility to care for their fetuses in utero, they would be only too happy to join in feminists' celebration of the gestational connection.[69]

A final consideration raised by some feminist critics of the adoption approach to surrogacy is that surrogacy is not really like adoption after all. According to Phyllis Chesler, adoption should be regarded as a child-centered practice whereby adults, willing to give children the kind of love they need to thrive, take into their homes and hearts *already-existing* children. It should not, insists Chesler, be regarded as an adult-centered practice whereby children are deliberately conceived and brought into existence so that adults can have someone to love them.[70]

Conclusion

Clearly, surrogacy puts special pressure on our decision as to which connections to children—genetic, gestational, intentional—create parental rights and relationships. The growing consensus among feminists, at least, is that *all* of these connections need to be honored. Nevertheless, feminists continue to debate the best way to order these connections in cases where the genetic, gestational, and rearing parents of a child do not wish to coalesce into one family. It is no wonder, then, that ectogenesis (the process of bringing an embryo to full term in an artificial placenta instead of a woman's womb) has struck some feminists as the ideal solution for surrogacy. Provided that personally unidentified eggs as well as sperm from gamete banks are used to create embryos in vitro, no one would be in a special relationship to the child at birth. Absent any genetic or gestational parental claims, fertile and infertile adults wishing to rear children would be on equal footing. They would need only to prove themselves fit for parenthood.

Whatever the advantages of ectogenesis might be, however, most feminists object to the combined "technological fix" of anonymous gamete bank, in-vitro fertilization, and artificial placenta—but not because there is something "unnatural" about this solution for the problems that currently plague surrogacy arrangements. Rather, most feminists object to this "Brave New World" approach to surrogacy arrangements because it lacks *courage*. They believe that we err when we choose the easy option of specifying no initial parent-child relationship over the difficult task of sorting through a complex network of relationships—a network that in surrogacy arrangements includes not only the relationships among genetic, gestational, and intentional parents but also those between fertile and infertile people. In the estimation of most feminists, then, the best solution to harmful surrogacy arrangements is not ectogenesis but a serious effort to address the large social problems that make such arrangements attractive: infertility, limited employment options for working-class women (the group of women from which most contracted mothers come), and labyrinthine laws. Only when these social problems are solved will we be in a position to work toward truly collaborative reproduction—whereby more than two people, able to fully share all parental blessings and burdens, together procreate a child whose best interests are paramount.

9

Feminist and Nonfeminist Perspectives on Genetic Screening, Diagnosis, Counseling, and Therapy

In order to understand the significance of the Human Genome Project, it is important to appreciate what it entails. The term 'human genome' refers to the complete set of genes, approximately 1,000,000 in number, contained in the 46 human chromosomes. In the mid-1980s, scientist Robert Sinsheimer promulgated the view that the entire human genome should be mapped and its genes sequenced. Then, on October 1, 1990, the National Institutes of Health and the Department of Energy began a fifteen-year, $3 billion effort to produce a database listing the location of each gene.[1] Developing a map of the human genome entails the identification of a large number of markers that serve as signposts along the length of each chromosome. These signposts are used as reference points for locating genes, including those that are correlated with genetic diseases, defects, and disorders.

Advocates of the Human Genome Project believe that scientists ought to investigate all aspects of reality, including the mysteries of human existence. They claim that such an investigation is valuable not only in and of itself but in an instrumental sense: The more we understand the mechanisms that determine our identity and behavior, the better we will be able to control them. Besides, there is no way to stop humans' quest for knowledge. Advocates of the Human Genome Project agree with Robert Oppenheimer, one of the developers of the atom bomb, that scientists cannot resist trying to discover more and more about reality: "If you are a scientist, you cannot stop such a thing. If you are a scientist, you believe that it is good to find out how the world works; that it is good to find out what the realities are; that it is good to turn over to mankind at large the greatest possible power to control the world."[2]

Conversely, critics of the Human Genome Project complain that it is not worth the enormous costs since, in their view, it will probably generate more "junk" information than truly helpful information about our genes. Moreover, they caution, even the helpful information generated by the project will not be an unalloyed blessing since it will contribute to the development of major ethical, legal, and social problems. Thus, critics of the Human Genome Project urge scientists to establish ethical rules, legal guidelines, and social norms in advance of the publication of their discoveries in order to avoid their misuse or abuse.

As it happens, advocates as well as critics of the Human Genome Project believe that this initiative should be carefully monitored. Yet no matter how willing scientists are to regulate their genetic research, it is uncertain that they will be able to achieve consensus about the nature of the rules, guidelines, and norms that should regulate the Human Genome Project. Although the twenty-five-nation Council of Europe wishes to negotiate an international bioethics treaty, this organization has not been able to achieve agreement as to how restrictive or permissive genetic research should be.[3] Peter Singer, head of the International Association of Bioethics, doubts that the nations engaged in the Human Genome Project will ever achieve a meeting of the minds. For example, Germany, still haunted by memories of Nazi eugenic programs, has enacted extremely restrictive genetic research and testing laws, whereas the United States, convinced that no one in our government is at all interested in reenacting the horrors of Hitler, is encouraging its genetic scientists to assume a leadership role in the quest to understand the biological composition of human beings.[4]

Nonfeminist Bioethical Perspectives on Genetic Screening, Diagnosis, and Counseling

Genetic Screening and Diagnosis

As society struggles to contend with the economic, political, social, and cultural effects of the Human Genome Project,[5] scientists are fast at work, developing techniques for genetically screening and diagnosing human beings at ever earlier stages in their development. Granted, scientists are currently able to detect only a few disorders in pre-embryos beyond cystic fibrosis and other single-gene diseases such as Duchenne muscular dystrophy, Tay-Sachs disease, hemophilia A and B, betathalassemia, sickle-cell disease, alpha-antitrypsin deficiency, and Lesch-Nyhan syndrome.[6] However, it is only a matter of time before pre-embryos can be screened for a wider variety of genetic diseases and disorders. The millennium will definitely see couples in IVF programs using genetic information to determine which of their pre-embryos to discard and which to implant.[7]

Much more developed than the techniques for preimplantation screening are those for embryo screening within the woman's womb. At present, there are three basic approaches to identifying fetal defects in utero. The first approach involves visualization, which can be either noninvasive (ultrasonography) or invasive (embryoscopy, fetoscopy, and endoscopy). The second approach involves analysis of fetal tissues (amniocentesis, chorionic villus sampling, cordocentesis [fetal blood sampling], skin biopsy, liver biopsy, and muscle biopsy). And the third approach involves laboratory studies (cytogenetics, biochemical analysis, and DNA analysis). All three approaches enable clinicians to determine whether fetuses have certain chromosomal abnormalities, including trisomies such as Down's syndrome, unbalanced translocations, mosaics, and sex-chromosome disorders. They also enable clinicians to determine whether fetuses have certain biochemical abnormalities at the genetic level, including Huntington's disease (HD), sickle-cell anemia, Tay-Sachs disease, and, through alpha-feto protein measurements, neural tube defects.[8] Currently, most health-care practitioners prefer not to offer prenatal diagnosis as a matter of routine to all pregnant women. Instead, they offer it for the following specific reasons: (1) advanced maternal age (age thirty-five and up); (2) a genetic history of abnormalities; (3) membership in an at-risk ethnic group (e.g., Tay-Sachs in Ashkenazi Jews, sickle-cell anemia in African-Americans, and beta-thalassemia in Mediterranean peoples); (4) a family history of infants with birth defects; and (5) multiple miscarriages.[9] In the future, however, health-care practitioners may change their policy if an increasing number of pregnant women demand, for example, that they have a right to know about the genetic condition of their fetus, even if they have no special medical reason for thinking that it is genetically imperiled.

Yet another form of screening, so-called newborn screening, targets babies. The conditions screened for are relatively few. For instance, all fifty U.S. states routinely screen infants for phenylketonuria (PKU), a disorder that, if undetected and untreated by a special diet low in phenylalanine, can lead to severe mental retardation. Other disorders that are routinely screened for in the United States are galactosemia, a disorder affecting the body's ability to process galactose in milk; congenital hypothyroidism, an endocrine disorder; and sickle-cell anemia, a blood disorder that can be fatal even before one year of age.[10] Significantly, all of the conditions just listed can be effectively treated or at least ameliorated if detected as early as possible.

Still another form of screening, so-called carrier screening, targets adult carriers of genes for autosomal recessive (AR) disorders and X-linked recessive disorders. Among the AR disorders typically screened for are cystic fibrosis (CF), sickle-cell anemia, betathalassemia, and Tay-Sachs. Among the X-linked recessive disorders typically screened for are Duchenne muscular dystrophy and fragile X syndrome. Lawyer John A. Robertson claims that the availability of carrier screening tests represents a "significant expansion of procreative choice for couples."[11] Presumably, most responsible individuals and couples want to know their carrier status before they start procreating.

A final form of screening, so-called pre-symptomatic screening, is not unique to a particular age group. Its aim is to uncover genetic disease before symptoms appear. Although such screening is relatively limited now, it may be used in the future to screen pre-embryos, fetuses, newborns, and adults not only for a variety of late-onset diseases such as Alzheimer's and Huntington's but also for genetic predispositions to a wide range of diseases including cancer and heart disease. Since many of these diseases are neither curable not treatable, however, individuals might have to bear the psychological burden of knowing that they are unhealthy without being able to do much to help themselves.

Since genetic screening and diagnosis techniques have been in use for quite some time, nonfeminist bioethicists have been debating their wisdom for more than twenty-five years. The issue that initially preoccupied bioethicists was whether genetic screening programs should be mandatory or voluntary. On the one hand, advocates of mandatory screening claimed among its *benefits* the following features: "(1) a reduction in pain and suffering where early detection of a treatable genetic disease is possible; (2) better informed choices by couples thinking of having children; (3) fewer genetic disabilities if couples forgo having children when there are high genetic risks; (4) reduction in the financial costs of caring for persons with genetic diseases; (5) less loss of individuals' potential 'productive input to society'; and (6) healthier people."[12] On the other hand, opponents of mandatory screening listed the following *harms:* (1) an erosion of such democratic values as liberty and individual choice; (2) feelings of hopelessness, since there are few treatments or cures for detected diseases; (3) discrimination toward persons identified as victims of or carriers for genetic diseases; and (4) the unnecessary anxiety or unjustified relief of individuals who are incorrectly screened.[13]

The episode that largely ended the mandatory versus voluntary debate in the United States was a social experiment in mandatory sickle-cell anemia screening. In this country the preponderance of people afflicted with sickle-cell anemia, an autosomal recessive disorder, are African-American. Indeed, approximately 1 in 10 African-Americans carry the sickle-cell anemia trait, with an incidence of 1 in 500 births. Significantly, few who have the carrier trait for sickle-cell anemia ever show symptoms of the disease, and those with the actual disease can be mildly, severely, or fatally afflicted.

Researchers developed inexpensive screening tests for sickle-cell anemia in 1970. Initially, many African-Americans urged federal and state authorities to provide subsidized sickle-cell anemia screening programs in black communities. Between 1971 and 1972, twelve states enacted *mandatory* sickle-cell anemia screening laws and secured federal funds to set up major screening programs. For the most part, screening took place at the time when an African-American couple applied for a marriage license. Regrettably, however, the results of these tests were not always respected as the private property of the couple. In fact, information about carrier status was often passed on to insurers and employers without the carriers' consent. Because some health-care insurers did not want to cover individuals with a high probability of procreating children affected with sickle-cell anemia, they frequently rejected carriers' applications for health-care insurance. In addition, some employers began to practice their own version of "cherry-picking." Failing to understand that *carriers* for recessive genetic diseases or disorders such as sickle-cell anemia are not usually afflicted by the condition themselves, these employers refused to hire carriers of the sickle-cell anemia trait on the grounds that they were too unhealthy to keep up with a demanding workload.[14] Serious misunderstandings of this sort contributed to African-Americans' growing suspicion that the real aim of *mandatory* sickle-cell screening programs was not to help them manage a health problem specific to their community but, rather, to discriminate against them. A few African-Americans even claimed that the white community was out to eliminate the black community—to starve it to death, or at least to pressure it into not procreating. Largely in response to the black community's reaction to what it had come to view as *racist* sickle-cell anemia laws and screening policies, the National Sickle-Cell Anemia Control Act was passed in 1972. It legislated that federal funds could be used only for voluntary screening programs. Almost over night, the states dropped their mandatory screening programs. Some switched to voluntary programs; others, to no programs whatsoever.

Although most nonfeminist bioethicists agree that this 1972 act was a step in the right direction, some of them point out that the line between voluntary and mandatory screening is all too easily crossed. In fact, one of the most controversial genetic screening programs to date has been a "voluntary," private-sector attempt to provide Tay-Sachs carrier screening to the Ashkenazi Jewish population, whose carrier frequency is 1 in 30. In 1983 Rabbi Joseph Ekstein, who himself had lost four children to

Tay-Sachs, began a Tay-Sachs carrier screening program called Dor Yeshorim (literally, "Generation of the Righteous"). Touted by its supporters as a model screening program for carriers of genetic diseases, Dor Yeshorim claims that it seeks to maintain confidentiality, to avoid discrimination, and to respect the ethnic, religious, and cultural values of the Ashkenazi Jews, a tightly bound community that favors "match-made" intermarriage. The program targets predominantly Jewish high schools and encourages male and female students of reproductive age to be screened (usually during the sophomore year, when they are around fifteen years old). Blood samples are coded by a number that is given to the screened individual; no name is associated with the sample, and no genetic counseling is provided. When a young man and woman begin to date, or when parents enter into match-making negotiations, someone (usually the matchmaker) calls up the numbers of the two individuals and the system indicates whether they are a suitable match. Continued dating or marriage between the individuals is discouraged if they are identified as being at risk for procreating a child afflicted with Tay-Sachs. Over the last ten years, the Dor Yeshorim program has reportedly reduced the number of children born with Tay-Sachs to Ashkenazi Jews by 65 to 85 percent.[15]

Despite these beneficial results, however, some nonfeminist bioethicists have expressed concern that the Dor Yeshorim program is not truly *voluntary*. Critics note that Dor Yeshorim brochures imply, first, that screening is not only a social necessity but also a religious duty; and, second, that not only the health of one's children but also the strength of one's marriage are a function of one's carrier status. Critics also point out that although Dor Yeshorim claims to have *two* goals—preventing Tay-Sachs and assisting parents of children with Tay-Sachs—it is clear that prevention is its preferred goal. Thus, the critics conclude, to the degree that the Ashkenazi community pressures its members to submit to screening, it is being coercive. Apparently, noncompliance brings with it the "penalty" of being branded as irresponsible or worse.

Conceding that voluntary screening programs such as Dor Yeshorim are not always fully voluntary, many nonfeminist bioethicists nonetheless support them on the grounds that, after all, people do have a right to know whether they or their potential reproductive partners are carriers of harmful genetic diseases and defects. Based on this information, they can decide whether to get married and whether to have children. For example, an engaged man and woman who are both carriers of cystic fibrosis, a somewhat less devastating disorder than Tay-Sachs, can choose among the following options: (1) not marrying, (2) marrying but deciding to adopt or to use either donor sperm or donor eggs, and (3) marrying and deciding to procreate with their own gametes. Carrier couples who decide to procreate with their own genetic material confront another series of options: (1) using pre-implantation screening with the intention of discarding CF-affected pre-embryos; (2) using prenatal screening with the intention of aborting CF-affected fetuses; (3) following through on the first or second of these options, but not necessarily with the intention of discarding or aborting CF-affected pre-embryos or fetuses; and (4) simply taking their one-in-four chance of giving birth to a CF-affected child.[16]

Given the availability of pre-implantation and prenatal screening, concerns about the moral status of pre-embryos and embryos associated with genetic technology are, not surprisingly, the same as those associated with reproductive technology. Full-protectionists insist that discarding pre-embryos, to no less degree than aborting embryos, constitutes murder. A person is a person, they insist; it matters not whether she or he is one day old or one year old, healthy or unhealthy, genetically fit or genetically diseased. In contrast, modified-protectionists and nonprotectionists argue that until a pre-embryo or embryo reaches a particular point in development (e.g., quickening, viability, or birth), it is not a person. Thus, they argue, there is nothing "murderous" about parents deciding to discard or abort their yet-to-be-born child before it becomes a person, especially if it has a serious genetic disorder. But, they add, this is not to say that there is nothing morally wrong about such discards and abortions. Although *Roe v. Wade* deems as irrelevant the reasons persons give for aborting a first-trimester fetus[17] (and hence, by parity of reasoning, for discarding an in-vitro blastocyst), many nonprotectionists and modified-protectionists as well as full-protectionists are disturbed when couples or individuals discard a pre-embryo or abort an embryo not because it has a serious genetic disease or because its existence conflicts with the life or health of its gestator, but simply because it has a minor genetic defect (e.g., cleft palate) or because it is the so-called wrong sex (e.g., a female when a male is desired or vice versa).

It is difficult to articulate why it is somehow morally worse (even if not "murderous") to kill a *nonperson* for a trivial or discriminatory reason rather than for a serious or nondiscriminatory reason. After all, why should nonpersons have any moral claim on us whatsoever? In response to this challenging query, some nonfeminist bioethicists observe that even if a pre-embryo or an embryo is not a person, its *potential* to become a person requires that we not end its existence in a cavalier manner as if it had no moral standing whatsoever. To the degree that human persons believe they owe animals and even nonsentient creatures some moral consideration, they should also believe that they owe human nonpersons some moral consideration.

Far less controversial among nonfeminist bioethicists is the matter of newborn screening. Since newborn screening involves information about genetic conditions that are largely treatable and that most parents want to have ameliorated for their children, few nonfeminist bioethicists express concern about the fact that, in most states, newborn screening is mandatory. What they do tend to worry about is its accuracy, availability, and confidentiality.[18] Many nonfeminist bioethicists point out that the extent of infant screening depends not only on a state's laws but also on the ability of a state to fully or partially fund screening programs. Although it seems desirable to screen newborns for any deleterious genetic condition that is treatable, it is probably not fiscally feasible to do so. What is more, it seems arbitrary to screen newborns for treatable genetic diseases and disorders but not for a condition such as HIV for which promising new drug treatments are increasingly available. In the case of HIV, however, such "arbitrariness" is probably not entirely unjustified. Because society tends to discriminate against individuals with HIV far more than against individuals with, say, PKU, fears about violations of confidentiality are heightened in the case of HIV. Special attention must be given to balancing the benefits that might come to an infant from treating it for HIV against the harms that might come to the infant should its HIV status be revealed to unsympathetic individuals. Unless parents can be adequately assured that their children will not be discriminated against simply on the basis of their health, there might someday be a need to shift from mandatory to *voluntary* newborn screening for any disease or defect, genetic or nongenetic, that is socially stigmatizing.

Finally, most nonfeminist bioethicists support pre-symptomatic testing of adults who may have genetic disorders, provided that such testing respects both the principle of beneficence and that of autonomy. Critics who put more of a premium on beneficence than on autonomy question whether individuals are well served when told that they are destined to develop a largely untreatable and presently incurable disease such as Huntington's. The fact that about 10 to 12 percent of HD victims commit suicide, and that 30 percent of those at risk plan to follow suit if told they have the disease, suggests that many HD victims are unable to handle the "bad news" about themselves.[19] Apparently, they are not easily comforted by the thought that they might live thirty, forty, or even fifty quality years before they begin to manifest the symptoms of this disease, which eventually destroys the body and mind. In response to these considerations, critics who stress autonomy over beneficence insist that, for better or worse, individuals have a right to know about their genetic destiny. They should have the choice to kill themselves in preference to dying from a painful and degenerating disease. And certainly, say the critics, they should have the privilege to reorganize their lives in a way that fits their knowledge about its approximate quantity and quality.

Another ethical concern some nonfeminist bioethicists voice about pre-symptomatic screening focuses not so much on pre-symptomatic individuals' well-being as on that of their families and friends. Huntington's disease (to continue the example) does not begin to manifest itself symptomatically until well into adulthood, usually between the ages of thirty and fifty. For this reason, according to some nonfeminist bioethicists, once pre-symptomatic HD victims have been informed of their condition, they have an obligation to inform potential or, as the case may be, actual spouses of this fact. Not everyone will want to marry someone with Huntington's disease, or to procreate with her or him—particularly if there has been insufficient time to develop a deep love relationship in which one partner cares not whether the other will make difficult demands on her or his time, energy, resources, and own health.

A final concern raised by some nonfeminist bioethicists about pre-symptomatic testing focuses on family members' participation in so-called linkage testing, whereby geneticists obtain genetic information from family members in order to ascertain the patient's genetic status. Nonfeminist bioethicists agree that any attempt to force unwilling individuals to undergo a genetic test would violate both the principle of autonomy and the right to bodily integrity. They also agree that courts would be unlikely to uphold such measures. Nevertheless, many nonfeminist bioethicists believe that family members have certain moral responsibilities to one another. In their view, since linkage testing is not particularly risky or painful, and since those who participate need not know the results, morally responsible individuals should cooperate in linkage testing.

Over and beyond these *specific* concerns raised by nonfeminist bioethicists about particular forms of genetic testing are their *general* concerns about all forms of genetic testing. In the main, these more global worries have centered on issues related to test accuracy, accessibility, cost, and confidentiality. For example, John A. Robertson argues that one of the main issues about screening in coming years "will be to determine when a carrier test is sensitive and specific enough that it should be routinely available to those for whom it is of interest."[20] Some nonfeminist bioethicists believe that unless a carrier test (or, for that matter, a pre-implantation, prenatal, newborn, or pre-symptomatic test) is extremely accurate, it should not be provided. Moreover, they insist, even when an accurate test is offered, screened individuals (or the guardians of screened individuals) should receive the results from a genetic counselor. Other nonfeminist bioethicists believe that individuals have the right to demand genetic tests, including those that pose considerable uncertainties. They also insist that it is up to individuals to decide whether they want to use the services of a genetic counselor subsequent to genetic screening. Some individuals, moreover, might prefer taking a screening test in their own homes (in the event that such home tests are developed, FDA-approved, and marketed) over being tested in a health-care practitioner's office. Home tests certainly afford individuals far greater privacy than do office tests. Not everyone wants to hear the assessments and advisements of knowledgeable strangers.

Like Robertson, bioethicists John Fletcher and Dorothy Wertz worry about the problem of accuracy. However, issues of test accessibility seem to concern them even more. Fletcher and Wertz note that the problem of accessibility has two dimensions: (1) unfairness in access to genetic services, and (2) insufficient services to meet needs. In the United States, those with little or no access to genetic services are often the same people who receive very late or no prenatal care—namely, women who lack adequate health-care insurance, or who are ill-informed about the nature and function of genetic services, or who live at a distance from a genetic screening center. In contrast, financially secure and well-educated U.S. women receive a disproportionate share of the genetic services available. Fletcher and Wertz caution that "if this trend continues, being genetically handicapped could become a mark of social class."[21]

Closely related to the problem of accessibility is, of course, the matter of test cost. Although many nonfeminist bioethicists insist that society is ethically obligated to include a range of genetic services in any adequate health-care package, they quickly add that "adequate" genetic services do not encompass *all* genetic services.[22] Not everyone can be screened for everything; rather, society is able to subsidize screening only for those individuals who are at considerable risk for serious genetic diseases or disorders. For example, federal and state programs cover the costs of Tay-Sachs screening for Ashkenazi Jews but not for the U.S. population as a whole, since very few carriers for Tay-Sachs are non-Ashkenazi Jews. Granted, any proposal that seeks to provide a health-care service to some on the basis of gender, race, or ethnicity, but not to all, may seem discriminatory; but since it does not make good medical sense to provide health-care services to people unlikely to benefit from them, such allegations of discrimination are surmountable.

Of even greater concern to nonfeminist bioethicists is the confidentiality problem. As discussed above, individuals do not always want family members or friends to know their genetic status. As a result, family members and friends are sometimes deprived of the information *they* need to make wise procreative decisions and/or difficult decisions about the course of their own lives. Among the guidelines to which nonfeminist bioethicists appeal when health-care practitioners ask whether they may breach patient confidentiality in order to spare family members harm are those proposed by the President's Commission for the Study of Ethical Problems in Medicine. According to this commission, confidentiality may be breached only in exceptional circumstances that meet four conditions:

> (1) reasonable efforts to elicit voluntary consent to disclosure have failed; (2) there is a high probability both that harm will occur if the information is withheld and that the disclosed information will actually be used to avert harm; (3) the harm that identifiable individuals would suffer would be serious; and (4) appropriate precautions are taken to insure that only the genetic information needed for diagnosis and/or treatment of the disease in question is disclosed.[23]

As clear as these guidelines are, nonfeminist bioethicists report that it is often difficult to determine whether some of the conditions that justify a breach of confidence have actually been met. With respect to a disease like HD, for example, it is enormously difficult to determine whether condition (2) has been met. Assuming that the harm society wants to avoid is the harm that results when people procreate children with serious genetic diseases or defects, is it the case that people will refrain from passing on to future generations the genetic disease or disorder from which they suffer? Some nonfeminist bioethicists claim that, although many individuals will so refrain, a large number of genetically disordered individuals will choose to procreate despite what they know about themselves. In short, knowing that one has the HD gene does not necessarily compel one to choose not to procreate. After all, the person in question, perhaps one who has had the opportunity to lead forty or more *quality* years of life, may well reason that her or his offspring would rather experience four good decades of life (even though they will be followed by some very bad years) than no life at all. Why, then, should health-care practitioners breach confidence when they suspect that their patients' family members will choose to procreate no matter what they know about their genetic condition?

Because most nonfeminist bioethicists believe that it is not their role to second-guess what actions family members or friends will or won't take once they know their genetic "destiny," they are usually able to justify breaches of confidence aimed at providing family members or friends with the kind of information they need to avoid significant harm to themselves. Whether family members or friends use this information for the intended purpose will, of course, be up to them. Significantly, most nonfeminist bioethicists are not willing to give the same informational advantage to institutional third parties such as insurance companies or corporations that they are willing to give to family members or friends. In fact, virtually all nonfeminist bioethicists agree that neither employers nor insurers should have access to personal genetic data about their employees or subscribers until laws prohibiting "genetic discrimination" are enacted. Most nonfeminist bioethicists go one step further in agreeing with Fletcher and Wertz that

> [e]ven when legal protections have been adopted, access to personal genetic data should only occur with the informed consent of the individual involved. In nations where private health insurance is a major industry, with third parties paying for health care, the industry should be regulated by government to discourage excessive premiums for those at higher genetic risk. Refusal of private health insurance to families at higher risk for genetic disease should be illegal. Another alternative is government underwriting of health insurance for those at genetic risk.[24]

What underlies these recommendations about the insurance industry, and similar recommendations about the workplace, is the conviction that unlike many other health problems, a genetic disease or defect is not within a person's control. Granted, this conviction is one that probably needs to be modified. Whereas a wide variety of genetic disorders are probably highly impervious to environmental cues (in the same way that one's race and sex are highly impervious to environmental cues), an equally wide variety of genetic disorders are probably very sensitive to environmental "triggers."

Genetic Counseling

Since genetic diagnosis and screening without genetic counseling often do more harm than good, nonfeminist bioethicists have recently focused increased attention on the nature, function, and quality of genetic counseling. Barbara Bowles Biesecker describes genetic counseling "as the interaction between a health-care provider and patient or family member on concerns about the birth of a child with medical problems, reproductive testing options, a family history of ill health, or the diagnosis of an inherited condition."[25] This interaction is threefold, in that genetic counseling has (1) a diagnostic component during which clinical geneticists glean genetic information from clients' family histories, medical records, and clinical examinations or test results; (2) an educational component during which genetic counselors and sometimes also geneticists discuss with clients a range of issues related to their own genetic condition or that of their children, embryos, pre-embryos, or yet unconceived children; and (3) a psychosocial component during which genetic counselors explore clients' emotional responses to the information presented, supporting them in a nonjudgmental manner and helping them make their own decisions about how they want to act (or not act) as a result of what they now know about themselves or their progeny.[26]

Because most nonfeminist bioethicists are concerned about the potential for anyone, including genetic counselors, to be tempted to practice eugenics, they favor so-called nondirective genetic counseling, which emphasizes client autonomy.[27] Indeed, until very recently, they have urged genetic counselors to keep their personal views and moral judgments to themselves. This rule of nondirectiveness is now less strict. For example, Fletcher and Wertz allow exceptions to it when a client's capacity to comprehend and participate in decisionmaking is impaired.[28] They claim that mentally ill, severely retarded, and substance-addicted clients are usually unable to make sense of the genetic information with which they are provided. They also claim that clients with poor educations, or whose cultural frameworks are markedly different from those of their genetic counselors, often have trouble understanding and interpreting the genetic information communicated to them. In such cases Fletcher and Wertz advocate giving *direct* moral advice either to the relatives of impaired counselees or to the impaired counselees themselves, especially when genetic harm to others is a potential danger.[29] Another exception to the rule of nondirectiveness advocated by nonfeminist bioethicists is the *direct* counseling of clients that because gender is not a disease or defect, it is morally wrong to terminate a pre-embryo's or embryo's life simply because it is the so-called wrong sex.[30] Finally, a few nonfeminist bioethicists call for explicit guidance in the event that a pre-embryo or embryo is seriously genetically disordered. For example, Margery Shaw insists that genetic counselors should *directly* advise individuals that knowingly giving birth to a seriously impaired child is tantamount to negligent fetal abuse, a harm no less serious than negligent child abuse.[31]

Arthur Caplan believes that the days of nondirective genetic counseling are numbered. As he sees it, "with a mountain of new information about the human genome looming in the not so distant future, genetic counseling can no longer afford to ignore the question of what sorts of disorders and diseases it wishes to discover, why, and what exactly it wants to say about them."[32] Caplan claims that genetic counselors could afford a "no-comment" policy in the past, when they were able to inform individuals only about the presence of serious genetic diseases and defects. Confident that their clients wanted to do the "right" thing for themselves, their families, and their future children, few genetic counselors worried that their clients would deliberately cause themselves or their offspring grievous pain and suffering. However, this "no-comment" policy does not work as well, says Caplan, when genetic counselors are able to inform individuals about the presence of all sorts of genetic conditions, only some of them "negative." No longer are genetic counselors able to assume that most of their clients will not be tempted to abort their fetus simply because it has, say, a predisposition for obesity. For this reason alone, Caplan concludes, nondirective genetic counseling cannot handle what may be blatantly immoral requests on the part of clients:

> If families come seeking testing and counseling so that they can indulge their taste for a child of a particular sex, or if, for some personal reasons, they want a child with a particular disease or handicap, or because they hope to create a tissue donor, the counselor bound by strict value neutrality can say nothing. As the range of traits and conditions correlated with genetic states begins to grow, the requests of parents are likely to grow as well. At some point parents are likely to begin making requests for testing and counseling that clearly fall in the realm of genetic improvement and enhancement rather than in the domain of dysfunction and disease. An ethic of value neutrality provides no foundation for counselors to try and dissuade parents from making choices that are frivolous, silly, or malicious.[33]

Perhaps the greatest concern many nonfeminist bioethicists have about the future of *good* genetic counseling is that genetic counselors will probably remain few even as their clients become dramatically more numerous. Moreover, since the general public is relatively uninformed about genetics, nonfeminist bioethicists worry that as genetic tests become more common and easier for health-care practitioners to provide, many patients may receive tests without adequate counseling and follow-up. As a result, these patients might experience unnecessary stigmatization and anxiety or, alternatively, unwarranted peace of mind and relief.[34]

Nonfeminist Bioethical Perspectives on Gene Therapy

Currently, most of the genetic diseases and defects for which geneticists screen are untreatable. Indeed, it is the fact that most of these disorders cannot be cured or ameliorated that makes the task of genetic counselors so difficult. Researchers and clinicians hope that this state of affairs will change in the near future—in other words, that they will be able to treat most genetic diseases and defects, thereby enabling individuals to avoid difficult moral decisions about the course of their own lives and those of their pre-embryos and embryos.

Although gene therapy is in its infancy, strides are being made each year. At present, there are two types of gene therapy: somatic cell gene therapy and germline cell gene therapy. Somatic cell gene therapy simply treats defective cells already differentiated (e.g., blood cells) with normal cells. This type of gene therapy can be accomplished ex vivo, in situ, or in vivo. In the ex vivo method, the most widely used method of gene therapy to date, the physician removes defective cells from the patient and adds the normal-functioning gene to them. The corrected cells are then reinserted into the patient's body. In the in situ method, the physician introduces the normal-functioning gene directly into the patient's body at the *site* of the disease. Since it is not usually possible to precisely locate a disease site, this technique has been used only rarely. In the future, researchers hope to develop the in vivo method as well. The procedure would involve simply injecting viral vectors into the bloodstream, which would then carry the normal-functioning gene directly into the proper tissue. If this method of somatic cell gene therapy does become fully developed, it will be just as easy to get "gene therapy" as it currently is to get a flu shot.[35]

The second form of gene therapy is germline cell gene therapy, which involves the insertion of genes into fertilized eggs or into pre-implantation embryos so that the normal-functioning genes enter germ cells or the cells that give rise to them. The main ethical difference between somatic cell and germline cell forms of germ therapy is that the former constitutes treatment for the individual only, whereas the latter constitutes treatment for all the descendants of the individual as well. At present, germline cell gene therapy is more of a possibility than an actual reality.

As long as the purposes of somatic cell gene therapy are "negative" and "medical"—that is, aimed at treating genetic conditions that society widely regards as diseases (e.g., cystic fibrosis)—most nonfeminist bioethicists have no special moral qualms about its use.[36] Indeed, they note that when directed to the treatment of serious genetic disorders, somatic cell gene therapy poses no ethical problems over and beyond those that accompany the administration of other experimental therapeutic procedures. Scientist Bernard Davis expresses this view clearly when he writes that "the incorporation of a gene to treat a disease in an individual seems morally not different from the repeated administration of the product of the gene, and even if it entails some risks it would be justified by the illness of that recipient."[37]

To the degree that most nonfeminist bioethicists are morally comfortable with somatic cell gene therapy whose purposes are "negative" and "medical," they are decidedly morally uncomfortable with somatic cell gene therapy whose purposes are "positive" and "nonmedical." Examples of somatic cell gene therapy used for so-called enhancement purposes include inserting a gene to increase the height of one's child, not because he would otherwise be a dwarf but simply to maximize his chances of becoming a basketball star or a tall, imposing business executive.[38] The issue here is whether the purpose of medicine is only to make possible or to restore normal human functioning, or whether it is also to help some or all individuals function better than normal whenever possible. Some nonfeminist bioethicists believe that the role of medicine is the limited one of eliminating diseases, defects, and disorders, and that people have no right to demand that medicine be used to make them "supermen" or "superwomen." In contrast, other nonfeminist bioethicists maintain that medicine has no "eternal" or "natural" purposes. Medicine is limited, they insist, only by the state of science and technology: Now that it is possible for medicine to make people better than "nature" unassisted makes them, it should do so. Thus, these nonfeminist bioethicists reason that if parents have the right to secure the services of cosmetic surgeons and orthodontists, educators and psychologists, sports trainers and body builders, to improve their children's bodies and minds, they also have a right to secure the services of physicians and other health-care practitioners to accomplish the similar goals at the genetic rather than environmental level.[39]

To the degree that nonfeminist bioethicists debate among themselves about the morality of using somatic cell gene therapy for "positive" and "nonmedical" purposes as well as for "negative" and "medical" purposes, they also debate among themselves about using germline cell gene therapy for any purposes whatsoever. Opponents of germline cell gene therapy usually raise three arguments against it. First, they claim that germline cell gene therapy poses so many unpredictable, uneliminable, and serious long-term risks to the altered subjects and their offspring that it cannot be justified.[40] In their estimation, the risk-benefit ratio is such that there is no real justification for using germline cell gene therapy to eliminate conditions such as cystic fibrosis, especially since this aim can largely be accomplished through far less risky means such as carrier screening, prenatal diagnosis followed by abortion, and somatic cell gene therapy (which affects only presently afflicted individuals). Second, opponents of germline cell gene therapy insist that it places multiple human generations in the role of unconsenting research subjects. As they see it, the present generation of human beings cannot serve as proxies capable of determining the best interests of individuals who will be born 100 or even 500 years after they die, since the present generation has no way of predicting "what genetic makeup future persons may find advantageous or desirable."[41] Third, opponents fear that the state—"Big Brother"—will be tempted to use this type of therapy to create a "Brave New World" of people permanently altered in ways that suit the interests of the collectivity rather than those of the individual.[42]

Advocates of germline cell gene therapy respond to the first of these objections by claiming that the risks of such therapy are quite small, especially when balanced against benefits such as the elimination of widely dreaded genetic diseases and defects. Indeed, say these advocates, there is a supporting argument to be made that germline cell gene therapy is morally preferable to somatic cell gene therapy in that it obviates the need to perform costly, risky somatic cell gene therapy in multiple generations.[43] For example, there is no good reason to think that a dreaded disease like Tay-Sachs will somehow become a blessing to the human community a hundred years hence. Thus, it makes sense to identify carriers of Tay-Sachs at the pre-embryo stage now and thereby eliminate this scourge once and for all.

With respect to the second argument that opponents have raised against germline cell gene therapy—namely, that when the current generation uses this type of therapy, it treats future generations as the unconsenting objects of risky scientific experiments—advocates respond that parents make all sorts of decisions for their children. And if we trust parents to act in the best interests of their children when they decide to procreate a child of a particular genetic makeup (namely, their own), then we should also trust this generation to act in the best interests of future generations as it proceeds to decide when and when not to use germline cell gene therapy. The fact that this generation can neither acquire the permission of future generations nor know their genetic "needs" and "preferences" is not a sound justification for banning germline cell gene therapy. If it were, says Ray Moseley, it would likewise be "unethical to do anything affecting future generations, including produce them."[44] Like many advocates of germline cell gene therapy, Moseley proposes that "[a] more reasonable and ethically sound guiding principle in regard to decisions affecting future generations should be that whatever is done must be ethically acceptable to existing persons and that the decision should not lead to *predictably* bad consequences for future persons."[45]

Finally, the advocates of germline cell gene therapy reply to opponents that no one's "Big Brother" is interested in using this type of therapy as the foundation for some major program of eugenics. Health-care costs, they insist, are already destroying or significantly eroding the economies of major industrialized nations. Thus rationing health care—eliminating all but the most medically necessary services—is the order of the day, rather than identifying more ways to spend already limited health-care dollars. If society needs to worry about anything, they add, it is not "Big Brother" using germline cell gene therapy to create a Master Race but, rather, wealthy consumers seeking to purchase desired genes on the free market in order to enhance their own welfare and / or that of their progeny.[46]

According to many nonfeminist bioethicists, a common concern underlies all their deliberations and debates about genetic screening, diagnosis, counseling, and therapy. They claim that the Human Genome Project is particularly significant in that it challenges our understanding of ourselves, our nature and significance, and our connections with our ancestors and descendants. As philosopher Thomas Murray describes it, in one way or another our understanding of ourselves as moral agents has depended on the conviction that we are responsible for our actions, provided that we have both cognitive awareness of their nature ("good" or "bad") and the physical and psychological ability to control them. As a culture, he says, we are preoccupied with issues of individual responsibility, especially when there is fault or blame to be assigned. We ask if alleged criminals are responsible for their behavior—morally blameworthy, legally culpable. We ask if unhealthy people are responsible for their condition. Did they drink, smoke, or eat to excess? Did they have their annual checkup? And beyond these issues of individual responsibility, we ask whether various racial or ethnic groups who do especially well (or especially poorly) in various social and economic realms experience the good (or bad) fortune they do because of their innate qualities, or because of their lack of educational and occupational opportunities, or because of their lack of hard work. Only if a group's bad fortune is due to some factor over which we believe the group had no control, Murray observes, do we say that the group is not to blame for its own bad fortune.[47]

Of all the explanations, excuses, and justifications for human behavior that we find compelling, however, none seems to have as much power as genetic explanations, excuses, and justifications. The Human Genome Project will only increase our tendency to explain all of our physical and psychological diseases, defects, and disorders as the simple product of our genetic structure. It will also increase our tendency to excuse and sometimes even justify our shortcomings, flaws, and sins as the product of forces beyond our control. Not having chosen our genes, we will plead not guilty whenever we are faulted for our behavior or our personality. As Murray and many other nonfeminist bioethicists see it, however, too much reliance on genetic explanations, excuses, and justifications for human behavior is morally dangerous. Although our genes provide us with clues for why we are the way we are and why we act the way we do, so too does our environment. Given the proper environment, we can overcome or compensate for many of our genetic limits. Thus, we do not want to cultivate an escapist or defeatist attitude that permits us to idly stand by as people suffer from all manner and fashion of disease, defect, disorder and disability on the grounds that there is nothing we can do to help. Nor do we want to fall into a "genomic" trap that encourages us to "solve" our social and economic woes simply by preventing the birth of any individual who promises to be a "problem." In sum, according to Murray and other nonfeminist bioethicists, the greatest risk that the Human Genome Project poses is the risk that we may come to think of ourselves either as merely the passive products of our genes or as the active manipulators of not only our own but everyone's genetic destiny.[48]

Feminist Bioethical Perspectives on Genetic Screening, Diagnosis, and Counseling

Genetic Screening and Diagnosis

As might be expected, the pre-embryo, embryo, or fetus is not the primary focus of feminist concerns about genetic screening, diagnosis, and counseling. Rather, what interests feminists is the role that gender plays in reproductive and genetic decisions. As is widely recognized, any information a couple or woman receives with reference to the embryo's genetic condition is mediated through the woman's body. So too is any decision a couple or a woman makes about the embryo's fate. Women are the ones who undergo amniocentesis and other prenatal genetic tests; and they are the ones who have abortions. Thus, compared to men, women ordinarily have to accept not only more physical intrusions into their bodies but also more responsibility for the ultimate fate of their embryos. Pre-implantation screening alters this state of affairs. If a pre-embryo is screened ex utero, both members of a couple would presumably have an equal right (and responsibility) to determine whether the pre-embryo should be discarded if it has, for example, Down's syndrome. To the degree that discarding a *pre-embryo* is analogous to aborting a very early *embryo*, then, there is a case to be made that when a man's desire to discard his and his wife's genetically defective pre-embryo supersedes his spouse's desire to implant it in her womb, it is *he* who is responsible for the "abortion" of their pre-embryo.

In this connection, some feminists cite *Davis v. Davis* (1992)[49] as enormously instructive. John A. Robertson summarizes this precedent-setting case as follows:

> A couple had frozen seven embryos pursuant to their efforts to have children via IVF. They subsequently decided to divorce but could not agree on disposition of the frozen embryos. The husband opposed thawing them and using them to start pregnancy, while the wife insisted that she or another person have them placed in her. The Tennessee Supreme Court finally resolved this issue by ruling that an agreement between the parties for disposition in the case of divorce would have been binding, and that in the absence of such an agreement, the relative burdens and benefits of a particular solution must be examined. In that case if the party wishing to retain the embryos had other means of obtaining embryos, such as going through IVF again with a new partner, that party's wish to have children could still be satisfied without foisting unwanted parenthood on the party who wished that the embryos

> not be used. On the other hand, if there was no other way for that party to be reasonably able to produce embryos, so that the existing embryos were the last resort or chance to have offspring, then they should be entitled to use them. In that case, fairness would require that the objecting party not have to provide child support. In the facts presented to it, the court ruled in favor of the husband, who did not want frozen embryos implanted after divorce, because the wife had alternative ways to reproduce.[50]

What bothers some feminists about the *Davis* decision is not the decision per se but, rather, how *quickly* the court acknowledged the importance of a *man's* right not to procreate, given that it took previous courts several years to acknowledge a *woman's* right not to procreate. When a woman wants to abort her embryo, the embryo's right to life is balanced against her right not to procreate. When a man wants to discard his pre-embryo, however, his right not to procreate trumps not only the woman's right to procreate but also the pre-embryo's right to life.

Assuming that pre-implantation screening will not become routinely used, on account of its cost and relative difficulty, prenatal screening will remain the order of the day. At present, women still have to submit to one or the other of two fairly invasive procedures—chorionic villus sampling or amniocentesis—in order to receive important information about the genetic status of their fetuses. In the future, however, women will no longer have to submit to such procedures. For example, when tests to identify fetal cells in maternal blood are perfected, the genetic condition of fetuses will be diagnosable at seven to eight weeks by a simple blood test. As wonderful as such a development seems to be, feminists who have reservations about genetic testing argue that just because a prenatal test can be performed very early and noninvasively, it does not follow that the test is an unalloyed blessing for women. Indeed, from the standpoint of these feminists, it is precisely because future prenatal tests will be so easy that society will probably label any woman who refuses them "irresponsible." Moreover, because at least half of society will not be eager to subsidize health care for genetically defective or diseased children, such tests are likely to pressure pregnant women not only to determine their fetus's condition but also to do the "right" thing (by which is presumably meant the scheduling of an abortion) in the event that the news is "bad."

In response to the point that women of the future might not be able to say "no" to early, noninvasive prenatal tests, feminists who favor genetic testing make the counterpoint that this does not matter, since most women will want to say "yes" to such tests. For these feminists, the real moral question to raise about genetic testing is whether the poor as well as the rich will have access to it. They argue that, for the most part, women do not want to bring unhealthy children into the world: Life is hard enough, after all, without being burdened from the moment of birth by serious physical and/or mental disabilities. Thus, these feminists recommend that the state provide genetic testing for *all* pregnant women, poor or rich, so that they have the opportunity to terminate their pregnancies in the event that their fetuses are found to be suffering from a serious genetic disease or defect. For example, an indigent pregnant woman might want to bring her child to term even though he suffers from Down's syndrome, a genetic disorder that, although costly to treat, does not prevent him from leading a meaningful life.

Significantly, pressure to discard or abort pre-embryos and embryos with serious genetic disorders comes from feminist as well as nonfeminist directions. Philosopher Adrienne Asch notes that, according to some feminists, having children with serious genetic diseases or defects is not in women's best interests.[51] These feminists reason that since it is women who usually care for disabled children and adults in their own homes, it is women who often have to give up not only their professional careers but also their personal pleasures in order to meet the many physical and psychological needs of those for whom they've assumed responsibility.[52] Although many women would prefer not to make these kinds of sacrifices, they make them anyway for fear of being branded otherwise as "selfish," "uncaring," or "cruel." For this and other reasons, some feminists advise carriers of serious genetic disorders not to procreate unless they do so with the assistance of one or more genetically healthy gamete donors. In the event that a carrier gets pregnant, the same feminists recommend that she submit to prenatal screening and abort her embryo should it have the serious genetic disorder she carries. To urge this woman to consider other options such as carrying her embryo to term and putting it up for adoption, or carrying the embryo to term and institutionalizing it, is, in the estimation of these feminists, to provide her with some very *bad* choices. In the first place, society will probably condemn her as irresponsible for putting her severely disabled child up for adoption, or for institutionalizing the child. Second, and even more problematically, society will probably make her feel guilty for trying to "get rid of" her severely disabled child by imposing on others' generosity.

Agreeing that having children with serious genetic disorders is not in *women's* best interests, other feminists nevertheless stress that the *primary* reason why women should abort embryos with serious genetic disorders is that it is not in these *embryos'* best interests that they be born. In this connection, feminist Laura Purdy has stated:

> When I look into my heart to see what it says about this matter I see, I admit, emotions I would rather not feel—reluctance to face the burdens society must bear, unease in the presence of some disabled persons. But most of all, what I see there are the demands of love: to love someone is to care desper-

> ately about their welfare and to want for them *only* good things. The thought that I might bring to life a child with serious physical or mental problems when I could, by doing something different, bring forth one without them, is utterly incomprehensible to me.[53]

Purdy believes that it may be wrong to bring into the world children with serious genetic diseases or defects. However, she would prefer that these children never be conceived rather than that they be aborted subsequent to conception. On the one hand, Purdy argues that since a nonexistent entity can neither be harmed nor deprived of the kind of rights only actual persons have, it is not wrong to prevent its conception. On the other hand, she says, prospective parents ought to have children only if they can provide them with a normal opportunity for a good life. Thus, Purdy concludes that, given what prospective parents presumably desire (namely, to nurture and love children who will be happy), carriers for genetic disorders that preclude a normal opportunity for a good life should not act on their desire to procreate children genetically related to them.[54]

Purdy's view has been challenged by both nonfeminists and feminists. Nonfeminist critics note that the genetic disorder upon which Purdy has based some of her arguments—namely, Huntington's disease—is one that many people do not think is incompatible with a normal opportunity for a good life. Many people with HD lead very good lives until, and even after, they begin to manifest the symptoms of the disease, sometime between the ages of thirty and fifty. Thus, it is not clear that carriers for HD are morally wrong to procreate. To this objection, Purdy responds that although she might have erred in focusing on Huntington's disease, this strategic error fails to defeat her general point—namely, that certain genetic diseases (e.g., Tay-Sachs) *are* in fact incompatible with a normal opportunity for a good life.

Purdy's feminist critics express concern that her view is all too compatible with the view of those who long for a society in which only perfect or nearly perfect people are tolerated—precisely the kind of society that women, who have been traditionally regarded as imperfect (deficient, secondary, deformed), should fear. According to some of these feminists, the very fact that our society is routinizing and normalizing genetic screening, especially prenatal screening, is a sign that our society might have eugenic aspirations after all. Whereas in the past clinicians recommended prenatal screening only for women over thirty-five, women or couples carrying genes for genetic disorders, and women or couples who had previously procreated a child with a genetic disorder, they now offer amniocentesis to women under thirty-five and to women or couples who simply want as much genetic information about their fetus as is available.[55] Indeed, what was once the exception with respect to prenatal screening is fast becoming the rule. Increasingly, pregnant women feel that they *must* have their embryos or pre-embryos screened, since this is what *all* rational pregnant women supposedly want to do. Worse, many of these women feel that no matter how much they want to bring their child to term, they are obliged not to do so in the event of a serious genetic defect. Since society seems to have little tolerance for "imperfect" babies, a woman who chooses to carry to term, for example, her Down's syndrome embryo is not likely to be hailed as a responsible/moral decisionmaker; on the contrary, she will probably be branded an irresponsible/immoral decisionmaker whose "selfish" decision has added to rather than subtracted from the human community's pool of pain.

Among the feminists who worry about where Purdy's line of reasoning might lead women is Adrienne Asch. Although Asch supports women's abortion rights as a general rule, she discourages women from choosing to abort a fetus simply because it has a *nonfatal* genetic disability. She argues that there is a significant moral difference between a woman deciding to abort her fetus because the man with whom she planned to rear it has suddenly decided to divorce her, on the one hand, and a woman deciding to abort her fetus because it has a limb deformity, on the other. In short, Asch argues, it is one thing to abort one's fetus because of something "wrong" about one's own life or circumstances, and quite another to abort one's fetus because of something "wrong" about it. Asch makes the further point that it perplexes her when feminists have no trouble seeing what is wrong about aborting a fetus simply because it is the "wrong" sex, but much trouble seeing what is wrong about aborting a fetus simply because it has Down's syndrome, spina bifida, cystic fibrosis, or muscular dystrophy (four genetic diseases that do not prevent those who have them from leading reasonably meaningful and productive lives). If feminists claim that what is wrong about aborting a fetus simply because it is a female is that it sends a very negative (ugly, chilling, scary) message to actual girls and women about their worth, then they should realize that what is wrong about aborting a fetus simply because it has Down's syndrome is that it sends a very negative message to actual persons with Down's syndrome: a message that conveys the sentiment "We wish you weren't here." In this connection, Asch claims that feminists should be as concerned about "ableism" as they are about "sexism." Discrimination is discrimination regardless of its object.

Genetic Counseling

Feminists disagree among themselves not only about whose interest is served when women (or couples) procreate children with severe or mild genetic disorders but also about how directive or nondirective genetic counseling should be. Interestingly, the majority of genetic counselors today are women, and most of them support nondirective genetic counseling. Some feminists speculate that female genetic counselors may be eager to insist on client autonomy precisely because they recognize that the lives of their clients, most of whom are women, will be affected more than their male partners by the decisions that are made in their offices.[56] Given the ways in which many women have been pressured, coerced, forced, or otherwise "led" to make procreative decisions that are not in their own best interests, a hands-off, no-comment policy seems a wise one for feminists to espouse. At the same time, however, there is the concern that "a blind adherence to autonomy to promote reproductive decision making without interference may result in a missed opportunity for genetic counselors to facilitate the clients' exploration of their own values, desire, and preferences."[57]

In some cases, then, the best way to increase a woman's true autonomy would be to discuss with her what other women in positions akin to hers have chosen to do, and with what results. Indeed, there might even be occasions when a genetic counselor should honestly answer the question "What would you do if you found yourself in my position?"

Although she does not want to make women feel guilty about their reproductive choices, Adrienne Asch suspects that many genetic counselors, contrary to what they say, are already more "directive" than "nondirective" in their approach toward women carrying "undesirable" fetuses. Their silence, combined with society's predisposition to eliminate whatever or whomever it perceives as "worse" in favor of whatever or whomever it perceives as "better," has the effect of permitting (even requiring) women to do the "right" thing—namely, to eliminate their less-than-best fetuses. With this state of affairs in mind, Asch suggests that if genetic counselors truly wished to increase women's autonomy, they should "urge women to obtain far more and very different information than they commonly get about people with disabilities, to examine what might lead them to abort for the 'wrong sex,' [and] to consider whether they could imagine carrying the fetus to term and giving up the child for adoption if they cannot face raising it (since they voluntarily undertook pregnancy).[58] Asch also implies that genetic counselors should encourage women to do this kind of thinking in the context of a consciousness-raising session during which they can examine "who they are, what they want out of being parents, and whether an abortion decision makes a statement about the value of the potential life they carry or about aspects of themselves."[59]

Asch's reflections suggest to some feminists that the analysis by Drs. Ezekiel and Linda Emanuel of the physician-patient relationship might be applied effectively to the genetic counselor-client relationship. According to the Emanuels, there are four major models of the physician-patient interaction—the paternalistic, the informative, the interpretive, and the deliberative.[60] Under the paternalistic model, the Emanuels say, physicians strive to make sure that their patients "receive the interventions that best promote their health and well-being."[61] Paternalistic physicians use their skills to determine which procedures they think patients ought to undergo, and then they guide their patients to assent to these procedures. Convinced that they and not their patients are the medical experts, and that their patients share their values and views about what constitutes a benefit, paternalistic physicians insist that there is nothing wrong with their approach. On the contrary, they insist, it is their *duty* to get patients to agree to the treatments they *know* will serve the patients' *best* interests. As the Emanuels see it, however, the paternalistic model is disturbing not only because it undermines patients' autonomy but also because it provides no opportunity for patients or physicians to reflect upon their supposedly shared values and views.

In contrast to the paternalistic model, the informative model gives free reign to patients' autonomy. According to the Emanuels, this model is based on a sharp distinction between facts and values. It also assumes that physicians are in the "fact" business only. Patients make their *own* decisions about what they value—choices that are none of the physicians' business. In short, it is the responsibility of physicians not to question patients' treatment goals but, rather, to provide patients with the information they need to determine which of several treatments *they* think is most likely to achieve their desired treatment goals. The Emanuels claim, in other words, that under the informative model, physicians are merely purveyors of technical expertise: "There is no role for the physician's values, the physician's understanding of the patient's values, or his or her judgement of the worth of the patient's values."[62]

The third model, the interpretive model, also puts a premium on patients' autonomy; but, in the Emanuels' estimation, it has the advantage of emphasizing how difficult it is to correctly identify what patients' *true* values and preferences are. Physicians who favor the interpretive model claim that patients are not always sure what they want or why they want it when they first arrive for a medical examination. For this reason, these physicians believe they have an obligation to help their patients get clearer on their own health-related values. Once assured that their patients really know what they want and why, however, these physicians readily defer to their patients' judgment and rely on a version of the *informative* model.

The final model presented by the Emanuels is the deliberative model. Under this model, physicians and patients engage in a discussion that permits both parties to articulate their values. If convinced that their patients' values are such that they will ultimately disserve the patients' best interests (in terms of health and well-being), physicians who favor the deliberative model do not hesitate to challenge those values—first, by revealing their own, very different values and, then, by inviting their patients to respond in kind. Through this give-and-take process, both parties are given the opportunity to reflect upon and express what course of action they each think will serve the patients' best interests, with the understanding that the "right" view—whether the physicians' *or* the patients'—is the one that should ultimately be followed.

Clearly, nondirective genetic counseling is most consistent with what the Emanuels term the informative model, whereby (1) there is no role for the counselor's judgment of the worth of the client's values, and (2) client autonomy is preserved in the sense that *the client*, and no one but the client, makes the choice say, to abort (or not abort) a "defective" fetus or to refrain from (or engage in) procreating. Because this "no-comment" approach isolates the client, however, it leaves the client wondering whether she or he has made a wise (and moral) decision. For this reason, many feminists believe that genetic counselors should adopt a deliberative style of counseling, enabling counselors as well as clients to sort out their own complex ideas about disease, defect, disability, imperfection, and so on.

Feminists who support "deliberative" genetic counseling realize that it runs counter to the idea that proper professional distance should be maintained between health-care practitioners and clients. Nevertheless, they maintain that the deliberative model seems more congenial to feminist methodology than the other three models discussed by the Emanuels. In the first place, this model encourages genetic counselors and their clients to ask each other the so-called woman question—that is, to raise not only general moral concerns about aborting "imperfect" children (in terms of risks, benefits, side effects, and so on) but also *feminist* moral concerns about how aborting "imperfect" children might be related to the oppression of women. Second, the deliberative model permits genetic counselors and their clients to raise each other's consciousness about the subtle as well as blatant forms of oppression that emerge in a society paradoxically intolerant of the differences that define it. Finally, the deliberative model enables clients to make decisions that will serve not only their own best interests but, indeed, those of all women, including disabled women and women who have chosen to carry their "defective" children to term.

Feminist Bioethical Perspectives on Gene Therapy

Feminists make many of the same for and against arguments about gene therapy as nonfeminists do. However, they also raise some considerations that nonfeminists do not. Feminists who favor both somatic cell gene therapy and germline cell gene therapy for "negative" and "medical" purposes reason that women will *want* to treat their embryos in utero for serious genetic diseases. There is, after all, no feminist argument against treating embryos, children, and adults for the conditions that would and do seriously limit their lives. Living with defects one cannot change is one matter; doing nothing about serious defects one can ameliorate is quite another. The fact that a child or adult with Down's syndrome can lead a productive and happy life does not mean that the same child or adult would turn down the opportunity to lead an even more productive and happy life—that is, a life not bound by the limitations that Down's syndrome imposes on its subjects.

When feminists who favor gene therapy for "negative" and "medical" purposes raise ethical concerns about it, they tend to focus, first, on whether the pregnant woman is not only able but also truly willing to accept the risks and burdens that some forms of gene therapy pose. Currently, a relatively high number of citizens seem prepared to punish women for "negligently, recklessly, or intentionally" engaging in lifestyle behaviors that result in serious, irreparable damage to their infants. Such behaviors are believed to encompass everything from engaging in unsafe sex with HIV-positive partners to not eating enough nutritious food, working in toxic environments, drinking too much caffeine, overexercising or underexercising, taking licit as well as illicit drugs that might imperil fetal well-being, or failing to follow physicians' orders. Already, many pregnant women have been prosecuted and, in a few instances, imprisoned for giving birth to cocaine-exposed infants.[63] What some feminists fear, then, is that if the concept of "fetal abuse" or "fetal negligence" captures the public's imagination, the public might decide to punish not only pregnant women who do not "take care of themselves" but also pregnant women who do not submit to gene therapy for their fetuses. These feminists also worry that a variety of social, political, medical, and psychological forces will pressure pregnant women to submit to surgeries or treatments even before they are perfected and made relatively risk-free. Comments Dr. David Perlman:

> Fetus and mother are connected via the umbilical cord and exchange blood, nutrients, waste products and antibodies, among other substances. If a retroversion containing spliced genes is used as the vehicle for delivering genetic changes to early concepti, sperm or ova, as has been proposed and recently attempted, then women may face the danger of having their own genetic material altered by these same retroversiers. Since no one currently knows the mechanism of human genetic recombination and whether proto-oncogenes or other activating factors in adult women might interact with fetal retroversion and cause genetic recombination of normal adult and fetal genes, there is a chance of genetic endangerment.[64]

A second ethical concern that feminists who favor gene therapy raise is that great care must be taken in defining what constitutes a serious genetic disease or defect so that the definition does not contribute to women's (or, for that matter, anyone else's) oppression. According to philosopher Arthur Caplan, a disease is an "abnormal, dysfunctional, and disvalued" mental or physical state.[65] On the basis of this definition, it is clear that Tay-Sachs is a disease: Relatively few people have it; it renders one unable to function mentally and physically; and it is universally dreaded on account of the suffering it causes. Conversely, the state of being six-feet tall, or being ordinary-looking, or being a female rather than a male (or vice versa), is not a disease. Many feminists are quick to add that because society can manipulate the criteria for disease to serve oppressive purposes—including that of subordinating women to men—feminists need to play a role in determining what genetic conditions do or do not count as serious genetic disease and disorders.

A third and final concern that feminists who favor gene therapy for "negative" and "medical" purposes express is that its cost is likely to be high and that only relatively advantaged women (or couples) are able to afford it. Told that her embryo or pre-embryo has a genetic disease or defect, an economically disadvantaged woman must choose either to end the embryo or pre-embryo's life or to carry it to term. No matter which "choice" she makes, however, she will be the object of social disapproval. If the chooses the former course of action, some will label her a "baby killer"; but if she chooses the latter, others will view her as "irresponsible." In contrast, a relatively advantaged woman has available to her a wider range of choices, including the option of gene therapy. Her money spares her from having to make an agonizing "choice" about her fetus's destiny. Thus, feminists who favor gene therapy aimed at treating diseases and defects urge that it be provided to all women, rich or poor, on the grounds that all women should have equal procreative freedom.

The fact that many feminists support gene therapy for "negative" and "medical" reasons does not mean that they also support it for "positive" and "nonmedical" purposes. On the contrary, many feminists are not comforted by the analogy between using gene therapy for the purposes of enhancing one's normal embryo, on the one hand, and using cosmetic surgery for the purposes of enhancing one's normal child, on the other. According to these feminists, when used for enhancement purposes *neither* gene therapy nor cosmetic surgery serves women's best interests. What counts as an "enhancement" is, in their opinion, even more socially and culturally bound than what counts as a "disease." The reason, they explain, is that there is a biological substratum to disease—a set of physical facts about it—that makes it difficult to argue that disease is simply a social or cultural construction. In contrast, many of the qualities favored by our society—for example, looking like Sylvester Stallone or Cheryl Tiegs—are peculiar to our circumstances, to the time and space in which we live. But a hundred years from now, when, due to gene therapy, every fourth person or so looks like Stallone or Tiegs, our society might no longer consider such people to be particularly attractive. As a result, that future society might demand that gene therapy be used for a new "enhancement" purpose—namely, the elimination of the Tiegs and Stallone types. Fearing this prospect, feminists question whether science and medicine should devote energy and expertise to serving ephemeral social preferences, especially those that tend to reinforce an iniquitous status quo. Given that all too many people will want their children to fit prevailing social norms, even when these norms happen to be sexist, racist, and classist in nature, gene therapy for enhancement purposes will only make the struggle for equity between men and women that much more difficult.

Conclusion

To be sure, some feminist bioethicists do not favor any form of gene therapy whatsoever—whether for "medical" and "negative" purposes or for "nonmedical" and "positive" purposes. In their view, along with gene therapy, genetic screening, diagnosis, and treatment, will come increased opportunities for society to control people in general and to oppress women in particular. That such a state of affairs might ensue is indeed a possibility. However, it is also possible that society might instead use the new genetic technologies in ways that contribute to people's well-being and freedom and serve the cause of gender equity.

In an article on society's responses to the new reproductive technologies, Norma Juliet Wikler makes some observations that apply equally to the new genetic technologies. She notes that "the key to understanding the import of the new technologies is to understand why the old ones were not used."[66] For example, given that artificial insemination is so easily accomplished—as noted earlier, with so simple an instrument as a turkey baster—why is it that women did not choose until very recently to inseminate themselves?[67] In order to answer this question, says Wikler, feminists must explore what factors in society's structure prevented women from even thinking to use a technology that would have increased their control over the procreative process. As Wikler sees it, such an exploration "will show that the most important link leads not from the laboratory to changes in the social structure, but the other way around."[68] Today, an increasing number of women are inseminating themselves not because scientists have just figured out the "mysteries" of artificial insemination but because changes have occurred in male-female relations, sexual morality, and the role and status of women. What is more, scientists are developing a wide panoply of assisted reproduction techniques and genetic services not because "science" beckons them to do so but because an increasing number of people want them. In other words, social forces are creating a "need" for IVF clinics and genetic services.

Clearly, the new reproductive and genetic technologies are not the real problem in most feminists' minds. On the contrary, it is people—particularly those who help create society's "needs." Although few feminists are enthusiastic about projects to create perfect people, they do not want to prevent women from learning about their genetic destiny and then taking steps to control it. In this connection, Ruth Cowan asks: "Which outcome is more to be feared? A future in which parents can freely choose the characteristics of fetuses that will be brought to term, or a future in which there are grounds on which a woman could be refused both information about her fetus and an abortion if she desired one?"[69] It is to be hoped that women will choose the characteristics of their fetuses in ways that will break down gender inequity and the host of other human oppressions to which it is related. In choosing for their fetuses, women will be choosing for themselves. The question, then, is not "What kind of people should there be in the future?" but "What kind of people do we want to be now?"

Epilogue

Feminist approaches to bioethics are not a substitute for traditional and alternative nonfeminist approaches to bioethics. They do not presume to have all the answers to all the moral questions that have been or will be raised in the biomedical or health-care realm. However, the fact that feminist approaches to bioethics do not seek to privilege themselves over other approaches to bioethics does not necessarily mean that they should be viewed as "optional" moral perspectives that nonfeminist bioethicists are free to ignore. On the contrary, they need to be recognized by nonfeminist bioethicists as partial, provisional, and suggestive perspectives on what counts as good clinical decisionmaking and wise public policymaking.

In some ways, feminist approaches to bioethics share complementary medicine's "maverick" status: Both are downplayed as somewhat "offbeat." However, the fact that increasing numbers of people are turning to complementary medicine suggests that the public is tiring of what mainstream medicine often offers them—namely, much in the way of high-tech, so-called state-of-the-art treatment for their diseased, defective, and disabled body parts, but relatively little in the way of human care for the whole person, for human minds and spirits as well as human bodies. Similarly, the growing number of thinkers exploring new approaches to bioethics should tell us that many theoreticians are dissatisfied with a moral decisionmaking process that relies too much on reason and critical analysis and too little on emotion and sympathetic interpretation.

Feminist approaches to bioethics offer nonfeminist approaches to bioethics some clues about why such good principles as autonomy, beneficence, nonmaleficence, and justice have trouble functioning well in the health-care system as it is presently organized. Trapped within conceptual as well as institutional structures of domination and subordination, autonomy can become an exercise of unreasonable demands in the name of exaggerated and egocentric "needs"; nonmaleficence, an exercise in undertreatment of patients in the name of "futility"; beneficence, an exercise in overtreatment of patients in the name of scientific expertise; and justice, a disguise for undemocratic modes of rationing in the name of the greater good.

Asking the so-called woman question and raising men's and women's consciousness about the subtle and blatant forms that gender oppression assumes in the world of medicine enables health-care practitioners and patients to see that what counts as a free choice for a man is not always a free choice for a woman, and that what serves the health needs of men does not always serve the health needs of women. But feminist approaches to bioethics offer nonfeminist approaches to bioethics more than just some significant opportunities for conceptual reinterpretations and terminological revision. They also permit, in behalf of these older approaches to bioethics, consideration of the possibility that an ontology of connectedness, of autokoenomy, as opposed to one of separateness, of autonomy, better supports the practice of medicine. And, indeed, medicine is a practice that not only permits but requires intimate relationships between the self and the other. Both health-care practitioners and patients must cultivate the virtues of honesty, courage, and justice if the practice of medicine is to survive, let alone thrive. Each time a physician is dishonest with a patient, not only that physician's relationship to the particular patient but the relationship of all physicians to all patients is weakened. Similarly, each time a patient sues a physician for frivolous reasons, not only that particular patient's relationship with the physician but the relationship of all patients to all physicians is distorted. No man—or woman—is an island in the world of medicine. In choosing for oneself, one is almost always choosing for others and, in some instances, for the entire practice of medicine.

In addition to offering nonfeminist approaches to bioethics an ontology that stresses the ways in which human beings are connected (notice, for instance, the difference between the expressions "maternal-fetal conflict" and "maternal-fetal relation"), feminist approaches to bioethics provide an epistemology of perspective, of *positionality*, as opposed to an epistemology of certitude, of Archimedean point. I know who I am. And what I see is a function of who I am—a white, middle-class, well-educated, postmenopausal, Catholic, heterosexual, married academic and mother of two boys. Likewise, what you see is a function of who you are—a self that is, no doubt, quite different from me. Yet to the degree that we are cognizant of the ways in which we are different as well as the ways in which we are alike, we are in a position to join together to achieve true objectivity. Without knowing what you see, however, I have no hope of correcting my myopic tendencies or removing the motes from my eyes. By the same token, what the patient typically sees is not what the physician typically sees; and for this reason both patient and physician are blind to each others' visions and will remain so unless they reveal in words their guarded thoughts and hidden feelings.

Finally, feminist approaches to bioethics offer nonfeminist approaches to bioethics an ethics of care combined with an ethics of power. At one and the same time, feminist bioethicists affirm the values that have been culturally linked with women (e.g., nurturance, caring, compassion, empathy, sympathy) and mistrust them. All too often women care too much, sacrificing their own personal and professional interests for the sake of their family members' and friends' interests, as if their own good counted for nothing. The fact that it is women who "dominate" the so-called helping professions (nursing, social work, child care) is a sign that our society still believes that women are especially suited to caring for the vulnerable: the elderly, infants, the sick, the distressed, and so on. Until men view themselves as caregivers and nurturers, women in the world of medicine will need to ask themselves and others why it is they, much more so than men, who wipe tears from patients' eyes, empty bedpans, and take rather than give orders.

To be sure, feminist approaches to bioethics have problems of their own. The very fact that some feminists focus on issues of choice, whereas other feminists focus on issues of control and still others on issues of connection, often causes feminists to engage in heated arguments as opposed to productive discussions about whether and how to regulate, say, assisted reproduction programs. Although I am convinced that most feminist bioethicists are indeed attracted to the philosophical framework I have described in this book, and although I believe that feminist bioethicists can and will develop consensus policies within this framework, I do not think there exists any *formula* that can guarantee consensus. For this reason, I have not attempted to develop any *specific* feminist policies here. Feminist policy cannot be conceived in the abstract; on the contrary, it has to be birthed in the concrete. In order to develop a feminist approach to a particular bioethical issue, feminist bioethicists must sit down together and challenge one another's perceptions about what sorts of systems, structures, and policies are most likely to serve the interests of women who, because of differences of race, class, ethnicity, age, marital status, health status, and so on, are obviously not all the same. Unless I actually sit down with a group of feminists who are actively doing bioethics, I dare not announce an imaginary conclusion to a discussion that has not actually occurred. There is no such thing as feminist armchair bioethics. Feminist approaches to bioethics require actual discourse, preferably face-to-face but at least computer-to-computer or phone-to-phone. Thus, I wish to end this book with a plea to all feminist bioethicists, including myself. We need to remember what our goal is—namely, to make the world of health care one that structures and organizes itself so as to serve men and women (as well as all races and classes) equally. If human beings have anything in common, it is our carnality and mortality. We all experience pain, suffering, and death; and since we are all equal in this way, it is the task of medicine to serve each of us as if we were the paradigm case of treatment for everyone. Feminist bioethicists are among the leaders in the movement to make medicine attentive to people's differences so that it can help people become the same—that is, equally autonomous and equally the recipients of beneficent clinical practices and just health-care policies. Beginning with an inquiry into the status of women in health care and medicine, and specifically with an investigation into those biomedical systems, structures and policies that subordinate women to men, feminist bioethicists aim to make medicine a practice that contributes not only to gender liberation but also to race and class liberation. After all, women cannot be fully liberated absent race and class liberation. A woman is always more than just a woman; her skin has a hue, and her wallet is either mostly full or mostly empty. Thus, feminist bioethicists' work is only beginning—and it will be quite some time before we know whether our thoughts and actions have actually secured our intended goal—namely, a health-care system, a style of medical practice, that takes women's interests, issues, values, and experiences as seriously as men's. As for me, I plan to live long enough to see feminist bioethicists help achieve this gender-equitous state of affairs. In defiance of the wisdom of the ancient Greeks, society will then have my permission to judge me happy *before* I die.

Notes

Introduction

1. Alison M. Jaggar, "Feminist Ethics: Projects, Problems, Prospects," in Claudia Card, ed., *Feminist Ethics* (Lawrence: University of Kansas Press, 1991), pp. 85–90.

Chapter One

1. Louis P. Pojman, *Discovering Right and Wrong* (Belmont, Calif.: Wadsworth, 1990), p. 2.
2. A. E. Taylor, trans., *Aristotle* (New York: Dover Publications, 1955), p. 91.
3. Aristotle, "Nicomachean Ethics," bk. 2, ch. 7 (trans. A. E. Wardman), in Renford Bambrough, ed., *The Philosophy of Aristotle* (New York: Mentor Books, 1963).
4. "American Medical Association Principles of Medical Ethics (1980)," in Thomas A. Mappes and Jane S. Zembaty, eds., *Biomedical Ethics* (New York: McGraw-Hill, 1991), p. 54.
5. Jeremy Bentham, "An Introduction to the Principles of Morals and Legislation," in Bentham, *Utilitarianism and Other Writings* (New York: New American Library, 1962), p. 65.
6. John Stuart Mill, "Utilitarianism," in Mill, *Utilitarianism, Liberty, and Representative Government* (London: J. M. Pent and Sons, 1936), pp. 7–8.
7. Immanuel Kant, *Groundwork of the Metaphysics of Morals*, trans. H. J. Paton (New York: Harper & Row, 1956), pp. 74–75.
8. David Hume, *Inquiry into the Principles of Morals* (New York: Liberal Arts Press, 1957), p. 105.
9. Ibid., p. 44.
10. Ibid., p. 57 (emphasis added).
11. Ronald Yezzi, *Medical Ethics: Thinking About Unavoidable Questions* (New York: Holt, Rinehart & Winston, 1980), p. 13.
12. Ibid.
13. Ibid., pp. 13–14.

14. Leon R. Kass, *Toward a More Natural Science: Biology and Human Affairs* (New York: Free Press, 1985), p. 348.
15. Thomas Hobbes, *Leviathan* (New York: E. P. Dutton, 1950), p. 104.
16. John Rawls, *A Theory of Justice* (Cambridge, Mass.: Belknap Press, 1971).
17. Ibid., p. 12.
18. Ibid., p. 154.
19. Ibid., p. 83.
20. David A.J. Richards, *The Moral Criticism of the Law* (Encino, Calif.: Dickenson, 1977), p. 46.
21. David A.J. Richards, *Sex, Drugs, Death, and the Law* (Totowa, N.J.: Rowman & Littlefield, 1982), p. 11.
22. Rawls, *A Theory of Justice*, pp. 92, 440.
23. Alasdair MacIntyre, *After Virtue* (Notre Dame, Ind.: University of Notre Dame Press, 1981), p. 177.
24. Ibid.
25. Ibid., p. 178.
26. Ibid., p. 181.
27. Ibid.
28. Lawrence A. Blum, *Friendship, Altruism and Morality* (London: Routledge and Kegan Paul, 1980), p. 2.
29. Jean-Paul Sartre, *Existentialism*, trans. Bernard Frectman (New York: Philosophical Library, 1947), p. 27.
30. Norman N. Greene, *Jean-Paul Sartre: The Existentialist Ethic* (Ann Arbor: University of Michigan Press, 1963), pp. 36–37.
31. David Sidorsky, ed., *John Dewey: The Essential Writings* (New York: Harper Torchbooks, 1977), p. 176.
32. William James, "On a Certain Blindness in Human Beings," in James, *Talks to Teachers on Psychology* (New York: W. W. Norton, 1958), p. 152.
33. Ibid., p. 144.
34. Robert L. Holmes, *Basic Moral Philosophy* (Belmont, Calif.: Wadsworth, 1993), pp. 44–45.
35. Ibid., p. 225.
36. William James, *The Principles of Psychology*, vol. 2 (New York: Dover Publications, 1950), p. 672.
37. Holmes, *Basic Moral Philosophy*, p. 225.
38. Jürgen Habermas, *Towards a Rational Society: Student Protest, Science, and Politics*, trans. J. J. Shapiro (Boston: Beacon Press, 1970), p. 75.
39. Jürgen Habermas, *Communication and the Evolution of Society*, trans. T. McCarthy (Boston: Beacon Press, 1979), p. 75.
40. Richard Rorty, *Contingency, Irony, and Solidarity* (Cambridge, Mass.: Cambridge University Press, 1987), p. 185.
41. Ibid., p. 61.
42. Michael Roth, "Review Essay: *Contingency, Irony, and Solidarity*," *History and Theory* 29, no. 3 (1990): 347.
43. Ibid.
44. Rorty, *Contingency, Irony, and Solidarity*, p. 186.

Chapter Two

1. Betty A. Sichel, "Different Strains and Strands: Feminist Contributions to Ethical Theory," *Newsletter on Feminism* 90, no. 2 (Winter 1991): 90.

2. Susan Sherwin, *No Longer Patient: Feminist Ethics and Health Care* (Philadelphia: Temple University Press, 1992), p. 42.

3. Ibid., pp. 42–43.

4. Carol Gilligan, *In a Different Voice* (Cambridge, Mass.: Harvard University Press, 1982).

5. Lawrence Kohlberg, "From Is to Ought: How to Commit the Naturalistic Fallacy and Get Away With It in the Study of Moral Development," in T. Mischel, ed., *Cognitive Development and Epistemology* (New York: Academic Press, 1971), pp. 164–165.

6. Gilligan, *In a Different Voice*, pp. 76–92.

7. Carol Gilligan, "Moral Orientation and Moral Development," in Eva Feder Kittay and Diana T. Meyers, eds., *Women and Moral Theory* (Totowa, N.J.: Rowman & Littlefield, 1987), p. 25.

8. Sandra Lee Bartky, "Feeding Egos and Tending Wounds: Deference and Disaffection in Women's Emotional Labor," in Bartky, ed., *Femininity and Domination*, p. 105.

9. Ibid., p. 106.

10. Ibid.

11. Ibid., p. 118.

12. Nel Noddings, *Caring: A Feminine Approach to Ethics and Moral Education* (Berkeley: University of California Press, 1984).

13. Ibid., pp. 3–4.

14. Sarah Lucia Hoagland, "Some Concerns About Nel Noddings' *Caring*," *Hypatia* 5, no. 1 (Spring 1990): 114.

15. Nel Noddings, "A Response," *Hypatia* 5, no. 1 (Spring 1990): 125.

16. Fyodor Dostoyevsky, *The Brothers Karamazov* (New York: Signet Classics, 1980).

17. Annette C. Baier, "What Do Women Want in a Moral Theory?" *Nous* 19, no. 1 (March 1985): 57.

18. Ibid., pp. 60–61.

19. Baier, "Trust and Antitrust Ethics," *Ethics* 96 (January 1986): 235.

20. Ibid.

21. Ibid., p. 238.

22. Ibid., p. 248.

23. Ibid., p. 241.

24. Ibid., p. 245.

25. Ibid.

26. Sara Ruddick, *Maternal Thinking: Toward a Politics of Peace* (Boston: Beacon Press, 1989).

27. Virginia Held, *Feminist Morality: Transforming Culture, Society, and Politics* (Chicago: University of Chicago Press, 1993).

28. Caroline Whitbeck, "The Maternal Instinct," in Joyce Trebilcot, ed., *Mothering: Essays in Feminist Theory* (Totowa, N.J.: Rowman & Allanheld, 1984).

29. Virginia Held, "Feminism and Moral Theory," in Eva Kittay and Diana Meyers, eds., *Women and Moral Theory* (Savage, Md.: Rowman & Littlefield, 1987), pp. 114–115.

30. Virginia Held, "Non-contractual Society: A Feminist View," in Marsha Hanen and Kai Nielsen, eds., *Science, Morality and Feminist Theory* (Calgary: University of Calgary Press, 1987), p. 130.

31. Ibid., p. 131.

32. Ibid., p. 132.

33. Annette Baier, "Cartesian Persons," in Baier, *Postures of the Mind: Essays on Mind and Morals* (Minneapolis: University of Minnesota Press, 1985), p. 84.

34. Patricia Ward Scoltsar, "Do Feminist Ethics Counter Feminist Aims?" in Eve Browning Cole and Susan Coultrip-McQuin, eds., *Explorations in Feminist Ethics* (Bloomington: Indiana University Press, 1992), p. 23.

35. Jeffner Allen, "Motherhood: The Annihilation of Women," in Trebilcot, ed., *Mothering: Essays in Feminist Theory*, p. 310.

36. Alison M. Jaggar, "Feminist Ethics," in Lawrence Becker, with Charlotte Becker, eds., *Encyclopedia of Ethics* (New York: Garland, 1992), pp. 363–364.

37. Jaggar, "Feminist Ethics," p. 361.

38. Alison M. Jaggar, "Feminist Ethics: Projects, Problems, Prospects," in Claudia Card, ed., *Feminist Ethics* (Lawrence: University of Kansas Press, 1991), p. 366.

39. Friedrich Wilhelm Nietzsche, *On the Genealogy of Morals*, trans. Walter Kaufman and R. Hollingdale (New York: Vintage Books, 1969).

40. Mary Daly, *Gyn/Ecology: The Metaethics of Radical Feminism* (Boston: Beacon Press, 1978), pp. 14–15.

41. Mary Daly, *Pure Lust: Elemental Feminist Philosophy* (Boston: Beacon Press, 1984), p. 275.

42. Ibid., p. 278.

43. Ibid., p. 279.

44. Sarah Lucia Hoagland, *Lesbian Ethics* (Palo Alto, Calif.: Institute of Lesbian Studies, 1989), p. 8.

45. Marilyn Frye, "A Response to *Lesbian Ethics*: Why Ethics?" in Claudia Card, ed., *Feminist Ethics* (Lawrence: University of Kansas Press, 1991), p. 53.

46. Ibid., p. 54.

47. Ibid., p. 13.

48. María Lugones, "Playfulness, 'World'-Travelling, and Loving Perception," *Hypatia* 2, no. 2 (Summer 1987): 13.

49. Hoagland, *Lesbian Ethics*, p. 246.

50. Virginia L. Warren, "Feminist Directions in Medical Ethics," *Health Care Ethics Committee Forum: An Interprofessional Journal on Healthcare Institutions' Ethical and Legal Issues* 4, no. 1 (1992): 20–22.

51. Jaggar, "Feminist Ethics," p. 364.

52. Ibid., pp. 363-364.

53. Ibid., p. 365.

54. Ibid.

55. Ibid.

Chapter Three

1. Tom L. Beauchamp and James F. Childress, *Principles of Biomedical Ethics*, 4th ed. (New York: Oxford University Press, 1994), p. 4.

2. K. Danner Clouser, "Bioethics," in Warren T. Reich, ed., *Encyclopedia of Bioethics*, vol. 1 (New York: Simon & Schuster/MacMillan, 1995), p. 116.

3. G. R. Dunstan, "Two Branches from One Stem," in Daniel Callahan and G. R. Dunstan, eds., *Biomedical Ethics: An Anglo-American Dialogue* (New York: New York Academy of Sciences, 1988), p. 4.

4. Clouser, "Bioethics," p. 119.

5. Edmund D. Pellegrino, "The Metamorphosis of Medical Ethics: A 30-Year Perspective," *Journal of the American Medical Association* 269, no. 9 (March 3, 1993): 1158–1162.

6. Ibid., p. 1159.

7. Stephen Toulmin, "Medical Ethics in Its American Context," in Callahan and Dunstan, eds., *Biomedical Ethics: An Anglo-American Dialogue*, p. 9.

8. Albert R. Jonsen, "The Birth of Bioethics," *Special Supplement Hastings Center Report* 23, no. 6 (November-December 1993): S1–S4.

9. Ibid., p. S2.

10. Ibid., pp. S2–S3.

11. Nancy Gibbs, "Love and Let Die," *Time*, March 19, 1990, p. 65.

12. "Last Rights," *Newsweek*, August 26, 1991, p. 41.

13. Jonsen, "The Birth of Bioethics," p. S4.

14. Clouser, "Bioethics," p. 125.

15. Ibid.

16. Ibid., p. 126.

17. Ibid.

18. Ibid.

19. Ibid.

20. David de Grazia, "Moving Forward in Bioethical Theory: Theories, Cases, and Specified Principlism," *The Journal of Medicine and Philosophy* 15, no. 2 (1990): 512.

21. Adapted from a table provided by Dr. Joan Gibson, "Thinking About the 'Ethics' in Bioethics," in B. R. Furrow, S. H. Johnson, T. S. Jost, and R. L. Schwartz, eds., *Bioethics: Healthcare Law and Ethics* (St. Paul, Minn.: West Publishing, 1991), p. 3.

22. Bernard Gert, *The Moral Rules* (New York: Harper & Row, 1973), pp. 44–60.

23. Ibid., p. 125.

24. K. Danner Clouser and Bernard Gert, "A Critique of Principlism," *Journal of Medicine and Philosophy* 15, no. 2 (1990): 235.

25. Albert R. Jonsen and Stephen Toulmin, *The Abuse of Casuistry* (Berkeley: University of California Press, 1988), p. 13.

26. Beauchamp and Childress, *Principles of Biomedical Ethics*, p. 19.

27. Albert Jonsen, "Casuistry," in Warren T. Reich, ed., *Encyclopedia of Bioethics*, vol. 1 (New York: Simon & Schuster/MacMillan, 1995), p. 349.

28. James H. Jones, *Bad Blood: The Tuskegee Syphilis Experiment—A Tragedy of Race and Medicine* (New York: The Free Press, 1981).

29. Jonsen, "The Birth of Bioethics," p. S2.

30. Beauchamp and Childress, *Principles of Biomedical Ethics,* p. 38.

31. Pellegrino, "The Metamorphosis of Medical Ethics: A 30-Year Perspective," p. 1160.

32. Ibid.

33. Edmund D. Pellegrino and David C. Thomasma, *For the Patient's Good: The Restoration of Beneficence in Health Care* (New York: Oxford University Press, 1988).

34. Clouser and Gert, "A Critique of Principlism," p. 233.

35. Ibid.

36. Ibid.

37. W. D. Ross, *The Right and the Good* (Oxford: Clarendon Press, 1930), p. 19.

38. Beauchamp and Childress, *Principles of Biomedical Ethics,* p. 34.

39. Robert Holmes, quoted in K. Danner Clouser and Loretta Kopelman, "Introduction: What Is Applied About Applied Philosophy?" *Journal of Medicine and Philosophy* 15, no. 2 (1990): 123.

40. Ibid., p. 157.

41. Ronald Green, "Method in Bioethics: A Troubled Assessment," *Journal of Medicine and Philosophy* 15, no. 2 (1990): 186.

42. Carl Elliott, "Where Ethics Comes From and What To Do About It," *Hastings Center Report* 22, no. 4 (July-August 1992): 30.

43. Ibid., pp. 30–31.

44. Ibid., p. 35.

45. Ibid.

46. Beauchamp and Childress, *Principles of Biomedical Ethics,* p. 501.

47. Ibid., p. 502.

48. Henry Richardson, "Specifying Norms As a Way to Resolve Concrete Ethical Problems," *Philosophy and Public Affairs* 19 (Fall 1990): 294.

49. Ibid., pp. 281–282.

50. Ibid., p. 283.

51. Ibid., p. 299.

52. Warren T. Reich, "History of the Notion of Care," in *Encyclopedia of Bioethics,* vol. 1 (New York: Simon & Schuster / MacMillan, 1995), p. 329.

53. Ibid.

54. Francis W. Peabody, "The Care of the Patient," in John Stoecke, ed., *Encounters Between Patients and Doctors: An Anthology* (Cambridge, Mass: MIT Press, 1927), pp. 387-401.

55. Eric J. Cassell, *The Nature of Suffering and the Goals of Medicine* (New York: Oxford University Press, 1991), p. 234.

56. Ibid., pp. 194–211.

57. Nancy S. Jecker and Warren T. Reich, "Contemporary Ethics of Care," in Warren T. Reich, ed., *Encyclopedia of Bioethics,* vol. 1 (New York: Simon & Schuster / MacMillan, 1995), p. 342.

58. Tristram Engelhardt, *The Foundations of Bioethics,* 2nd ed. (New York: Oxford University Press: 1996), pp. 8–13.

59. Ibid., p. 41.

60. Ibid., pp. 41–42.

61. Ibid., p. 123.

62. Ibid.

Chapter Four

1. Alison M. Jaggar, *Feminist Politics and Human Nature* (Totowa, N.J.: Rowman and Allanheld, 1983), p. 7.

2. See, for example, Jaggar, *Feminist Politics and Human Nature*, and Zillah Eisenstein, *The Radical Future of Liberal Feminism* (Boston: Northeastern University Press, 1986).

3. See, for example, Richard Schmitt, *Introduction to Marx and Engels* (Boulder, Colo.: Westview Press, 1987), and Michele Barrett, *Women's Oppression Today* (London: Verso, 1980).

4. Adrienne Rich, "Compulsory Heterosexuality and Lesbian Existence," *Signs: Journal of Women in Culture and Society* 5, no. 4 (Summer 1980): 648–649.

5. Juliet Mitchell, *Woman's Estate* (New York: Vintage Books, 1971).

6. Juliet Mitchell, *Psychoanalysis and Feminism* (New York: Vintage Books, 1971).

7. Jaggar, *Feminist Politics and Human Nature*, pp. 316–317.

8. Gerda Lerner, "Reconceptualizing Differences Among Women," *Journal of Women's History* 1, no. 3 (Winter 1990): 106–122.

9. Ximena Bunster-Bunalto, "Surviving Beyond Fear: Women and Torture in Latin America," in June Nash and Helena Safa, eds., *Women and Change in Latin America* (Westport, Conn.: Greenwood Publishing Group, 1986), pp. 297–324.

10. Ynestra King, "Healing the Wounds: Feminism, Ecology, and Nature/Culture Dualism," in Nancy Tuana and Rosemarie Tong, eds., *Feminism and Philosophy: Essential Readings in Theory, Reinterpretation, and Application* (Boulder, Colo.: Westview Press, 1995).

11. Simone de Beauvoir, *The Second Sex*, trans. and ed. H. M. Parshley (New York: Vintage Books, 1974), p. xxxiii.

12. Dorothy Kaufmann McCall, "Simone de Beauvoir, *The Second Sex*, and Jean-Paul Sartre," *Signs: Journal of Women in Culture and Society* 5, no. 2 (Winter 1979): 210.

13. Dorothy Dinnerstein, *The Mermaid and the Minotaur: Sexual Arrangements and Human Malaise* (New York: Harper & Row, 1977).

14. Nancy Chodorow, *The Reproduction of Mothering* (Berkeley: University of California Press, 1978).

15. Sheila Mullett, "Shifting Perspectives: A New Approach to Ethics," in Lorraine Code, Sheila Mullett, and Christine Overall, eds., *Feminist Perspectives* (Toronto: University of Toronto, 1989), pp. 119–120.

16. 'Phallogocentric' refers to a worldview centered on the penis—that is, on the man. ('Phallus' means penis or testes, 'logos' means the word as metaphysical presence and 'centric' means centered on.)

17. de Beauvoir, *The Second Sex*, p. 51.

18. Hélène Cixous, "The Laugh of the Medusa," in Elaine Marks and Isabelle de Courtiuron, eds., *New French Feminisms* (New York: Schocken Books, 1981), p. 242.

19. Elaine Marks and Isabelle de Courtiuron, "Introduction III," in Marks and Courtiuron, eds., *New French Feminisms*, p. 36.

20. Cixous, "The Laugh of the Medusa," p. 256.

21. Ibid.

22. Ibid., p. 251.

23. María Lugones and Elizabeth Spelman, "Have We Got a Theory for You! Feminist Theory, Cultural Imperialism, and the Demand for 'The Woman's

Voice,'" in Janet A. Kourany, James P. Sterba, and Rosemarie Tong, eds., *Feminist Philosophies* (Englewood Cliffs, N.J.: Prentice-Hall, 1992), pp. 382–383.

24. Andree Nicola McLaughlin, "Black Women, Identity, and the Quest for Humanhood and Wholeness: Wild Women in the Whirlwind," in Alison M. Jaggar and Paula S. Rothenberg, eds., *Feminist Frameworks* (New York: McGraw-Hill, 1993), p. 275.

25. Robin West, "Jurisprudence and Gender," *University of Chicago Law Review* 55, no. 1 (Winter 1988): 6–7.

26. Schmitt, *Introduction to Marx and Engels*, pp. 7–8.

27. Ibid.

28. Karl Marx, *A Contribution to the Critique of Political Economy* (New York: International Publishers, 1972), pp. 20–21.

29. Chodorow, *The Reproduction of Mothering*, pp. 174–176.

30. Dinnerstein, *The Mermaid and the Minotaur*, p. 83.

31. West, "Jurisprudence and Gender," p. 3.

32. Ibid., p. 29.

33. See, for example, Caroline Whitbeck, "A Different Reality: Feminist Ontology," in Ann Garry and Marilyn Pearsall, eds., *Women, Knowledge, and Reality* (Boston: Urwin Hyman, 1989), pp. 51–76.

34. West, "Jurisprudence and Gender," p. 29.

35. Ibid., pp. 29–36.

36. King, "Healing the Wounds: Feminism, Ecology, and the Nature/Culture Dualism," p. 353.

37. Katherine T. Bartlett, "Feminist Legal Methods (1990)," in D. Kelly Weisberg, ed., *Feminist Legal Theory: Foundations* (Philadelphia: Temple University Press, 1993), pp. 383–393.

38. Gloria Cowan, L. W. Warren, and J. L. Young, "Medical Perceptions of Menopausal Symptoms," *Psychology of Women Quarterly* 9 (1985): 3–14.

39. Susan Bordo, "Feminism, Postmodernism, and Gender Skepticism," in Linda J. Nicholson, ed., *Feminism/Postmodernism* (New York: Routledge, 1990), p. 152.

40. Sandra Harding, *The Science Question in Feminism* (Ithaca: Cornell University Press, 1986), p. 191.

41. Jaggar, *Feminist Politics and Human Nature*, p. 370.

42. Ibid.

43. Betty A. Sichel, "Different Strains and Strands: Feminist Contributions to Ethical Theory," *Newsletter on Feminism* 90, no. 2 (Winter 1990): 90.

44. Katharine T. Bartlett, "Feminist Legal Methods," in D. Kelly Weisberg, ed., *Feminist Legal Theory* (Philadelphia: Temple University Press, 1993), p. 551.

45. Simone de Beauvoir, *The Second Sex*, trans. H. M Parsley (New York: Vintage Books, 1952).

46. Bartlett, "Feminist Legal Methods," p. 551.

47. Catharine A. MacKinnon, "Feminism, Marxism, Method and the State: An Agenda for Theory," *Signs* 7, no. 3 (Spring 1982): 519.

48. Ibid., pp. 519–520.

49. Ibid., p. 544.

50. Adrienne Rich, *Of Woman Born* (New York: W. W. Norton, 1979), pp. 38–39.

51. Susan Sherwin, *No Longer Patient: Feminist Ethics and Health Care* (Philadelphia: Temple University Press, 1992), p. 32.

52. Mary Mahowald, *Women and Children in Health Care: An Unequal Majority* (New York: Oxford University Press, 1993), p. 4.

53. Ibid., p. 16.

54. Susan M. Wolf, ed., *Feminism & Bioethics: Beyond Reproduction* (New York: Oxford University Press, 1996).

55. Sarah Lucia Hoagland, *Lesbian Ethics* (Palo Alto, Calif.: Institute of Lesbian Studies, 1989), p. 12.

56. Bartlett, "Feminist Legal Methods (1990)," p. 389.

57. Ibid., p. 390.

58. Alison M. Jaggar, "Toward a Feminist Conception of Moral Reasoning," in James Sterba, ed., *Moral and Social Justice* (Lanham, Md.: Rowman and Littlefield, 1995), p. 115.

59. Ibid., p. 118.

60. Ibid., pp. 131–132 (emphasis added).

61. Lugones and Spelman, "Have We Got a Theory for You!" p. 383.

62. Ibid., pp. 132–135.

Chapter Five

1. James W. Knight and Joan C. Callahan, *Preventing Birth: Contemporary Methods and Related Moral Controversies* (Salt Lake City: University of Utah Press, 1989), p. 13.

2. St. Bonaventure, quoted in "Birth Control: The Pill and the Church," *Newsweek*, July 6, 1964, p. 51.

3. Norman St. John-Stevas, *Life, Death and the Law* (Bloomington: Indiana University Press, 1961), p. 84.

4. An exception to this tenet of natural law has been expressed by Michael Novak: "I do not understand why it is 'unnatural' to block the spatial flow of sperm so that it does not fertilize the ovum—to block it by diaphragm, or condom, say (however disagreeable such devices are)—and yet not 'unnatural' to time the placement of the sperm so that it does not fertilize the ovum. In either case, human intelligence is directing the process so that the ovum will not be fertilized. In the first case, a physical spatial object is inserted in the process; in the second case, an equally physical temporal gap is deliberately (and with such care!) inserted in the process. I do not understand why spatial objects are blameworthy while temporal gaps are not. Both are equally 'natural' (or 'unnatural')." See Novak, "Frequent, Even Daily, Communion," in Daniel Callahan, ed., *The Catholic Case for Contraception* (New York: Macmillan, 1969), p. 94.

5. Thomas A. Mappes and Janet S. Zembaty, eds., *Social Ethics: Morality and Social Policy* (New York: McGraw-Hill, 1977), p. 335.

6. Nicholas D. Kristof, "China's Birth Rate on Rise Again As Official Sanctions Are Ignored," *New York Times*, April 21, 1987, p. 1.

7. Patrick E. Tyler, "Population Control in China Falls to Coercion and Evasion," *New York Times*, June 25, 1995, pp. 1, 6.

8. Robert Hatcher et al., *Contraceptive Technology: 1986–1987* (New York: Irvington Publishers, 1986), p. 232.

9. *Carey v. Population Services International*, 431 U.S. 678 (1977).

10. A. M. Kenney, J. D. Forest, and A. Torres, "Storm over Washington: The Parental Notification Proposal," *Family Planning Perspectives* 14, no. 4 (July-August 1982): 185.

11. Ibid., p. 189.

12. L. Brown and Karen Garloch, "From Cradle to Grave," *Charlotte Observer*, November 27, 1989, p. B1.

13. E. R. McAnarney and W. R. Hendee, "Adolescent Pregnancy and Its Consequences," *Journal of the American Medical Association* 262, no. 1 (July 7, 1989): 74.

14. Barbara Kantrowitz and Pat Wingert, "The Norplant Debate," *Newsweek*, February 15, 1993, p. 40.

15. Arthur Caplan, quoted in ibid., p. 37.

16. George J. Annas, "Sterilization of the Mentally Retarded: A Decision for the Courts," *Hastings Center Report* 11, no. 4 (August 1981): 18.

17. *In the Matter of Lee Ann Grady*, 426A 2d 467, N.J. (1981).

18. Annas, "Sterilization of the Mentally Retarded," p. 18.

19. *Skinner v. Oklahoma*, 62 Sup. Ct. Rep. 1110 (1942).

20. 189 Okla. 235; 115 P. 2d 123 (141).

21. *Skinner v. Oklahoma*, 62 Sup. Ct. Rep. 1110 (1942).

22. Lisa C. Bower, "The Trope of the Dark Continent in the Fetal Harm Debates: 'Africanism' and the Right to Choice," in Patricia Boling, ed., *Expecting Trouble: Surrogacy, Fetal Abuse, & New Reproductive Technologies* (Boulder, Colo.: Westview Press, 1995), p. 146.

23. James W. Knight and Joan C. Callahan, *Preventing Birth: Contemporary Methods and Related Moral Controversies* (Salt Lake City: University of Utah Press, 1989), pp. 108–109.

24. Ibid., pp. 75-76.

25. R. A. Hatcher, F. Stewart, J. Trussel, D. Kowal, F. Guest, G. K. Stewart, and W. Cates, *Contraceptive Technology: 1990–1992* (New York: Irvington Publishers, 1990).

26. N. C. Lee, G. L. Rubin, H. W. Ory, and R. T. Burkman, "Type of Intrauterine Device and the Risk of Pelvic Inflammatory Disease," *Obstetrics and Gynecology* 62, no. 1 (1983): 1–10.

27. J. Shiver, Jr., "Dalkon Shield Company Files for Bankruptcy," *Los Angeles Times*, August 22, 1985, sec. 1, p. 20.

28. Susan Sherwin, *No Longer Patient: Feminist Ethics and Health Care* (Philadelphia: Temple University Press, 1992), p. 128.

29. Phillida Bunkle, "Calling the Shots? The International Politics of Depo-Provera," in Rita Arditti, Renate Duelli Klein, and Shelley Minden, eds., *Test-Tube Women: What Future for Motherhood?* (London: Pandora Press, 1985), pp. 165–187.

30. Anita Petra Hardon, "The Needs of Women Versus the Interests of Family Planning Personnel, Policy-Makers and Researchers: Conflicting Views on Safety and Acceptability of Contraceptives," *Social Science and Medicine* 35, no. 6 (1992): 762.

31. Ellen H. Moskowitz, Bruce Jennings, and Daniel Callahan, "Long-Acting Contraceptives: Ethical Guidelines for Policymakers and Health Care Providers," *Special Supplement: Hastings Center Report* (January-February 1995): S2.

32. "Contraceptives Raise Ethical Concerns," *Medical Ethics Advisor* 9, no. 2 (February 1993): 17.

33. Moskowitz et al., "Long-Acting Contraceptives," p. S4.

34. Bonnie Steinbock, "Coercion and Long-Term Contraceptives," *Special Supplement: Hastings Center Report* (January-February 1995): S21.

35. Ibid., p. S22.

36. Nancy Nevelopp Dubler and Amanda White, "Fertility Control," in Warren T. Reich, ed., *Encyclopedia of Bioethics*, vol. 1 (New York: Simon & Schuster/MacMillan, 1995), p. 84.

37. John A. Robertson, *Children of Choice: Freedom and the New Reproductive Technologies* (Princeton, N.J.: Princeton University Press, 1994), p. 70.

38. George F. Brown, "Long-Acting Contraceptives: Rationale, Current Development, and Ethical Implications," *Special Supplement: Hastings Center Report* (January-February 1995): S12.

39. Philip J. Hilts, "Birth-Control Backlash," *New York Times Magazine*, December 16, 1990, p. 74.

40. Ibid., p. 41.

41. Doug Podolsky, with Marjory Roberts, "Sorry, Not Sold in the U.S.," *U.S. News & World Report*, December 24, 1990, p. 65.

42. Dr. C. Wayne Bardin, quoted in Karen Heller, "Birth and Control," *Charlotte Observer*, May 2, 1993, p. 8E.

43. Heller, "Birth and Control," p. 8E.

44. Hilts, "Birth-Control Backlash," p. 55.

45. Michelle Ingrassia, "Still Fumbling in the Dark," *Newsweek*, March 13, 1995, p. 60.

46. Kaplan and Tong, *Controlling Our Reproductive Destiny: A Technological and Philosophical Perspective*, pp. 128–130.

47. Adele Clark, "Subtle Forms of Sterilization Abuse: A Reproductive Rights Analysis," in Arditti, Klein, and Minden, eds., *Test-Tube Women: What Future for Motherhood?* p. 198.

48. Helen Rodriguez-Trias, "Sterilization Abuse," in Ruth Hubbard, Mary Sue Henifin, and Barbara Fried, eds., *Biological Woman: The Convenient Myth* (Cambridge, Mass.: Schenkman, 1982), p. 150.

49. Clark, "Subtle Forms of Sterilization Abuse: A Reproductive Rights Analysis," p. 189.

50. Ibid., pp. 193–196.

51. Knight and Callahan, *Preventing Birth: Contemporary Methods and Related Moral Controversies*, pp. 143–144.

52. Hilts, "Birth-Control Backlash," p. 70.

53. Leanne Kleinmann, "The Most Intimate Crisis," *Health* (February 1987): 27.

54. William J. Bennett, "Sex and the Education of Our Children," *America* 156 (February 14, 1987): 122.

55. Kaplan and Tong, *Controlling Our Reproductive Destiny: A Technological and Philosophical Perspective*, p. 115.

56. Carol Gilligan, *In a Different Voice* (Cambridge, Mass.: Harvard University Press, 1982), p. 68.

57. Ibid., p. 109.

58. Ibid., pp. 112–115.

59. Mary Ann O'Loughlin, "Responsibility and Moral Maturity in the Control of Fertility—or, A Woman's Place Is in the Wrong," *Social Research* 50, no. 3 (Autumn 1983): 574.

60. Mary Mahowald, *Women and Children in Health Care: An Unequal Majority* (New York: Oxford University Press, 1992), p. 79.

61. Knight and Callahan, *Preventing Birth: Contemporary Methods and Related Moral Controversies*, p. 308.

62. C. L. Chung, "The Male Role in Contraception: Implications for Health Education," *Journal of School Health* 3 (March 1983): 197–201.

63. Marisa Fox, "New-Tech Contraception," *Health* (February 1987): 32.

64. R. Kangil, "Lord, But It's Hard to Sell a Male Contraceptives," *Johns Hopkins Magazine* (August 1984): 16–20.

65. Anne Woodhouse, "Sexuality, Femininity and Fertility Control," *Women's Studies International Forum* 5, no. 1 (1982): 1–15.

Chapter Six

1. Frederick S. Jaffe, "Enacting Religious Beliefs in a Pluralistic Society," *Hastings Center Report* 8, no. 4 (August 1978): 14.

2. Ibid.

3. John T. Noonan, Jr., "An Almost Absolute Value in History," in Richard Wasserstrom, ed., *Today's Moral Problems* (New York: Macmillan, 1975), p. 151.

4. Mary Anne Warren, "On the Moral and Legal Status of Abortion," in Tom L. Beauchamp and LeRoy Walters, eds., *Contemporary Issues in Bioethics* (Belmont, Calif.: Wadsworth, 1978), p. 224.

5. *Roe v. Wade*, 410 U.S. 113, 93 S.Ct. 705 (January 22, 1973).

6. Daniel Callahan, "How Technology Is Reframing the Abortion Debate," *Hastings Center Report* 16, no. 1 (February, 1986): 34.

7. Thomas A. Shannon and Allan B. Wolter, "Reflections on the Moral Status of the Pre-Embryo," *Theological Studies* 61 (1990): 621.

8. Bruce M. Carlson offers this further explanation: "Within the fertilized ovum lies the capability to form an entire organism. In many vertebrates the individual cells resulting from the first few divisions after fertilization retain this capability. In the jargon of embryology, such cells are described as totipotent. As development continues, the cells gradually lose the ability to form all the types of cells that are found in the adult body." See *Patten's Foundations of Embryology*, 5th ed. (New York: McGraw-Hill, 1988), p. 23.

9. Karen Gervais and Steven Miles, *RU-486: New Issues in the American Abortion Debate* (Minneapolis: Center for Biomedical Ethics, 1990), p. 13.

10. Ellen Willis, "Putting Women Back into the Abortion Debate," *Village Voice*, July 16, 1985, p. 15.

11. Ibid.

12. Judith Jarvis Thomson, "A Defense of Abortion," in Richard Wasserstrom, ed., *Today's Moral Problems*, 3rd ed. (New York: Macmillan, 1985), p. 425.

13. Ibid., p. 423.

14. Ibid., pp. 420–421.

15. Ibid., p. 426.

16. Christine Overall, *Human Reproduction: Principles, Practices, Policies* (Toronto: Oxford University Press, 1993), p. 67.

17. Ibid., p. 69.

18. Hadley Arkes, *First Things: An Inquiry into the First Principles of Morals and Justice* (Princeton, N.J.: Princeton University Press, 1986), p. 378.

19. Overall, *Human Reproduction*, p. 72.

20. Ibid.

21. Ibid., p. 74.

22. Anne Donchin, "The Growing Feminist Debate over the New Reproductive Technologies," *Hypatia* 4, no. 3 (Fall 1989): 144.

23. Overall, *Human Reproduction*, p. 75.

24. Ibid., pp. 76–77.

25. Alison Jaggar, "Abortion and a Woman's Right to Decide," in Carol C. Gould and Marx W. Wartofsky, eds., *Women and Philosophy: Toward a Theory of Liberation* (New York: Putnam's, 1976), pp. 352–353.

26. Ibid., p. 353.

27. Ibid.

28. Jonathan B. Imber, *Abortion and the Private Practice of Medicine* (New Haven, Conn.: Yale University Press, 1986).

29. In 1995, 31 percent of obstetrical residency programs did not offer training in how to do abortions—compared to 7.5 percent in 1976. See Joan Beck, "Give Doctors a 'Choice' on Abortion," *Charlotte Observer*, February 24, 1995, p. 9A.

30. Tamar Lewin, "Hurdles Increase for Many Women Seeking Abortions," *New York Times*, March 15, 1992, p. 11.

31. Lisa Belkin, "Kill for Life," *New York Times Magazine*, October 30, 1994, pp. 47–80.

32. Sandra G. Boodman, "The Death of Abortion Doctors," *Washington Post*, April 20, 1993, p. 7.

33. *Roe v. Wade*, 410 U.S., 113, S.Ct. 705, 35 L.ed. 2D. 147 (1973); cited in *Congressional Record*, vol. 119, no. 29 (February 26, 1973), p. 5.

34. *Maher v. Roe*, 432 U.S. (1977); *Beal v. Roe*, 432 U.S. (1977).

35. *ACLU Report*, October 1987, pp. 25–49.

36. "Portrait of Injustice," *Reproductive Freedom in the States* (New York: Center for Reproductive Law and Policy, February 25, 1995).

37. Public Agenda Foundation, "The Battle over Abortion: Seeking Common Ground in a Divided Nation" (Dayton, Ohio: National Issues Forum, 1990), p. 22.

38. "The Status of a Woman's Right to Choose Abortion," *Reproductive Freedom in the States* (New York: Center for Reproductive Law and Policy, September 8, 1994), p. 2.

39. "Restrictions on Young Women," *Reproductive Freedom in the States* (New York: Center for Reproductive Law and Policy, September 8, 1994).

40. *Akron, Ohio, Codified Ordinances*, Ch. 1879, 1870. 03 (1978).

41. *Thornburgh v. American College of Obstetricians and Gynecologists*, 476 U.S. 747 (1986).

42. *City of Akron v. Akron Center for Reproductive Health Services*, 462 U.S.416 (1983).

43. *Thornburgh v. American College of Obstetricians and Gynecologists*, 476 U.S. 747 (1986).

44. *Planned Parenthood of Southeastern Pennsylvania v. Casey*, 112 S.Ct. 279 (1992).

45. *Rust v. Sullivan*, 111 S.Ct. 1759 (1991).

46. Ellen Goodman, "Court Says the Government That Pays Your Rent Can Buy Your Speech," *Charlotte Observer*, May 27, 1991, p. 11A.

47. Carole Joffe, "Fertility Control: Social Issues," in Warren T. Reich, ed., *Encyclopedia of Bioethics*, vol. 1 (New York: Simon & Schuster/MacMillan, 1995), p. 829.

48. *Planned Parenthood Association of Kansas City v. Ashcroft*, 103 S.Ct. 1532 (1983); *Simopoulos v. Virginia*, 103 S.Ct. (1983); *City of Akron v. Akron Center for Reproductive Health*, 106 S.Ct. 1517 (1983).

49. *Planned Parenthood of Southeastern Pennsylvania v. Casey*, 112 S.Ct. 2791 (1992).

50. "The Status of a Woman's Right to Choose Abortion," p. 2.

51. Janet Benshoof, "*Planned Parenthood v. Casey*: The Impact of the New Undue Burden Standard on Reproductive Health Care," *Trends in Health Care, Law and Ethics* 8, no. 3 (Summer 1993): 27.

52. Edwin Cher, "House OKs Ban on Abortion Technique," *Charlotte Observer*, March 28, 1996, p. 11A.

53. *Webster v. Reproductive Health Services*, No. 88–605, 109 S.Ct. 3040 (1989).

54. *Turnock v. Ragsdale*, 112 S.Ct. 1309 (1992).

55. Chief Justice Rehnquist, quoted in Linda Greenhouse, "Change in Course," *New York Times*, July 4, 1989, p. 1.

56. Greenhouse, "Change in Course." p. 1.

57. Alice Lake, "The New French Pill," *McCall's*, March 1990, p. 62.

58. Andrea Sachs, "Abortion Pills on Trial," *Time*, December 5, 1994, p. 45.

59. Lake, "The New French Pill," p. 59.

60. Ibid.

61. Sachs, "Abortion Pills on Trial," p. 45.

62. Ruth Macklin, "Abortion: Contemporary Ethical and Legal Aspects," in Warren T. Reich, ed., *Encyclopedia of Bioethics*, vol. 1 (New York: Simon & Schuster/MacMillan, 1995), p. 14.

63. Anne M. Maloney, "Women and Children First," in Alison M. Jaggar, ed., *Living with Contradictions: Controversies in Feminist Social Ethics* (Boulder, Colo.: Westview Press, 1994), pp. 274–275.

64. Catharine A. MacKinnon, "Roe v. Wade: A Study in Male Ideology," in Lewis M. Schwartz, *Arguing About Abortion* (Belmont, Calif.: Wadsworth, 1993): 223.

65. Catharine A. MacKinnon, "Abortion: On Public and Private," in Jaggar, ed., *Living with Contradictions*, pp. 275–280.

66. Russell L. McIntyre, "Abortion and the Search for Public Policy," *Health Care, Law & Ethics* 8, no. 3 (Summer 1993), p. 15; emphasis added.

67. Ibid.

68. Beverly Smith, "Choosing Ourselves: Black Women and Abortion," in Jaggar, ed., *Living with Contradictions*, p. 291.

69. Jaggar, "Abortion and a Woman's Right to Decide," p. 357.

70. Gilligan, *In a Different Voice*, p. 26.

71. Ibid., pp. 28–29.

72. Gilligan, *In a Different Voice*, p. 92.

73. Nel Noddings, *Caring: A Feminine Approach to Ethics and Moral Education* (Berkeley: University of California Press, 1984), p. 9.

74. Ibid., p. 47.

75. Ibid., p. 151.

76. Ibid., p. 143.

77. Ibid., p. 152.

78. Ibid.

79. Ibid.

80. Susan Sherwin, *No Longer Patient: Feminist Ethics and Health Care* (Philadelphia: Temple University Press, 1992), p. 100.

81. Ibid., p. 102.

82. Ibid., p. 107.

83. Rosalind Pollack Petchsky, "Fetal Images: The Power of Visual Culture in the Politics of Reproduction," *Feminist Studies* 13, no. 2 (1987).

84. Sherwin, *No Longer Patient*, p. 109.

85. Ibid.

86. Ibid., p. 110.

87. Public Agenda Foundation, "Respecting Differences: Private Lives and the Public Interest," p. 34.

88. Wendy Brown, "Reproductive Freedom and the Right to Privacy: A Paradox for Feminists," in Irene Diamond, ed., *Families, Politics, and Public Policy: A Feminist Dialogue on Women and the State* (New York: Longman, 1983), p. 335.

89. M. Carlson, "Abortion's Hardest Cases," *Time*, July 9, 1990, p. 24.

Chapter Seven

1. John Robertson, *Children of Choice: Freedom and the New Reproductive Technologies* (Princeton, N.J.: Princeton University Press, 1994), pp. 4–5.

2. There are two types of artificial insemination: artificial insemination by husband (AIH) and artificial insemination by donor (AID). In order to avoid confusion between the acronym AID and the acronym AIDS (auto-immune-disease syndrome), some infertility specialists prefer to refer to AID as DI, or donor insemination.

3. U.S. Congress, Office of Technology Assessment, *Infertility: Medical and Social Choices* (Washington, D.C.: Government Printing Office, 1988).

4. V. Davajan and D. R. Mishell, Jr., "Evaluation of the Infertile Couple," in D. R. Mishell, Jr., and V. Davajan, eds., *Infertility, Contraception, and Endocrinology* (Oradell, N.J.: Medical Economics, 1986), p. 381.

5. Robertson, *Children of Choice*, p. 98.

6. Ibid., p. 97.

7. Leon Kass, "Babies by Means of In Vitro Fertilization: Unethical Experiments on the Unborn?" *New England Journal of Medicine* 285 (1971): 1177.

8. Peter Singer and Deanne Wells, *Making Babies: The New Science and Ethics of Conception* (New York: Charles Scribner's Sons, 1985), p. 48.

9. U.S. Congress, Office of Technology Assessment (OTA), *Artificial Insemination: Practice in the United States: Summary of a 1987 Study* (Washington, D.C.: 1988).

10. Catholic Church, Congregation for the Doctrine of the Faith, *Instruction on Respect for Human Life in its Origin and on the Dignity of Procreation* (Vatican City, 1987).

11. Singer and Wells, *Making Babies: The New Science and Ethics of Conception*, p. 38.

12. Barbara Menning, "Donor Insemination: The Psychosocial Issues," *American College of Gynecology and Obstetrics* 18 (1981): 155–171.

13. Ibid.

14. Robin Rowland, "The Social and Psychological Consequences of Secrecy in Artificial Insemination by Donor (AID) Programmers," *Social Science Medicine* 21, no. 4 (1985): 395.

15. George Annas, "Beyond the Best Interests of the Sperm Donor," *Child Welfare* 13, no. 13 (March 1981): 7.

16. L. T. Styron, "Artificial Insemination: A New Frontier for Medical Malpractice and Medical Products Liability," *Loyola Law Review* 32 (1986): 411–446.

17. Mary Warnock, *A Question of Life: The Warnock Report on Human Fertilization and Embryology* (Oxford: Basil Blackwell, 1985), p. 11.

18. Maureen McGuire and Nancy J. Alexander, "Artificial Insemination of Single Women," *Fertility and Sterility* 43, no. 2 (1985): 182–184.

19. Rowland, "The Social and Psychological Consequences of Secrecy," p. 395.

20. Gena Corea, *The Mother Machine: Reproductive Technologies from Artificial Insemination to Artificial Wombs* (New York: Harper & Row, 1985), p. 25.

21. Singer and Wells, *Making Babies: The New Science and Ethics of Conception*, pp. 42–46.

22. Lawrence J. Kaplan and Rosemarie Tong, *Controlling Our Reproductive Destiny: A Technological and Philosophical Perspective* (Cambridge, Mass.: MIT Press, 1994), p. 261.

23. Warren E. Leary, "New Focus on Sperm Brings Fertility Successes, *New York Times*, September 13, 1990, p. B11.

24. Christine Overall, *Reproduction: Principles, Practices, Policies* (Toronto: Oxford University Press, 1993), p. 27.

25. Ibid., pp. 27–28.

26. Lori B. Andrews, *New Conceptions: A Consumer's Guide to the Newest Infertility Treatments* (New York: Balantyne Books, 1985), p. 138.

27. John Robertson, "Procreative Liberty and the Control of Conception, Pregnancy, and Childbirth," *Virginia Law Review* 69 (April 1983): 450.

28. Maura J. Ryan, "The Argument for Unlimited Procreative Liberty: A Feminist Critique," *Hastings Center Report* 20, no. 4 (July-August 1990): 7.

29. Ibid., p. 12.

30. Overall, *Reproduction: Principles, Practices, Policies*, p. 29.

31. Corea, *The Mother Machine*, p. 101.

32. Tract Weber and Julie Marquis, "Staffers at Top Fertility Center Tell Horror Stories," *Charlotte Observer*, July 16, 1995, pp. 1A, 4A.

33. Otto Friedrich, "A Legal, Moral, Social Nightmare," *Time*, September 10, 1984, p. 55.

34. Laura Muha, "She Lost Her Husband But Saved Their Dream," *Redbook*, May 1995, p. 80.

35. Ibid., p. 83.

36. *Strnad v. Strnad*, 78 N.Y. Supplement, 2nd Ser. (1948), at 391–392.

37. *People v. Sorenson*, 68 Cal. 2nd 280, 66 Cal. Rpt. (1968), at 437.

38. B. J. Jensen, "Artificial Insemination and the Law," *Brigham Young University Law Review* (1982): 955–956.

39. Walter Wadlington, "Reproductive Technologies: Artificial Insemination," in Warren T. Reich, ed., *Encyclopedia of Bioethics* (New York: Simon & Schuster/ MacMillan, 1995), p. 2219.

40. Kamran S. Moghissi, "The Technology of AID," in Linda M. Whiteford and Marilyn L. Poland, eds., *New Approaches to Human Reproduction*, (Boulder, Colo.: Westview Press, 1989), p. 129.

41. Singer and Wells, *Making Babies: The New Science and Ethics of Conception*, p. 154.

42. Maureen McGuire and Nancy J. Alexander, "Artificial Insemination of Single Women," *Fertility and Sterility* 43, no. 2 (1985): 182–184.

43. Mary B. Mahowald, *Women and Children in Health Care: An Unequal Majority* (New York: Oxford University Press, 1993), p. 30.

44. Renate Duelli Klein, "Doing It Ourselves: Self Insemination," in Rita Arditti, Renate Duelli Klein, and Shelly Minden, eds., *Test-Tube Women: What Future for Motherhood?* (Boston: Pandora Press, 1985), pp. 382–385.

45. Ibid., p. 388.

46. Lawrence J. Kaplan and Carolyn M. Kaplan, "Natural Reproduction and Reproduction-Aiding Technologies," in Kenneth D. Alpern, ed., *The Ethics of Reproductive Technology* (New York: Oxford University Press, 1992), p. 24.

47. Robin Hemran, "When the 'Father' Is a Sperm Donor," *Washington Post Health*, February 11, 1992, p. 14.

48. Jan Fisher, "4 Charged in Illegal Sperm Bank," *New York Times*, April 27, 1992, p. B2.

49. B. Drummond Ayres, Jr., "Fertility Doctor Accused of Fraud," *New York Times*, November 21, 1991.

50. Corea, *The Mother Machine*, p. 49.

51. *C.M. v. C.C.*, 170 N.J. Superior Ct. 586, 407 A. 2nd 849, 852 (Juv. & Dom. Rel. Ct. 1979).

52. Ruth Marcus, "Court Lets Sperm Donor Sue for Parental Rights," *New York Times*, April 24, 1990, p. A4.

53. Carlyle C. Douglas, "Lesbian Child-Custody Cases Redefine Family Law," *New York Times*, April 10, 1990.

54. Ibid.

55. Herman, "When the 'Father' Is a Sperm Donor," p. 10.

56. Nadine Brozan, "Babies from Donated Eggs: Growing Use Stirs Questions," *New York Times*, January 18, 1988, p. 9.

57. Glanville Williams, *The Sanctity of Life and the Criminal Law* (New York: Alfred A. Knopf, 1970), p. 120, emphasis added.

58. George J. Annas, "Artificial Insemination: Beyond the Best Interests of the Donor," *Hastings Center Report* 9, no. 4 (August 1979): 14.

59. Patricia P. Mahlstedt, cited in Herman, "When the 'Father' Is a Sperm Donor," p. 10.

60. Alison Kornet, "Should Donors Be Anonymous?" *New Women*, November 1995. Some sperm banks have "openness" policies. For example, the California Cryobank in Los Angeles responds to AID offspring's requests by contacting genetic fathers and giving them a choice about whether they want to be identified. Comments Kornet: "It does not require men to decide upon donating whether contact with their offspring will be important to them in 20 years, but unlike the yes-donor policy, the openness policy cannot guarantee AID offspring the information they want" (p. 144).

61. Simone B. Novaes, "Semen Banking and Artificial Insemination by Donor in France: Social and Medical Discourse," *International Journal of Technology Assessment in Health Care* 2, no. 2 (1986): 221–222.

62. Lindsey Van Gelder, "A Lesbian Family," in Alison M. Jaggar, ed., *Living with Contradictions* (Boulder, Colo.: Westview Press, 1994), p. 450.

63. Kaplan and Tong, *Controlling Our Reproductive Destiny: A Technological and Philosophical Perspective*, pp. 258–264.

64. Peter Singer, "Technology and Procreation: How Far Should We Go?" *Technology Review* 88, no. 2 (February-March 1985): 27.

65. Clifford Grobstein, "Statement to the Ethics Advisory Board," *Technology Review* 88, no. 2 (February-March 1985): 27.

66. Leon Kass, "'Making Babies' Revisited," *The Public Interest* no. 54 (Winter 1979): 33.

67. Singer and Wells, *Making Babies: The New Science and Ethics of Conception*, p. 86.

68. Ibid., p. 87.

69. *Davis v. Davis*, 842 S.W.2d 588, 602–03 (Tenn. 1992).

70. Leon R. Kass, "'Making Babies'—The New Biology and the 'Old' Morality," *The Public Interest* no. 26 (Winter 1972): 49.

71. Leroy Walters, "Human In Vitro Fertilization: A Review of the Ethical Literature," *Hastings Center Report* 9, no. 4 (August 1979): 24.

72. Ibid., p. 32.

73. Ibid., p. 40.

74. Ibid., pp. 39–40.

75. Bernard Häring, *Ethics of Manipulation: Issues in Medicine, Behavior Control, and Genetics* (New York: Seabury Press, 1975), pp. 198–199.

76. Joel Feinberg, *Social Philosophy* (Englewood Cliffs, N.J.: Prentice-Hall, 1973), p. 47.

77. Richard T. Hull, ed., *Ethical Issues in the New Reproductive Technologies* (Belmont, Calif.: Wadsworth, 1990), p. 92. See also Robertson, *Children of Choice*, p. 114.

78. Robert H. Blank, *Rationing Medicine* (New York: Columbia University Press, 1988).

79. Overall, *Human Reproduction: Principles, Practices, Policies*, p. 151.

80. Gena Corea and Susan Ince, "Report of a Survey of IVF Clinics in the U.S.," in Patricia Spallone and P. L. Steinberg, eds., *Made to Order: The Myth of Reproductive and Genetic Progress* (Oxford: Pergamon Press, 1987), pp. 142–143.

81. Mary Anne Warren, "IVF and Women's Interests: An Analysis of Feminist Concerns," *Bioethics* 2, no. 1 (1988): 38.

82. Christine Crow, "'Women Want It': In-Vitro Fertilization and Women's Motivations for Participation," *Women's Studies International Forum* 8, no. 6 (1986): 551.

83. Robertson, *Children of Choice*, p. 226.

84. L. R. Shover, R. L. Collins, M. M. Quigley, J. Blanstein, and G. Kanoti, "Psychological Follow-up of Women Evaluated as Oocyte Donors," *Human Reproduction* 6, no. 10 (1991): 1491.

85. Martha E. Gimiııez, "Feminism, Pronatalism, and Motherhood," in Joyce Trebilcot, ed., *Mothering* (Totowa, N.J.: Roman and Allenheld), pp. 300–301.

86. Corea, *The Mother Machine: Reproductive Technologies from Artificial Insemination to Artificial Wombs*, p. 170.

87. Schover et al., "Psychological Follow-up of Women Evaluated As Oocyte Donors," p. 1491.

88. Mahowald, *Women and Children in Health Care: An Unequal Majority*, p. 104.

89. Shover et al., "Psychological Follow-up of Women Evaluated As Oocyte Donors," p. 1488.

90. Ibid.

91. Mahowald, *Women and Children in Health Care: An Unequal Majority*, p. 104.

92. Mary O'Brien, *The Politics of Reproduction* (Boston: Routledge and Kegan Paul, 1981), p. 58.

93. Gena Corea, "Egg Snatchers," in Arditti, Klein, and Minden, eds., *Test-Tube Women*, p. 45.

94. Robyn Rowland, "Reproductive Technologies: The Final Solution to the Woman Question," in Arditti, Klein, and Minden, eds., *Test-Tube Women*, p. 45.

95. Gena Corea, "Effects of NRAs on Women" (unpublished manuscript), p. 8.

96. As Dr. Margery Shaw has noted, once a pregnant woman decides to carry her fetus to term, she ensures a "conditional prospective liability" for negligent acts toward her fetus should it be born alive: "These acts could be considered negligent fetal abuse resulting in an injured child. A decision to carry a genetically defective fetus to term would be an example. Abuse of alcohol or drugs during pregnancy, . . . [w]ithholding of necessary prenatal care, improper nutrition, [and] exposure to the mother's defective intrauterine environment caused by her genotype . . . could all result in an injured infant who might claim that his right to be born physically and mentally sound had been invaded. See M. S. Henifin, R. Hubbard, and J. Norsigian, "Prenatal Screening," in Sherill Cohen and Nadine Taub, eds., *Reproductive Laws for the 1990s* (Clifton, N.J.: Humana Press, 1989), p. 167.

97. Joseph Fletcher, *Humanhood: Essays in Biomedical Ethics* (Buffalo, N.Y.: Prometheus Books, 1979), p. 90.

Chapter Eight

1. R. D. Kempers, ed., "Surrogate Mothers," *Fertility and Sterility* (September 1986): 625.

2. Peter Singer and Deanne Wells, *Making Babies: The New Science and Ethics of Conception* (New York: Charles Scribner's Sons, 1984), p. 96.

3. Leon R. Kass, "Making Babies—The New Biology and the 'Old' Morality," *The Public Interest* no. 26 (Winter 1972): 49.

4. Immanuel Kant, *Foundation of the Metaphysics of Morals*, trans. L. W. Beck (Indianapolis: Bobbs-Merrill Educational Publishing, 1959), p. 39.

5. Roger Rosenblatt, "Baby M—Emotion for Sale," *Time*, April 6, 1987, p. 88.

6. Ibid.

7. Herbert T. Krimmel, "The Case Against Surrogate Parenting," *Hastings Center Report* (October 1983): 38.

8. John A. Robertson, *Children of Choice: Freedom and the New Reproductive Technologies* (Princeton, N.J.: Princeton University Press, 1994), p. 132.

9. David A. J. Richards, "Commercial Sex and the Rights of the Person: A Moral Argument for the Decriminalization of Prostitution," *University of Pennsylvania Law Review* 127 (May 1979): 1257–1259.

10. Arlie Hochschild, "The Managed Heart," in Robert N. Bellah et al., eds., *Individualism and Commitment in American Life* (New York: Harper & Row, 1987), p. 176.

11. H. A. Davidson, "What Will Surrogate Mothering Do to the Fabric of the American Family?" *Public Welfare* (Fall 1983): 12.

12. D. Gelman and D. Shapiro, "Infertility: Babies by Contract," *Newsweek*, November 4, 1985, p. 74.

13. Robertson, *Children of Choice*, p. 139.

14. Robertson, "Embryos, Families, and Procreative Liberty: The Legal Structure of the New Reproduction," *Southern California Law Review* 59, no. 5 (July 1986): 1001.

15. Ibid.

16. Ibid.

17. John A. Robertson, "Surrogate Mothers: Not So Novel After All," *Hastings Center Report* 13, no. 5 (October 1983): 29.

18. "Excerpts from Decision by New Jersey Supreme Court in the Baby M Case," *New York Times*, February 4, 1988, p. B6.

19. Lori B. Andrews, "The Aftermath of Baby M: Proposed State Laws on Surrogate Motherhood," *Hastings Center Report* 17 (October-November 1987): 32.

20. B. Cohen, "Surrogate Mothers: Whose Baby Is It?" *American Journal of Law and Medicine* 10, no. 3 (Fall 1984): 255.

21. Surrogacy Arrangements Act 1985, United Kingdom, Chapter 49, p. 2: section (1), (a), (b), and (c).

22. Ibid., p. 3: sections (1) through (5).

23. Ibid., p. 46.

24. Phyllis Chesler, *The Sacred Bond: The Legacy of Baby M* (New York: Time Books, 1988), pp. 197–203.

25. "Rumpelstiltskin Revisited: The Unalienable Right of Surrogate Mothers," *Harvard Law Review* 99 (1986): 1953–1954.

26. See Singer and Wells, *Making Babies: The New Science and Ethics of Conception*, pp. 103–104.

27. "Surrogate Motherhood: Contracted Issues and Remedies Under Legislative Proposals," *Washburn Law Journal* 23 (1983–1984): 622n.

28. Lori B. Andrews, "Alternative Modes of Reproduction," in Sherill Cohen and Nadine Taub, eds., *Reproductive Laws for the 1990's* (Clifton, N.J.: Humana Press, 1989), pp. 365–366.

29. Andrew Sachs, "When the Lullaby Ends," *Time*, June 4, 1990, p. 82.

30. Mary Beth Whitehead, "A Surrogate Mother Describes Her Change of Heart—and Her Fight to Keep the Baby Two Families Love," *People Weekly* 26 (October 26, 1986): 47.

31. George J. Annas, "Regulating the New Reproductive Technologies," in Cohen and Taub, eds., *Reproductive Laws for the 1990's*, p. 414.

32. Corea, *The Mother Machine* (New York: Harper & Row, 1985), p. 276.

33. Hilde Lindemann Nelson and James Lindemann Nelson, "Cutting Motherhood in Two: Some Suspicions Concerning Surrogacy," *Hypatia* 4, no. 3 (Fall 1989): 91.

34. Ibid., p. 93.

35. Ibid.

36. Corea, *The Mother Machine*, p. 279.

37. R. H. Miller, "Surrogate Parenting: An Infant Industry Presents Society with Legal, Ethical Questions," *Ob-Gyn News* 18, no. 3 (February 1–14, 1983): 4.

38. Corea, *The Mother Machine*, p. 214.

39. Uma Narayan, "The 'Gift' of a Child," in Patricia Boling, ed., *Expecting Trouble: Surrogacy, Fetal Abuse, & New Reproductive Technologies* (Boulder, Colo.: Westview Press, 1995), p. 182.

40. Corea, *The Mother Machine*, p. 231.

41. Patricia A. Avery, "Surrogate Mothers: Center of a New Storm," *U.S. News & World Report*, June 6, 1983, p. 76.

42. "A Surrogate's Story of Loving and Losing," *U.S. News & World Report*, June 6, 1983, p. 77.

43. "Grandmother, 48, Is Surrogate for Daughter," *Boston Globe*, April 8, 1987, p. 17A.

44. Marge Piercy, *Woman on the Edge of Time* (New York: Fawcett Crest Books, 1976).

45. Ibid., p. 102.

46. Ibid., pp. 105–106.

47. Chesler, *The Sacred Bond: The Legacy of Baby M*, p. 38.

48. Narayan, "The 'Gift' of a Child," p. 194.

49. Ibid., p. 189.

50. Ibid., p. 180.

51. Robertson, *Children of Choice*, p. 40.

52. Mary Lyndon Shanley, "'Surrogate Mothering' and Women's Freedom: A Critique of Contracts for Human Reproduction," in Boling, ed., *Expecting Trouble: Surrogacy, Fetal Abuse, & New Reproductive Technologies*, p. 157.

53. Heidi Malm, "Commodification or Compensation: A Reply to Ketchum," in Helen B. Holmes and Laura M. Purdy, eds., *Feminist Perspectives in Medical Ethics* (Bloomington: Indiana University Press, 1992).

54. Robertson, *Children of Choice*, p. 140.

55. Carmel Shalev, *Birth Power* (New Haven, Conn.: Yale University Press, 1989), pp. 157, 94.

56. Andrews, "Alternative Modes of Reproduction," p. 365.

57. Laura M. Purdy, "Another Look at Contract Pregnancy," in Laura M. Purdy, ed., *Reproducing Persons: Issues in Feminist Bioethics* (Ithaca, N.Y.: Cornell University Press, 1996), p. 211.

58. Andrews, "Alternative Modes of Reproduction," p. 369.

59. Marjorie Maguire Schultz, "Reproductive Technology and Intention-based Parenthood: An Opportunity for Gender Neutrality," *Wisconsin Law Review* 2 (1990): 377–378.

60. Phyllis Chesler, *Sacred Bond: The Legacy of Baby M* (New York: Times Books, 1988), p. 164.

61. Iris Young, "Pregnant Embodiment: Subjectivity and Alienation," in *"Throwing Like a Girl" and Other Essays in Feminist Philosophy and Social Theory* (Bloomington: Indiana University Press, 1990), p. 167.

62. Shanley, "'Surrogate Mothering' and Women's Freedom: A Critique of Contracts for Human Reproduction," p. 162.

63. Anne Taylor Fleming, "Our Fascination with Baby M," *New York Times Magazine*, March 20, 1987, p. 38.

64. Barbara Katz-Rothman, *Recreating Motherhood: Ideology and Technology in a Patriarchal Society* (New York: W. W. Norton, 1989) pp. 254–255.

65. Sara Ann Ketchum, "New Reproductive Technologies and the Definition of Parenthood: A Feminist Perspective." Paper presented at Feminism and Legal Theory: Women and Intimacy, a conference sponsored by the Institute for Legal Studies at the University of Wisconsin–Madison (1987).

66. Sherman Elias and George J. Annas, "Noncoital Reproduction," *Journal of American Medical Association* 225 (January 3, 1986): 67.

67. George J. Annas, "Death Without Dignity for Commercial Surrogacy: The Case of Baby M," *Hastings Center Report* 18, no. 2 (1988): 23–24.

68. Ellen Goodman, "Whose Child?" *Charlotte Observer* (October 28, 1990), p. 3C.

69. Lawrence J. Nelson and Nancy Milliken, "Compelled Medical Treatment of Pregnant Women: Life, Liberty, and Law in Conflict," in Richard T. Hull, ed., *Ethical Issues in the New Reproductive Technologies* (Belmont, Calif.: Wadsworth, 1990), pp. 224–240.

70. Chesler, *Sacred Bond: The Legacy of Baby M*, pp. 109–146.

Chapter Nine

1. Eric T. Juengst, "The Human Genome Project and Bioethics," *Kennedy Institute of Ethics Journal* 1, no. 1 (March 1991): 71.

2. Robert Oppenheimer, quoted in George J. Annas and Sherman Elias, "The Major Social Policy Issues Raised by the Human Genome Project," in George J.

Annas and Sherman Elias, eds., *Gene Mapping: Using Law and Ethics As Guides* (New York: Oxford University Press, 1992), pp. 4–5.

3. Peter Aldhous, "Who Needs a Genome Ethics Treaty?" *Nature* 351 (June 13, 1991): 507.

4. Ibid.

5. Thomas H. Murray, "Ethical Issues in Human Genome Research," *FASEB Journal* 5 (January 1991): 55.

6. Alan H. Handyside, "Genetic Testing and Screening: Preimplantation Diagnosis," in Warren T. Reich, ed., *Encyclopedia of Bioethics*, vol. 1 (New York: Simon & Schuster / MacMillan, 1995), p. 985.

7. Ibid.

8. Alan H. Handyside, "Preimplantation Diagnosis of Genetic Defects," in James O. Drife and Alexander A. Templeton, eds., *Infertility: Proceedings of the Twenty-Fifth Study Group of the Royal College of Obstetricians and Gynecologists* (London: Springer-Verlag, 1992), pp. 331–344.

9. Mark Lappé, "The Predictive Power of the New Genetics," *Hastings Center Report* 14 (October 1984): 19.

10. Margaretta Seashore, "Newborn Screening," in Warren T. Reich, ed., *Encyclopedia of Bioethics*, vol. 1 (New York: Simon & Schuster / MacMillan, 1995), p. 991.

11. John A. Robertson, "Procreative Liberty and Human Genetics," *Emory Law Journal* 39 (1990): 698.

12. Ronald Yezzi, *Medical Ethics: Thinking About Unavoidable Questions* (New York: Holt, Rinehart and Winston, 1980), p. 92.

13. Ibid., p. 93.

14. Philip Reilly, *Genetics, Law and Society* (Cambridge, Mass.: Harvard University Press, 1977).

15. M. Kaback, "The Control of Genetics Disease by Carrier Screening and Antenatal Diagnosis: Social, Ethical, and Medicological Issues," *Birth Defects: Original Article Series* 18 (1983): 243–254.

16. John A. Robertson, *Children of Choice: Freedom and the New Reproductive Technologies* (Princeton, N.J.: Princeton University Press, 1994), p. 156.

17. Ibid.

18. Seashore, "Newborn Screening," p. 991.

19. Ronald Munson, *Intervention and Reflection: Basic Issues in Medical Ethics* (Belmont, Calif.: Wadsworth Publishing Co., 1992), p. 405.

20. Robertson, *Children of Choice*, p. 155.

21. John C. Fletcher and Dorothy C. Wertz, "Ethics, Law, and Medical Genetics: After the Human Genome Is Mapped," *Emory Law Journal* 39, no. 3 (Summer 1990): 762.

22. Ibid., p. 787.

23. Ibid., p. 780.

24. Ibid., p. 789.

25. Barbara Bowles Biesecker, "Practice of Genetic Counseling," in Warren T. Reich, ed., *Encyclopedia of Bioethics*, vol. 1 (New York: Simon & Schuster / MacMillan, 1995), p. 923.

26. Diane M. Bartels, Bonnie S. LeRoy, and Arthur L. Caplan, eds., *Prescribing Our Future: Ethical Challenges in Genetic Counseling* (New York: Aldine de Gruyer, 993).

27. Mary Yarborough, Joan A. Scott, and Linda K. Dixon, "The Role of Beneficence in Clinical Genetics: Nondirective Counseling Reconsidered," *Theoretical Medicine* 10, no. 2 (1989): 139–149.

28. Fletcher and Wertz, "Ethics, Law, and Medical Genetics: After the Human Genome Is Mapped," p. 765.

29. Ibid., p. 790.

30. Ibid., pp. 772–773.

31. Margery W. Shaw, "The Potential Plaintiff: Preconception and Prenatal Torts," in Aubrey Milunsky and George J. Annas, eds., *Genetics and the Law II* (New York: Plenum, 1980), pp. 225–232.

32. Arthur L. Caplan, "Neutrality Is Not Morality: The Ethics of Genetic Counseling," in Bartels, LeRoy, Caplan, eds., *Prescribing Our Future: Ethical Challenges in Genetic Counseling*, p. 163.

33. Ibid.

34. Thomas H. Murray and Jeffrey R. Botkin, "Genetic Testing and Screening: Ethical Issues," in Warren T. Reich, ed., *Encyclopedia of Bioethics*, vol. 1 (New York: Simon & Schuster / MacMillan, 1995), p. 1007.

35. W. French Anderson and Theodore Friedman, "Strategies for Gene Therapy," in Warren T. Reich, ed., *Encyclopedia of Bioethics*, vol. 1 (New York: Simon & Schuster / MacMillan, 1995), p. 908.

36. Edward M. Berger and Bernard M. Gert, "Genetic Disorders and the Ethical Status of Germ-Line Gene Therapy," *Journal of Medicine and Philosophy* 16 (1991): 669–670.

37. Bernard D. Davis, "The Two Faces of Genetic Engineering in Man," *Science* (1983): 219, 245.

38. W. French Anderson, "Human Gene Therapy: Why Draw a Line?" *Journal of Medicine and Philosophy* 14 (1989): 685–689.

39. Robertson, *Children of Choice: Freedom and the New Reproductive Technologies*, pp. 149–172.

40. Berger and Gert, "Genetic Disorders and the Ethical Status of Germ-Line Gene Therapy," pp. 677–681.

41. Ray Moseley, "Commentary: Maintaining the Somatic / Germ-Line Distinction: Some Ethical Drawbacks" *Journal of Medicine and Philosophy* 16 (1991): 642.

42. Jeremy Rifkin, *Algeny* (New York: Viking Press, 1983).

43. Bruce K. Zimmerman, "Human Germ-Line Therapy: The Case for Its Development and Use," *Journal of Medicine and Philosophy* 16 (1991): 596–598.

44. Moseley, "Commentary: Maintaining the Somatic / Germ-Line Distinction: Some Ethical Drawbacks," p. 643.

45. Ibid.

46. Norma Juliet Wikler, "Society's Response to the New Reproductive Technologies: The Feminist Perspective," *Southern California Law Review* 59 (1986): 1053–1054.

47. Thomas Murray, "The Human Genome Project and Genetic Testing: Ethical Implications," in *The Genome, Ethics and the Law* (Washington, D.C.: Association for the Advancement of Science, June 14–16, 1991), pp. 49–78.

48. Tom Wilkie, *Perilous Knowledge: The Human Genome Project and Its Implications* (Berkeley: University of California Press, 1993), pp. 166–191.

49. *Davis v. Davis*, 8425-W.2d 588 (Tenn. 1992).

50. John A. Robertson, "Reproductive Technologies: Cryopreservation of Sperm, Ova, and Embryos," in Warren T. Reich, ed., *Encyclopedia of Bioethics*, vol. 1 (New York: Simon & Schuster / MacMillan, 1995), p. 2232.

51. Adrienne Asch, "Can Aborting 'Imperfect' Children Be Immoral?" in John D. Arras and Bonnie Steinbock, eds., *Ethical Issues in Modern Medicine* (Mountain View, Calif.: Mayfield Publishing Company, 1995), p. 386.

52. Naomi Breslaw, David Sulhener, and Kathleen S. Staruck, "Women's Labor Force Activity and Responsibilities for Disabled Dependents: A Study of Families with Disabled Children," *Journal of Health and Social Behavior* 23, no. 2 (1982): 169–183.

53. Laura M. Purdy, "Loving Future People," in Laura M. Purdy, ed., *Reproducing Persons: Issues in Feminist Bioethics* (Ithaca, N.Y.: Cornell University Press, 1996), p. 58.

54. Ibid., pp. 50–74.

55. Asch, "Can Aborting 'Imperfect' Children Be Immoral?" p. 387.

56. Deborah F. Pencarinha, Nora K. Bell, Janice G. Edwards, and Robert G. Best, "Ethical Issues in Genetic Counseling: A Comparison of U.S. Counselor and Medical Geneticist Perspectives," *Journal of Genetic Counseling* 1, no. 1 (1992): 19–30.

57. Benjamin Wilford and Diane Baker, "Meaning What I Say Is Not Saying What I Mean: Genetic Counseling, Non-Directiveness and Clients' Values," *Journal of Clinical Ethics* 6, no. 2 (Summer 1995): 181.

58. Asch, "Can Aborting 'Imperfect' Children Be Immoral?" p. 389.

59. Ibid.

60. Ezekiel J. Emanuel and Linda L. Emanuel, "Four Models of the Physician-Patient Relationship," in Arras and Steinbock, eds., *Ethical Issues in Modern Medicine*, pp. 67–77.

61. Ibid., p. 67.

62. Ibid., p. 68.

63. Henry Eichel, "S.C. Lawsuit Spotlights Debate on How to Treat Pregnant Cocaine Users," *Charlotte Observer*, January 31, 1994, pp. 1A, 5A.

64. David Perlman, "The Ethics of Germ-Line Gene Therapy: Challenges to Mainstream Approaches by a Feminist Critique," *Trends in Health Care, Law & Ethics* 8 (Fall 1993): 43.

65. Arthur L. Caplan, "If Gene Therapy Is the Cure, What Is the Disease?" in Annas and Elias, eds., *Gene Mapping: Using Law and Ethics As Guides*, p. 134.

66. Wikler, "Society's Response to the New Reproductive Technologies," p. 1056.

67. Ibid.

68. Ibid.

69. Ruth Schwartz Cowan, "Genetic Technology and Reproductive Choice: An Ethics for Autonomy," in Daniel J. Devlen and Leroy Hood, eds., *The Code of Codes* (Cambridge, Mass.: Harvard University Press), p. 259.

About the Book and Author

No other cluster of medical issues affects the genders as differently as those related to procreation—contraception, sterilization, abortion, artificial insemination, in-vitro fertilization, surrogate motherhood, and genetic screening. Yet the moral diversity among feminists has led to political fragmentation, foiling efforts to create policies that are likely to serve the interests of the largest possible number of women. In this remarkable book, Rosemarie Tong offers an approach to feminist bioethics that serves as a catalyst, bringing together varied perspectives on choice, control, and connection. Emphasizing the complexity of feminist debates, she guides feminists toward consensus in thought, cooperation in action, and a world that would have no room for domination and subordination.

Tong fairly and comprehensively presents the traditions of both feminist and nonfeminist ethics and bioethics. Although feminist approaches to bioethics derive many insights from nonfeminist ethics and bioethics, Tong shows that their primary source of inspiration is feminist ethics, leading feminist bioethicists to ask the so-called woman question in order to raise women's consciousness about the systems, structures, and relationships that oppress them. Feminist bioethicists are, naturally, committed to acting locally in the worlds of medicine and science. But their different feminist voices must also be raised at the policy table in order to make gender equity a present reality rather than a mere future possibility. Inability to define a plan that guarantees liberation for all women must not prevent feminists from offering a plan that promises to improve the welfare of many women. Otherwise, a perspective less appealing to women may fill the gap.

Rosemarie Tong is Thatcher Professor of Philosophy and Medical Humanities at Davidson College. She is the author of *Feminist Thought* (Westview Press, 1989) and coeditor, with Nancy Tuana, of *Feminism and Philosophy* (Westview Press, 1995).

Index